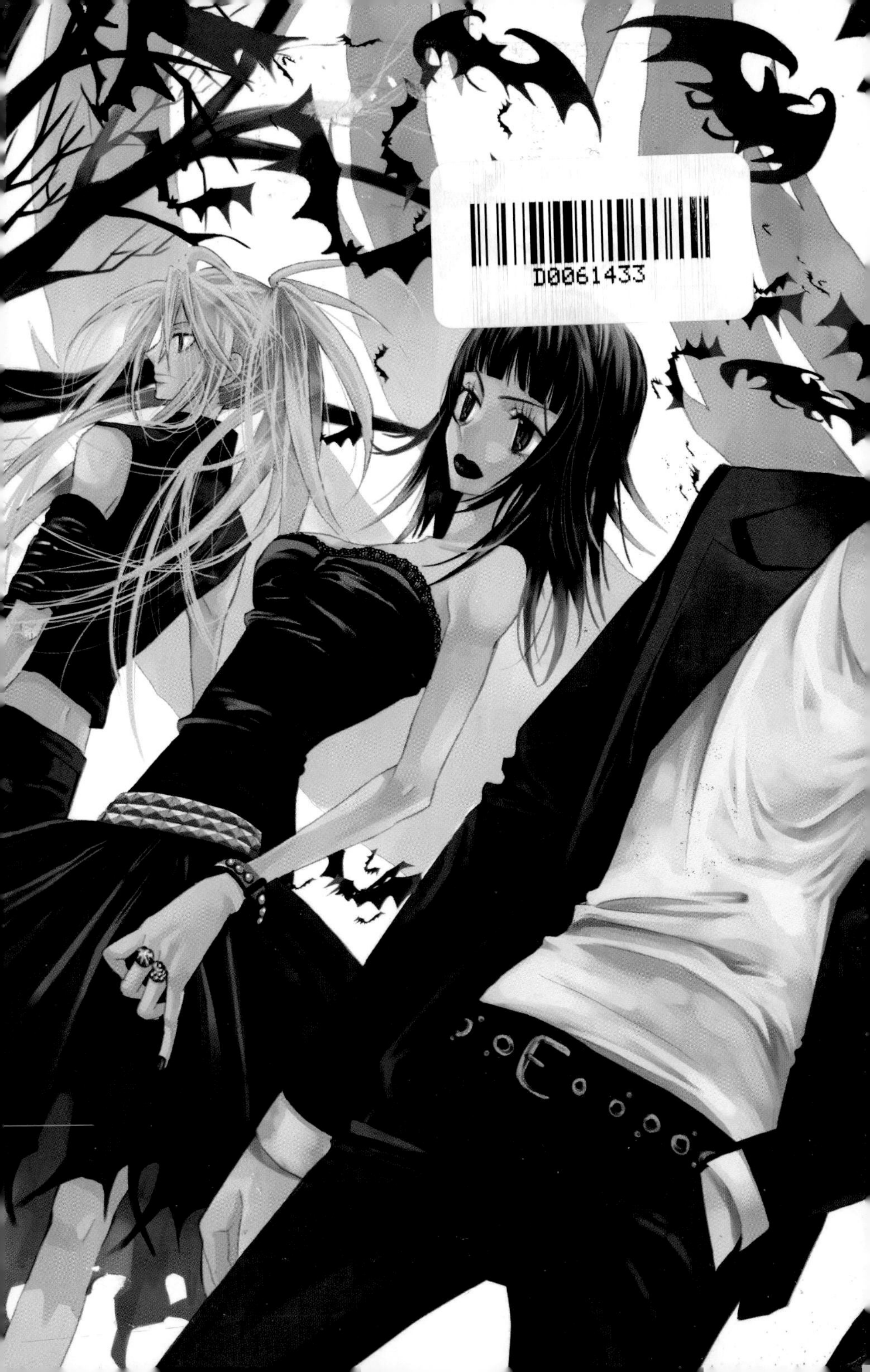

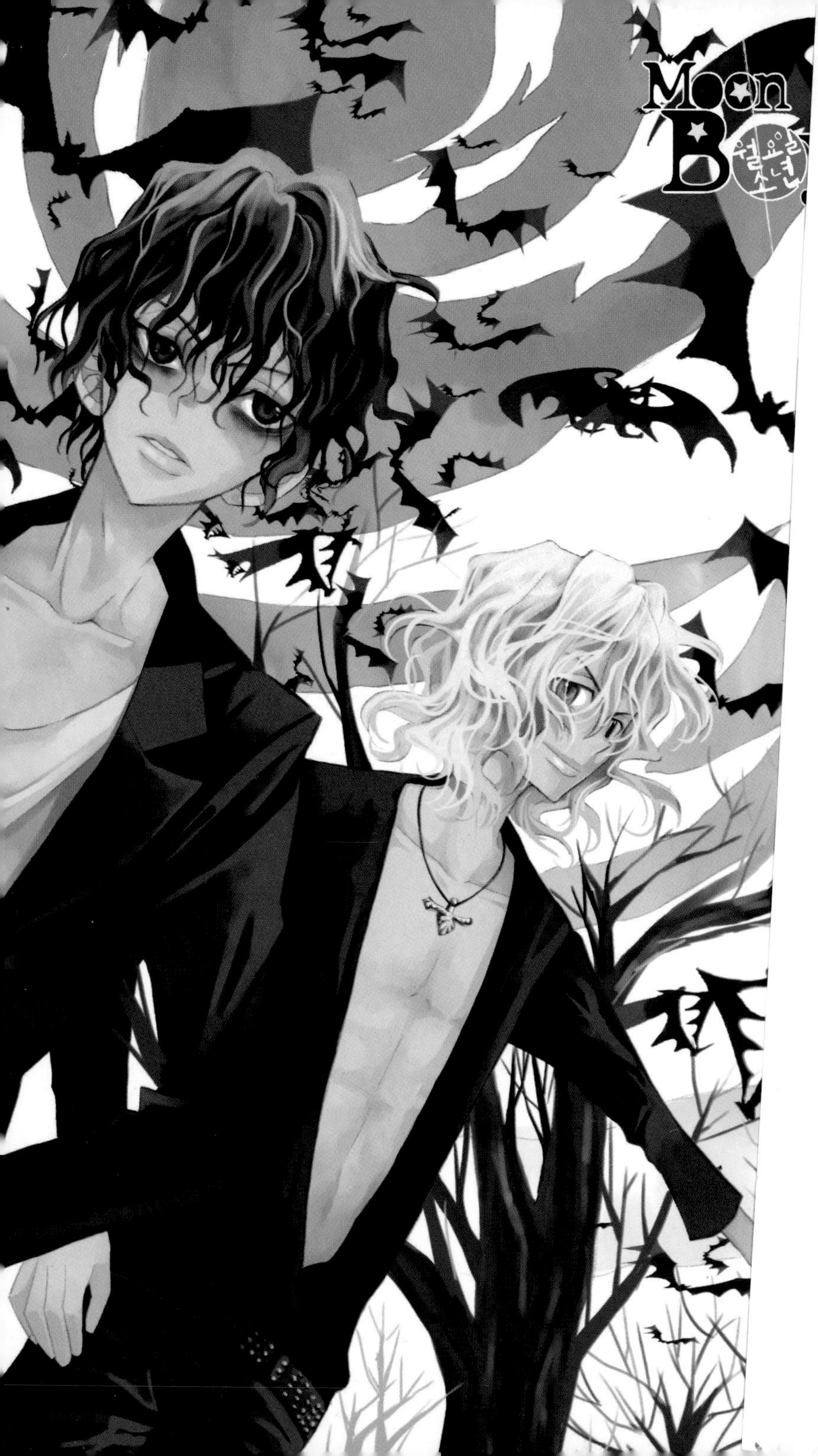
Moon
B
월요일 소년

MoonBoy

vol.3

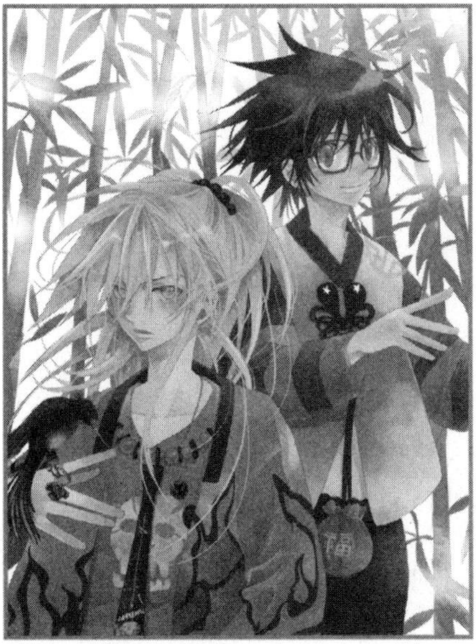

Lee YoungYou

Yen Press

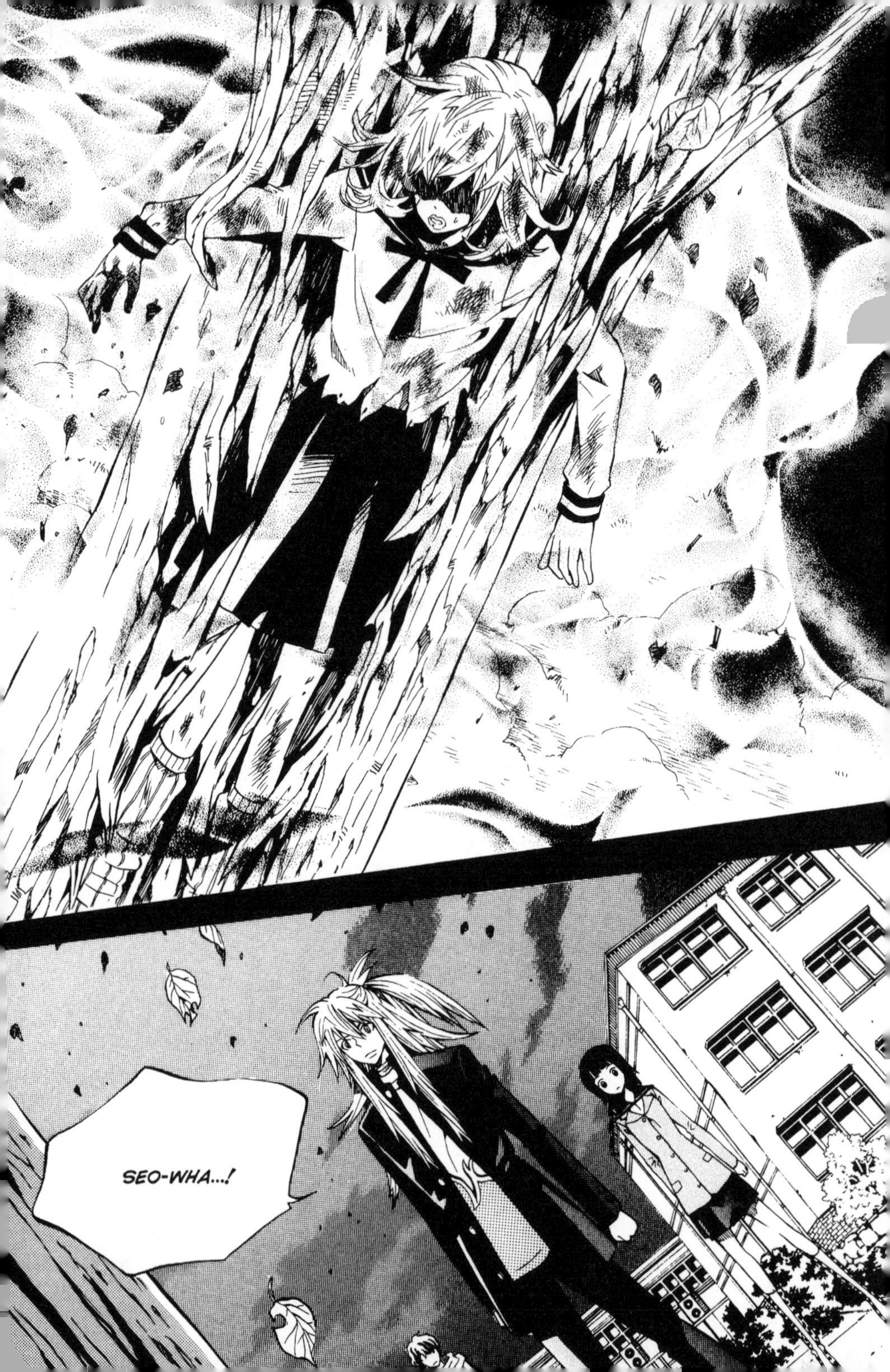
SEO-WHA...!

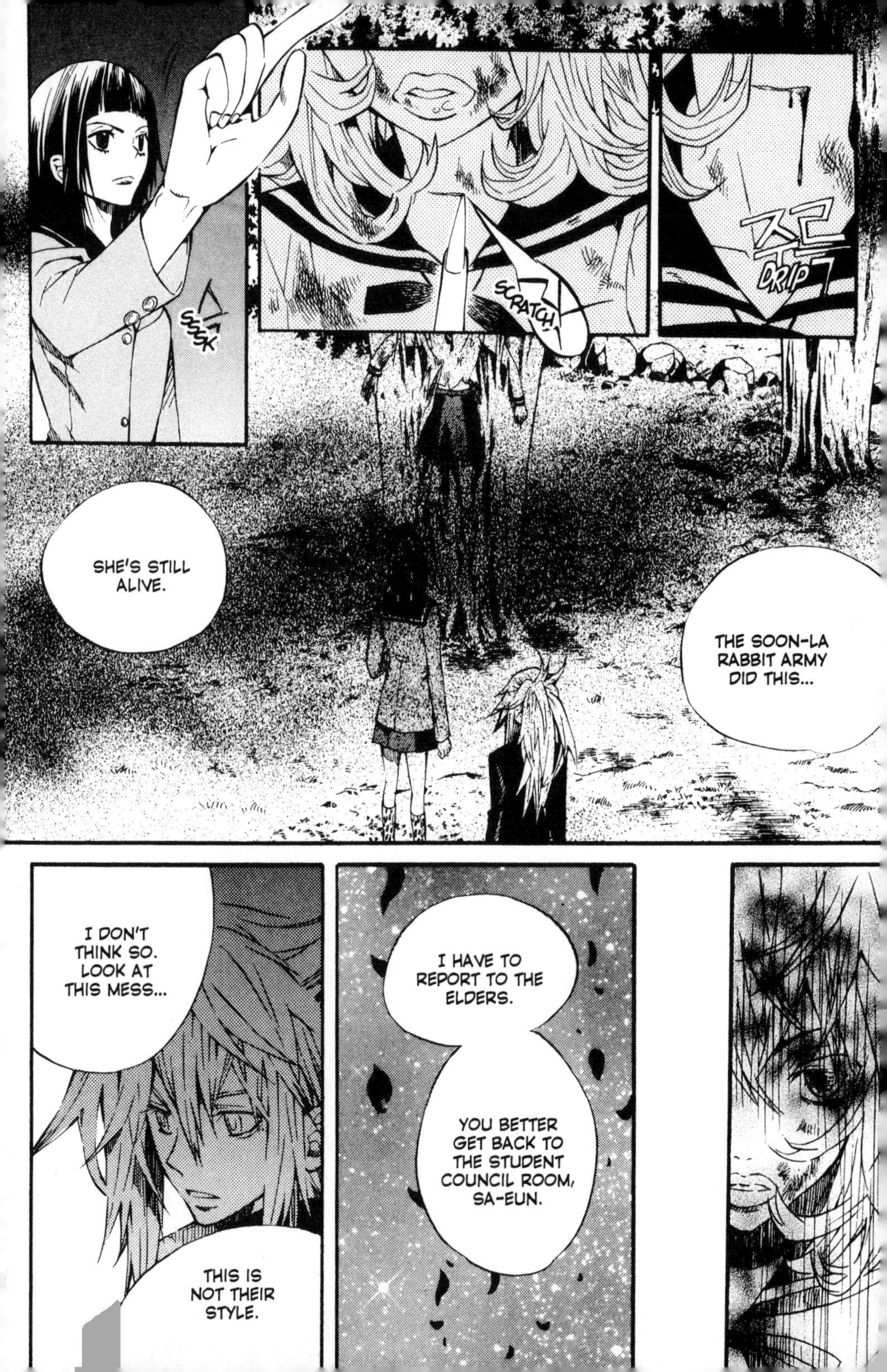
SSSK
SCRATCH
주르
DRIP
SHE'S STILL ALIVE.
THE SOON-LA RABBIT ARMY DID THIS...
I DON'T THINK SO. LOOK AT THIS MESS...
THIS IS NOT THEIR STYLE.
I HAVE TO REPORT TO THE ELDERS.
YOU BETTER GET BACK TO THE STUDENT COUNCIL ROOM, SA-EUN.

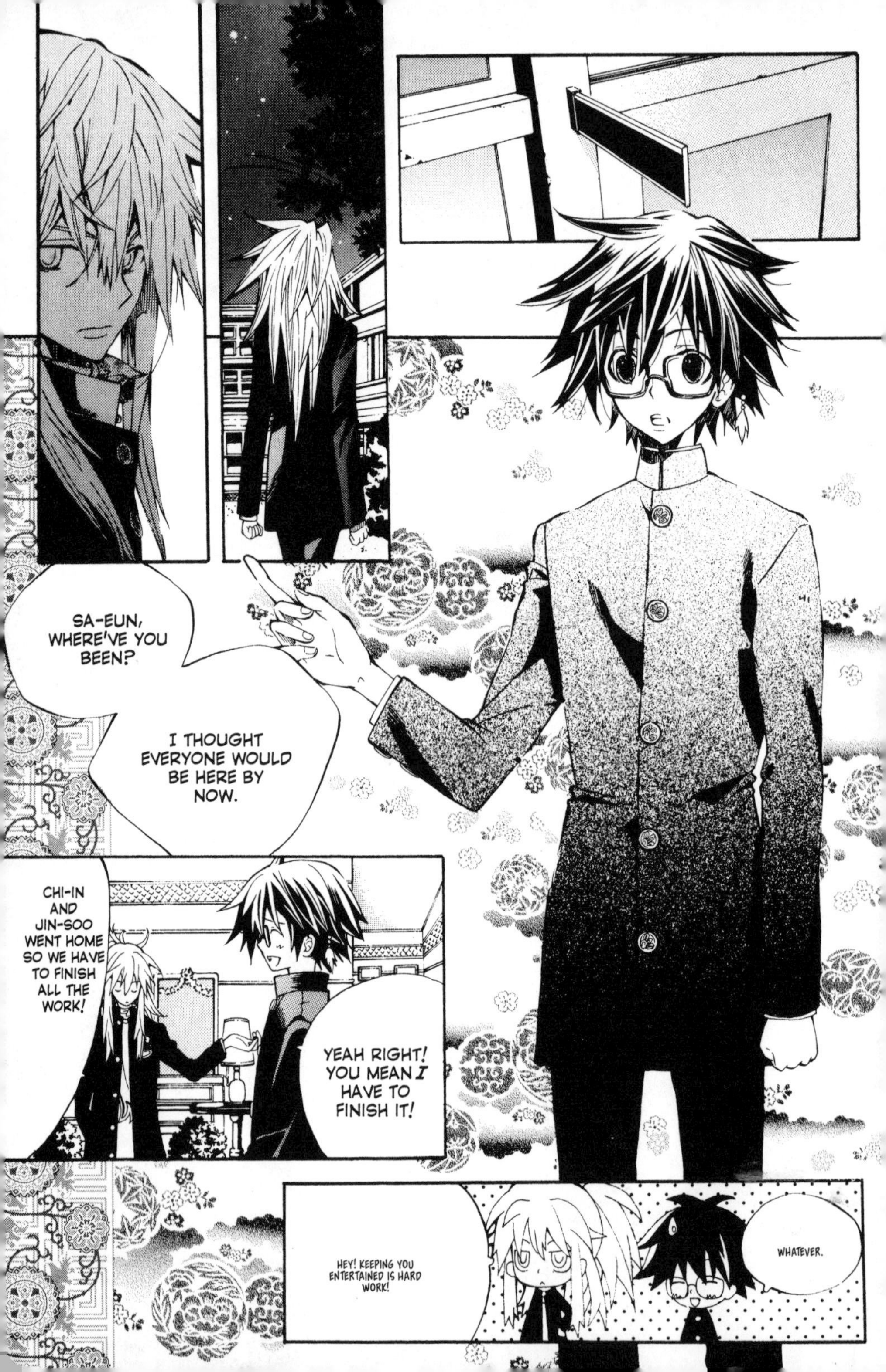
SA-EUN, WHERE'VE YOU BEEN?
I THOUGHT EVERYONE WOULD BE HERE BY NOW.
CHI-IN AND JIN-SOO WENT HOME SO WE HAVE TO FINISH ALL THE WORK!
YEAH RIGHT! YOU MEAN *I* HAVE TO FINISH IT!
HEY! KEEPING YOU ENTERTAINED IS HARD WORK!
WHATEVER.

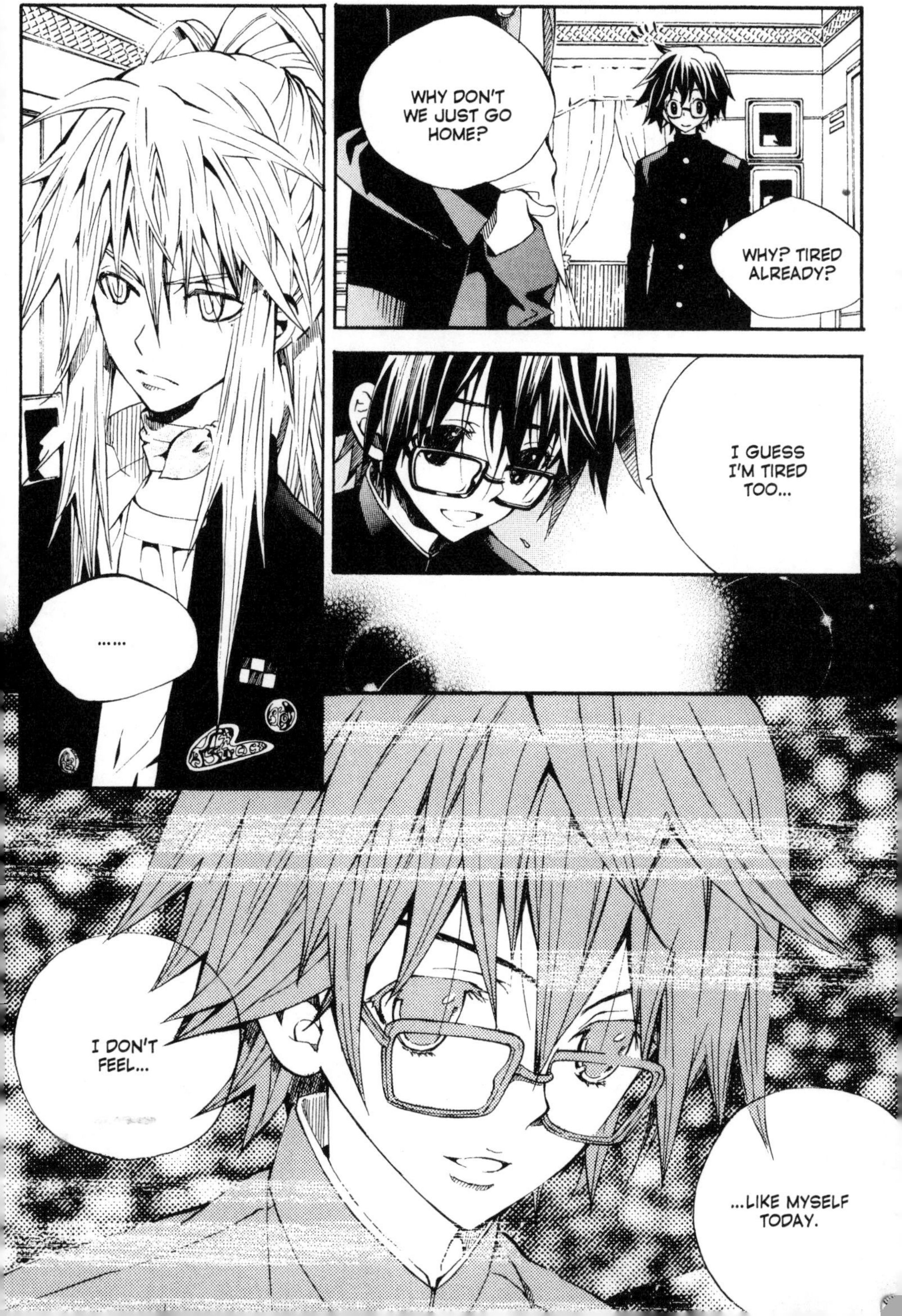
......
WHY DON'T WE JUST GO HOME?
WHY? TIRED ALREADY?
I GUESS I'M TIRED TOO...
I DON'T FEEL...
...LIKE MYSELF TODAY.

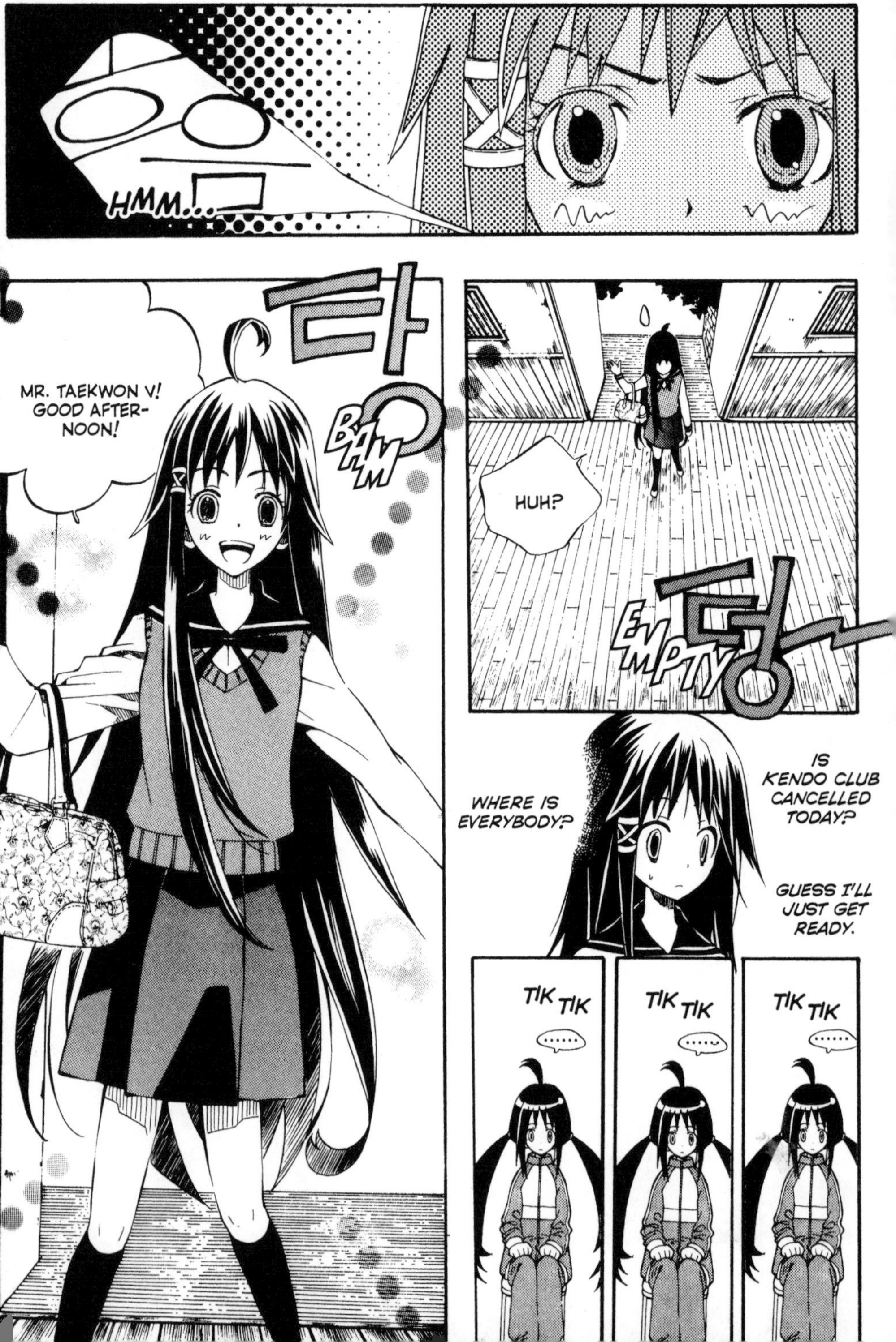
HMM...
MR. TAEKWON V! GOOD AFTER-NOON!
탕
BAM
HUH?
텅
EMPTY
WHERE IS EVERYBODY?
IS KENDO CLUB CANCELLED TODAY?
GUESS I'LL JUST GET READY.
TIK TIK
......
TIK TIK
......
TIK TIK
......

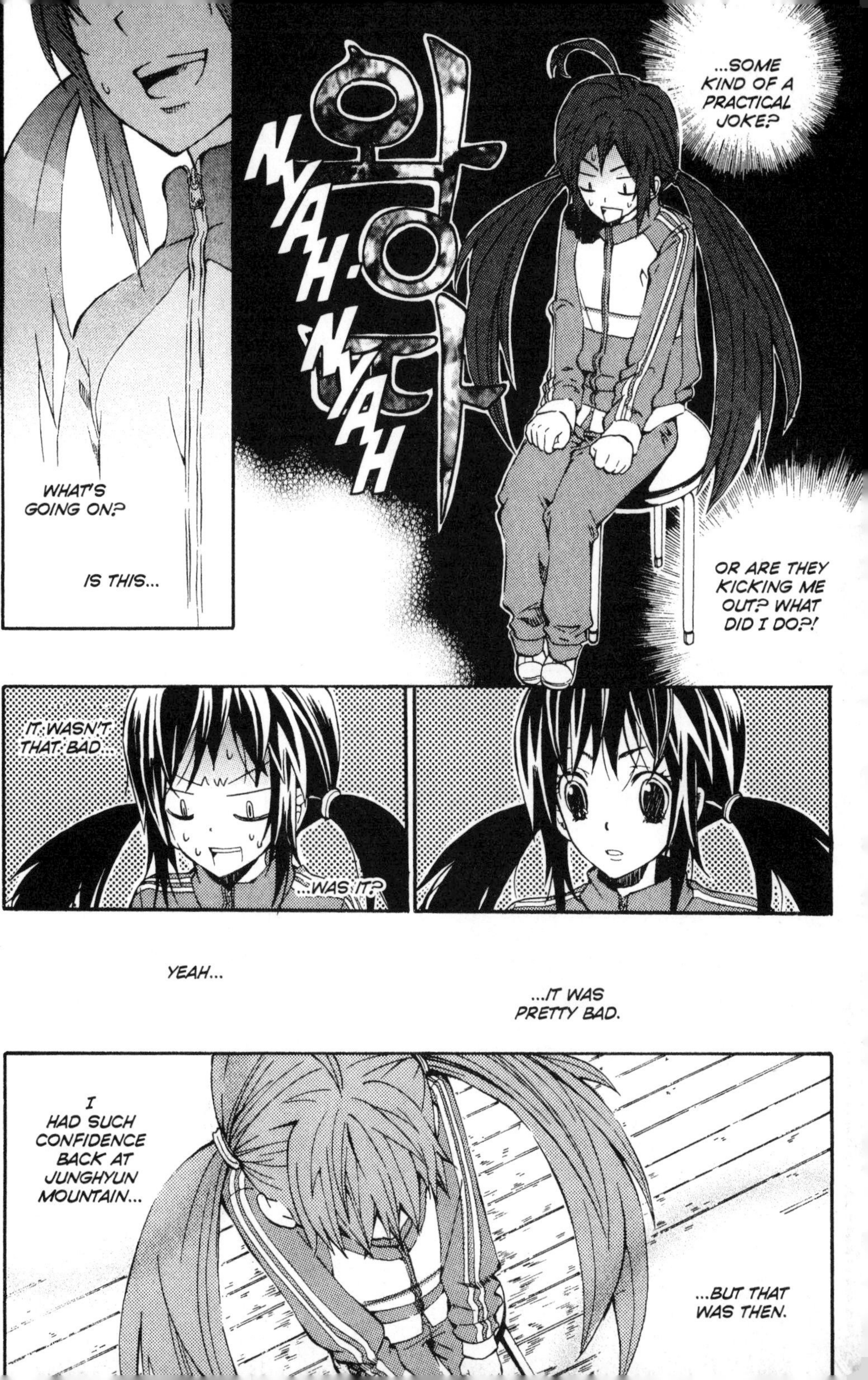
WHAT'S GOING ON?
IS THIS...
NYAH-NYAH-NYAH
...SOME KIND OF A PRACTICAL JOKE?
OR ARE THEY KICKING ME OUT? WHAT DID I DO?!
IT WASN'T THAT BAD...
...WAS IT?
YEAH...
...IT WAS PRETTY BAD.
I HAD SUCH CONFIDENCE BACK AT JUNGHYUN MOUNTAIN...
...BUT THAT WAS THEN.

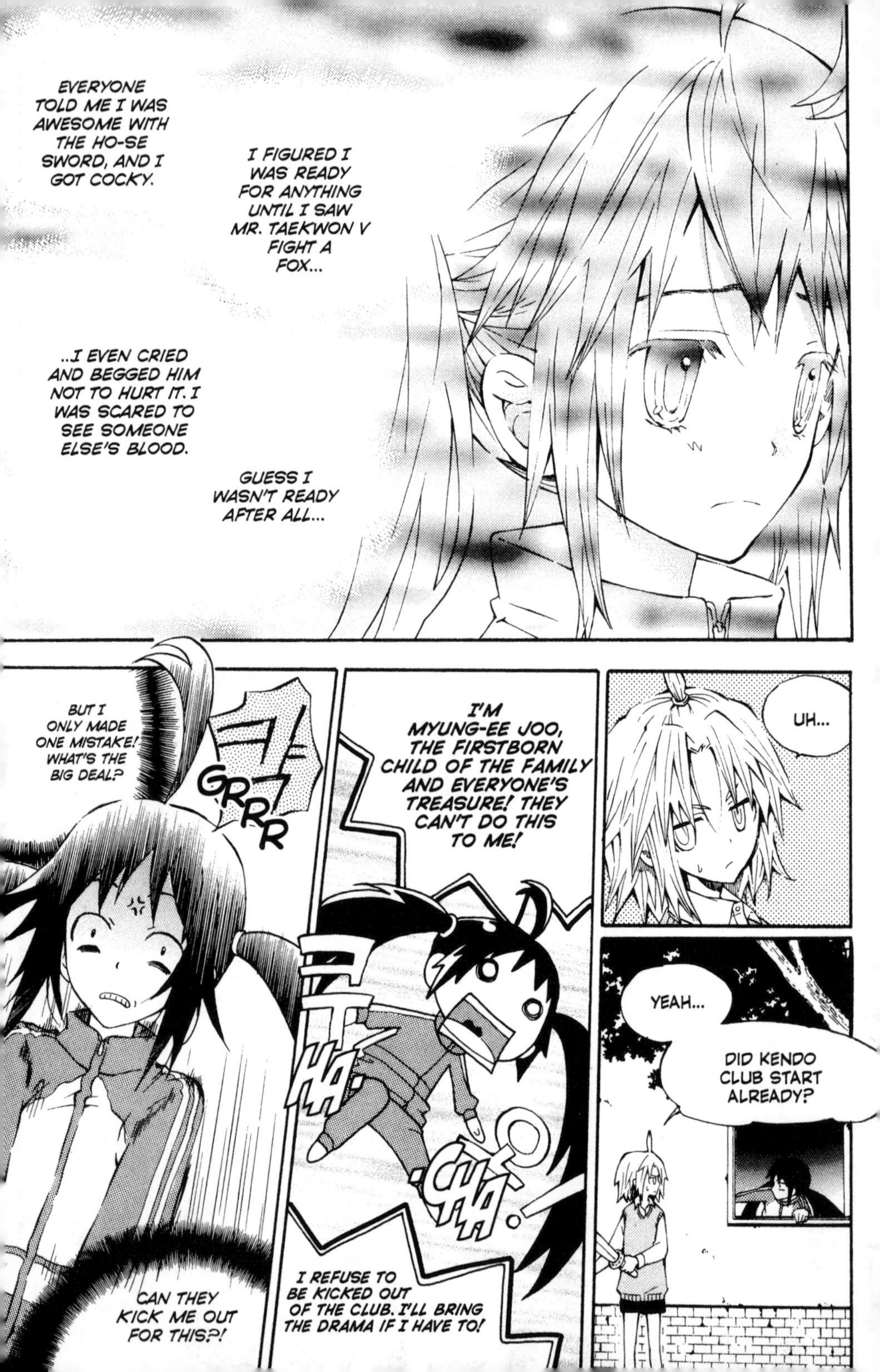
EVERYONE TOLD ME I WAS AWESOME WITH THE HO-SE SWORD, AND I GOT COCKY.
I FIGURED I WAS READY FOR ANYTHING UNTIL I SAW MR. TAEKWON V FIGHT A FOX...
...I EVEN CRIED AND BEGGED HIM NOT TO HURT IT. I WAS SCARED TO SEE SOMEONE ELSE'S BLOOD.
GUESS I WASN'T READY AFTER ALL...
BUT I ONLY MADE ONE MISTAKE! WHAT'S THE BIG DEAL?
GRRRR
CAN THEY KICK ME OUT FOR THIS?!
I'M MYUNG-EE JOO, THE FIRSTBORN CHILD OF THE FAMILY AND EVERYONE'S TREASURE! THEY CAN'T DO THIS TO ME!
HA
CHA
I REFUSE TO BE KICKED OUT OF THE CLUB. I'LL BRING THE DRAMA IF I HAVE TO!
UH...
YEAH...
DID KENDO CLUB START ALREADY?

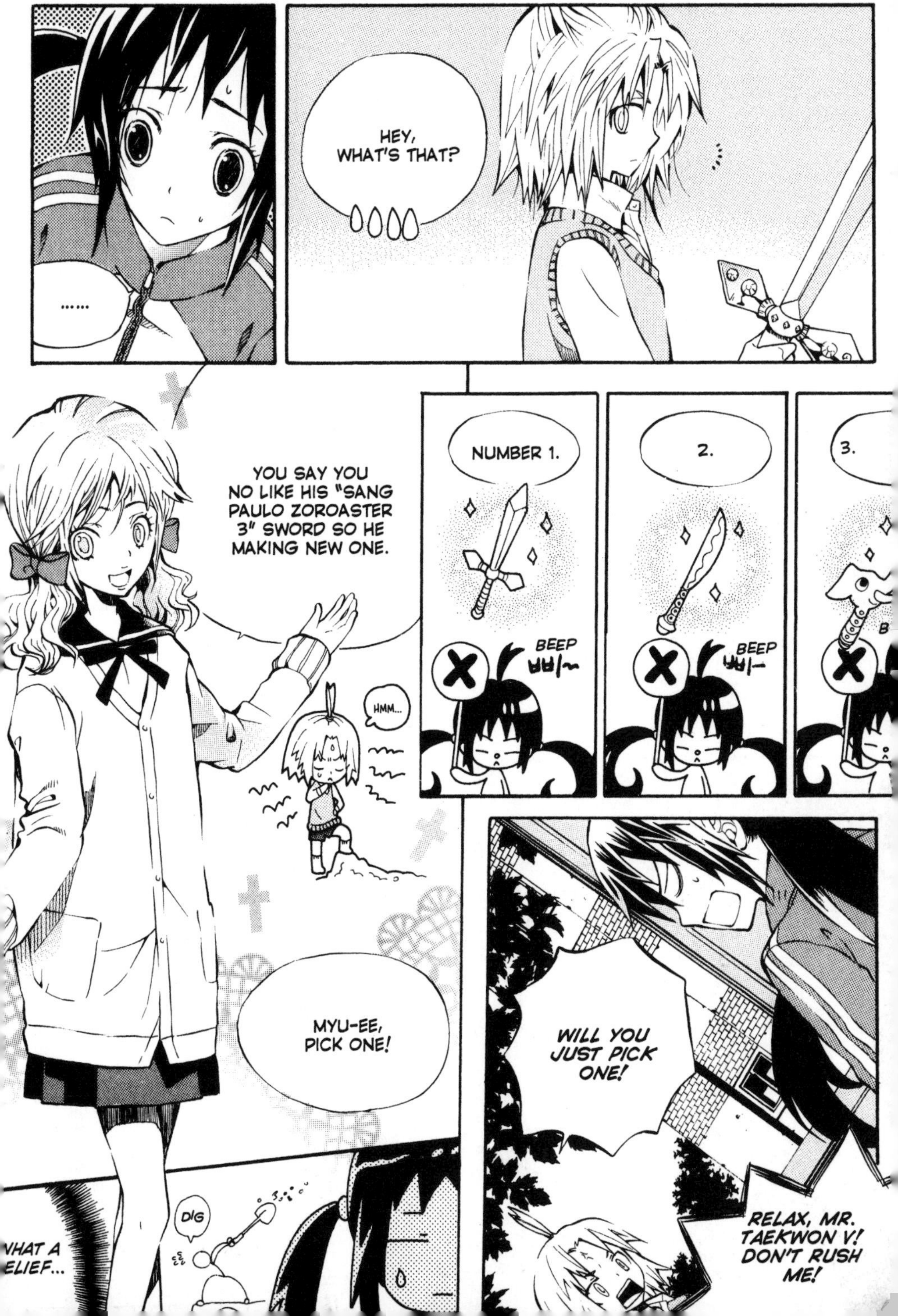
......
HEY, WHAT'S THAT?
YOU SAY YOU NO LIKE HIS "SANG PAULO ZOROASTER 3" SWORD SO HE MAKING NEW ONE.
HMM...
MYU-EE, PICK ONE!
NUMBER 1.
BEEP
삐~
2.
BEEP
삐-
3.
WILL YOU JUST PICK ONE!
RELAX, MR. TAEKWON V! DON'T RUSH ME!
DIG

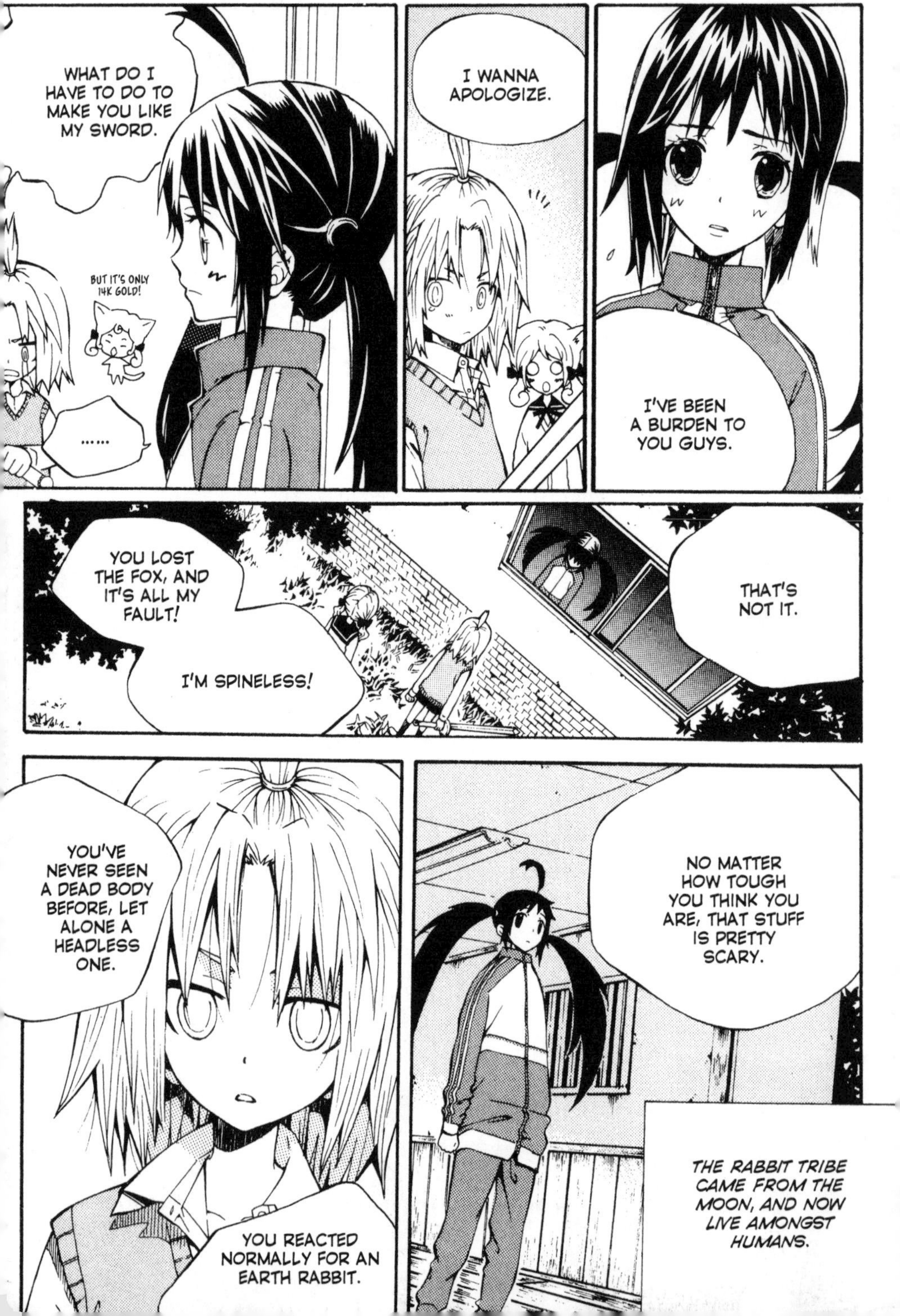
WHAT DO I HAVE TO DO TO MAKE YOU LIKE MY SWORD.
BUT IT'S ONLY 14K GOLD!
......
I WANNA APOLOGIZE.
I'VE BEEN A BURDEN TO YOU GUYS.
YOU LOST THE FOX, AND IT'S ALL MY FAULT!
I'M SPINELESS!
THAT'S NOT IT.
YOU'VE NEVER SEEN A DEAD BODY BEFORE, LET ALONE A HEADLESS ONE.
YOU REACTED NORMALLY FOR AN EARTH RABBIT.
NO MATTER HOW TOUGH YOU THINK YOU ARE, THAT STUFF IS PRETTY SCARY.
THE RABBIT TRIBE CAME FROM THE MOON, AND NOW LIVE AMONGST HUMANS.

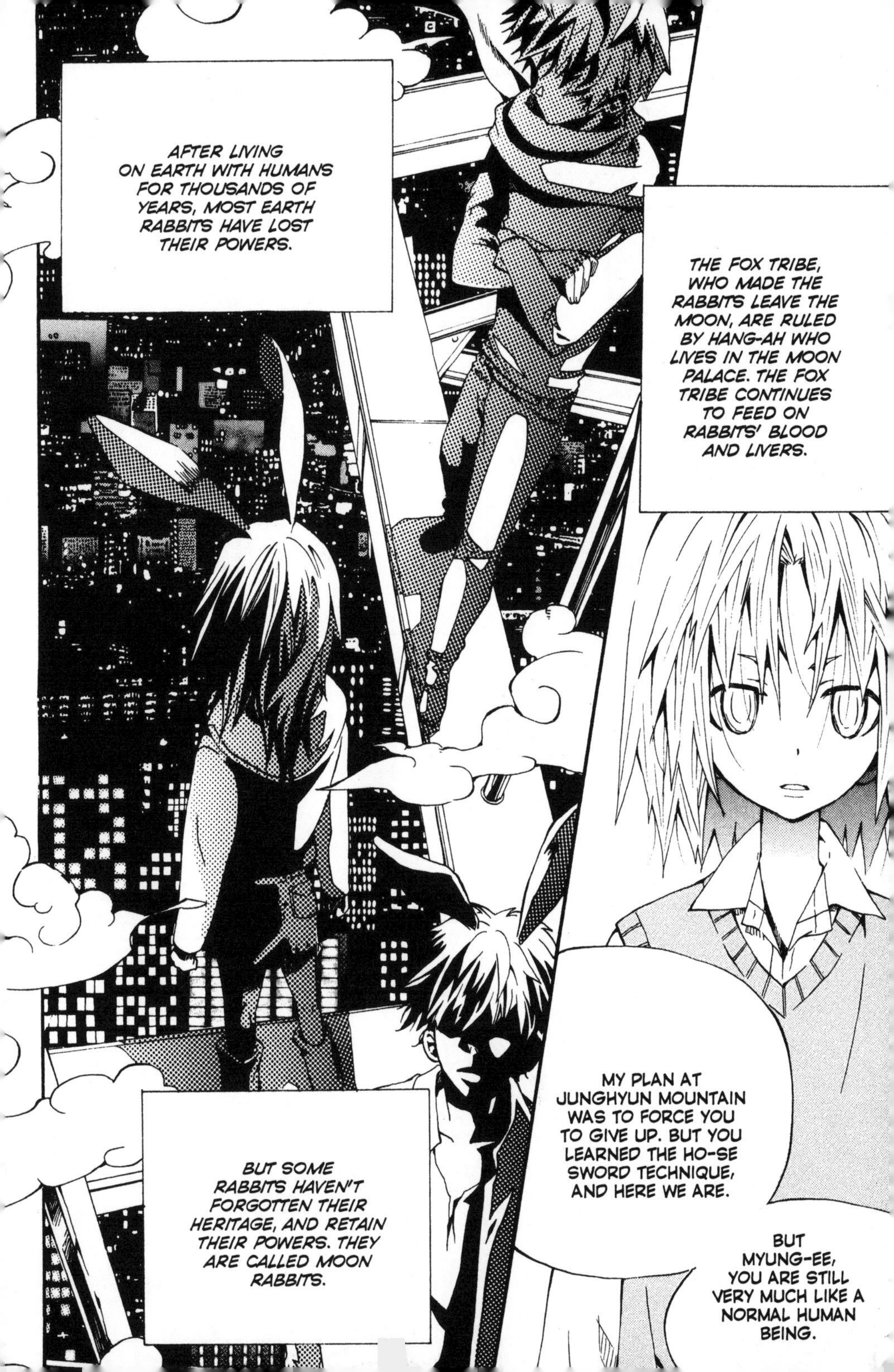
AFTER LIVING ON EARTH WITH HUMANS FOR THOUSANDS OF YEARS, MOST EARTH RABBITS HAVE LOST THEIR POWERS.
THE FOX TRIBE, WHO MADE THE RABBITS LEAVE THE MOON, ARE RULED BY HANG-AH WHO LIVES IN THE MOON PALACE. THE FOX TRIBE CONTINUES TO FEED ON RABBITS' BLOOD AND LIVERS.
BUT SOME RABBITS HAVEN'T FORGOTTEN THEIR HERITAGE, AND RETAIN THEIR POWERS. THEY ARE CALLED MOON RABBITS.
MY PLAN AT JUNGHYUN MOUNTAIN WAS TO FORCE YOU TO GIVE UP. BUT YOU LEARNED THE HO-SE SWORD TECHNIQUE, AND HERE WE ARE.
BUT MYUNG-EE, YOU ARE STILL VERY MUCH LIKE A NORMAL HUMAN BEING.

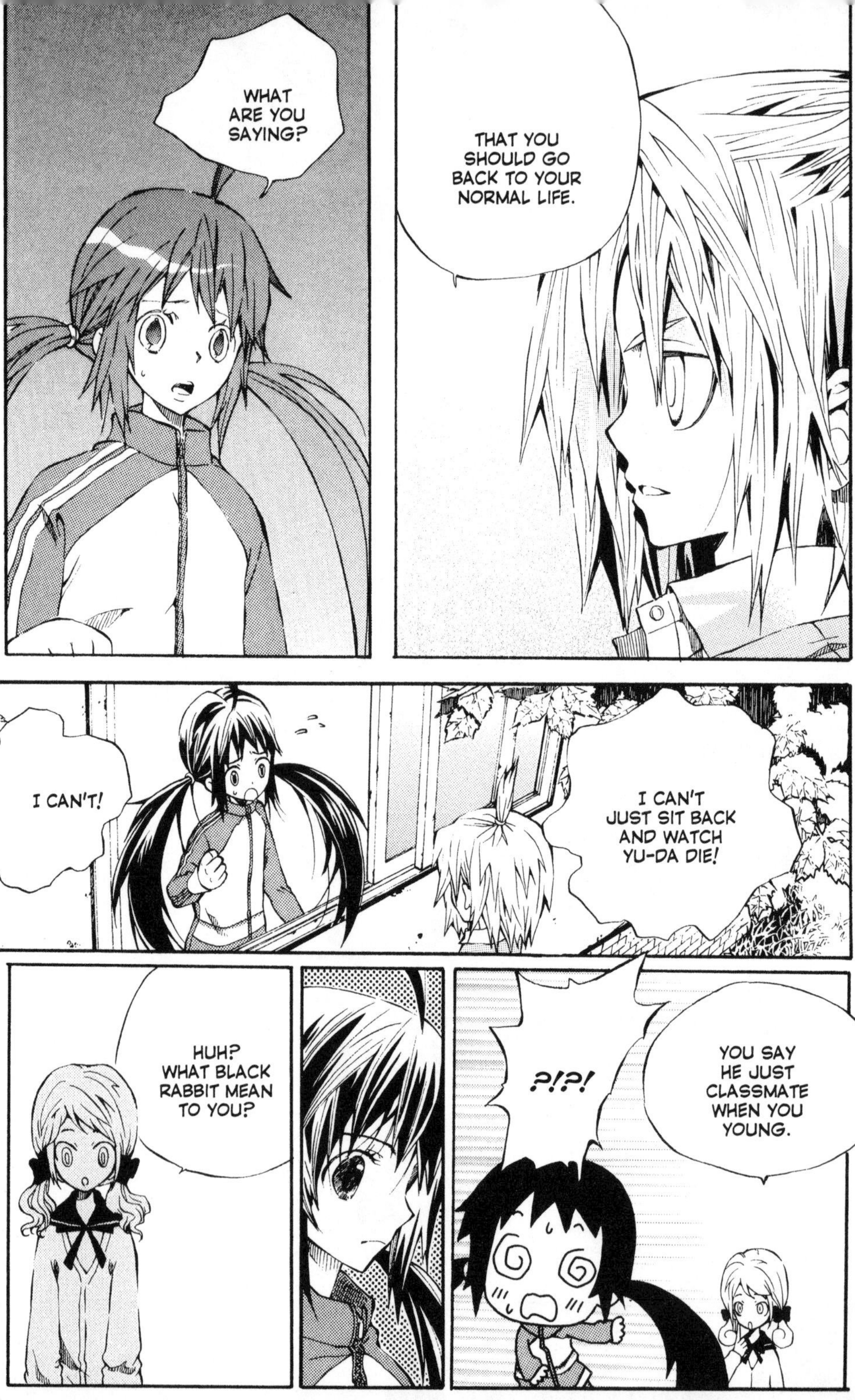
WHAT ARE YOU SAYING?
THAT YOU SHOULD GO BACK TO YOUR NORMAL LIFE.
I CAN'T!
I CAN'T JUST SIT BACK AND WATCH YU-DA DIE!
HUH? WHAT BLACK RABBIT MEAN TO YOU?
?!?!
YOU SAY HE JUST CLASSMATE WHEN YOU YOUNG.

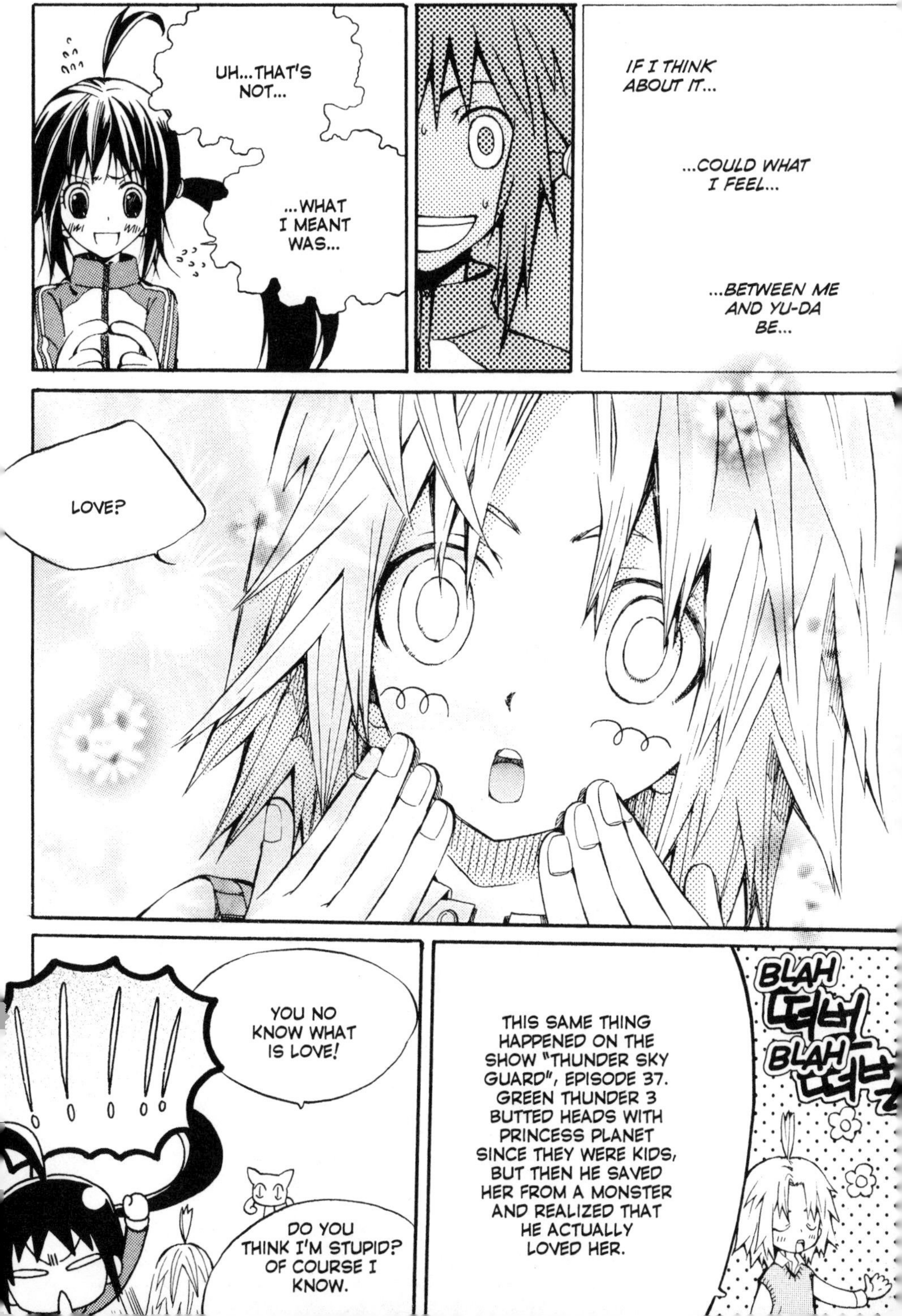
UH...THAT'S NOT...
...WHAT I MEANT WAS...
IF I THINK ABOUT IT...
...COULD WHAT I FEEL...
...BETWEEN ME AND YU-DA BE...
LOVE?
YOU NO KNOW WHAT IS LOVE!
DO YOU THINK I'M STUPID? OF COURSE I KNOW.
THIS SAME THING HAPPENED ON THE SHOW "THUNDER SKY GUARD", EPISODE 37. GREEN THUNDER 3 BUTTED HEADS WITH PRINCESS PLANET SINCE THEY WERE KIDS, BUT THEN HE SAVED HER FROM A MONSTER AND REALIZED THAT HE ACTUALLY LOVED HER.
BLAH 떠벌
BLAH 떠벌

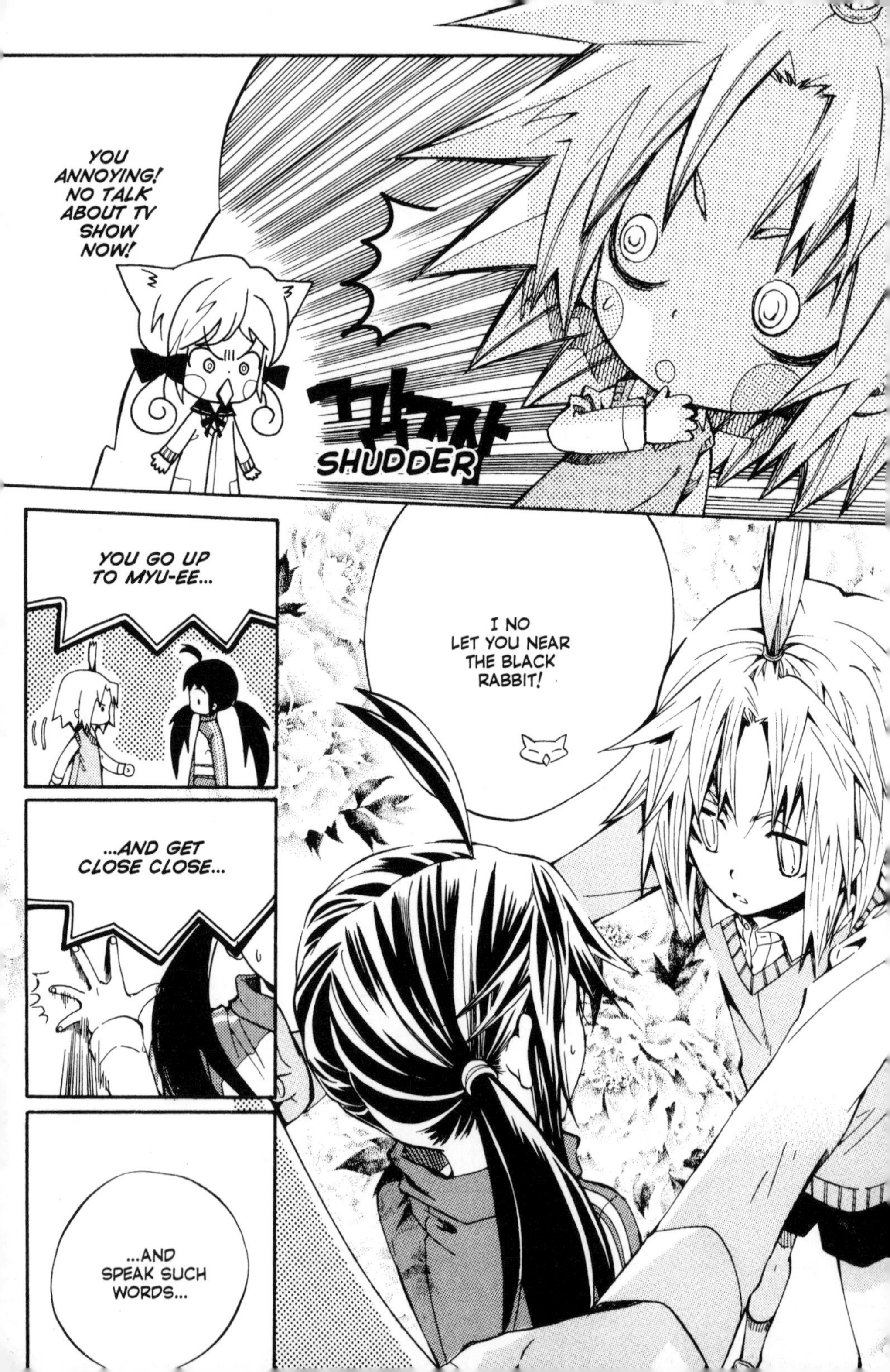
YOU ANNOYING! NO TALK ABOUT TV SHOW NOW!
SHUDDER
YOU GO UP TO MYU-EE...
...AND GET CLOSE CLOSE...
...AND SPEAK SUCH WORDS...
I NO LET YOU NEAR THE BLACK RABBIT!

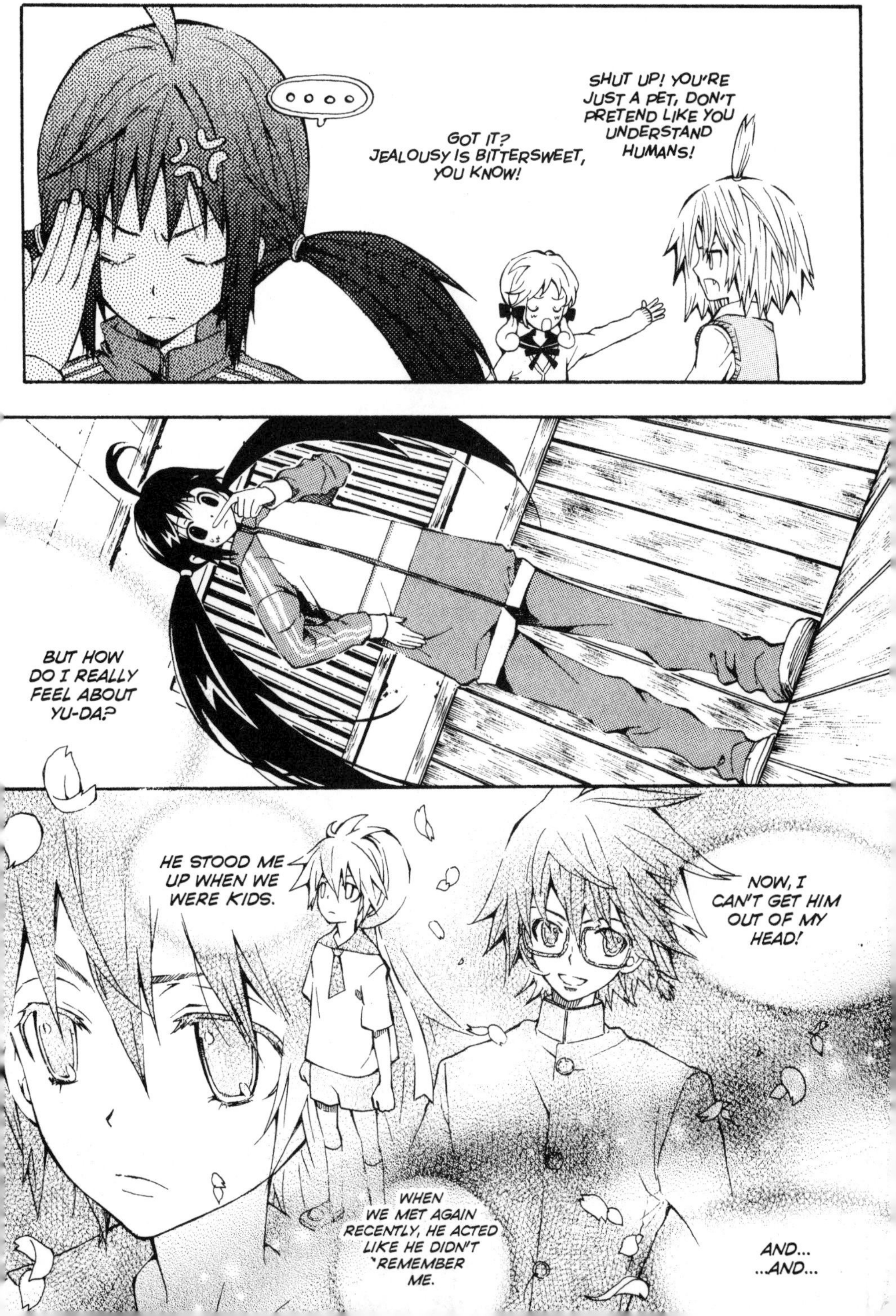
....
GOT IT? JEALOUSY IS BITTERSWEET, YOU KNOW!
SHUT UP! YOU'RE JUST A PET, DON'T PRETEND LIKE YOU UNDERSTAND HUMANS!
BUT HOW DO I REALLY FEEL ABOUT YU-DA?
HE STOOD ME UP WHEN WE WERE KIDS.
NOW, I CAN'T GET HIM OUT OF MY HEAD!
WHEN WE MET AGAIN RECENTLY, HE ACTED LIKE HE DIDN'T REMEMBER ME.
AND... ...AND...

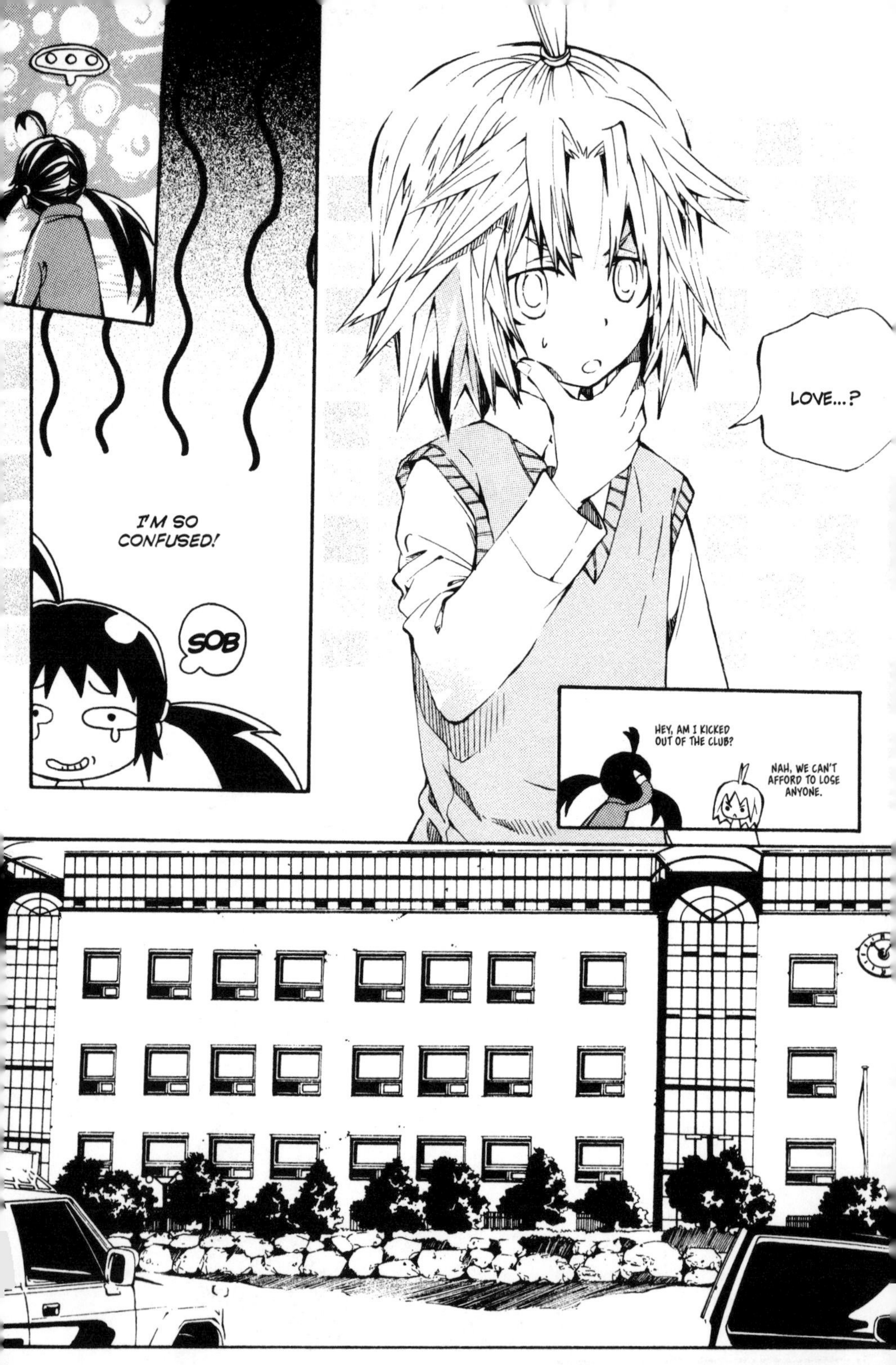
...
I'M SO CONFUSED!
SOB
LOVE...?
HEY, AM I KICKED OUT OF THE CLUB?
NAH, WE CAN'T AFFORD TO LOSE ANYONE.

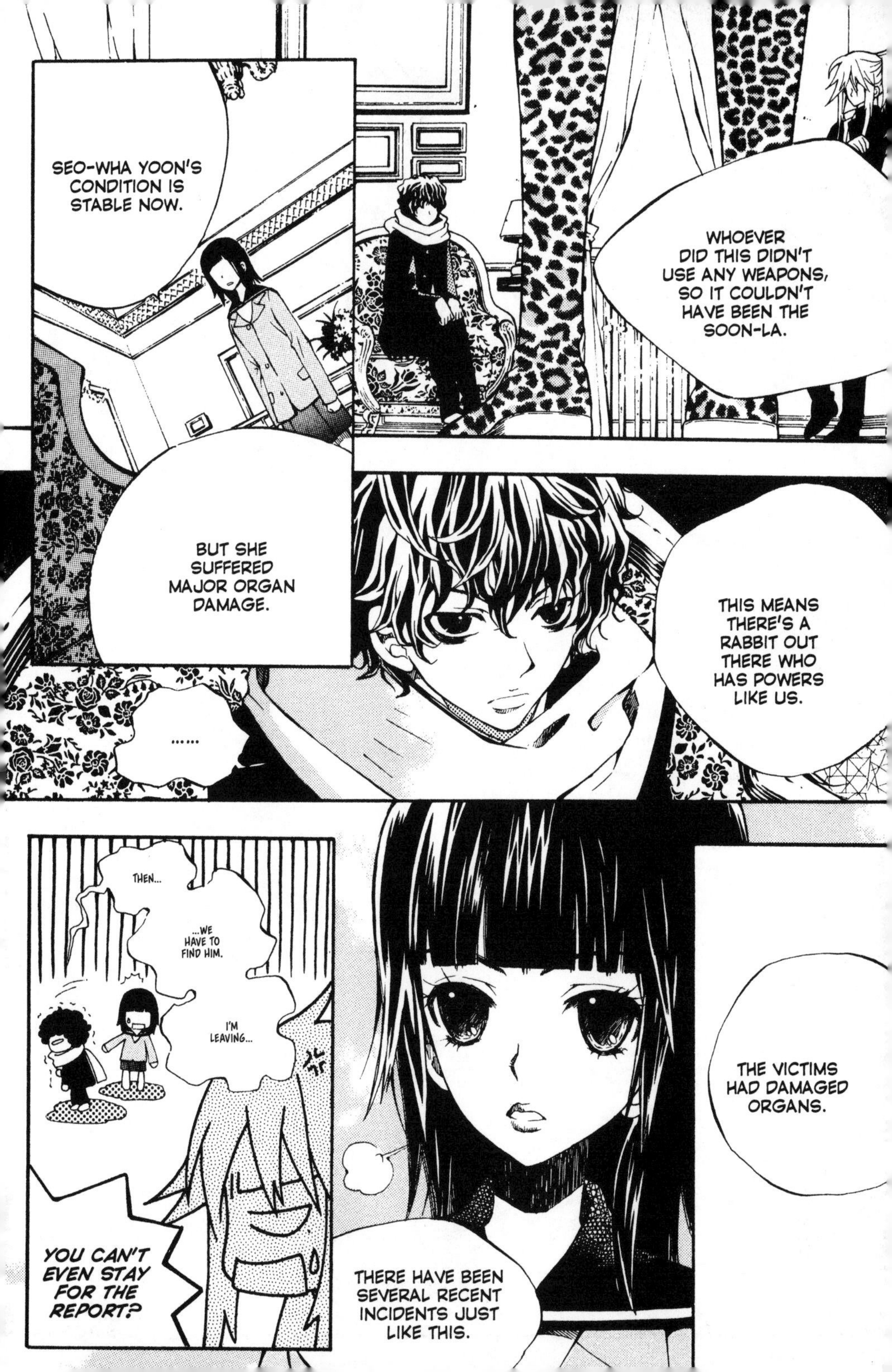

SEO-WHA YOON'S CONDITION IS STABLE NOW.
BUT SHE SUFFERED MAJOR ORGAN DAMAGE.
WHOEVER DID THIS DIDN'T USE ANY WEAPONS, SO IT COULDN'T HAVE BEEN THE SOON-LA.
THIS MEANS THERE'S A RABBIT OUT THERE WHO HAS POWERS LIKE US.
......
THEN...
...WE HAVE TO FIND HIM.
I'M LEAVING...
YOU CAN'T EVEN STAY FOR THE REPORT?
THE VICTIMS HAD DAMAGED ORGANS.
THERE HAVE BEEN SEVERAL RECENT INCIDENTS JUST LIKE THIS.

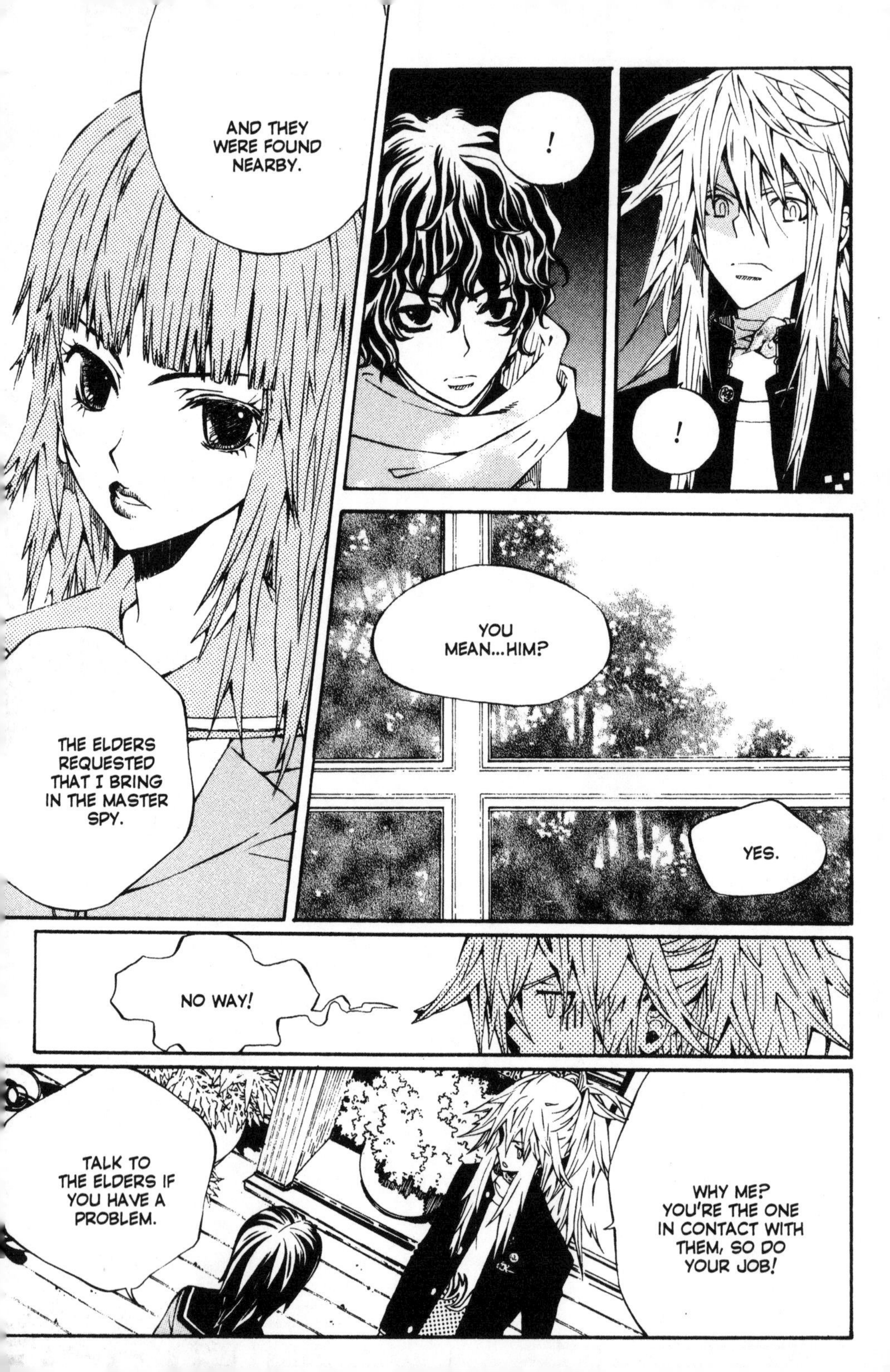

AND THEY WERE FOUND NEARBY.
THE ELDERS REQUESTED THAT I BRING IN THE MASTER SPY.
!
!
YOU MEAN...HIM?
YES.
NO WAY!
TALK TO THE ELDERS IF YOU HAVE A PROBLEM.
WHY ME? YOU'RE THE ONE IN CONTACT WITH THEM, SO DO YOUR JOB!

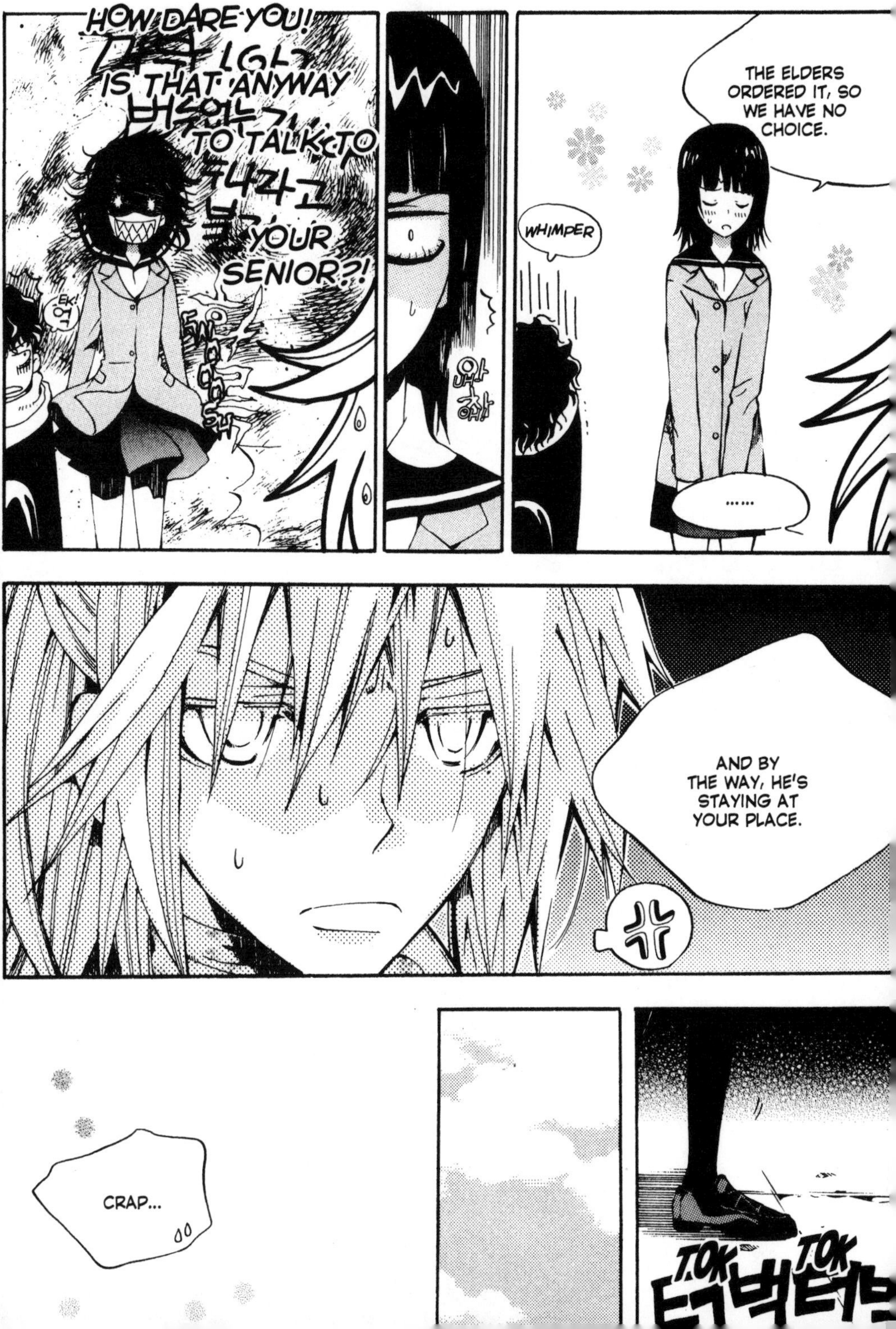
HOW DARE YOU!
IS THAT ANYWAY TO TALK TO YOUR SENIOR?!
EK!
WHIMPER
THE ELDERS ORDERED IT, SO WE HAVE NO CHOICE.
......
AND BY THE WAY, HE'S STAYING AT YOUR PLACE.
CRAP...
T.OK T.OK

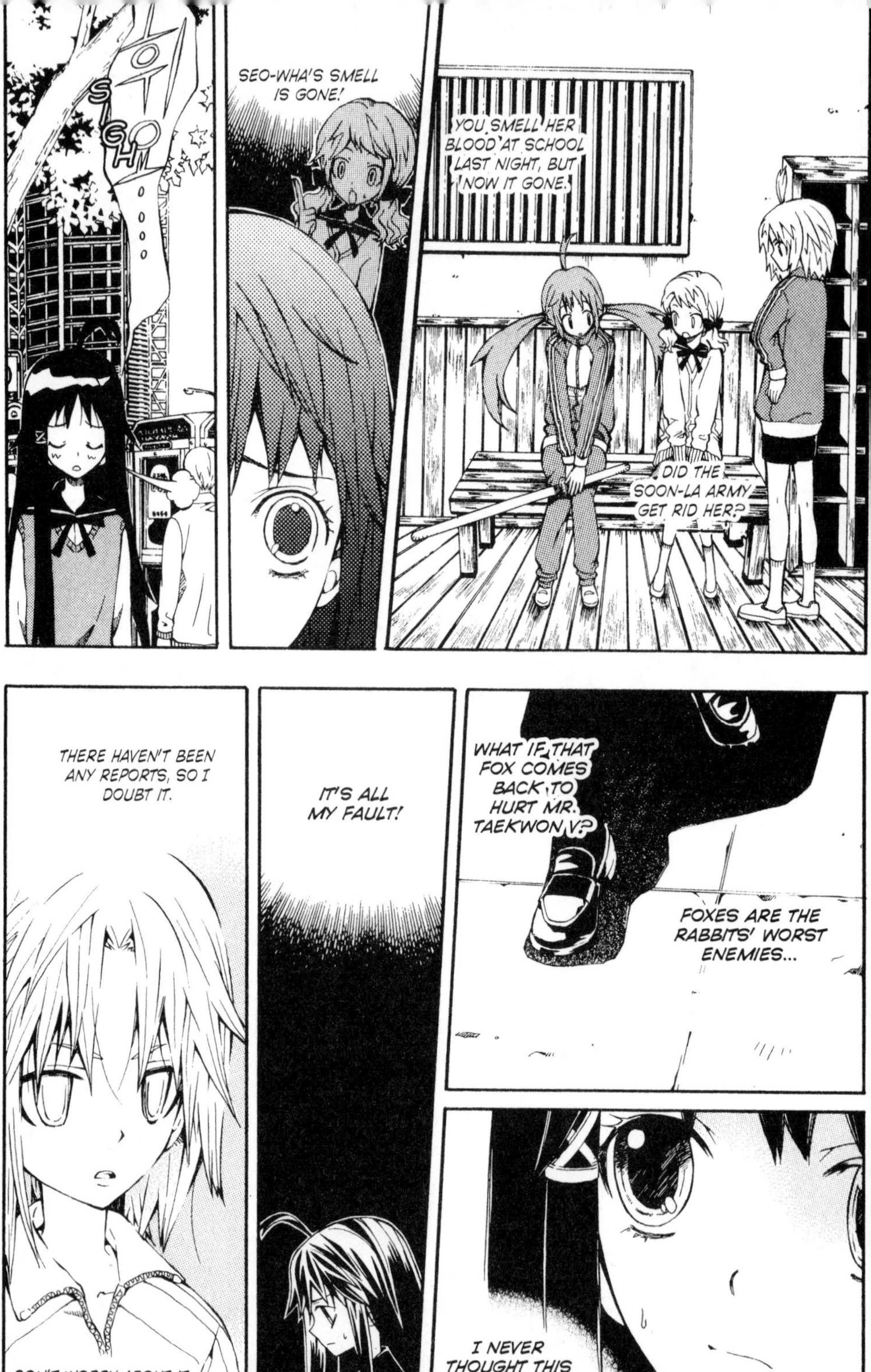
HO SIGH
SEO-WHA'S SMELL IS GONE!
YOU SMELL HER BLOOD AT SCHOOL LAST NIGHT, BUT NOW IT GONE.
DID THE SOON-LA ARMY GET RID HER?
THERE HAVEN'T BEEN ANY REPORTS, SO I DOUBT IT.
DON'T WORRY ABOUT IT.
IT'S ALL MY FAULT!
WHAT IF THAT FOX COMES BACK TO HURT MR. TAEKWON V?
FOXES ARE THE RABBITS' WORST ENEMIES...
I NEVER THOUGHT THIS COULD HAPPEN.

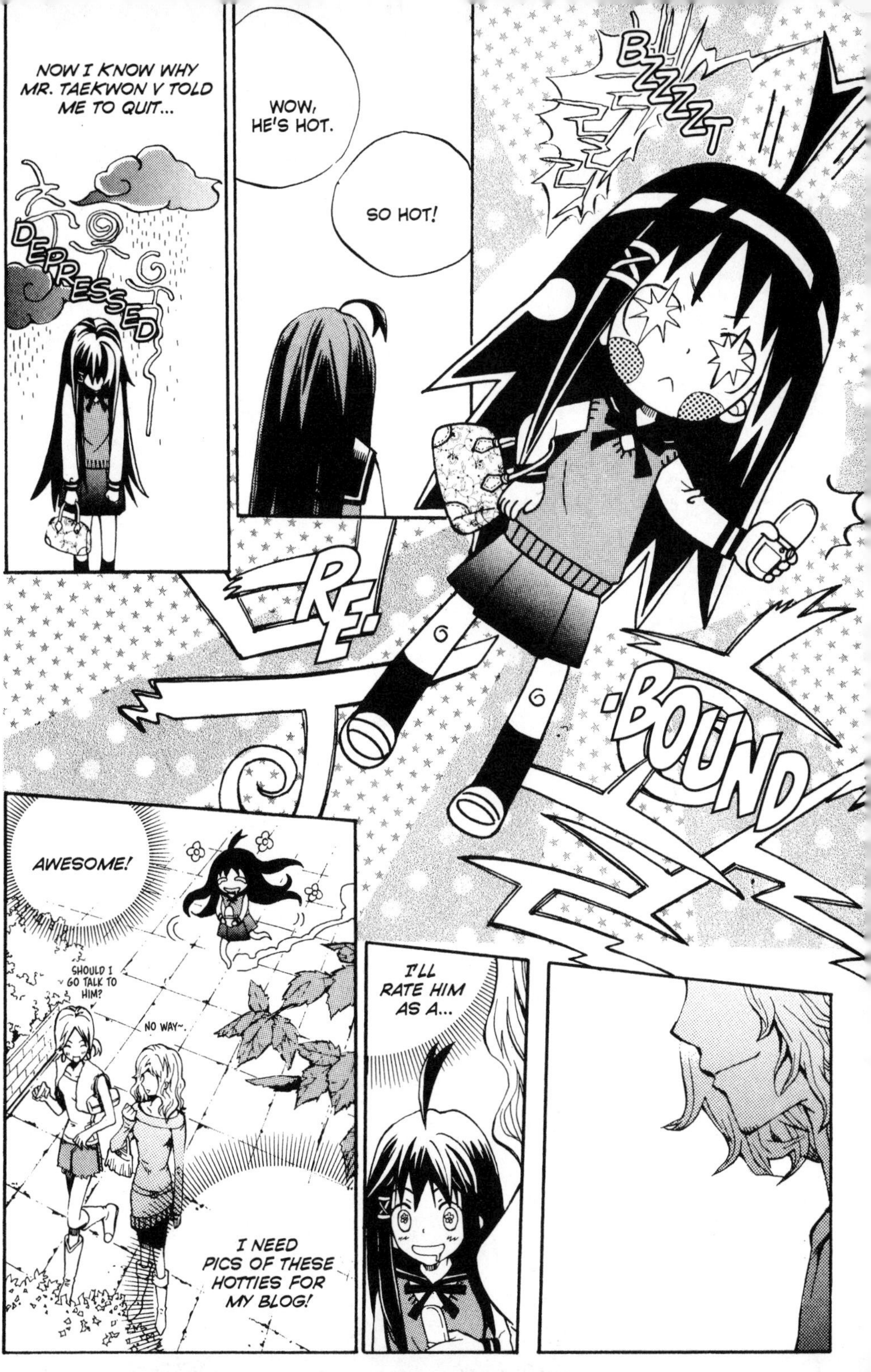
NOW I KNOW WHY MR. TAEKWON V TOLD ME TO QUIT...
DEPRESSED
WOW, HE'S HOT.
SO HOT!
BZZZZT
RE-
-BOUND
AWESOME!
SHOULD I GO TALK TO HIM?
NO WAY~.
I NEED PICS OF THESE HOTTIES FOR MY BLOG!
I'LL RATE HIM AS A...

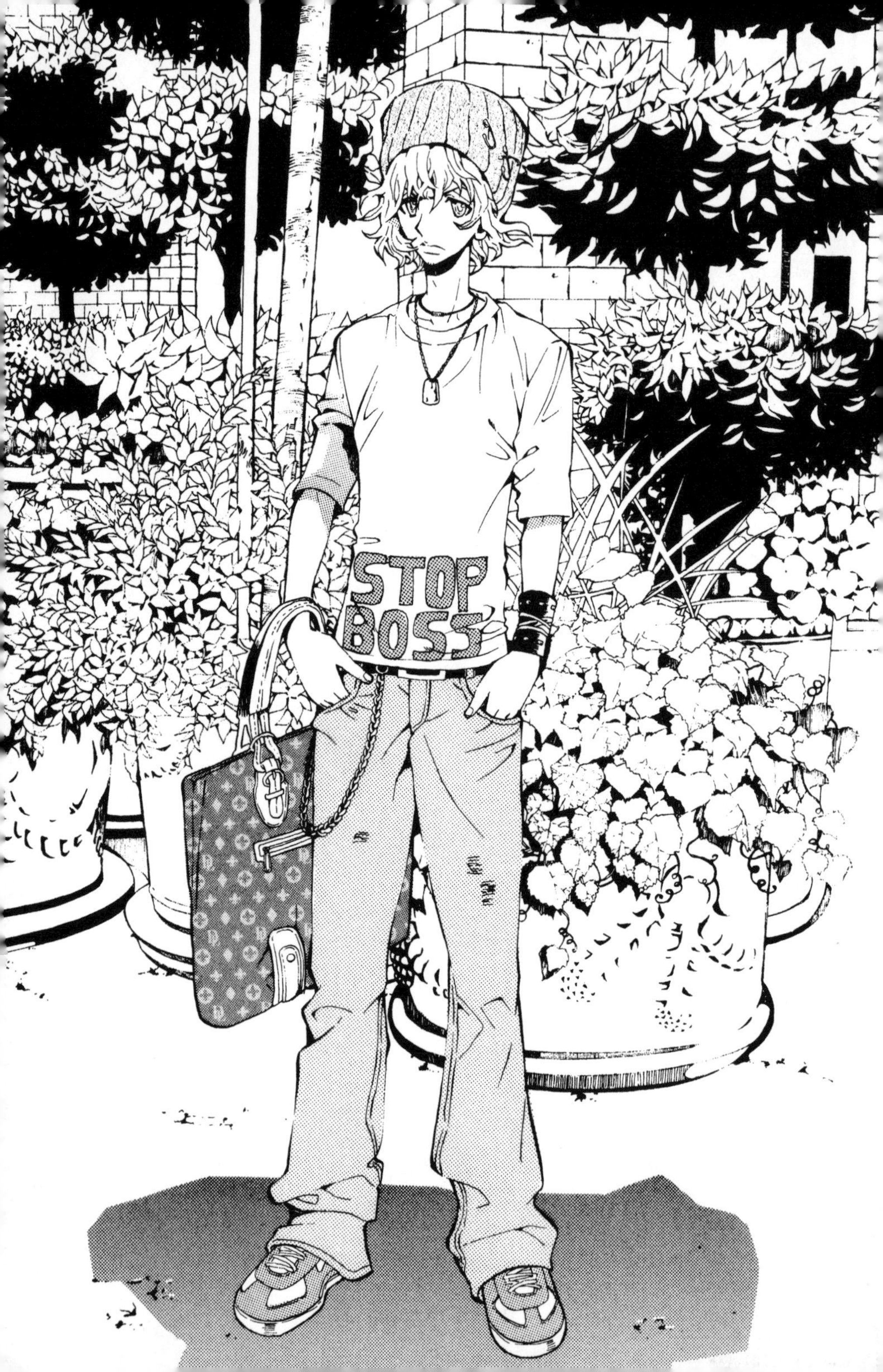
STOP
BOSS

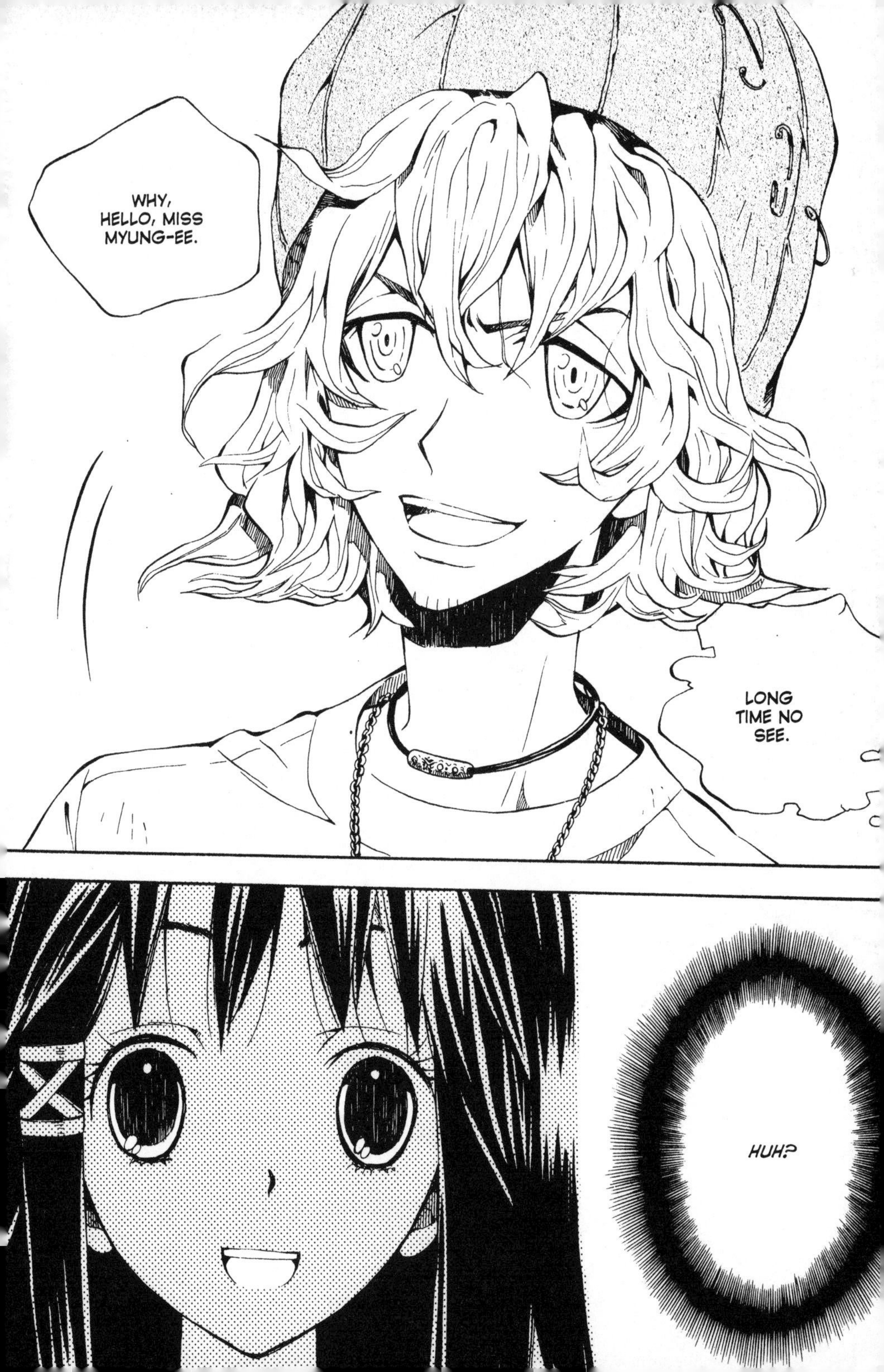
WHY, HELLO, MISS MYUNG-EE.
LONG TIME NO SEE.
HUH?

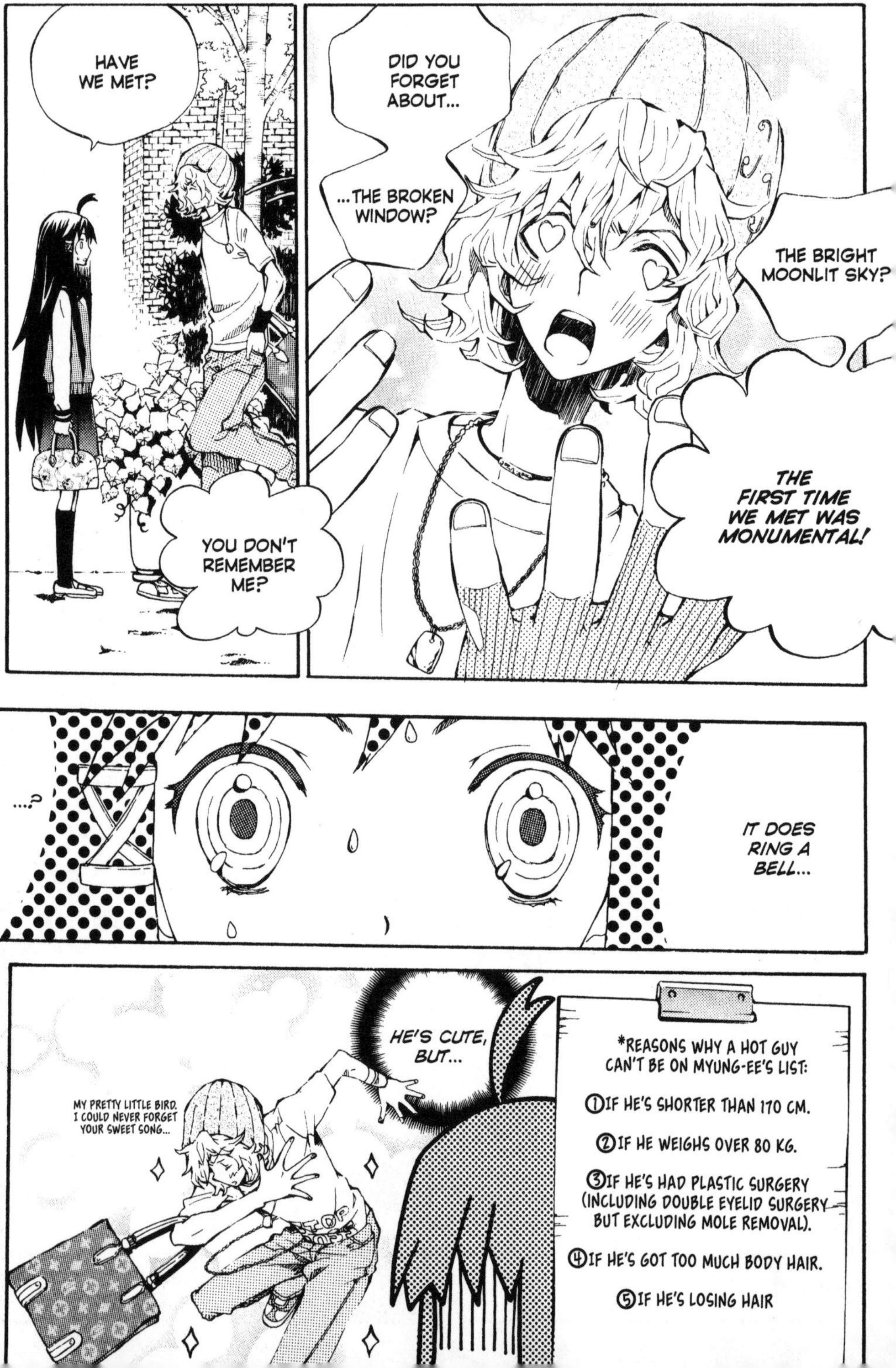
HAVE WE MET?
YOU DON'T REMEMBER ME?
DID YOU FORGET ABOUT...
...THE BROKEN WINDOW?
THE BRIGHT MOONLIT SKY?
THE FIRST TIME WE MET WAS MONUMENTAL!
...?
IT DOES RING A BELL...
HE'S CUTE, BUT...
MY PRETTY LITTLE BIRD. I COULD NEVER FORGET YOUR SWEET SONG...
*REASONS WHY A HOT GUY CAN'T BE ON MYUNG-EE'S LIST:
①IF HE'S SHORTER THAN 170 CM.
②IF HE WEIGHS OVER 80 KG.
③IF HE'S HAD PLASTIC SURGERY (INCLUDING DOUBLE EYELID SURGERY BUT EXCLUDING MOLE REMOVAL).
④IF HE'S GOT TOO MUCH BODY HAIR.
⑤IF HE'S LOSING HAIR

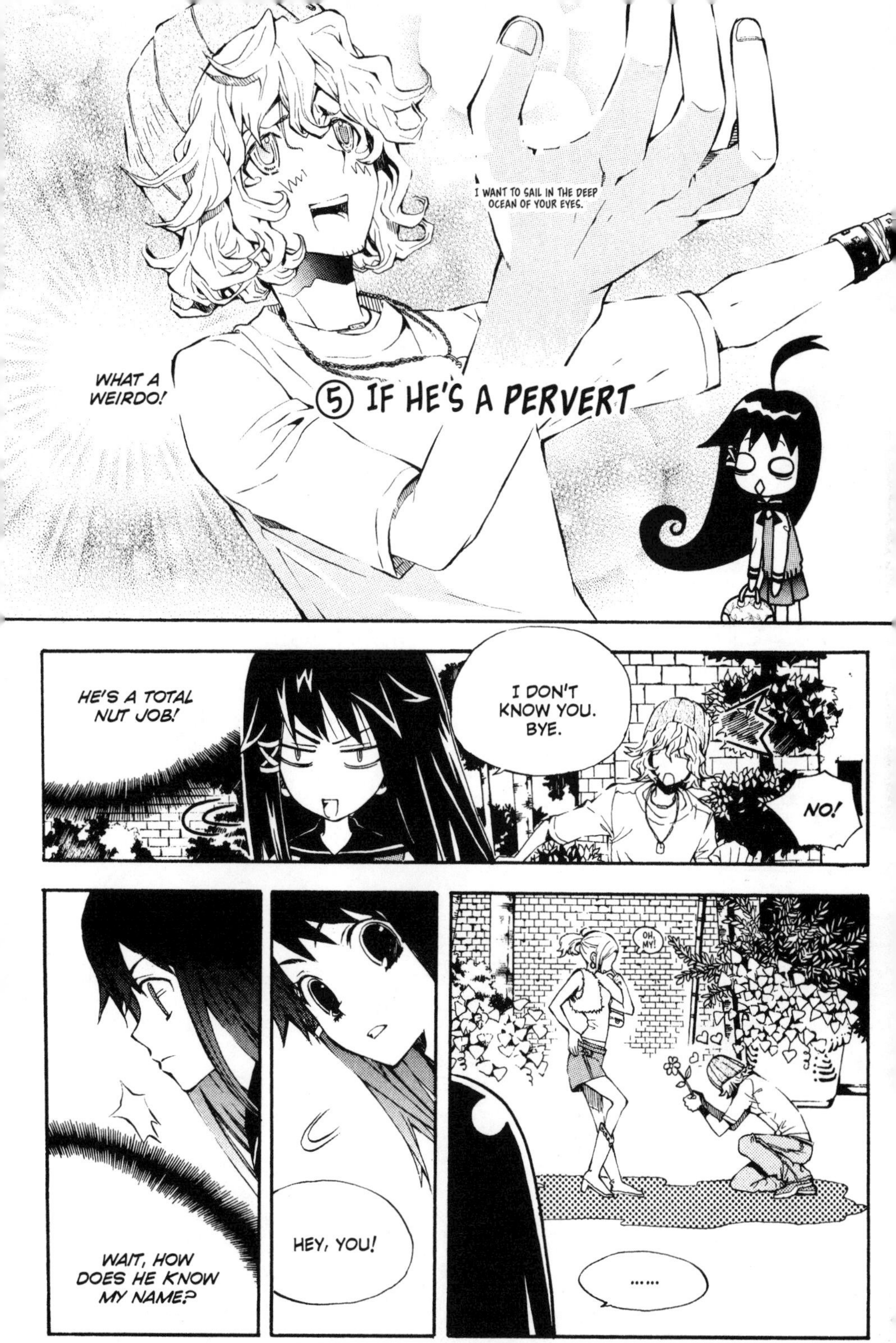
I WANT TO SAIL IN THE DEEP OCEAN OF YOUR EYES.
WHAT A WEIRDO!
5 IF HE'S A PERVERT
HE'S A TOTAL NUT JOB!
I DON'T KNOW YOU. BYE.
NO!
WAIT, HOW DOES HE KNOW MY NAME?
HEY, YOU!
OH, MY!
......

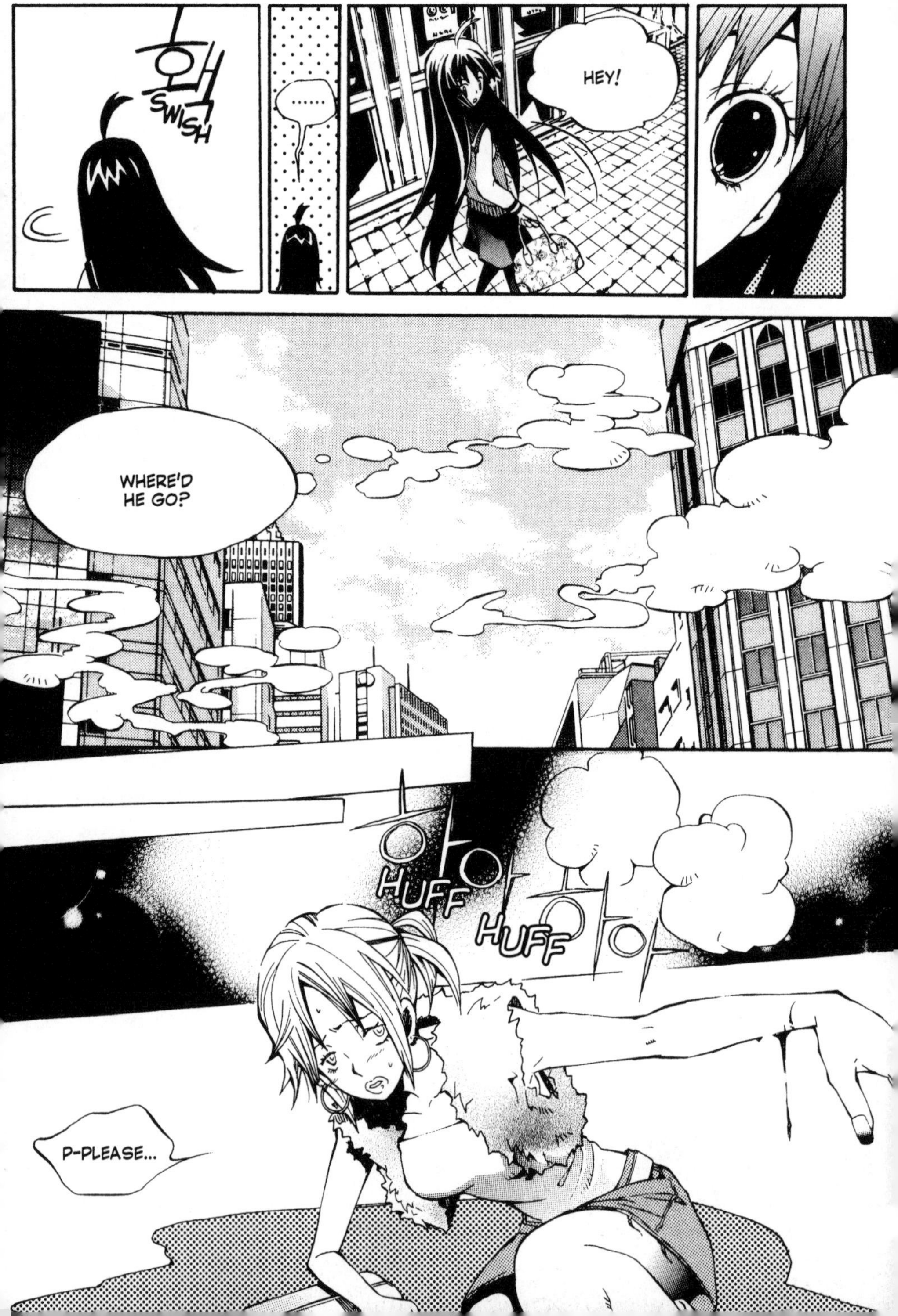
SWISH
....
HEY!
WHERE'D HE GO?
HUFF
HUFF
P-PLEASE...

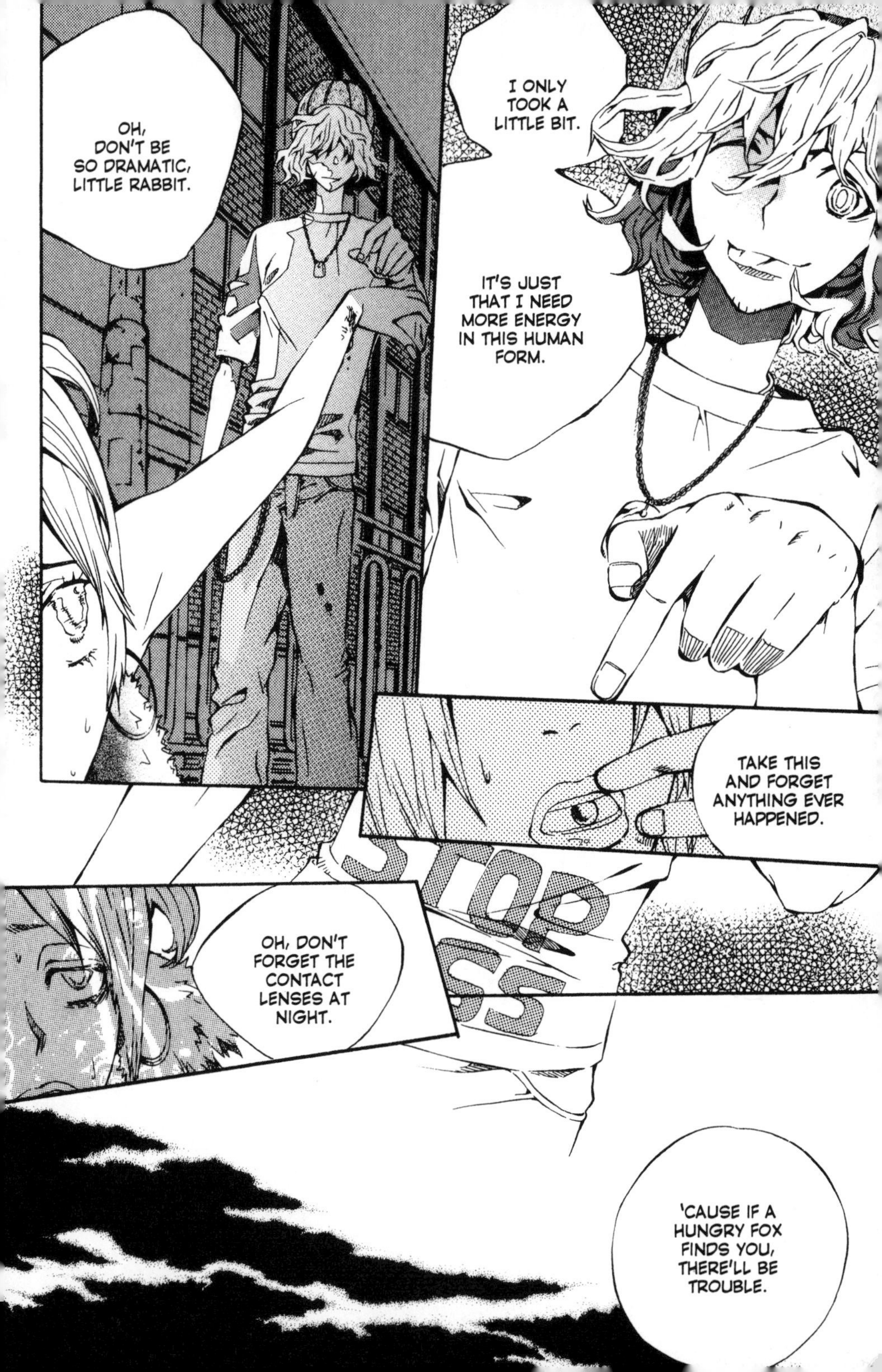
OH, DON'T BE SO DRAMATIC, LITTLE RABBIT.
I ONLY TOOK A LITTLE BIT.
IT'S JUST THAT I NEED MORE ENERGY IN THIS HUMAN FORM.
TAKE THIS AND FORGET ANYTHING EVER HAPPENED.
OH, DON'T FORGET THE CONTACT LENSES AT NIGHT.
'CAUSE IF A HUNGRY FOX FINDS YOU, THERE'LL BE TROUBLE.

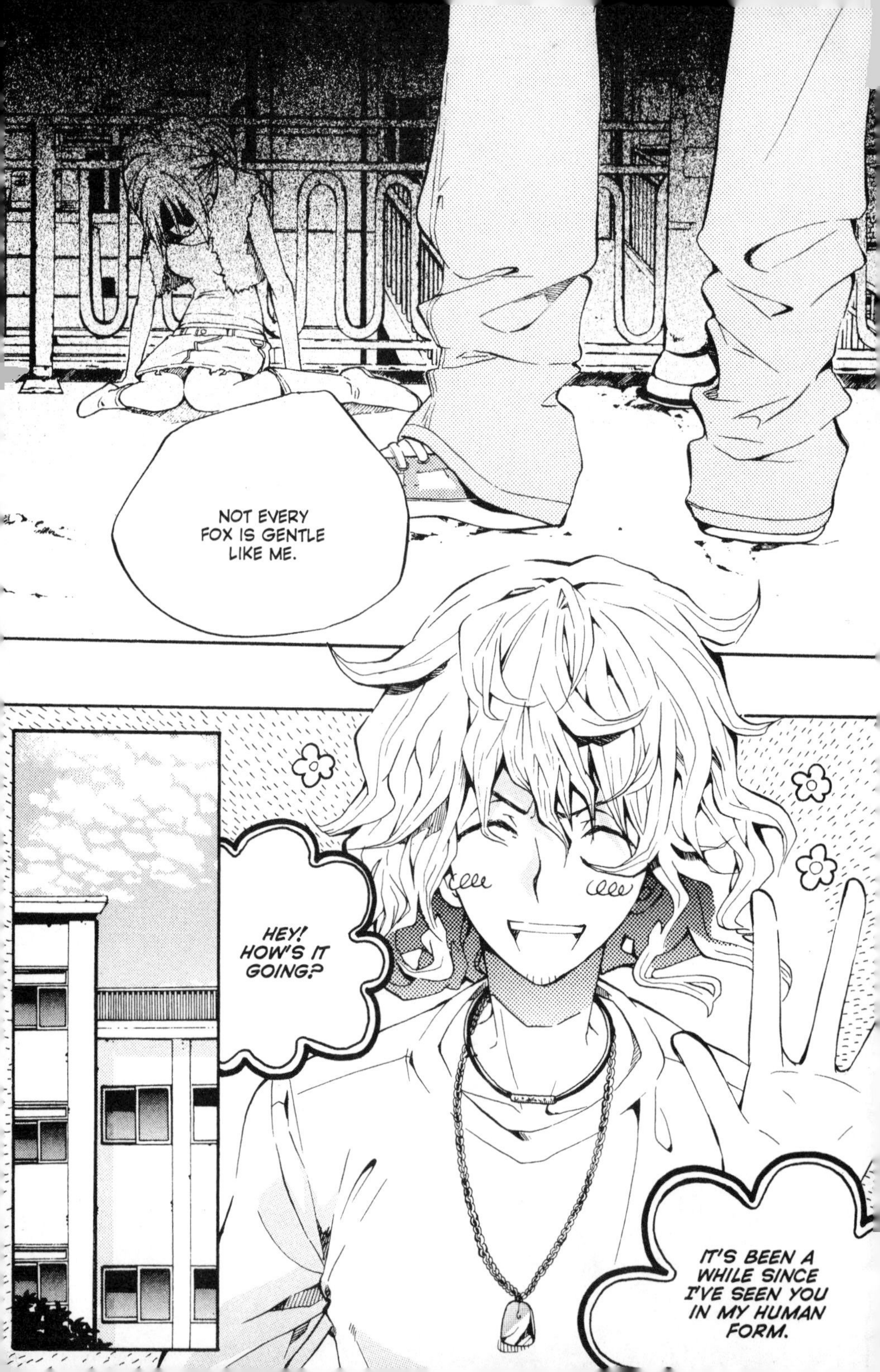
NOT EVERY FOX IS GENTLE LIKE ME.
HEY! HOW'S IT GOING?
IT'S BEEN A WHILE SINCE I'VE SEEN YOU IN MY HUMAN FORM.

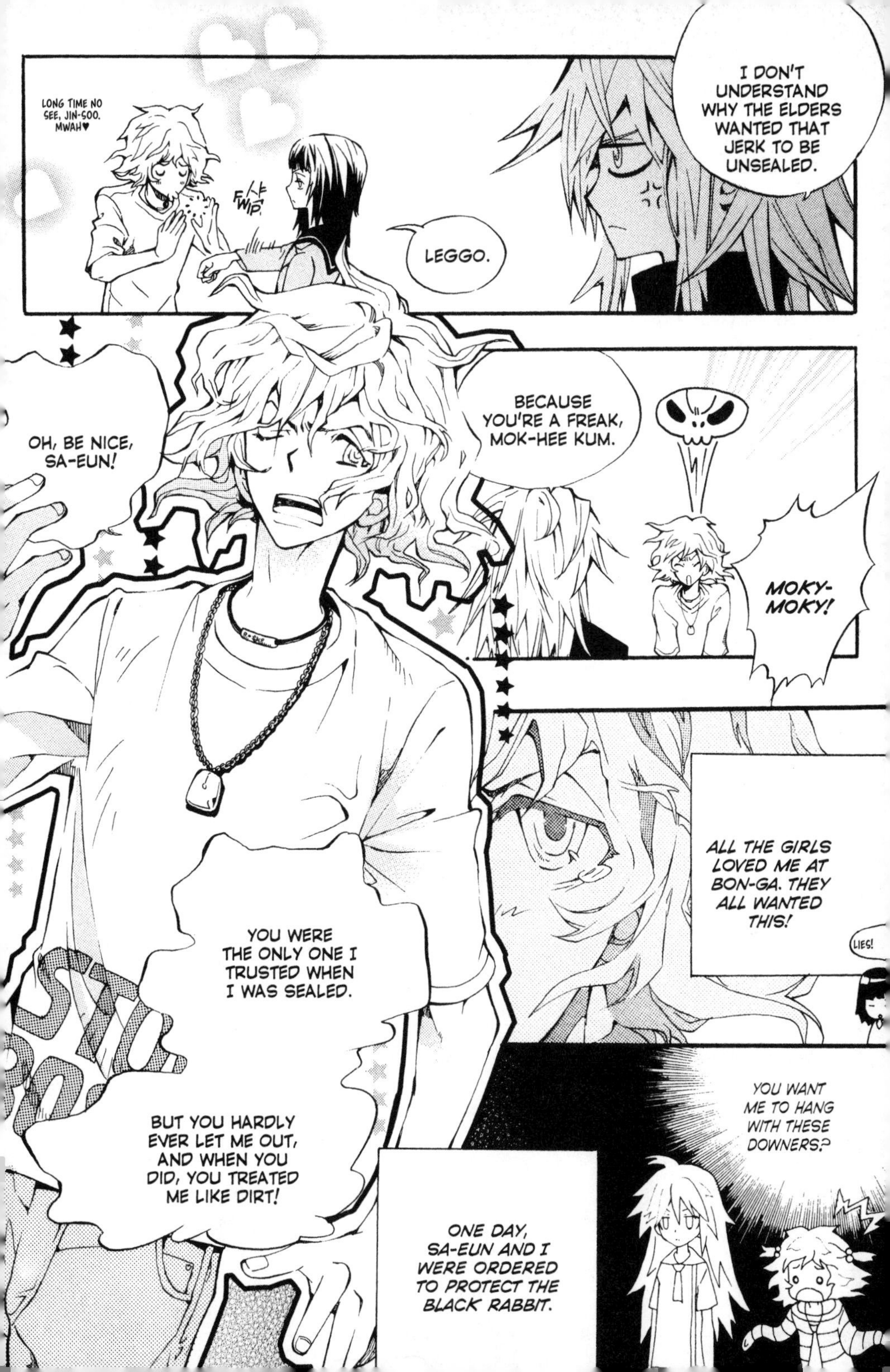
LONG TIME NO SEE, JIN-SOO. MWAH♥
FWIP!
LEGGO.
I DON'T UNDERSTAND WHY THE ELDERS WANTED THAT JERK TO BE UNSEALED.
OH, BE NICE, SA-EUN!
YOU WERE THE ONLY ONE I TRUSTED WHEN I WAS SEALED.
BUT YOU HARDLY EVER LET ME OUT, AND WHEN YOU DID, YOU TREATED ME LIKE DIRT!
BECAUSE YOU'RE A FREAK, MOK-HEE KUM.
MOKY-MOKY!
ALL THE GIRLS LOVED ME AT BON-GA. THEY ALL WANTED THIS!
LIES!
ONE DAY, SA-EUN AND I WERE ORDERED TO PROTECT THE BLACK RABBIT.
YOU WANT ME TO HANG WITH THESE DOWNERS?

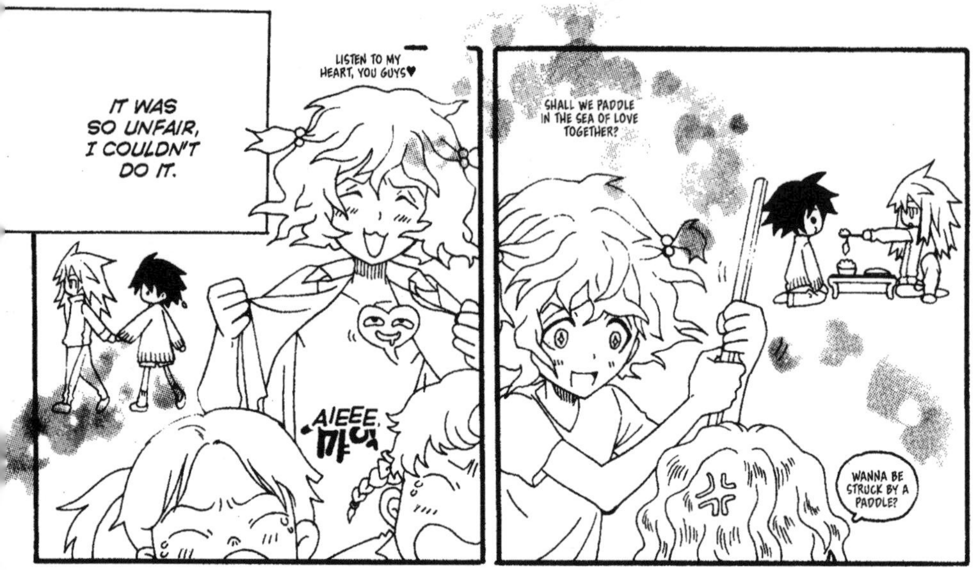
IT WAS SO UNFAIR, I COULDN'T DO IT.
LISTEN TO MY HEART, YOU GUYS♥
AIEEE.
SHALL WE PADDLE IN THE SEA OF LOVE TOGETHER?
WANNA BE STRUCK BY A PADDLE?

DO YOUR JOB!

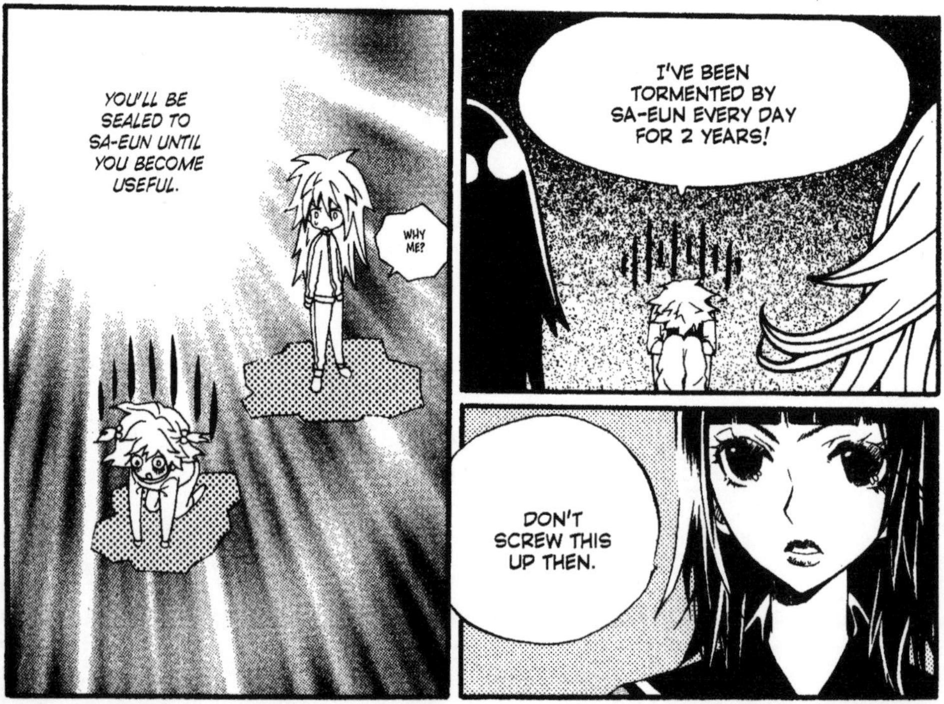
YOU'LL BE SEALED TO SA-EUN UNTIL YOU BECOME USEFUL.
WHY ME?
I'VE BEEN TORMENTED BY SA-EUN EVERY DAY FOR 2 YEARS!
DON'T SCREW THIS UP THEN.

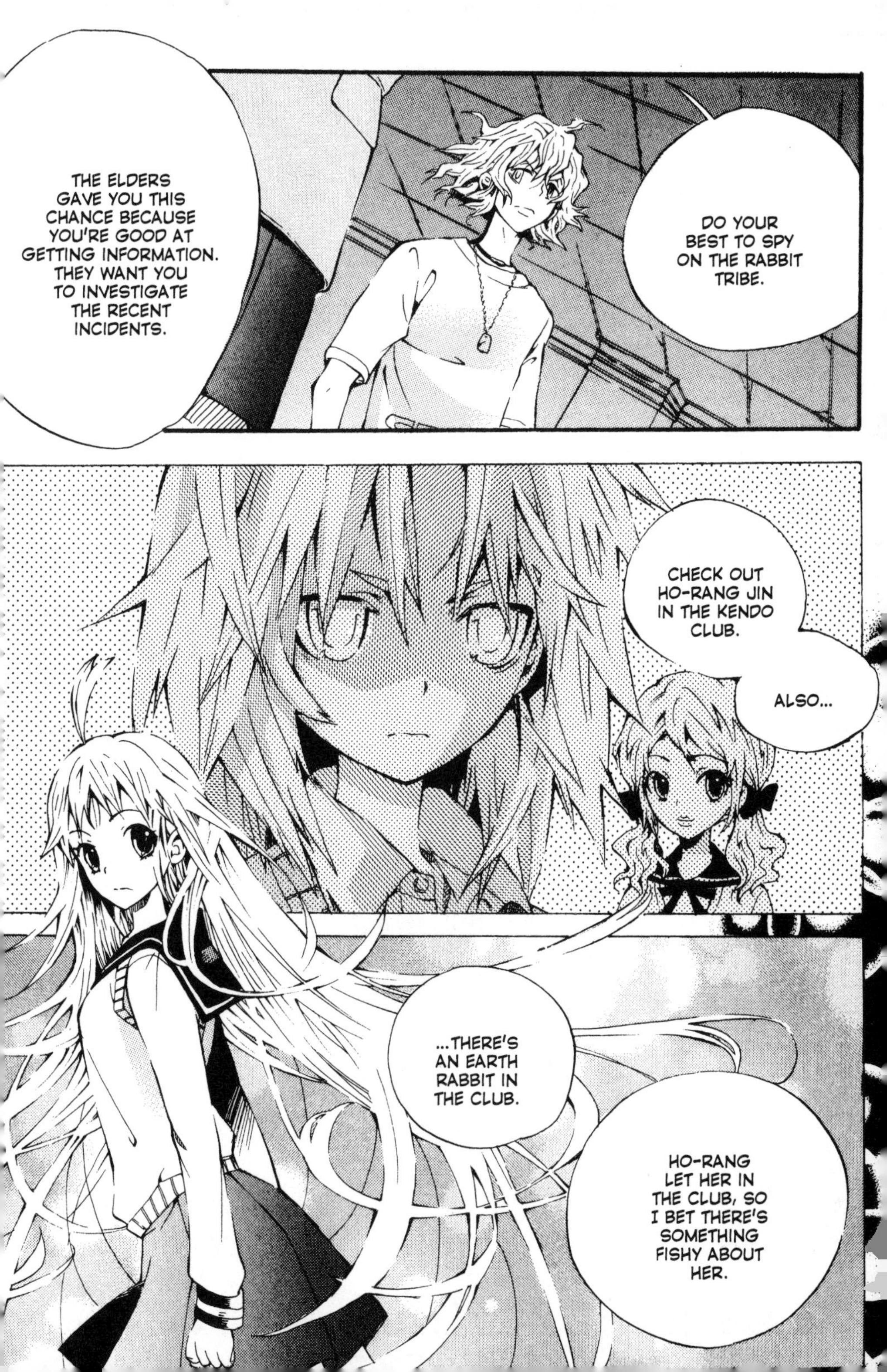
THE ELDERS GAVE YOU THIS CHANCE BECAUSE YOU'RE GOOD AT GETTING INFORMATION. THEY WANT YOU TO INVESTIGATE THE RECENT INCIDENTS.
DO YOUR BEST TO SPY ON THE RABBIT TRIBE.
CHECK OUT HO-RANG JIN IN THE KENDO CLUB.
ALSO...
...THERE'S AN EARTH RABBIT IN THE CLUB.
HO-RANG LET HER IN THE CLUB, SO I BET THERE'S SOMETHING FISHY ABOUT HER.

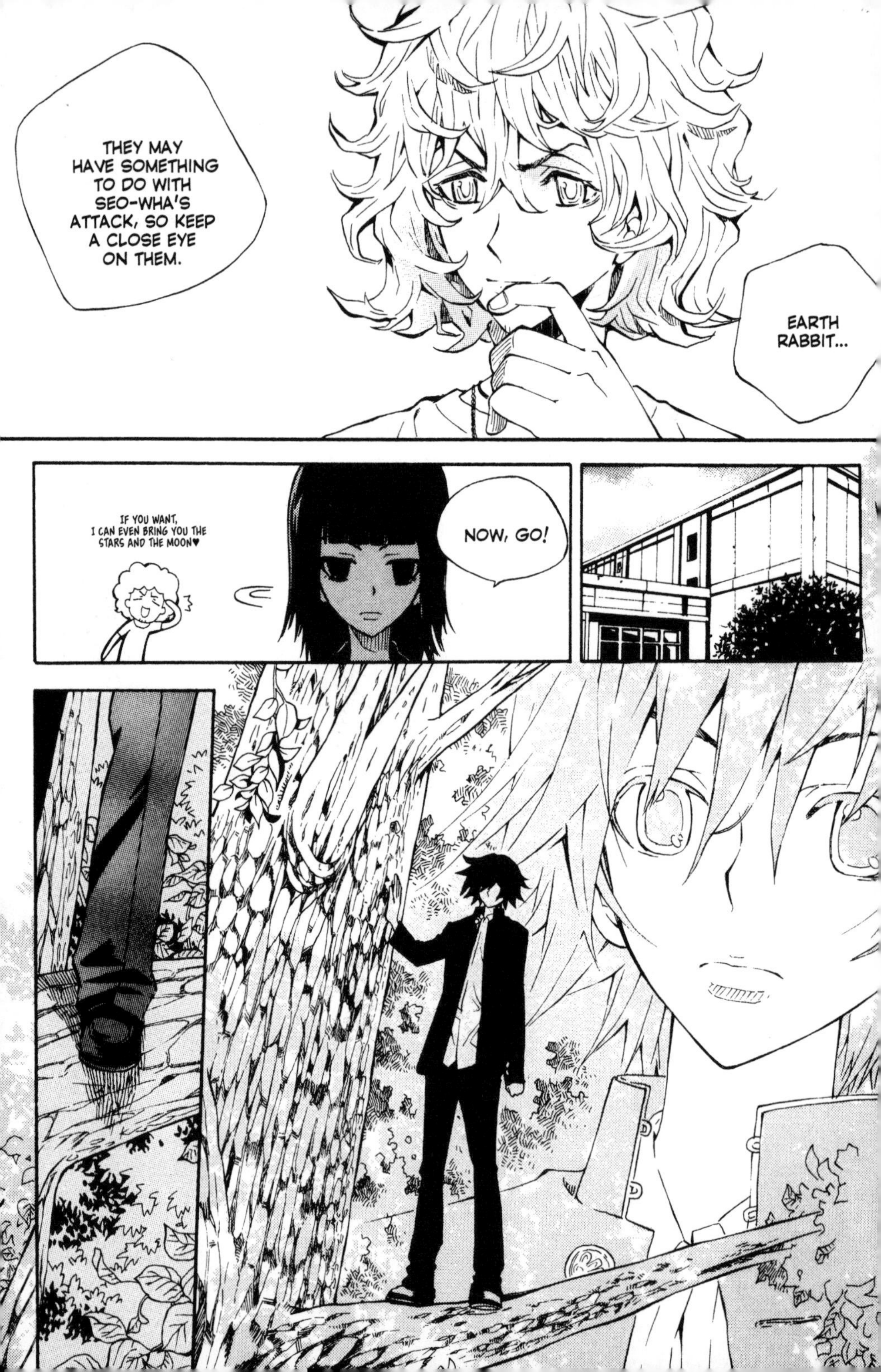
THEY MAY HAVE SOMETHING TO DO WITH SEO-WHA'S ATTACK, SO KEEP A CLOSE EYE ON THEM.
EARTH RABBIT...
IF YOU WANT, I CAN EVEN BRING YOU THE STARS AND THE MOON♥
NOW, GO!

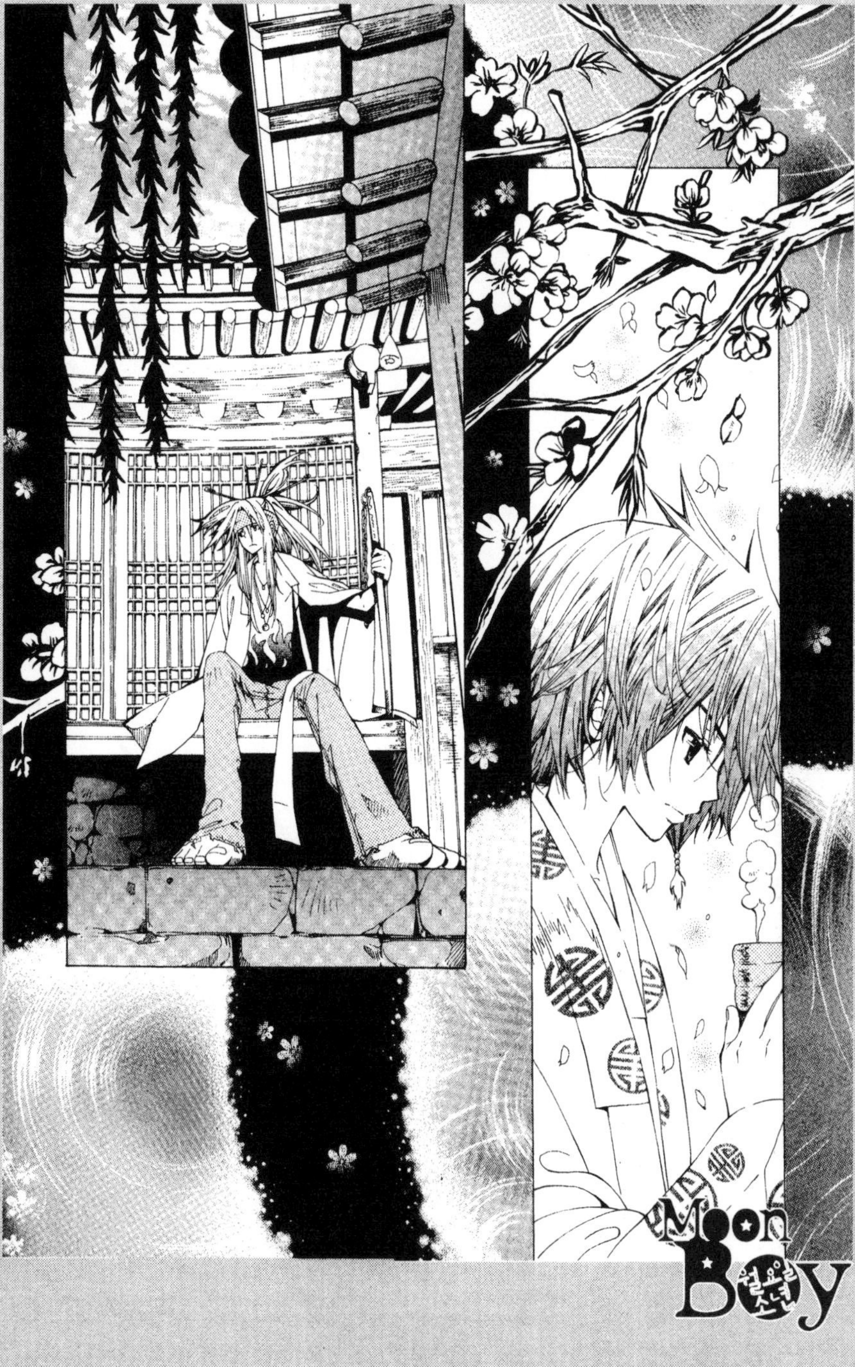
Moon Boy
월요일 소년

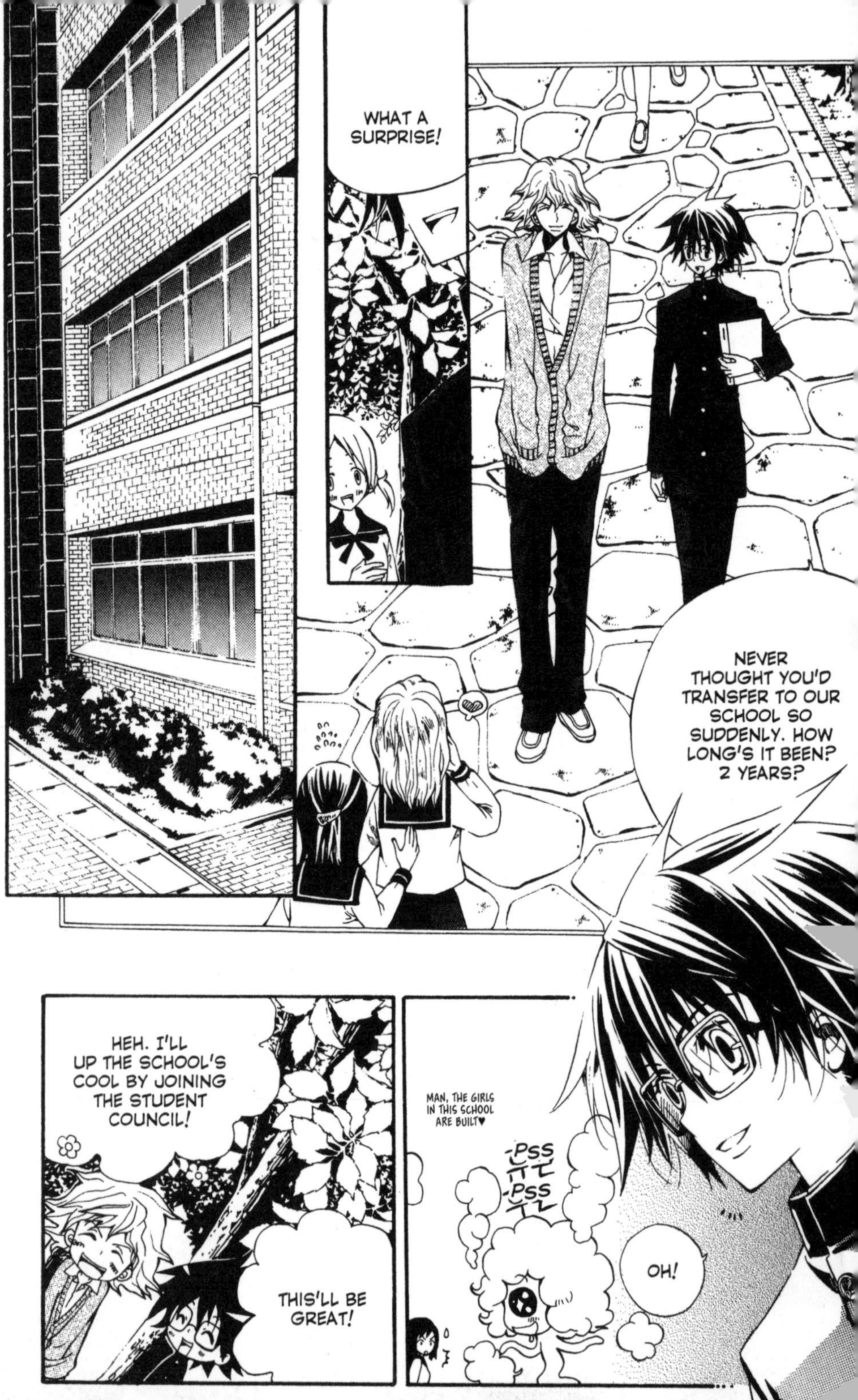
WHAT A SURPRISE!
NEVER THOUGHT YOU'D TRANSFER TO OUR SCHOOL SO SUDDENLY. HOW LONG'S IT BEEN? 2 YEARS?
HEH. I'LL UP THE SCHOOL'S COOL BY JOINING THE STUDENT COUNCIL!
THIS'LL BE GREAT!
MAN, THE GIRLS IN THIS SCHOOL ARE BUILT♥
-PSS
-PSS
OH!

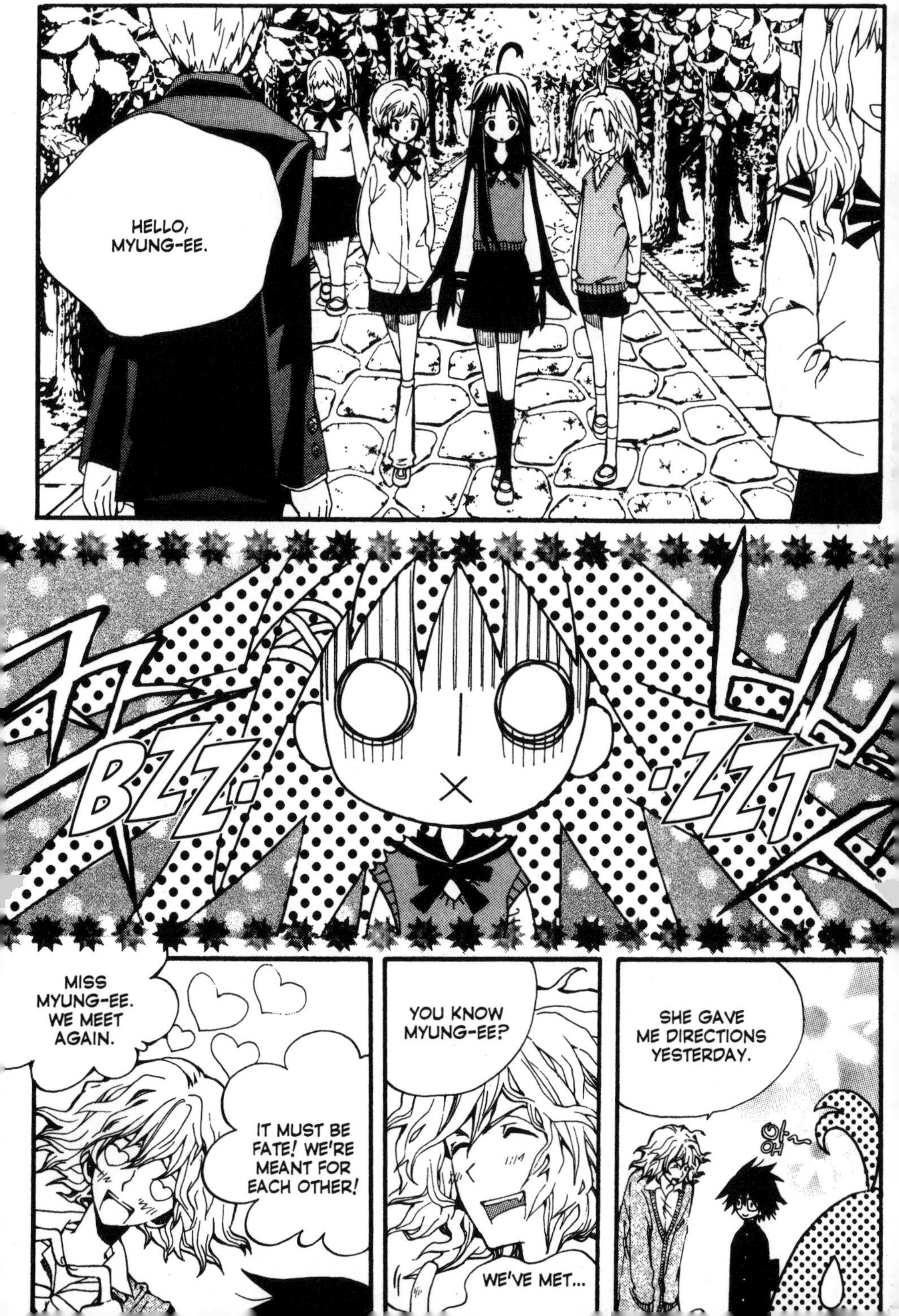
HELLO, MYUNG-EE.
BZZ-ZZT
MISS MYUNG-EE. WE MEET AGAIN.
IT MUST BE FATE! WE'RE MEANT FOR EACH OTHER!
YOU KNOW MYUNG-EE?
WE'VE MET...
SHE GAVE ME DIRECTIONS YESTERDAY.
아~ OH~

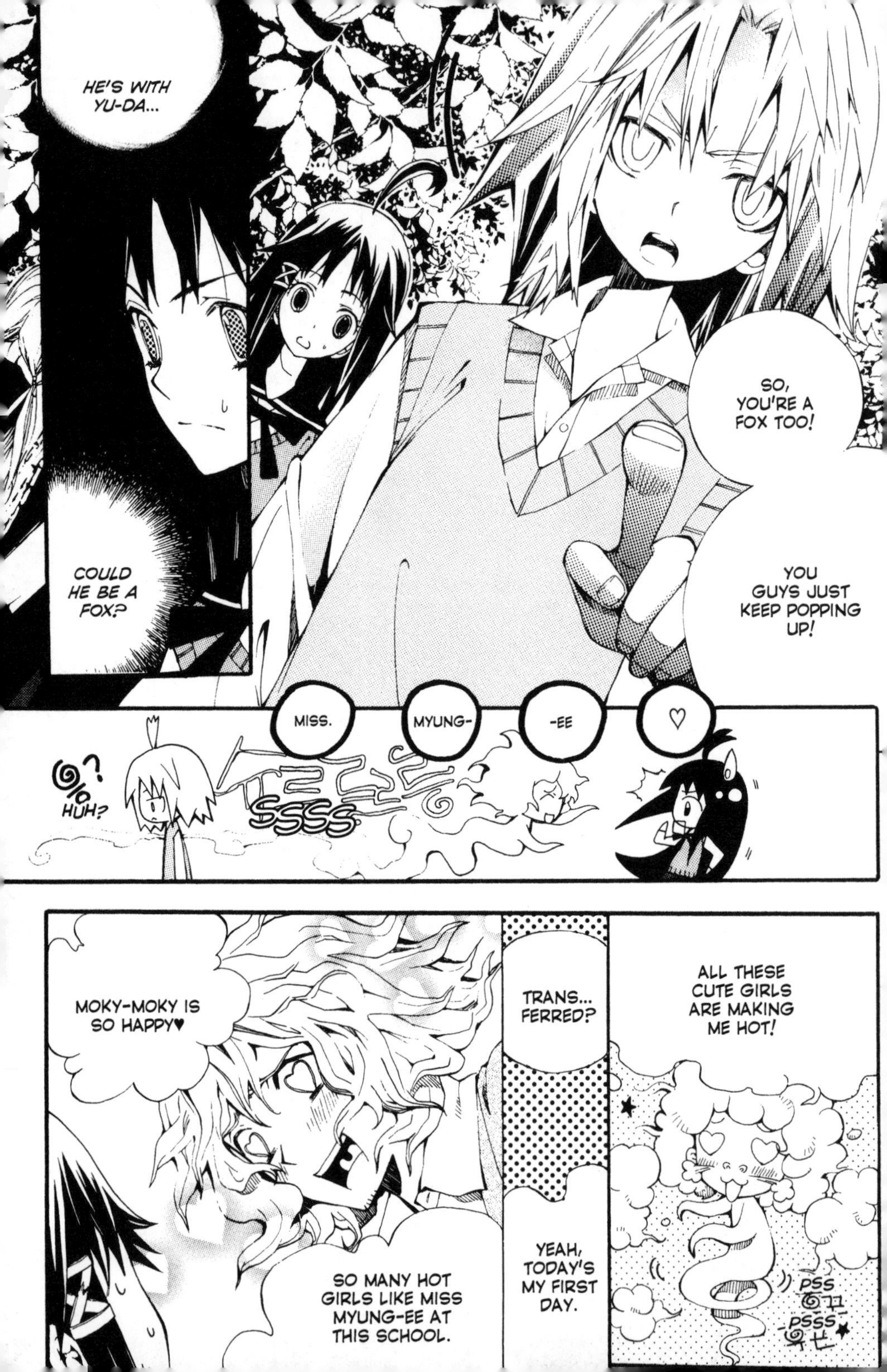
HE'S WITH YU-DA...
COULD HE BE A FOX?
SO, YOU'RE A FOX TOO!
YOU GUYS JUST KEEP POPPING UP!
HUH?
SSSS
MISS.
MYUNG-
-EE
♥
MOKY-MOKY IS SO HAPPY♥
SO MANY HOT GIRLS LIKE MISS MYUNG-EE AT THIS SCHOOL.
TRANS... FERRED?
YEAH, TODAY'S MY FIRST DAY.
ALL THESE CUTE GIRLS ARE MAKING ME HOT!
PSS
PSSS

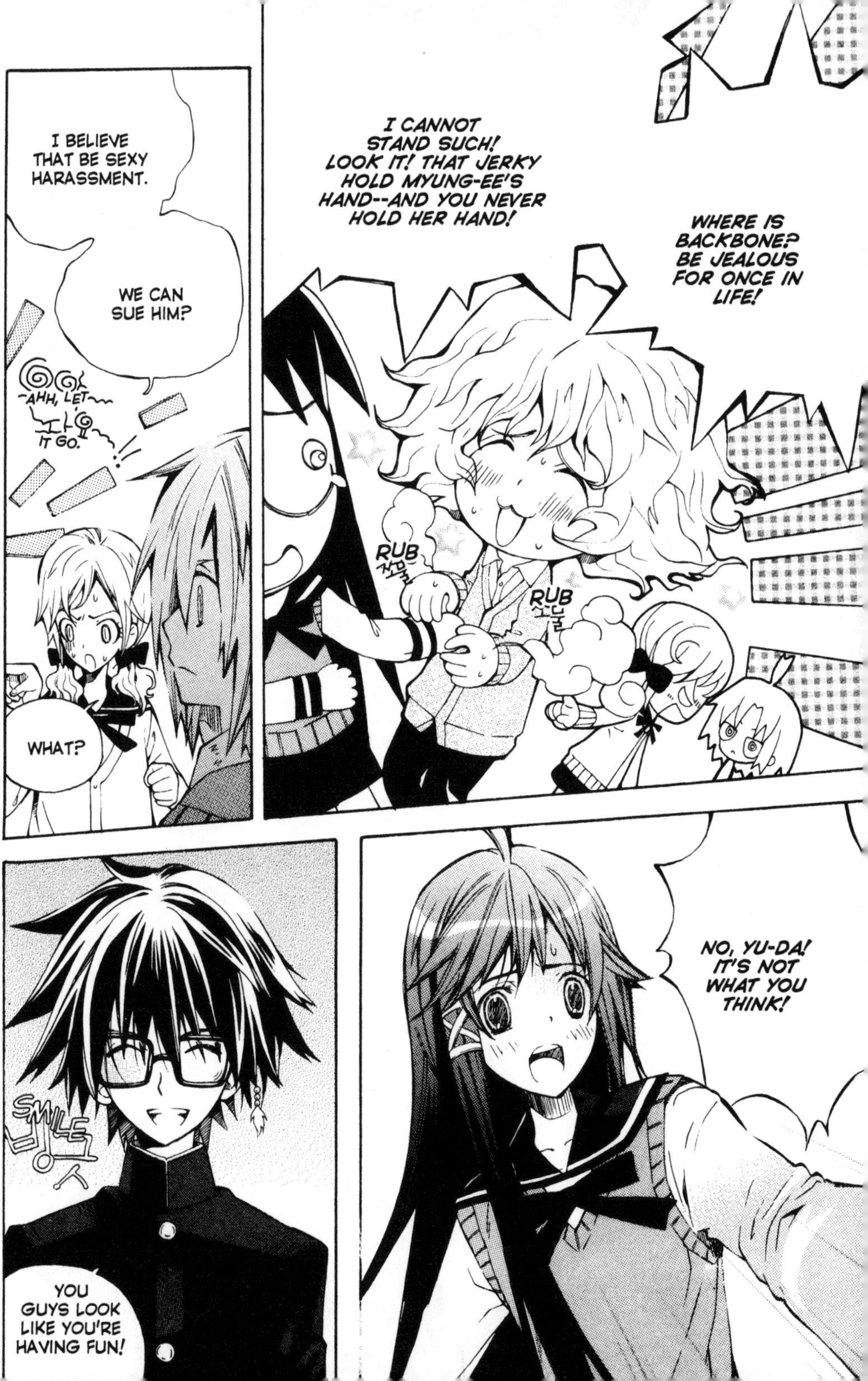
I BELIEVE THAT BE SEXY HARASSMENT.
WE CAN SUE HIM?
-AHH, LET IT GO.
WHAT?
I CANNOT STAND SUCH! LOOK IT! THAT JERKY HOLD MYUNG-EE'S HAND--AND YOU NEVER HOLD HER HAND!
WHERE IS BACKBONE? BE JEALOUS FOR ONCE IN LIFE!
RUB
RUB
SMILE
YOU GUYS LOOK LIKE YOU'RE HAVING FUN!
NO, YU-DA! IT'S NOT WHAT YOU THINK!

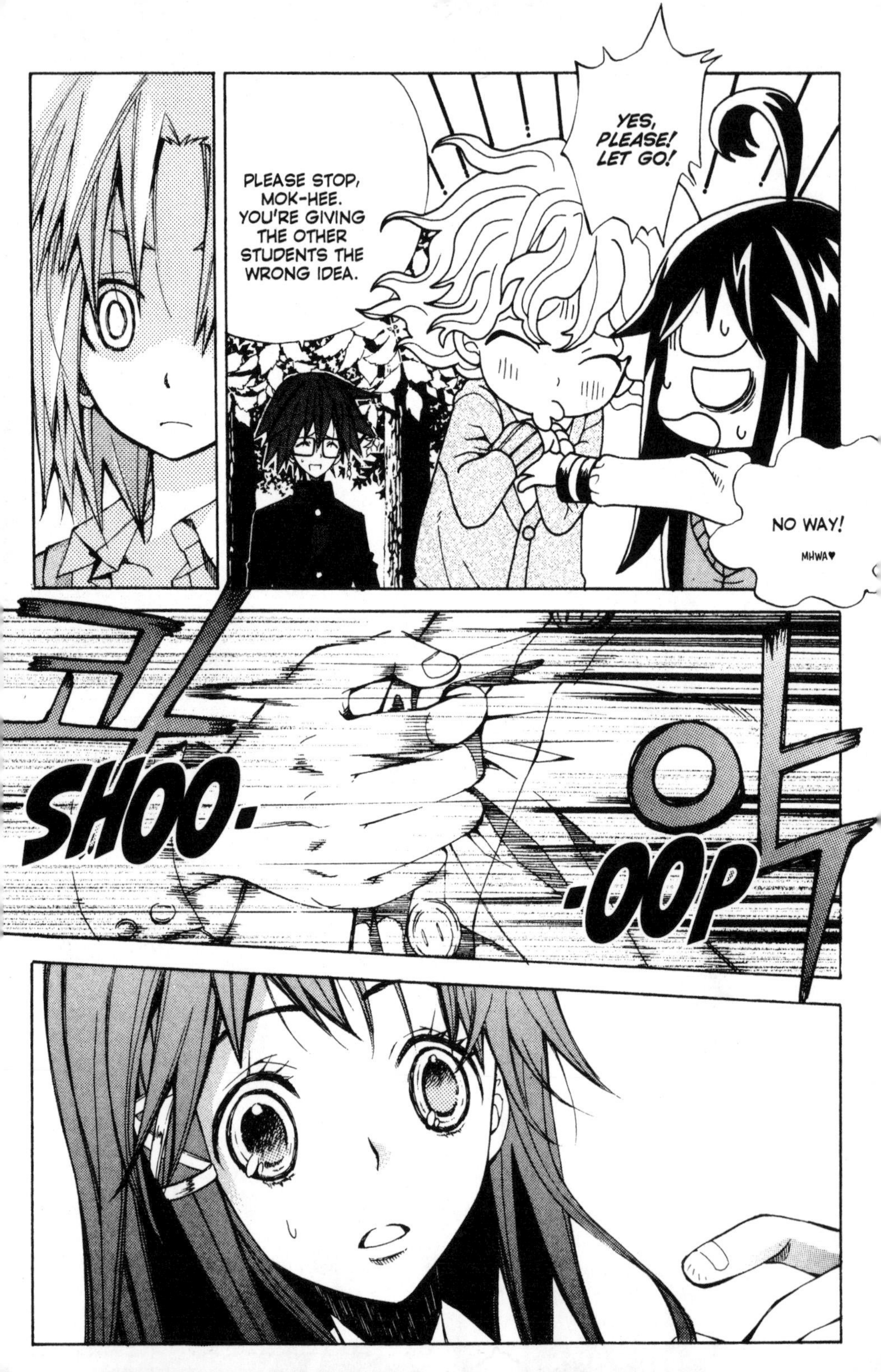
PLEASE STOP, MOK-HEE. YOU'RE GIVING THE OTHER STUDENTS THE WRONG IDEA.
YES, PLEASE! LET GO!
NO WAY!
MHWA♥
SHOO-
-OOP

LET HER GO,
IF YOU KNOW
WHAT'S GOOD
FOR YOU.

SHE NEVER
SAID SHE HAD
A BOYFRIEND.

I WAS JUST
JOKING. YOU
CAN SWITCH
OFF ATTACK
MODE, DUDE.
SERIOUSLY.

OKAY, OKAY.
MY BAD!

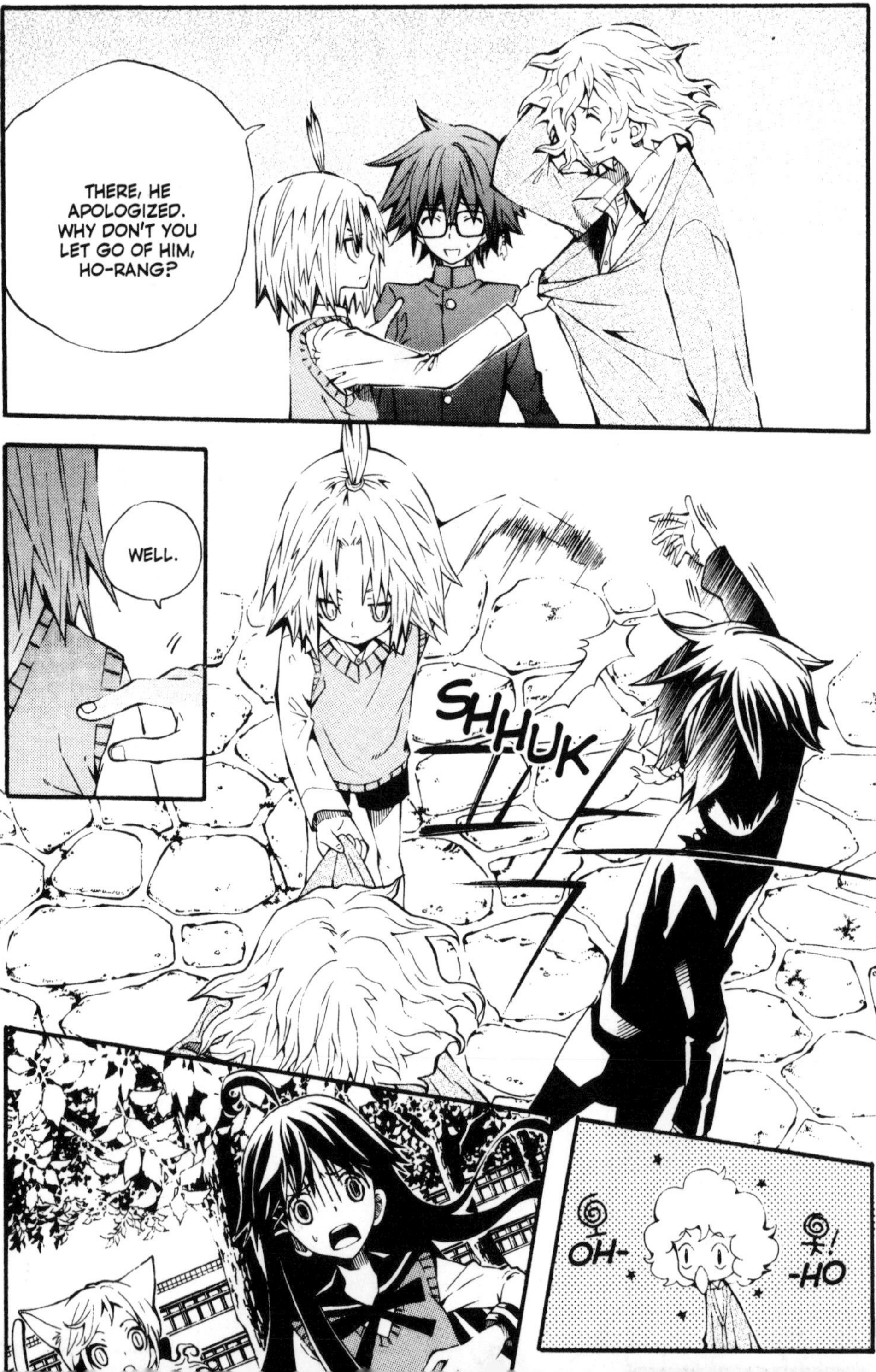
THERE, HE APOLOGIZED. WHY DON'T YOU LET GO OF HIM, HO-RANG?
WELL.
SHHUK
OH-
-HO

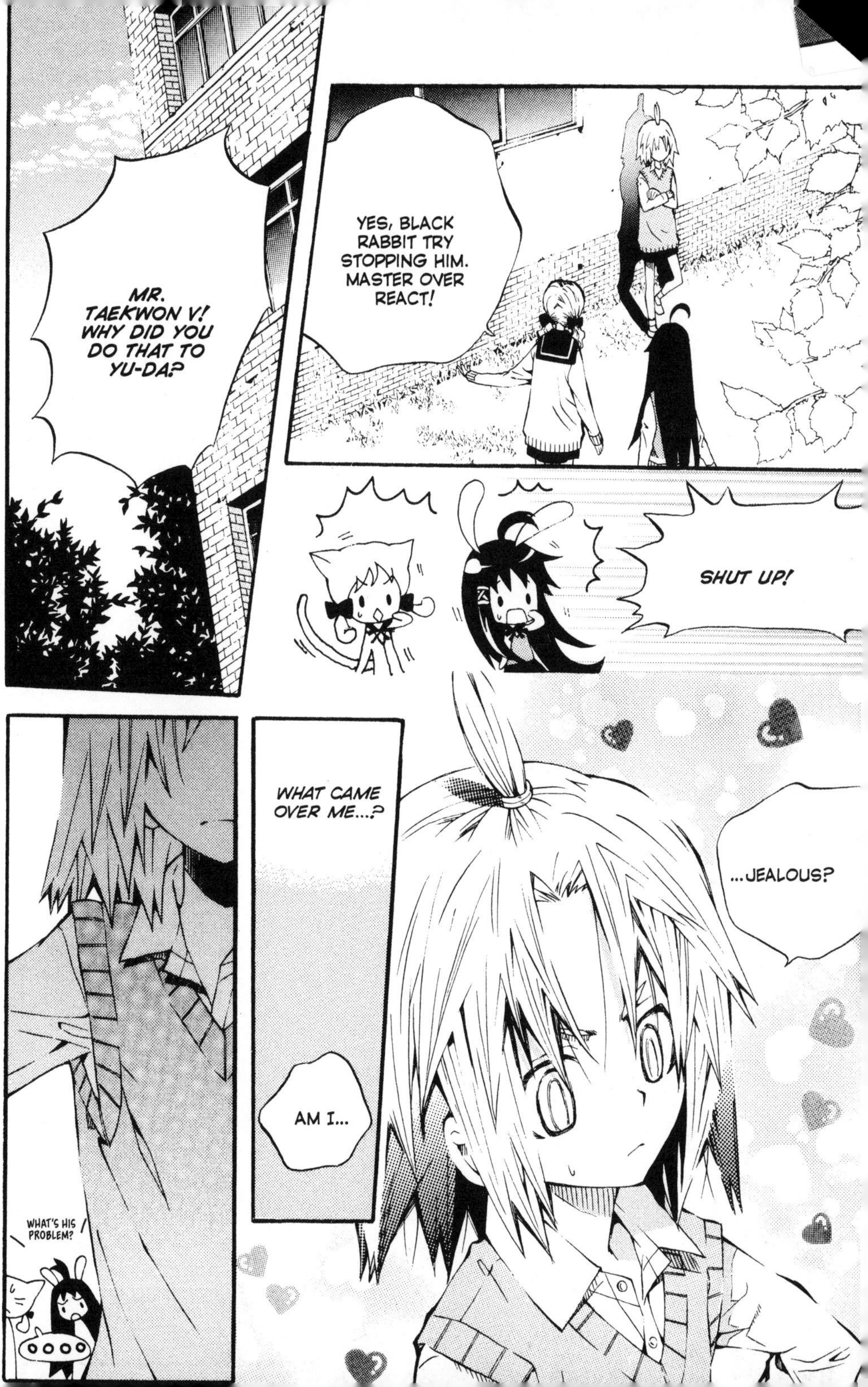
MR. TAEKWON V! WHY DID YOU DO THAT TO YU-DA?
YES, BLACK RABBIT TRY STOPPING HIM. MASTER OVER REACT!
SHUT UP!
WHAT'S HIS PROBLEM?
WHAT CAME OVER ME...?
AM I...
...JEALOUS?

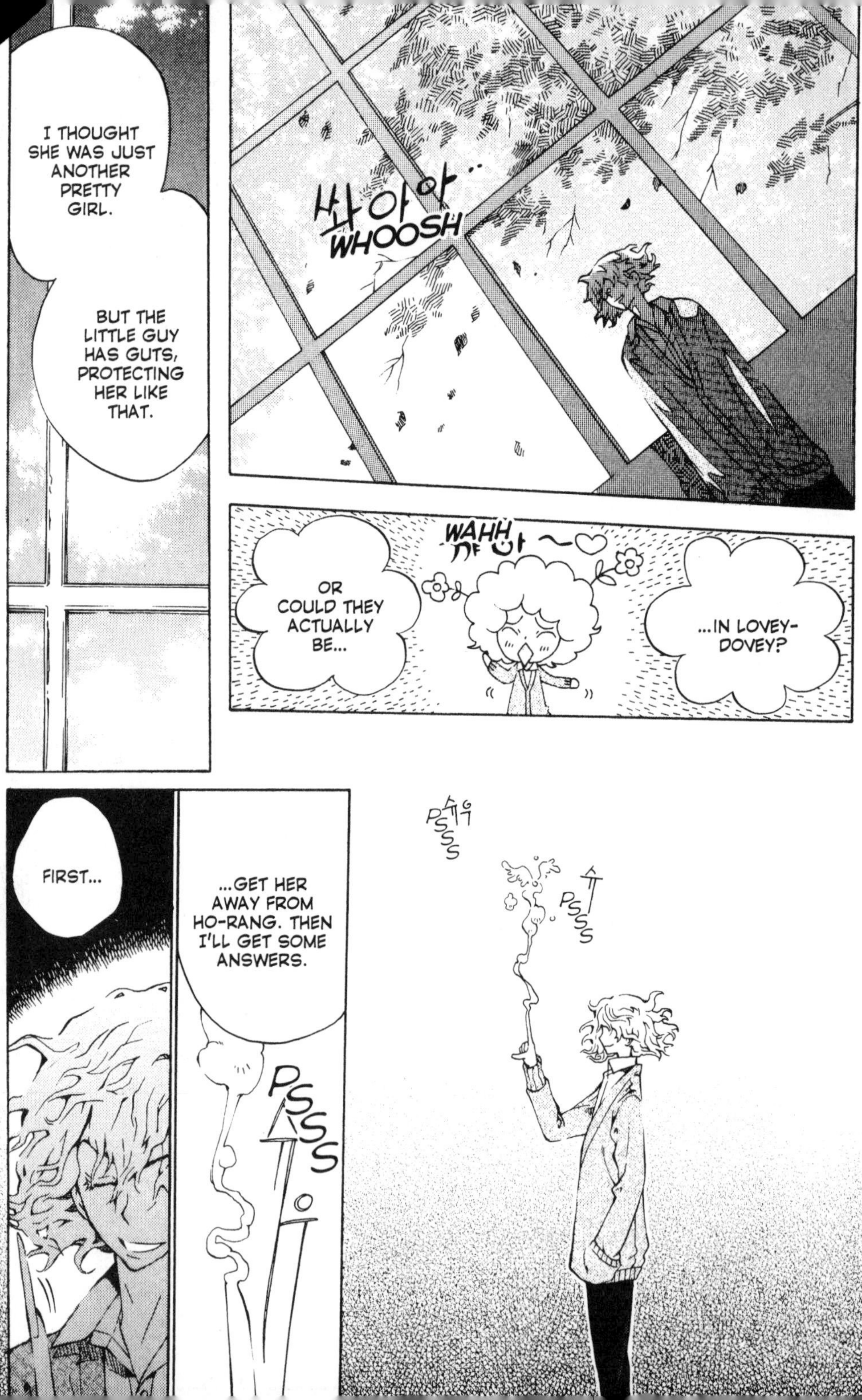
I THOUGHT SHE WAS JUST ANOTHER PRETTY GIRL.
BUT THE LITTLE GUY HAS GUTS, PROTECTING HER LIKE THAT.
쏴아
WHOOSH
WAHH
OR COULD THEY ACTUALLY BE...
...IN LOVEY-DOVEY?
FIRST...
...GET HER AWAY FROM HO-RANG. THEN I'LL GET SOME ANSWERS.
PSSS
PSSS
PSSS

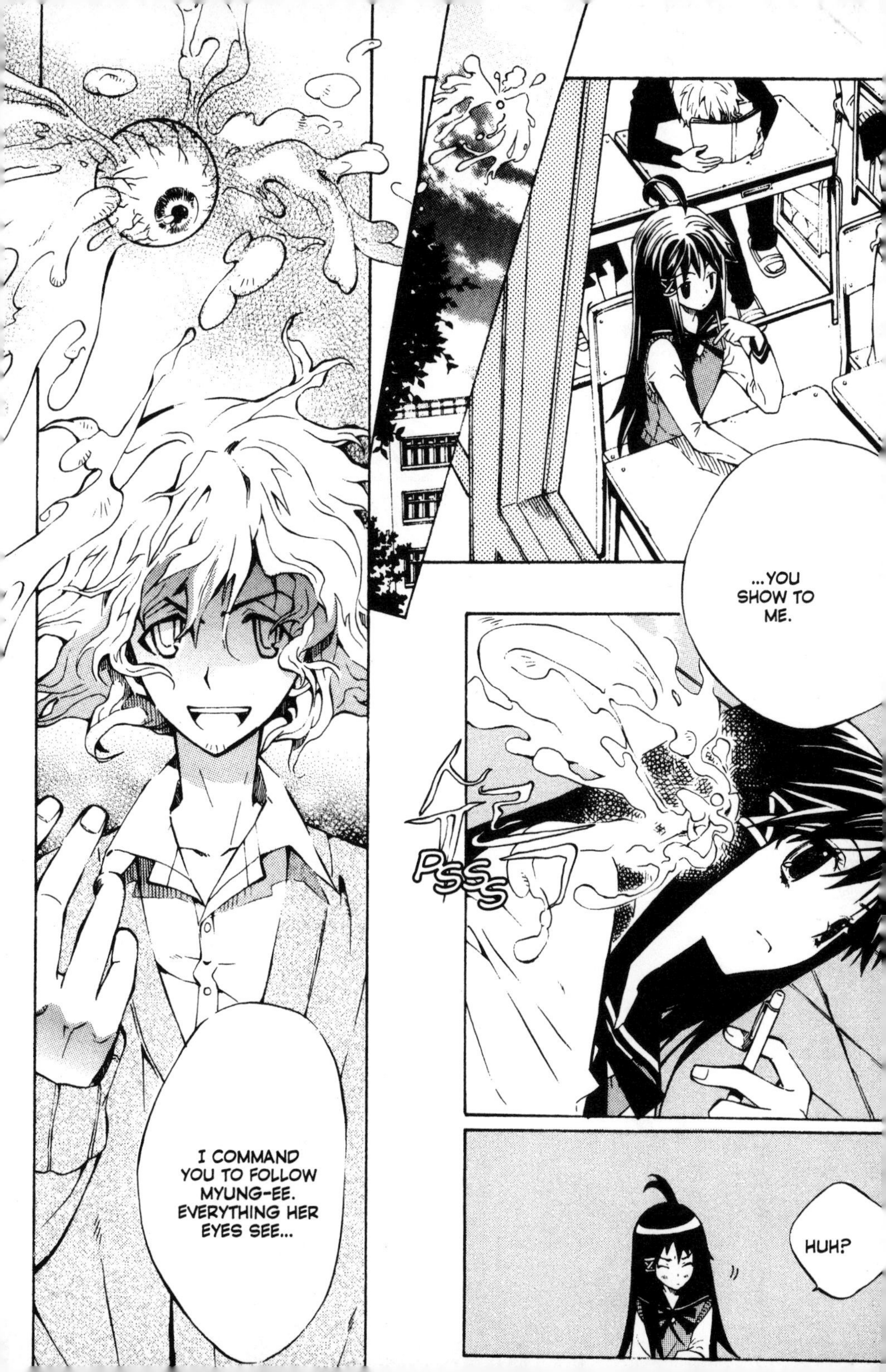
I COMMAND YOU TO FOLLOW MYUNG-EE. EVERYTHING HER EYES SEE...
...YOU SHOW TO ME.
PSSS
HUH?

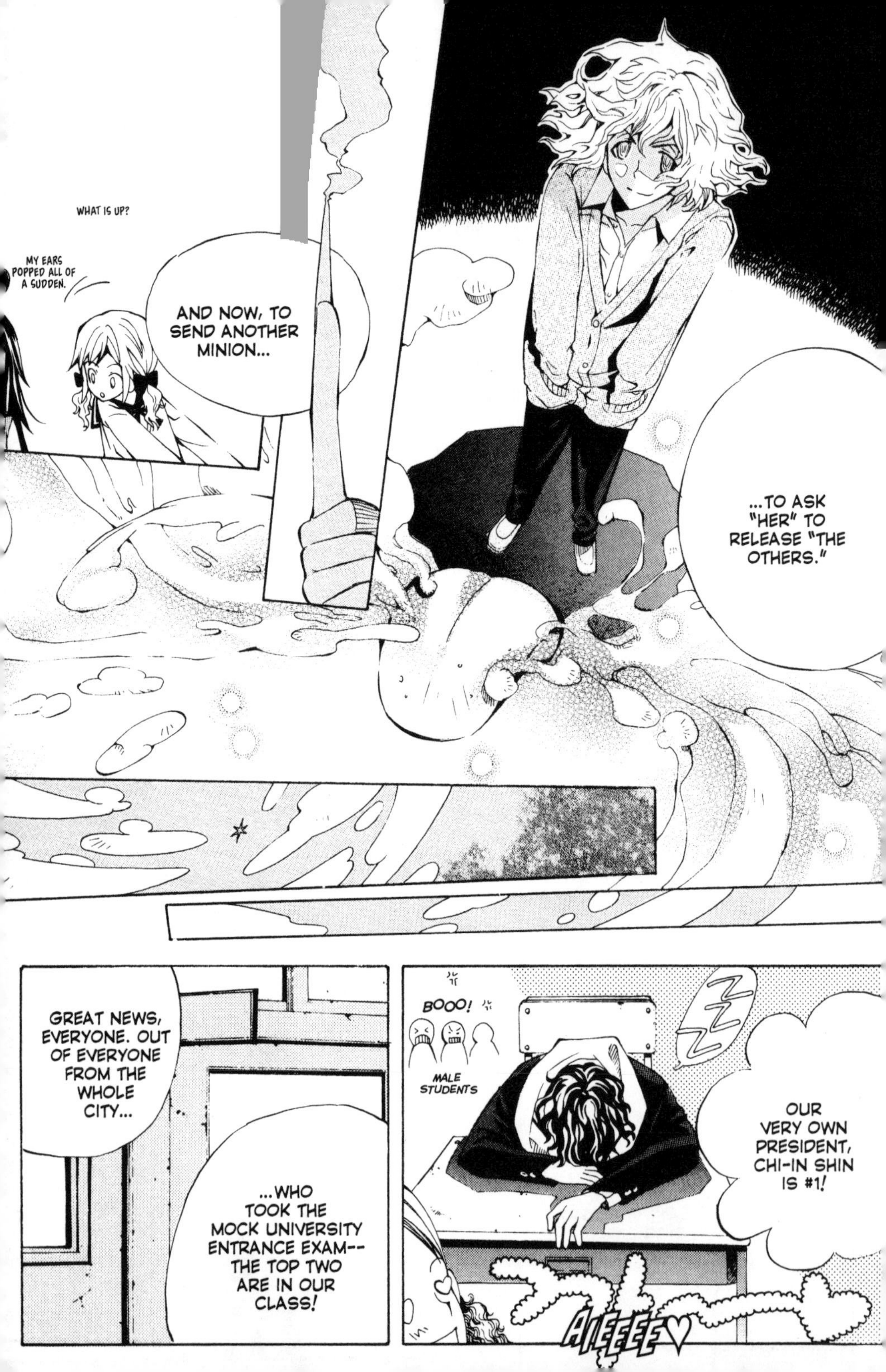
WHAT IS UP?
MY EARS POPPED ALL OF A SUDDEN.
AND NOW, TO SEND ANOTHER MINION...
...TO ASK "HER" TO RELEASE "THE OTHERS."
GREAT NEWS, EVERYONE. OUT OF EVERYONE FROM THE WHOLE CITY...
...WHO TOOK THE MOCK UNIVERSITY ENTRANCE EXAM-- THE TOP TWO ARE IN OUR CLASS!
BOOO!
MALE STUDENTS
OUR VERY OWN PRESIDENT, CHI-IN SHIN IS #1!
AIEEEE♥

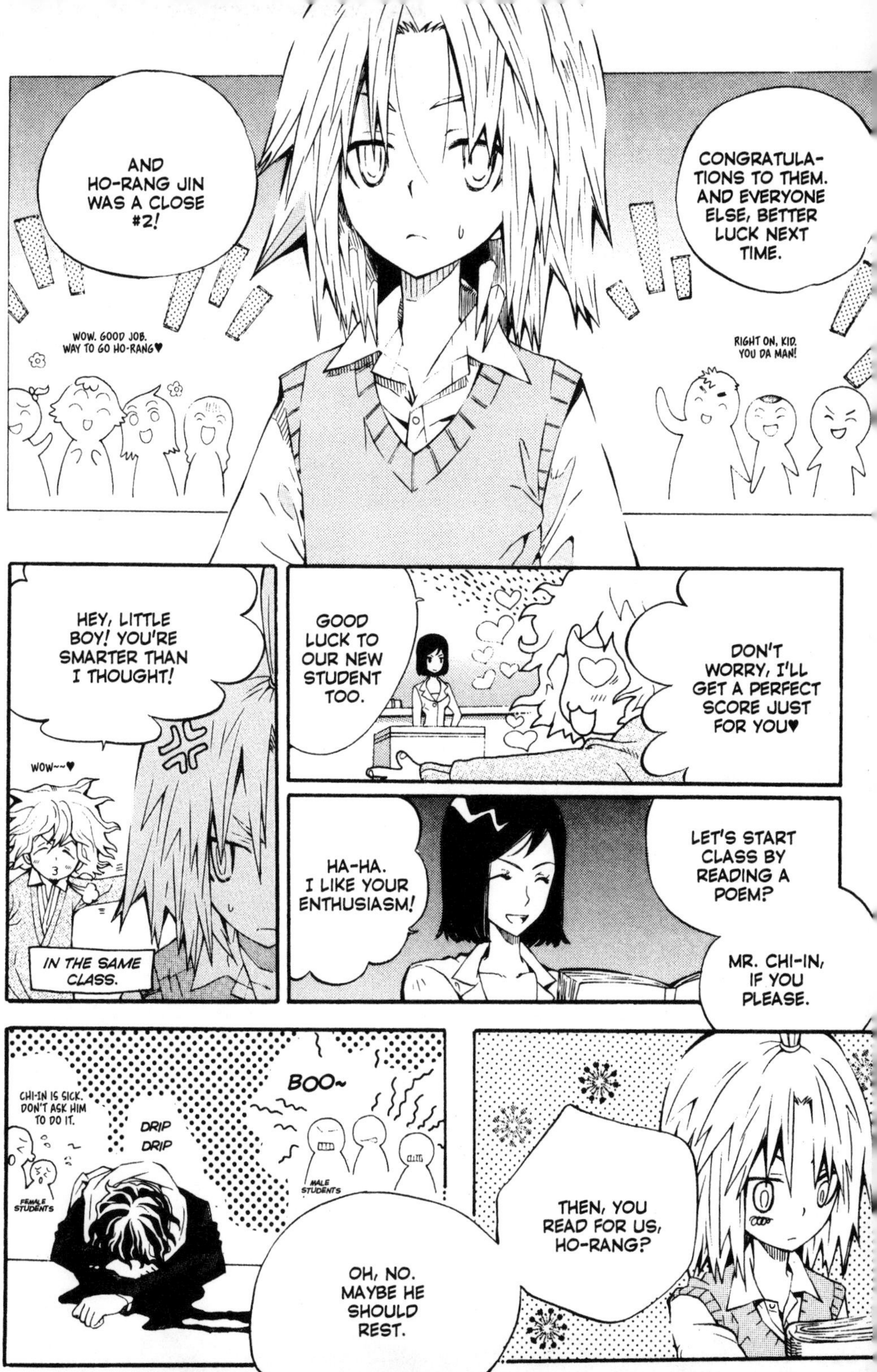
AND HO-RANG JIN WAS A CLOSE #2!
WOW. GOOD JOB. WAY TO GO HO-RANG♥
CONGRATULA-TIONS TO THEM. AND EVERYONE ELSE, BETTER LUCK NEXT TIME.
RIGHT ON, KID. YOU DA MAN!
HEY, LITTLE BOY! YOU'RE SMARTER THAN I THOUGHT!
WOW~~♥
IN THE SAME CLASS.
GOOD LUCK TO OUR NEW STUDENT TOO.
DON'T WORRY, I'LL GET A PERFECT SCORE JUST FOR YOU♥
HA-HA. I LIKE YOUR ENTHUSIASM!
LET'S START CLASS BY READING A POEM?
MR. CHI-IN, IF YOU PLEASE.
CHI-IN IS SICK. DON'T ASK HIM TO DO IT.
DRIP
DRIP
FEMALE STUDENTS
BOO~
MALE STUDENTS
OH, NO. MAYBE HE SHOULD REST.
THEN, YOU READ FOR US, HO-RANG?

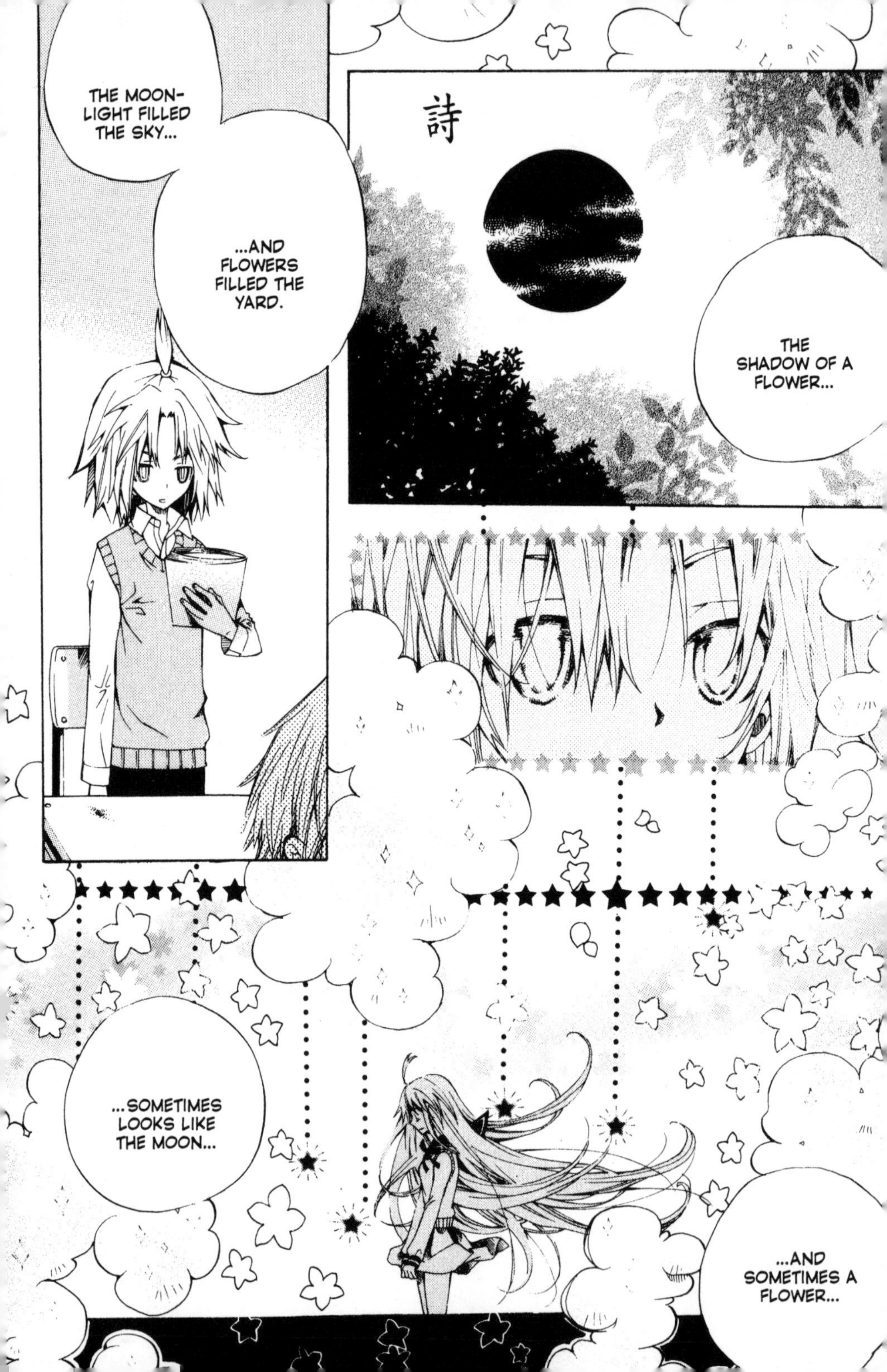
THE MOON-LIGHT FILLED THE SKY...
...AND FLOWERS FILLED THE YARD.
詩
THE SHADOW OF A FLOWER...
...SOMETIMES LOOKS LIKE THE MOON...
...AND SOMETIMES A FLOWER...

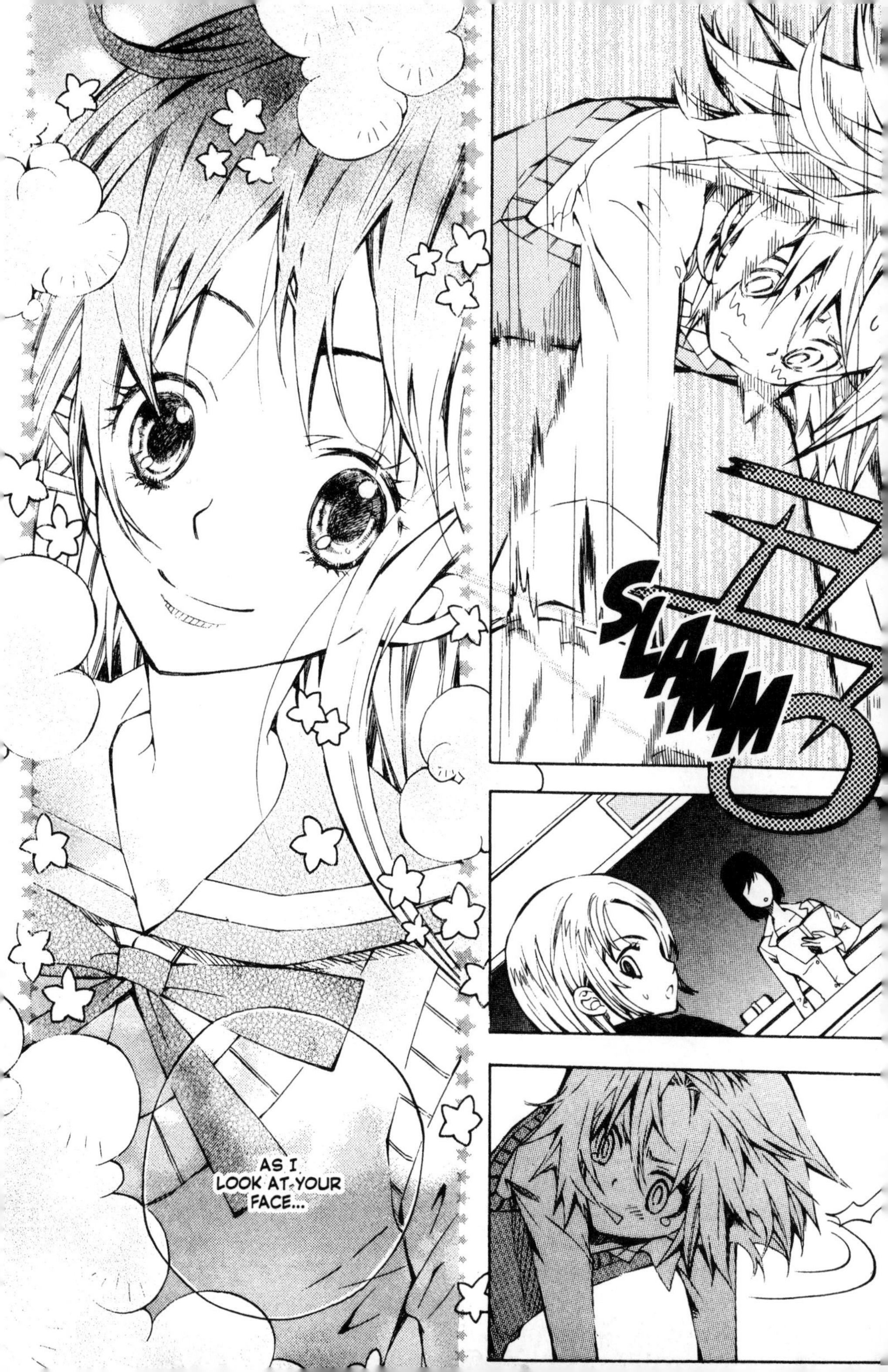
AS I LOOK AT YOUR FACE...
SLAMM

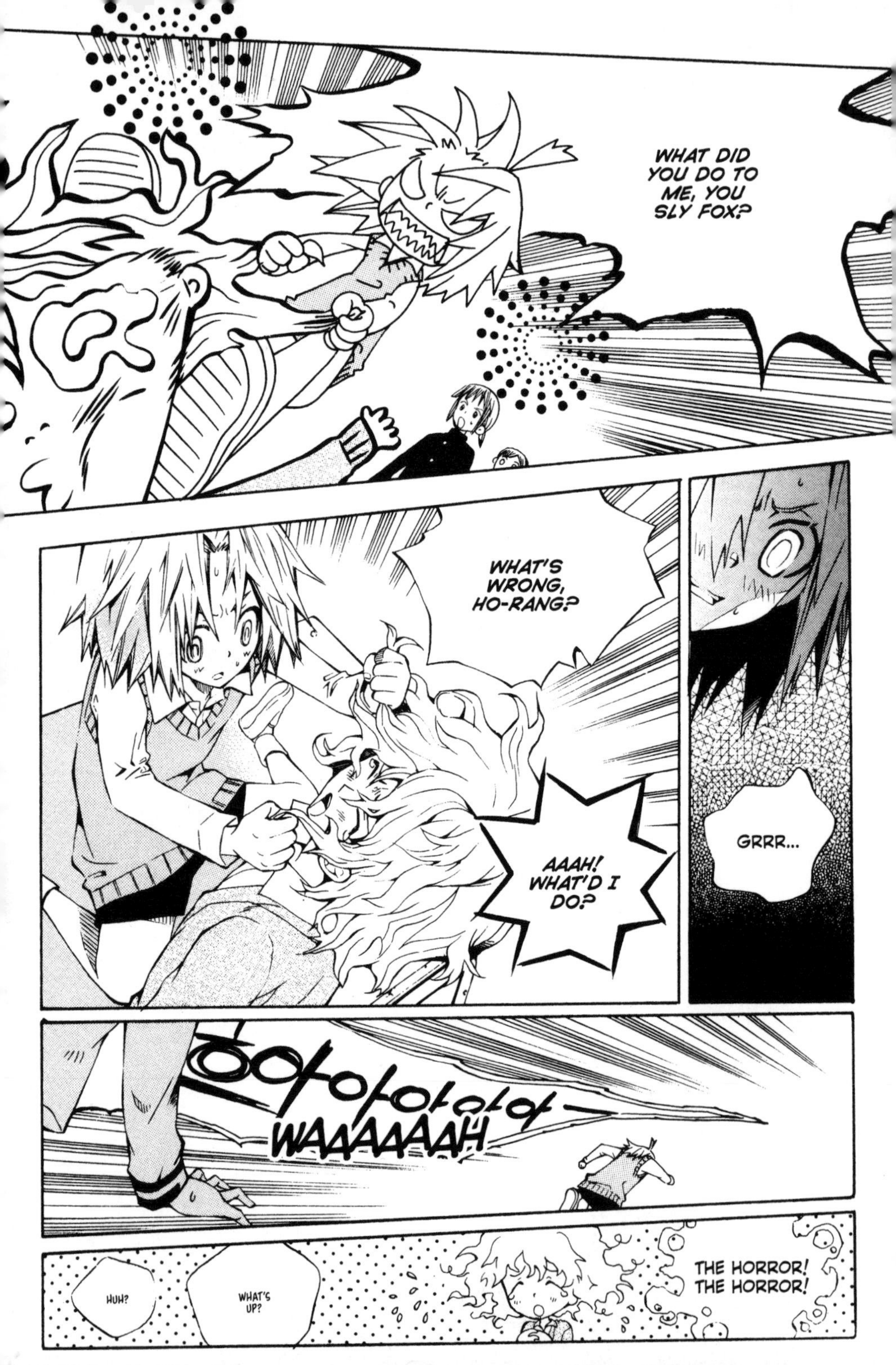
WHAT DID YOU DO TO ME, YOU SLY FOX?
WHAT'S WRONG, HO-RANG?
AAAH! WHAT'D I DO?
GRRR...
WAAAAAAH
HUH?
WHAT'S UP?
THE HORROR! THE HORROR!

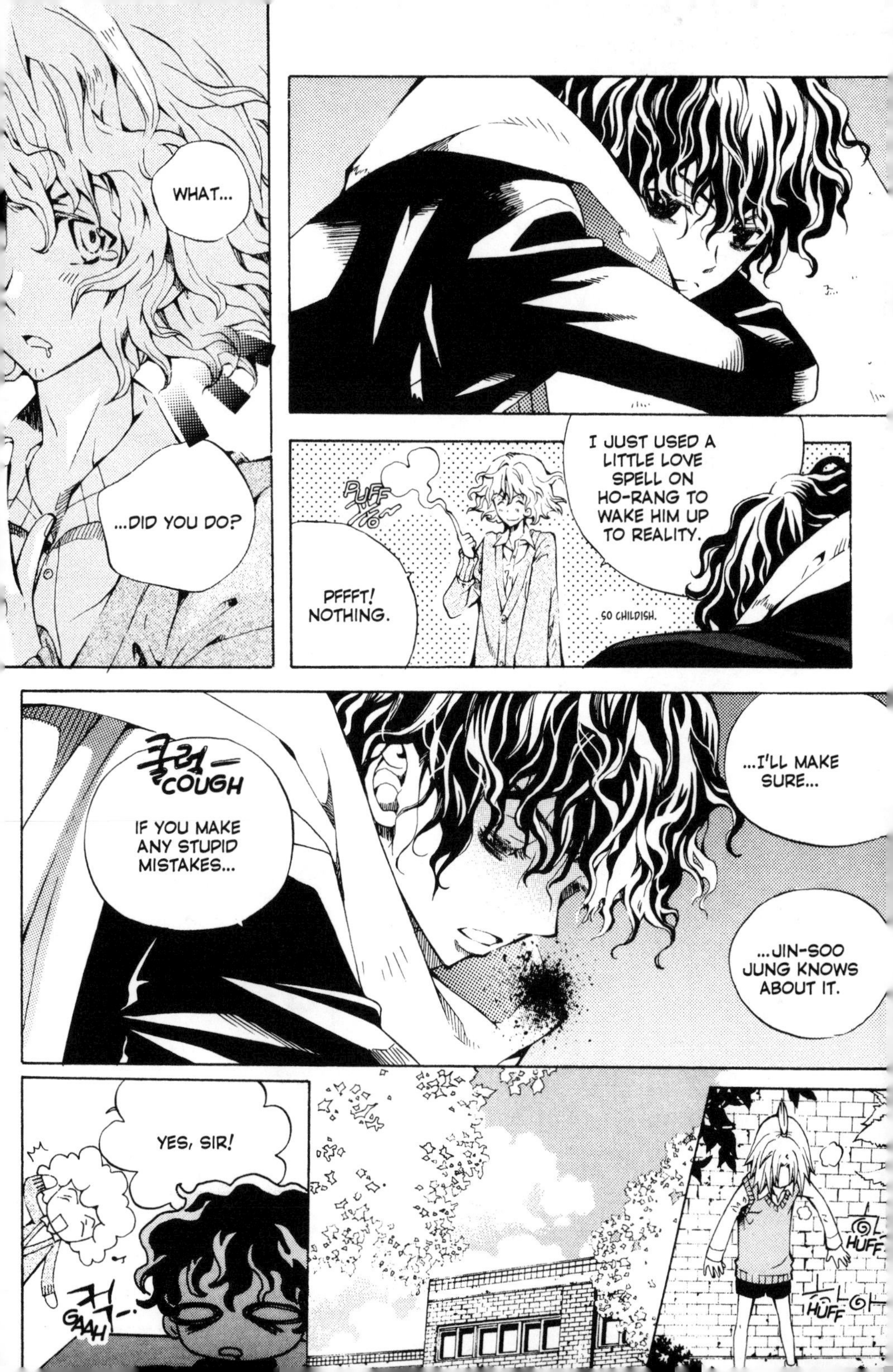
WHAT...
...DID YOU DO?
PUFF
I JUST USED A LITTLE LOVE SPELL ON HO-RANG TO WAKE HIM UP TO REALITY.
PFFFT! NOTHING.
SO CHILDISH.
콜럭— COUGH
IF YOU MAKE ANY STUPID MISTAKES...
...I'LL MAKE SURE...
...JIN-SOO JUNG KNOWS ABOUT IT.
YES, SIR!
GAAH
HUFF
HUFF

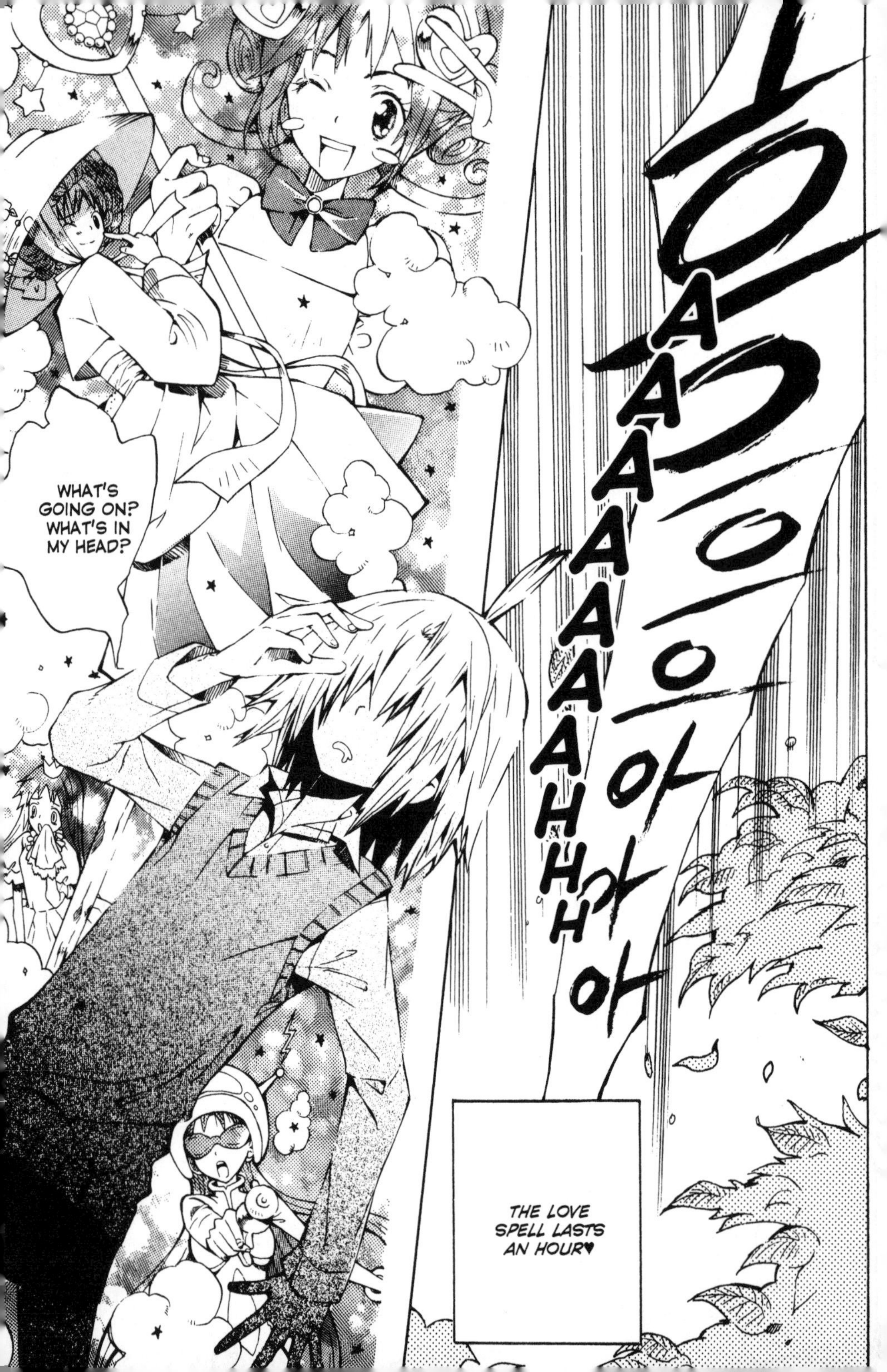
WHAT'S GOING ON? WHAT'S IN MY HEAD?
AAAAAAAAHHH
THE LOVE SPELL LASTS AN HOUR♥

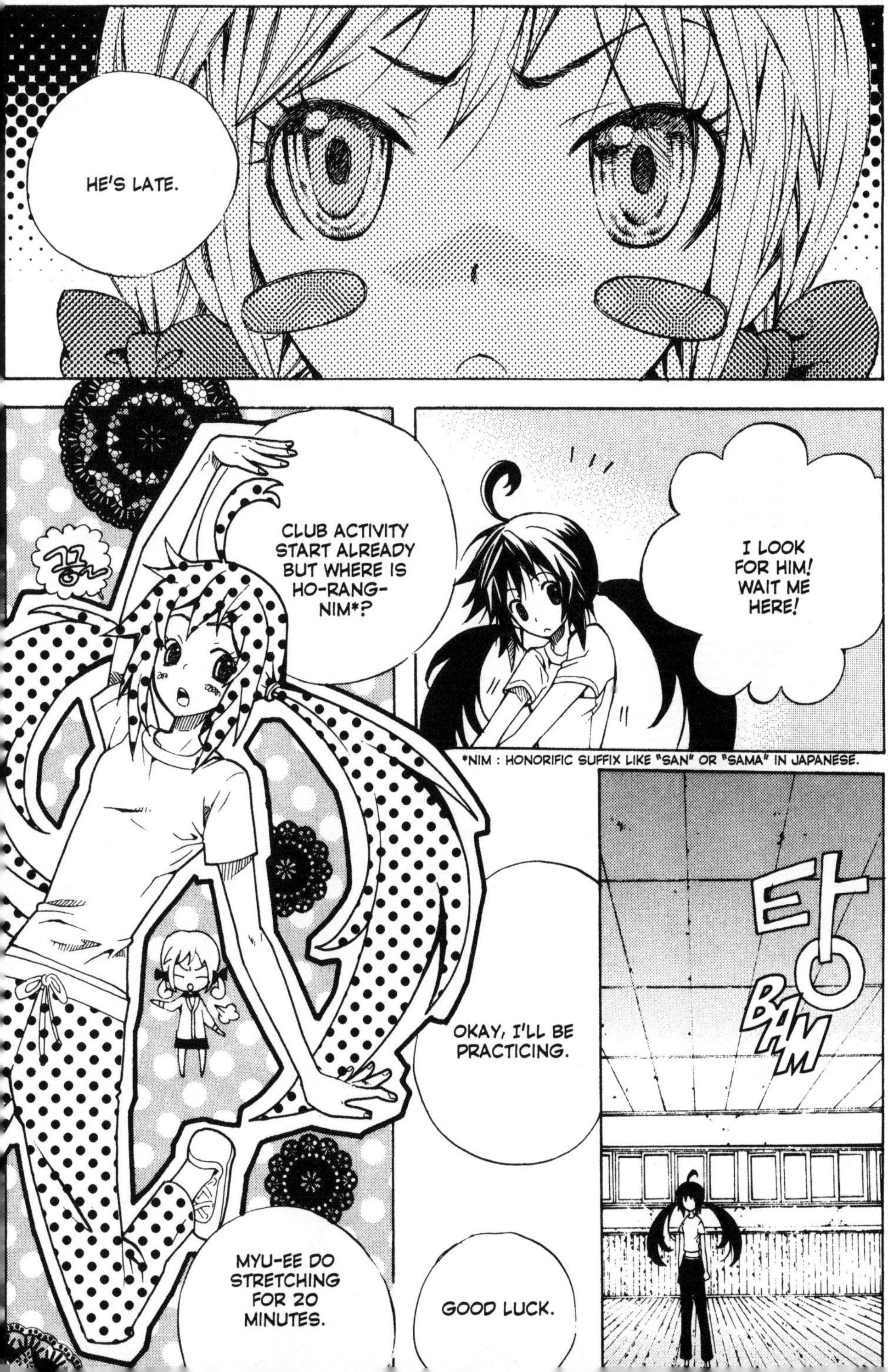
HE'S LATE.
CLUB ACTIVITY START ALREADY BUT WHERE IS HO-RANG-NIM*?
MYU-EE DO STRETCHING FOR 20 MINUTES.
I LOOK FOR HIM! WAIT ME HERE!
OKAY, I'LL BE PRACTICING.
GOOD LUCK.
탕
BAM

*NIM : HONORIFIC SUFFIX LIKE "SAN" OR "SAMA" IN JAPANESE.

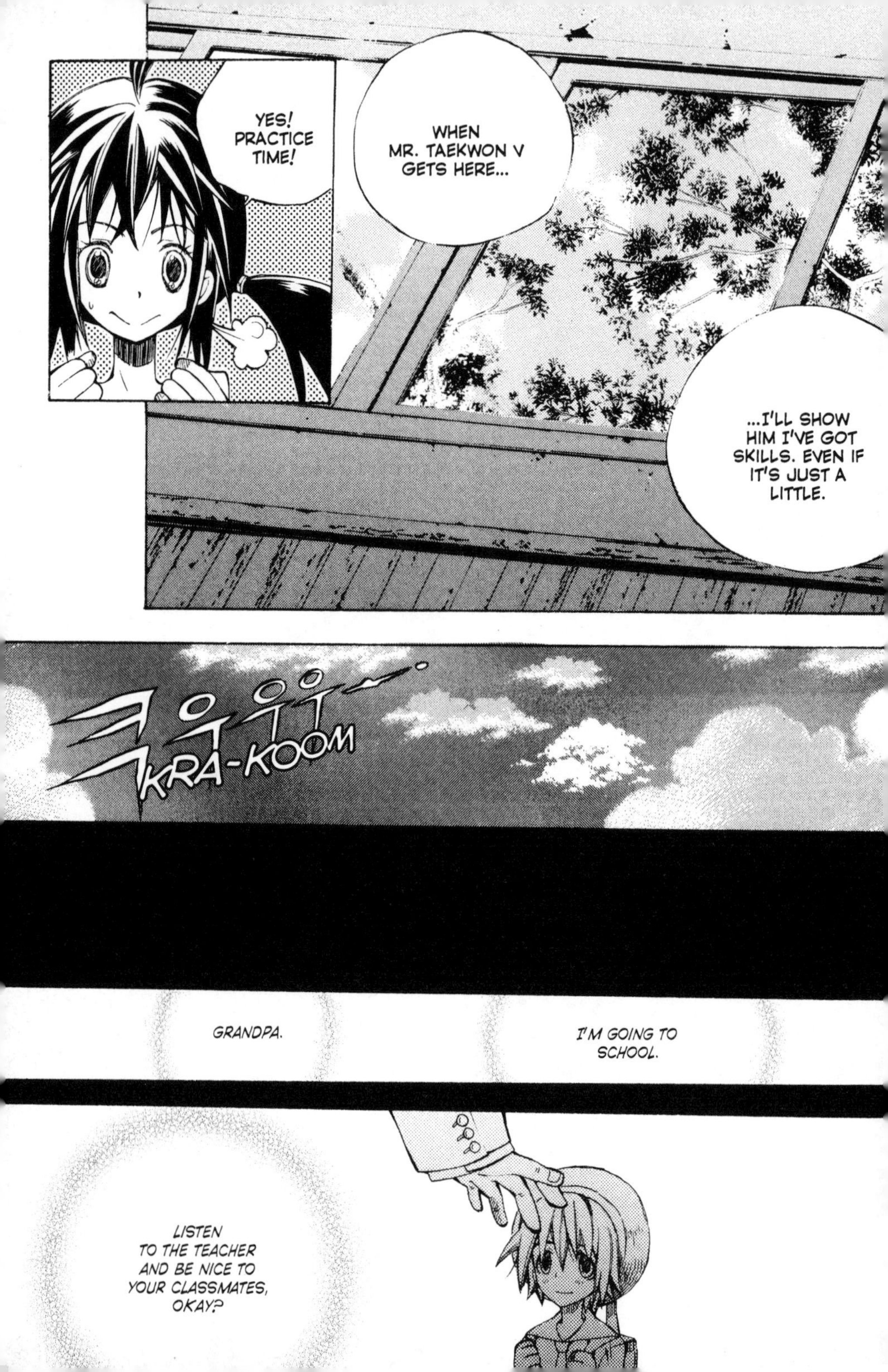
YES! PRACTICE TIME!
WHEN MR. TAEKWON V GETS HERE...
...I'LL SHOW HIM I'VE GOT SKILLS. EVEN IF IT'S JUST A LITTLE.
KRA-KOOM
GRANDPA.
I'M GOING TO SCHOOL.
LISTEN TO THE TEACHER AND BE NICE TO YOUR CLASSMATES, OKAY?

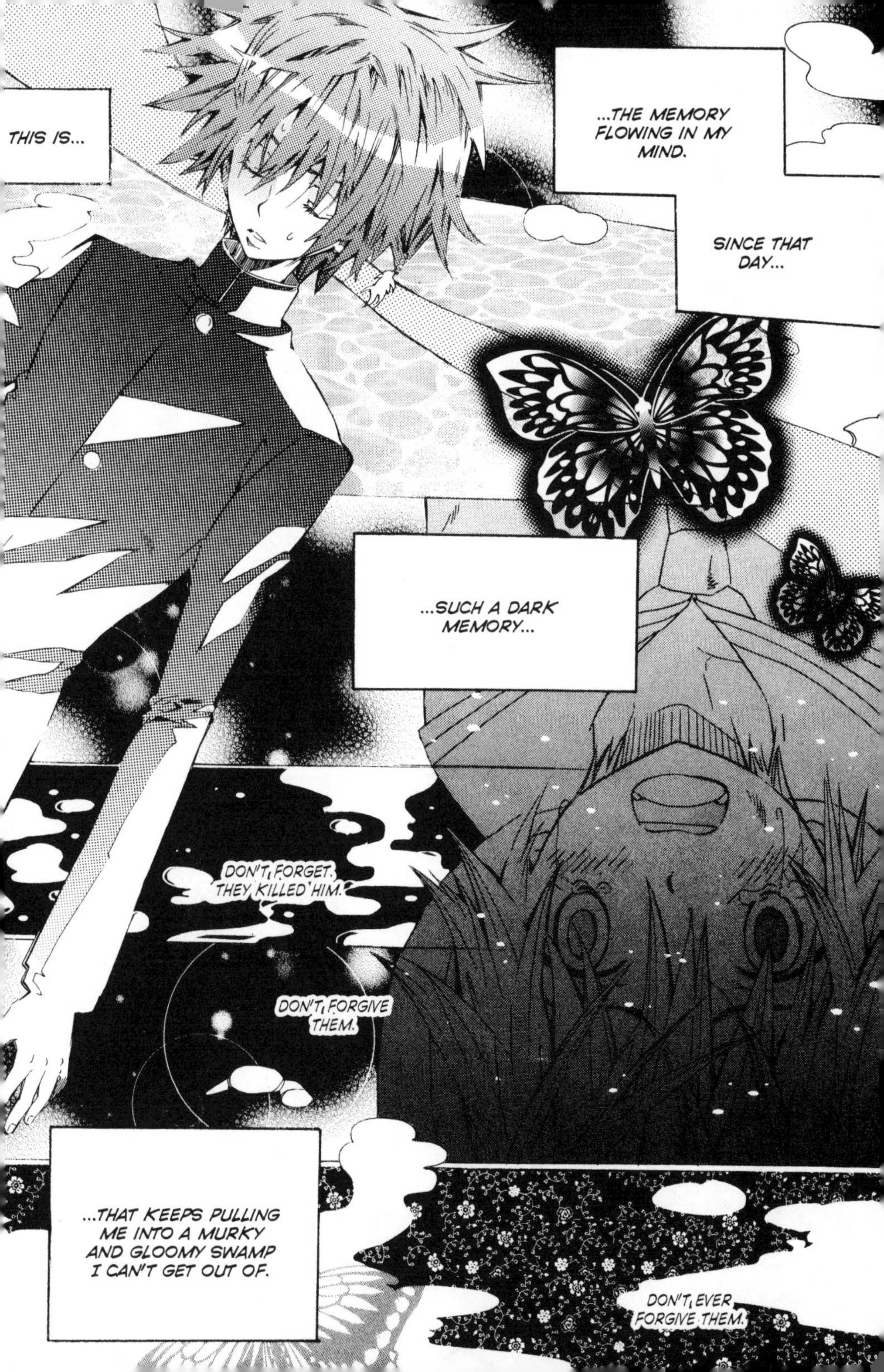
THIS IS...
...THE MEMORY FLOWING IN MY MIND.
SINCE THAT DAY...
...SUCH A DARK MEMORY...
DON'T FORGET. THEY KILLED HIM.
DON'T FORGIVE THEM.
...THAT KEEPS PULLING ME INTO A MURKY AND GLOOMY SWAMP I CAN'T GET OUT OF.
DON'T EVER FORGIVE THEM.

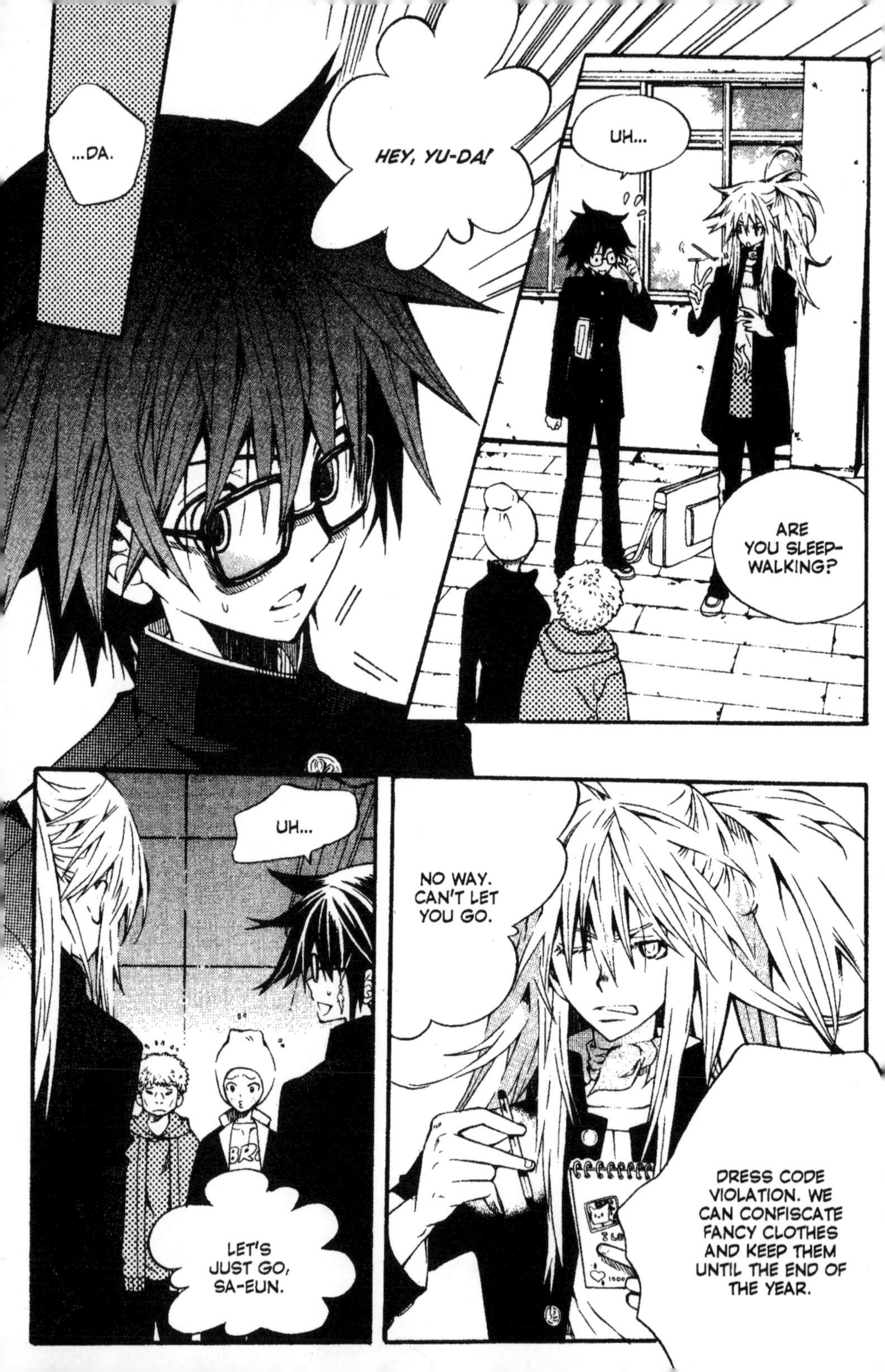
...DA.
HEY, YU-DA!
UH...
ARE YOU SLEEP-WALKING?
UH...
LET'S JUST GO, SA-EUN.
NO WAY. CAN'T LET YOU GO.
DRESS CODE VIOLATION. WE CAN CONFISCATE FANCY CLOTHES AND KEEP THEM UNTIL THE END OF THE YEAR.

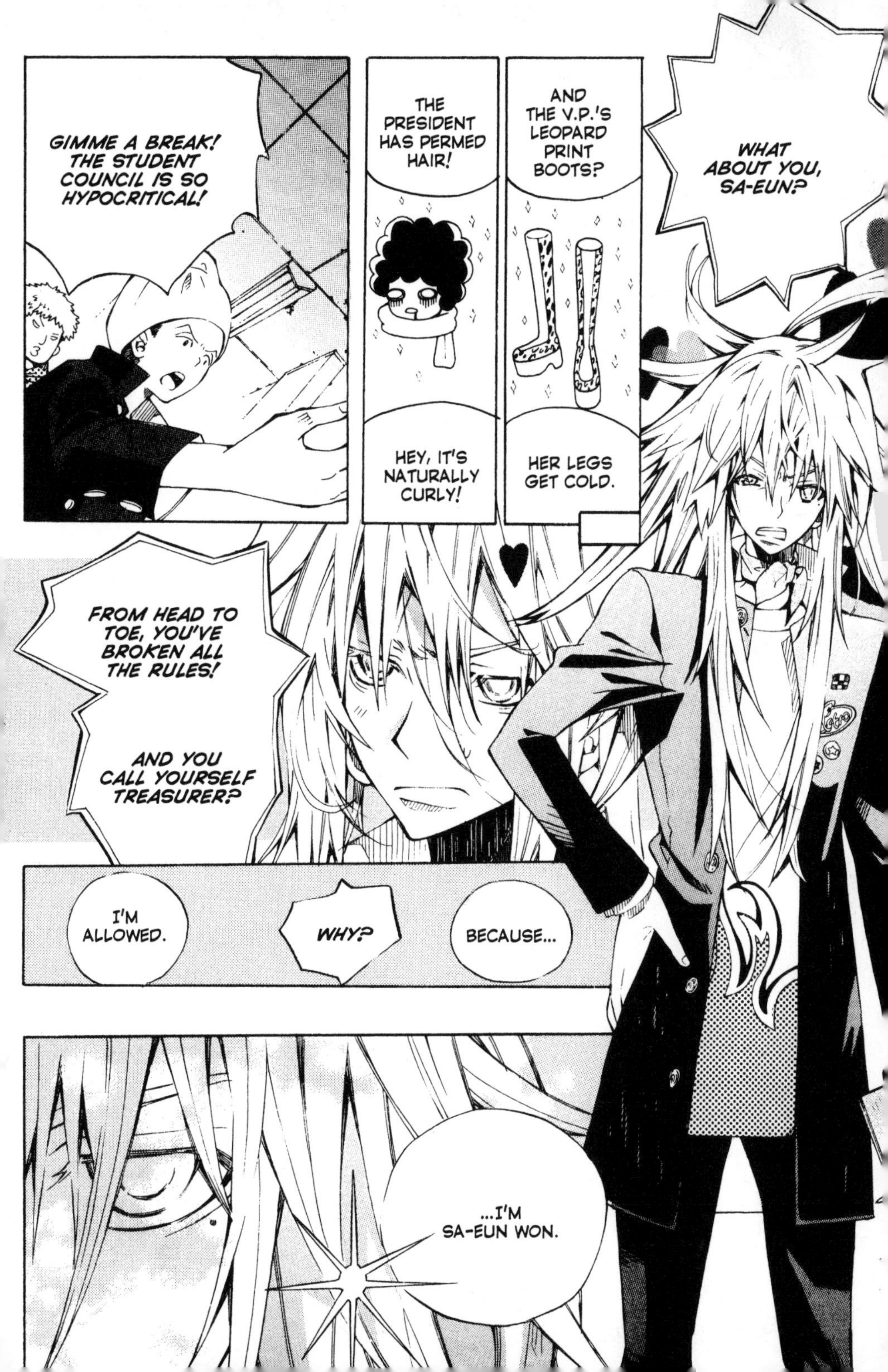
GIMME A BREAK! THE STUDENT COUNCIL IS SO HYPOCRITICAL!
THE PRESIDENT HAS PERMED HAIR!
HEY, IT'S NATURALLY CURLY!
AND THE V.P.'S LEOPARD PRINT BOOTS?
HER LEGS GET COLD.
WHAT ABOUT YOU, SA-EUN?
FROM HEAD TO TOE, YOU'VE BROKEN ALL THE RULES!
AND YOU CALL YOURSELF TREASURER?
I'M ALLOWED.
WHY?
BECAUSE...
...I'M SA-EUN WON.

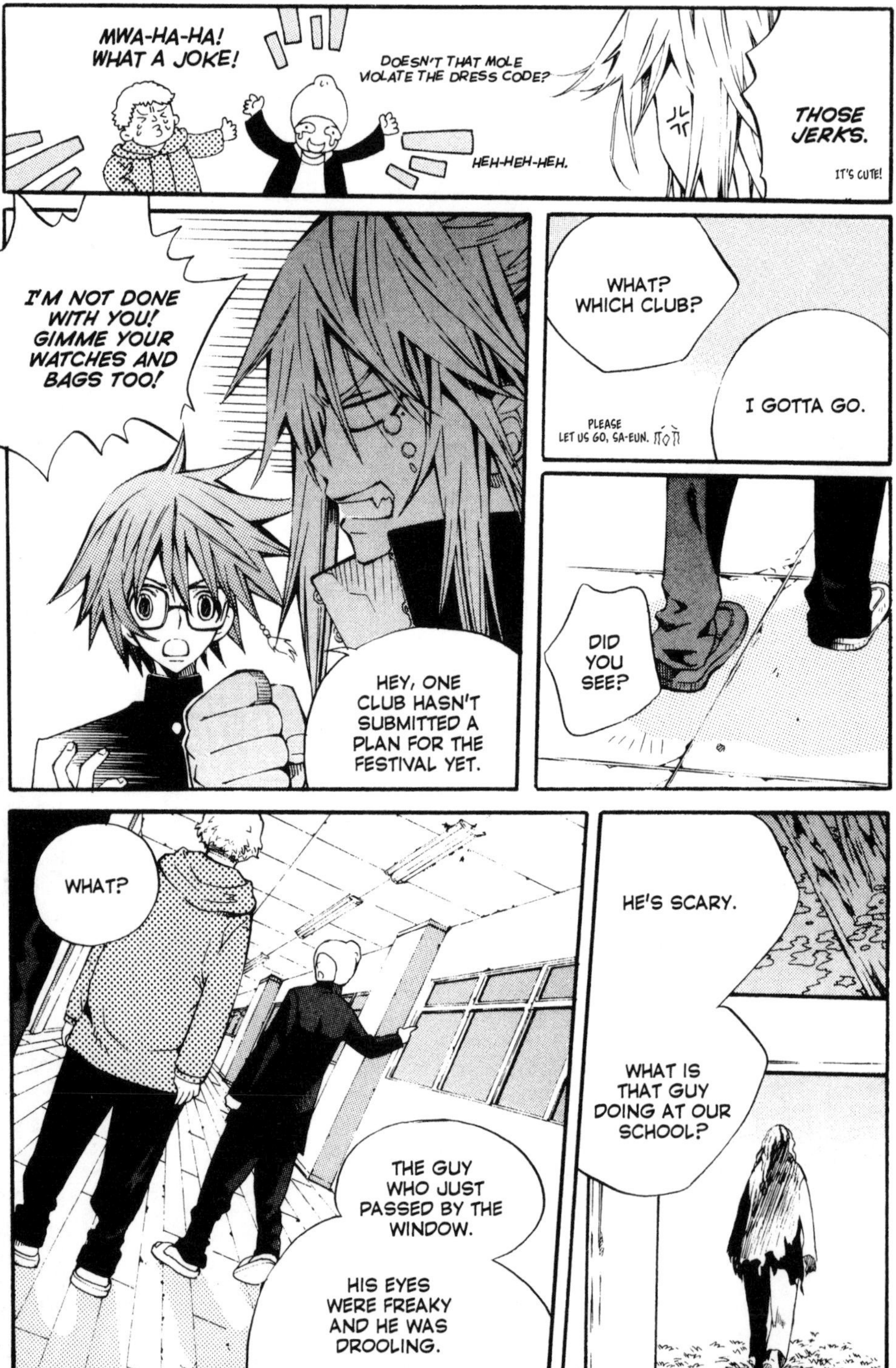
MWA-HA-HA! WHAT A JOKE!
DOESN'T THAT MOLE VIOLATE THE DRESS CODE?
HEH-HEH-HEH.
THOSE JERKS.
IT'S CUTE!
I'M NOT DONE WITH YOU! GIMME YOUR WATCHES AND BAGS TOO!
HEY, ONE CLUB HASN'T SUBMITTED A PLAN FOR THE FESTIVAL YET.
WHAT? WHICH CLUB?
PLEASE LET US GO, SA-EUN.
I GOTTA GO.
DID YOU SEE?
WHAT?
THE GUY WHO JUST PASSED BY THE WINDOW.
HIS EYES WERE FREAKY AND HE WAS DROOLING.
HE'S SCARY.
WHAT IS THAT GUY DOING AT OUR SCHOOL?

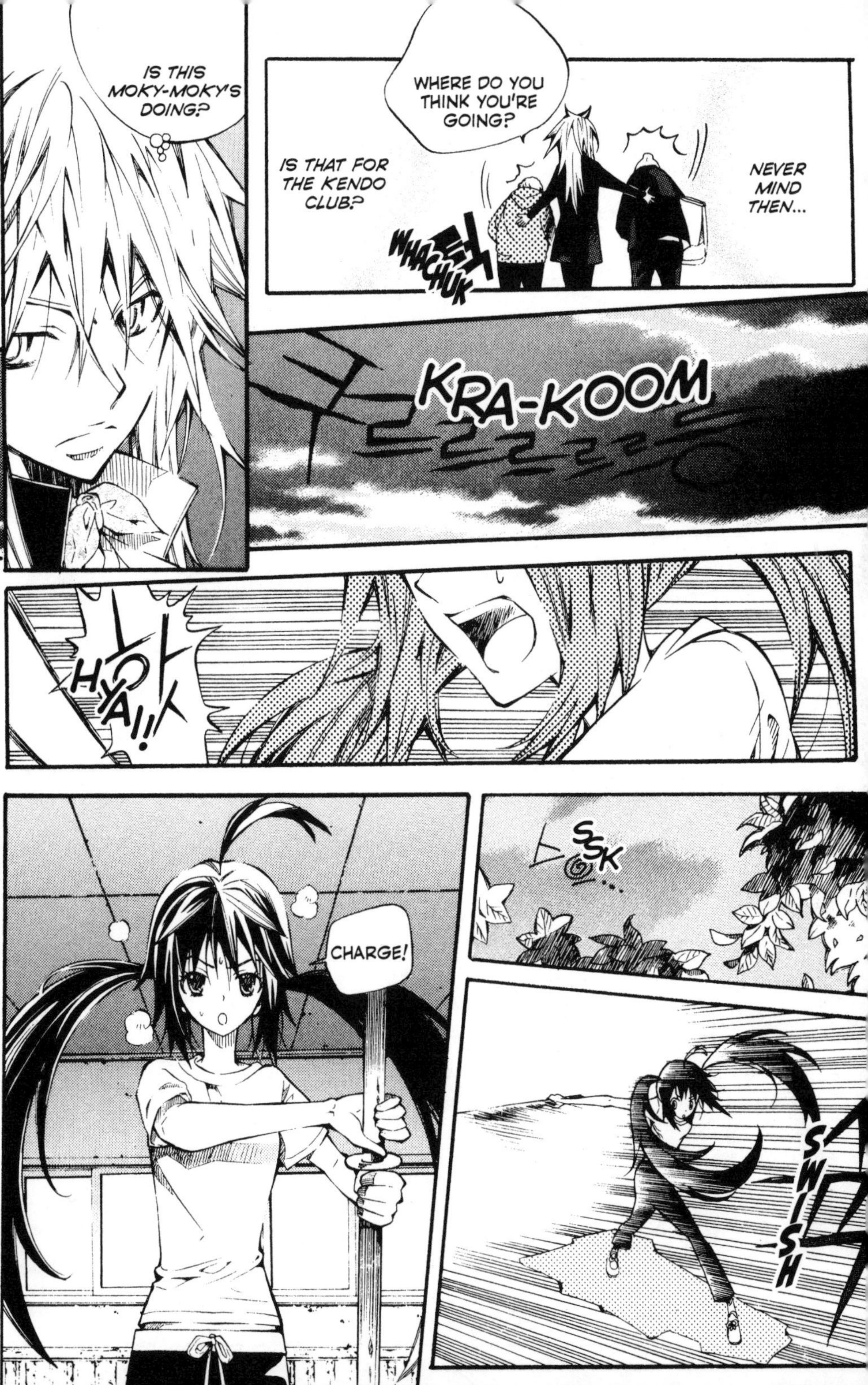

IS THIS MOKY-MOKY'S DOING?
WHERE DO YOU THINK YOU'RE GOING?
IS THAT FOR THE KENDO CLUB?
NEVER MIND THEN...
WHACHUK
KRA-KOOM
HYAII!!
CHARGE!
SSK...
SWISH

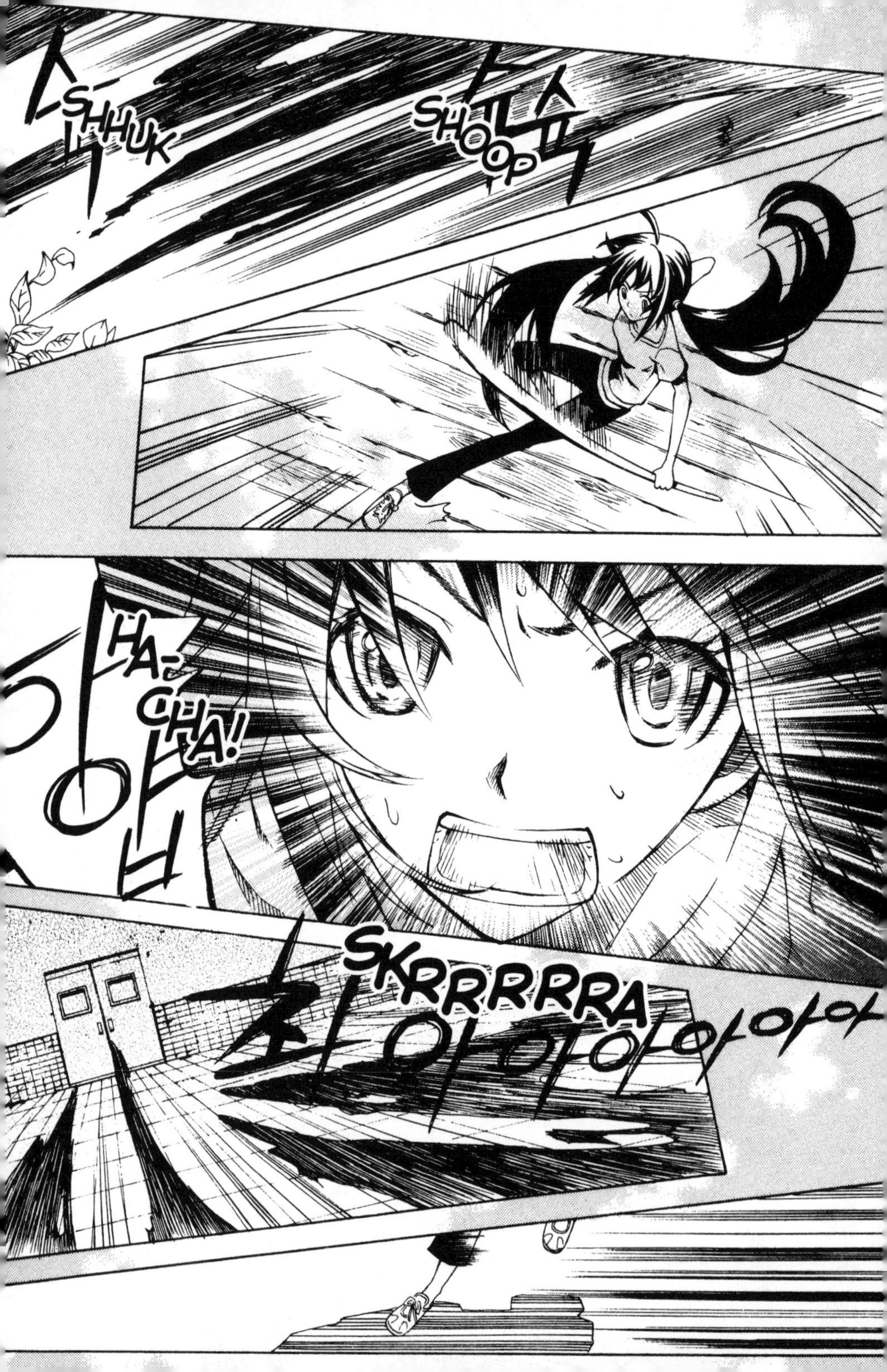
SHHUK
SHOOP
HA-CHA!
SKRRRRRA

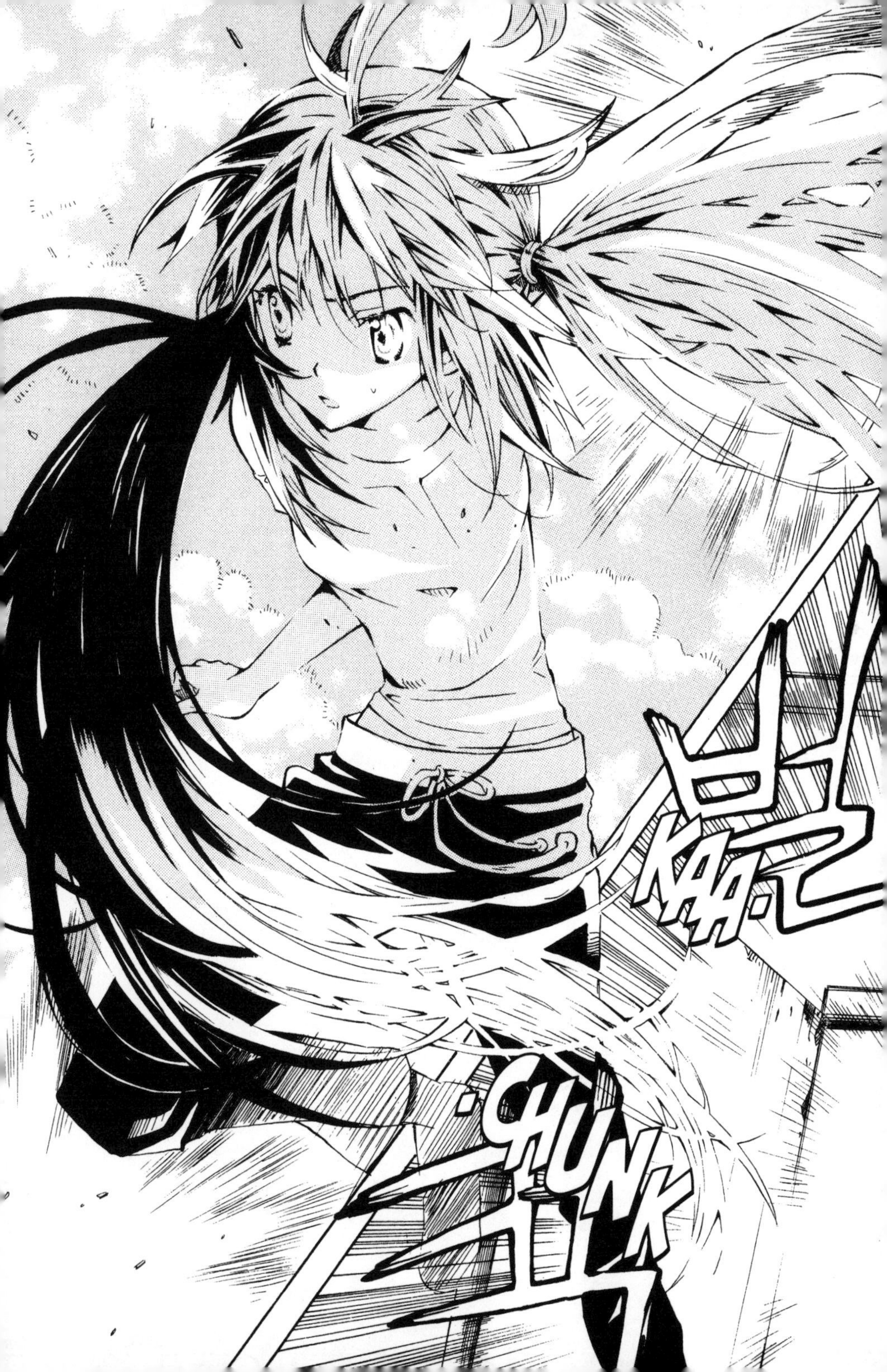
KAA-
CHUNK

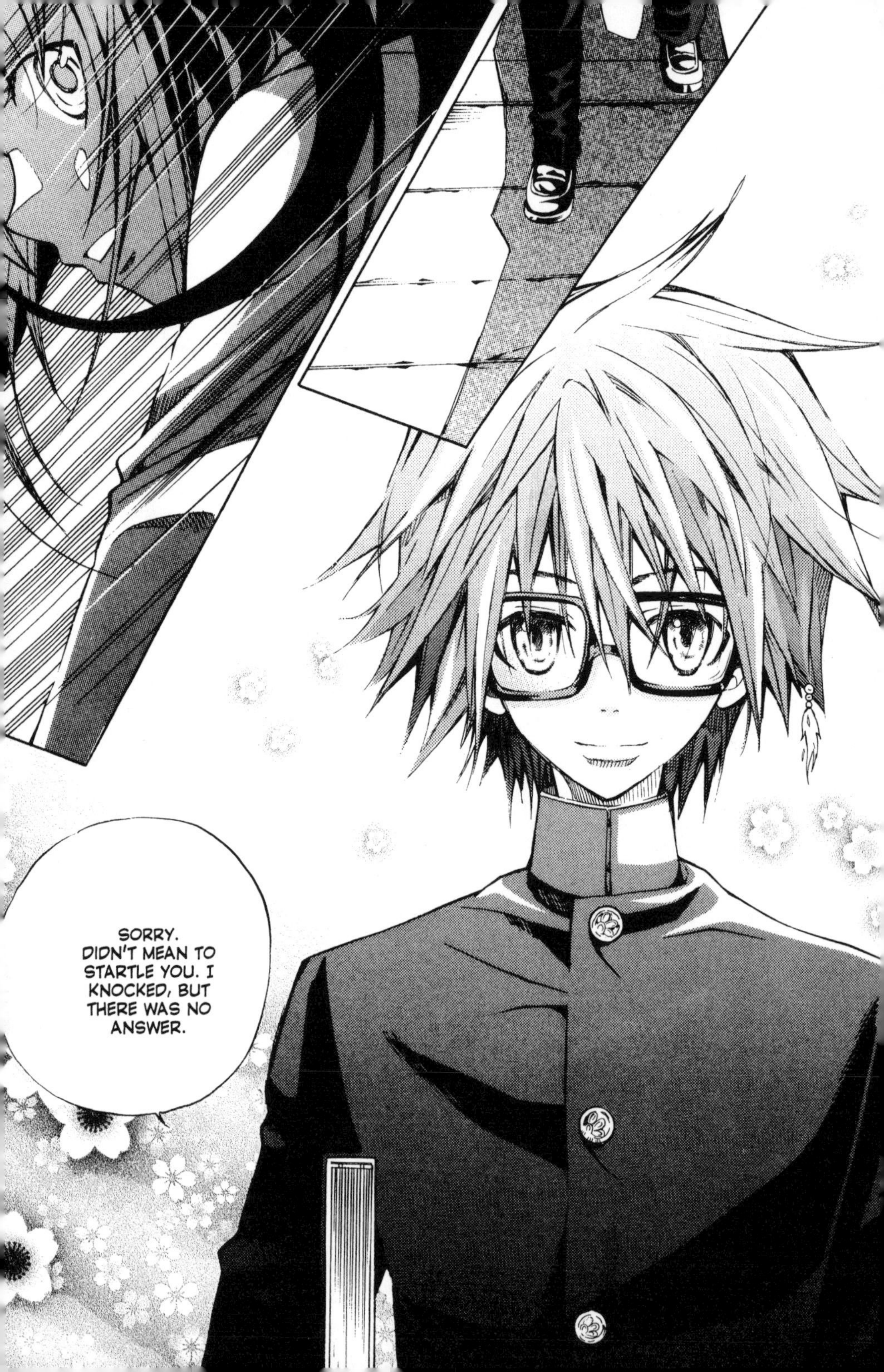
SORRY. DIDN'T MEAN TO STARTLE YOU. I KNOCKED, BUT THERE WAS NO ANSWER.

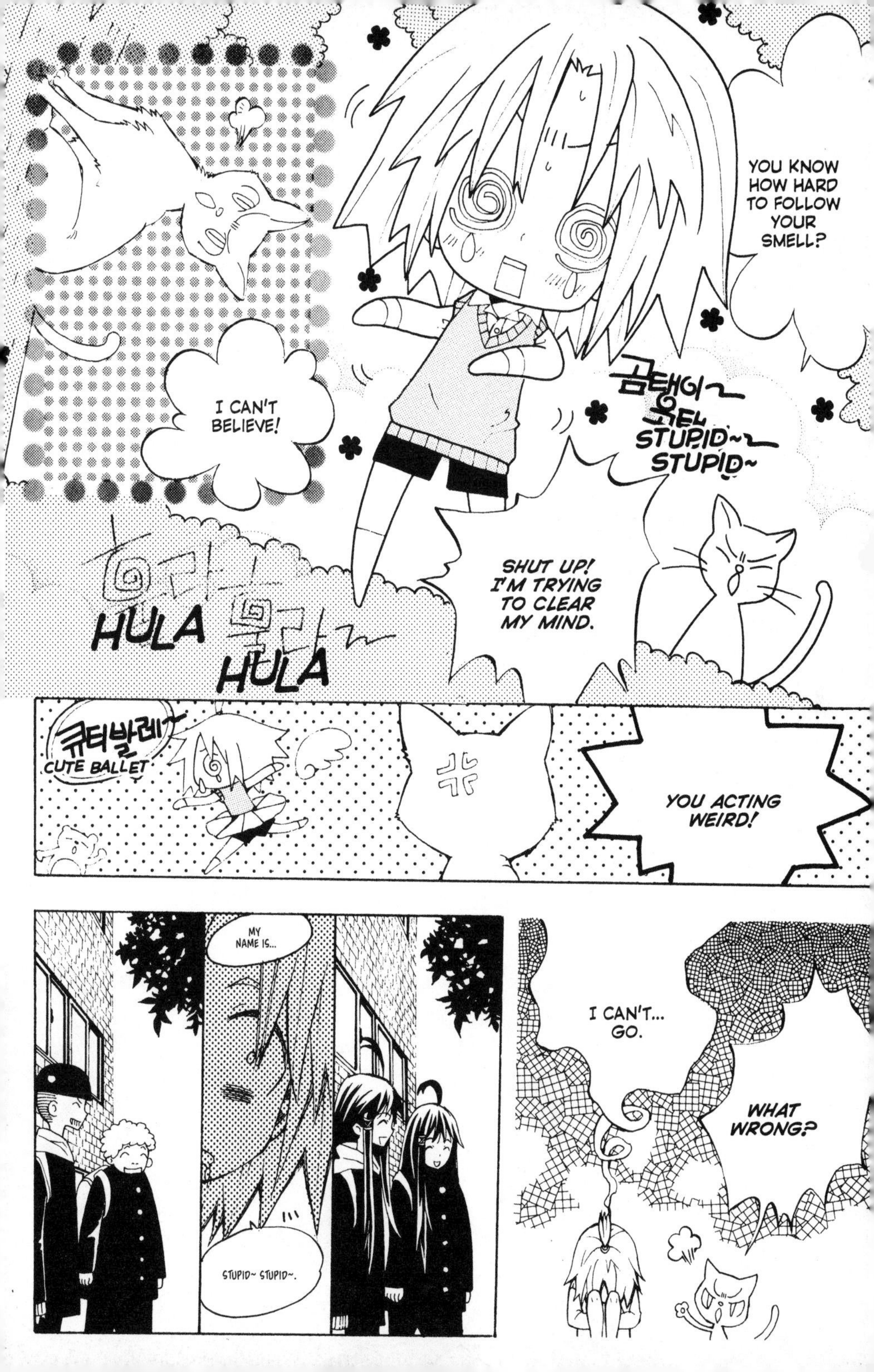

I CAN'T BELIEVE!
YOU KNOW HOW HARD TO FOLLOW YOUR SMELL?
곰탱이~
STUPID~ STUPID~
SHUT UP! I'M TRYING TO CLEAR MY MIND.
HULA HULA
CUTE BALLET
YOU ACTING WEIRD!
MY NAME IS...
STUPID~ STUPID~.
I CAN'T... GO.
WHAT WRONG?

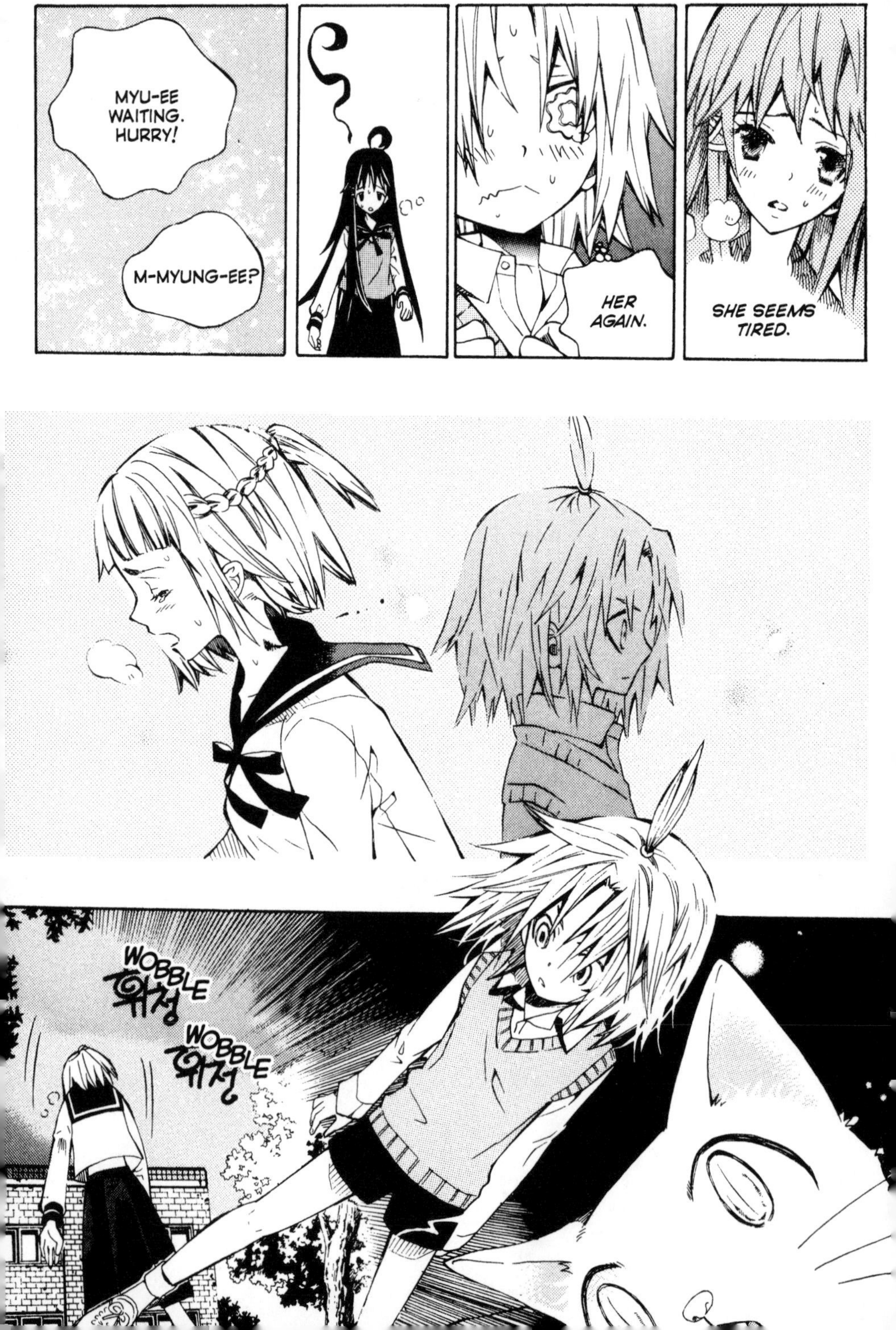
MYU-EE WAITING. HURRY!
M-MYUNG-EE?
HER AGAIN.
SHE SEEMS TIRED.
WOBBLE 휘청
WOBBLE 휘청

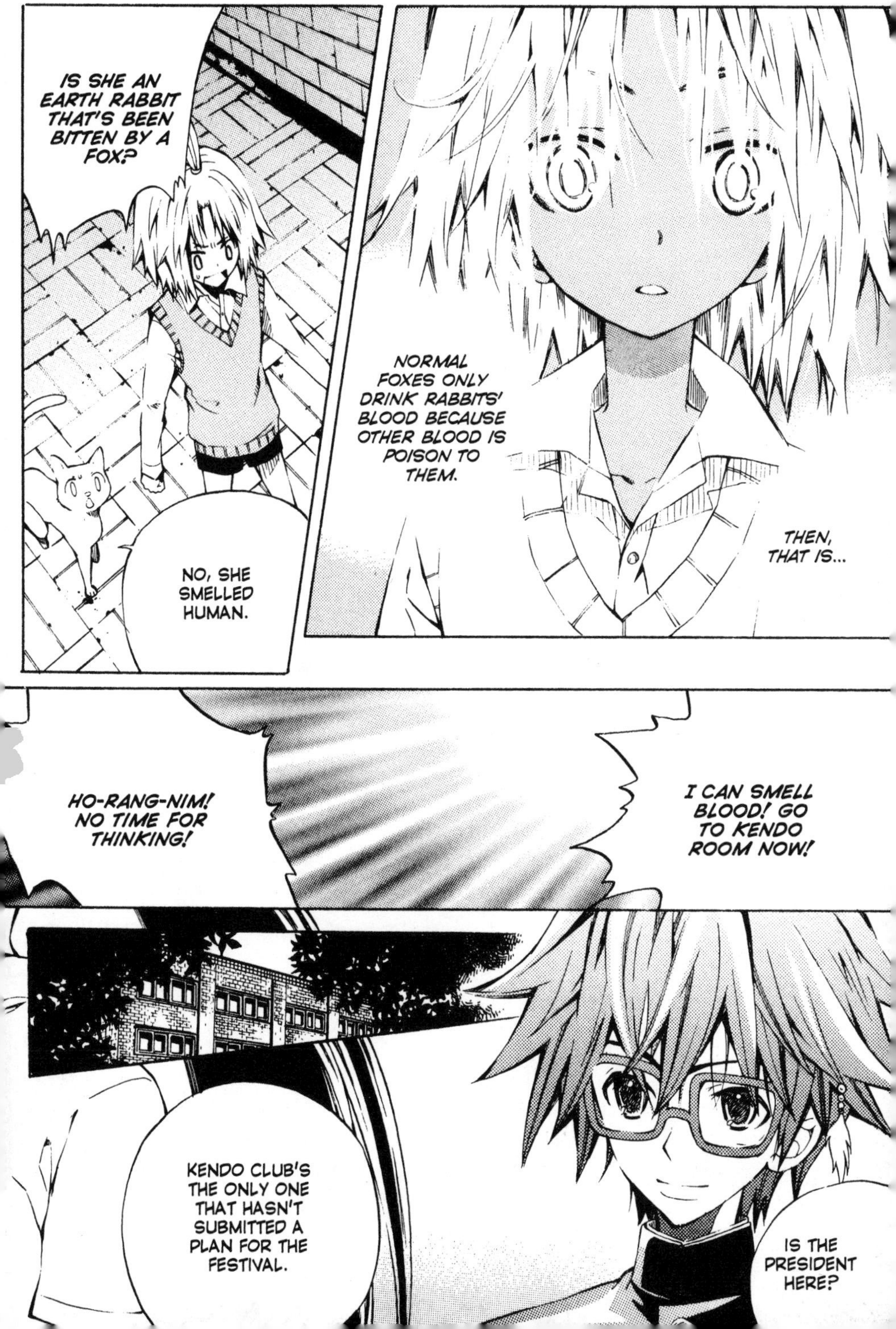
IS SHE AN EARTH RABBIT THAT'S BEEN BITTEN BY A FOX?
NO, SHE SMELLED HUMAN.
NORMAL FOXES ONLY DRINK RABBITS' BLOOD BECAUSE OTHER BLOOD IS POISON TO THEM.
THEN, THAT IS...
HO-RANG-NIM! NO TIME FOR THINKING!
I CAN SMELL BLOOD! GO TO KENDO ROOM NOW!
KENDO CLUB'S THE ONLY ONE THAT HASN'T SUBMITTED A PLAN FOR THE FESTIVAL.
IS THE PRESIDENT HERE?

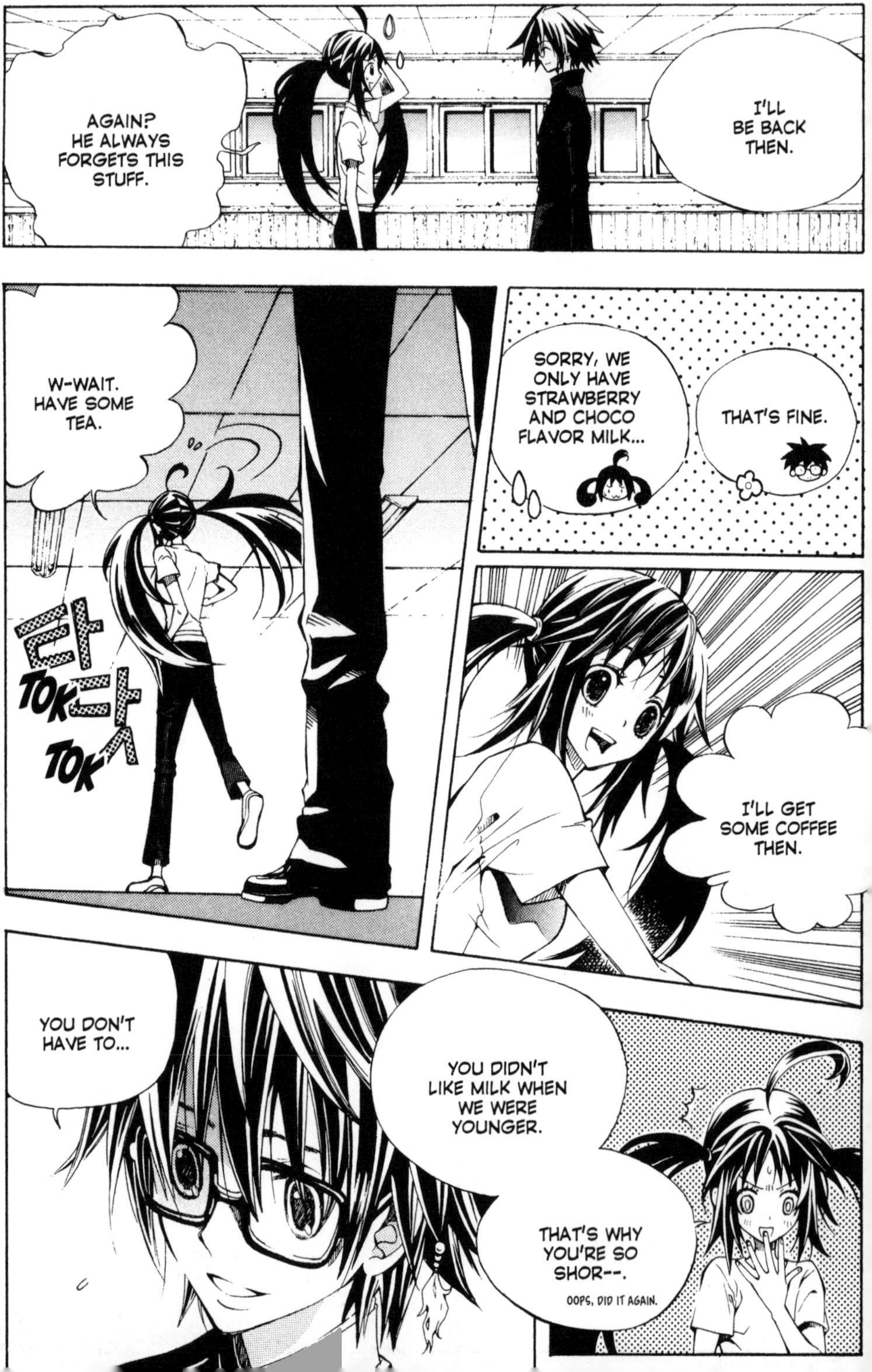
AGAIN? HE ALWAYS FORGETS THIS STUFF.
I'LL BE BACK THEN.
W-WAIT. HAVE SOME TEA.
타다닥
TOK TOK
SORRY, WE ONLY HAVE STRAWBERRY AND CHOCO FLAVOR MILK...
THAT'S FINE.
I'LL GET SOME COFFEE THEN.
YOU DON'T HAVE TO...
YOU DIDN'T LIKE MILK WHEN WE WERE YOUNGER.
THAT'S WHY YOU'RE SO SHOR--.
OOPS, DID IT AGAIN.

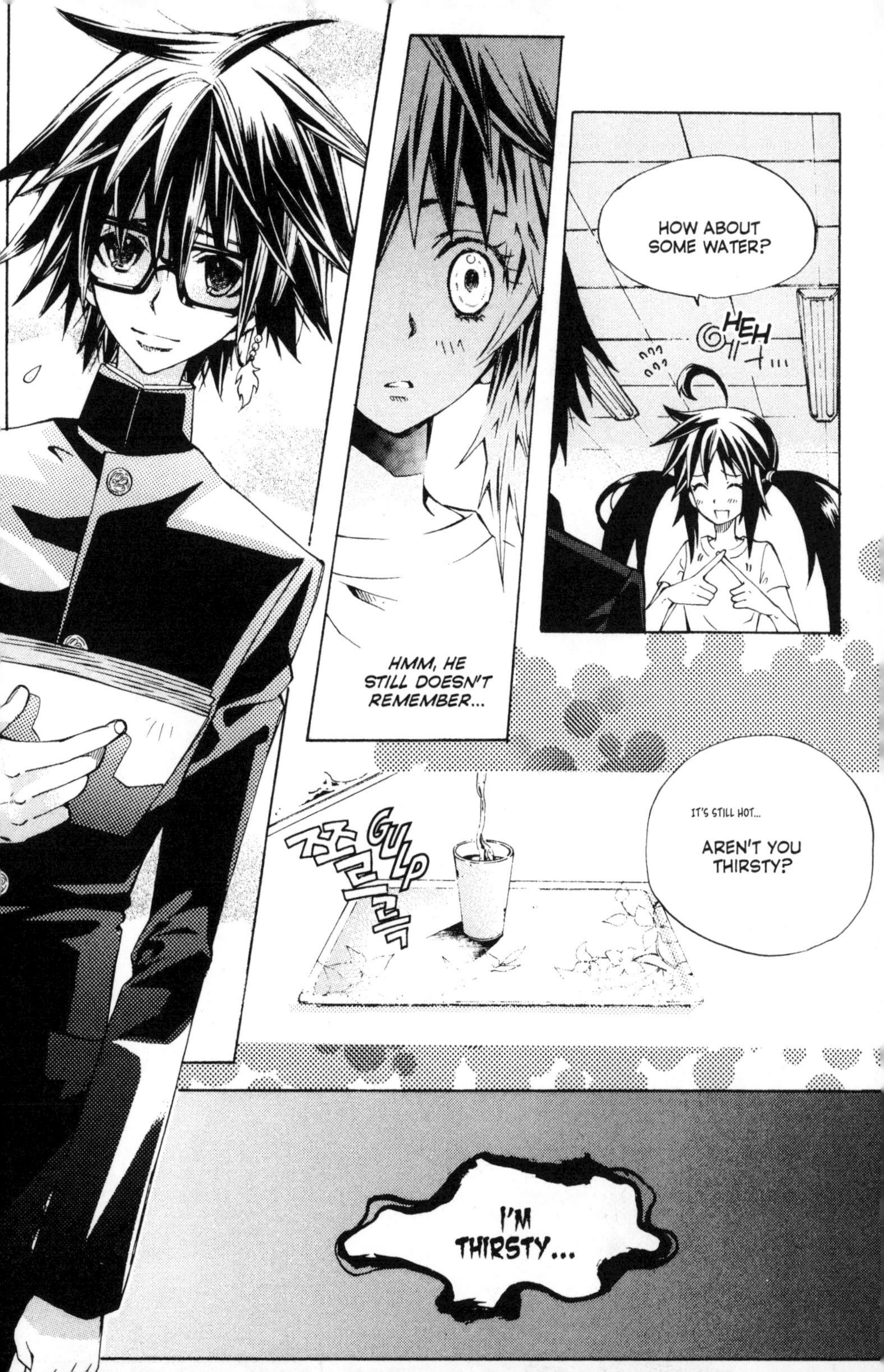
HMM, HE STILL DOESN'T REMEMBER...
HOW ABOUT SOME WATER?
HEH
GULP
IT'S STILL HOT...
AREN'T YOU THIRSTY?
I'M THIRSTY...

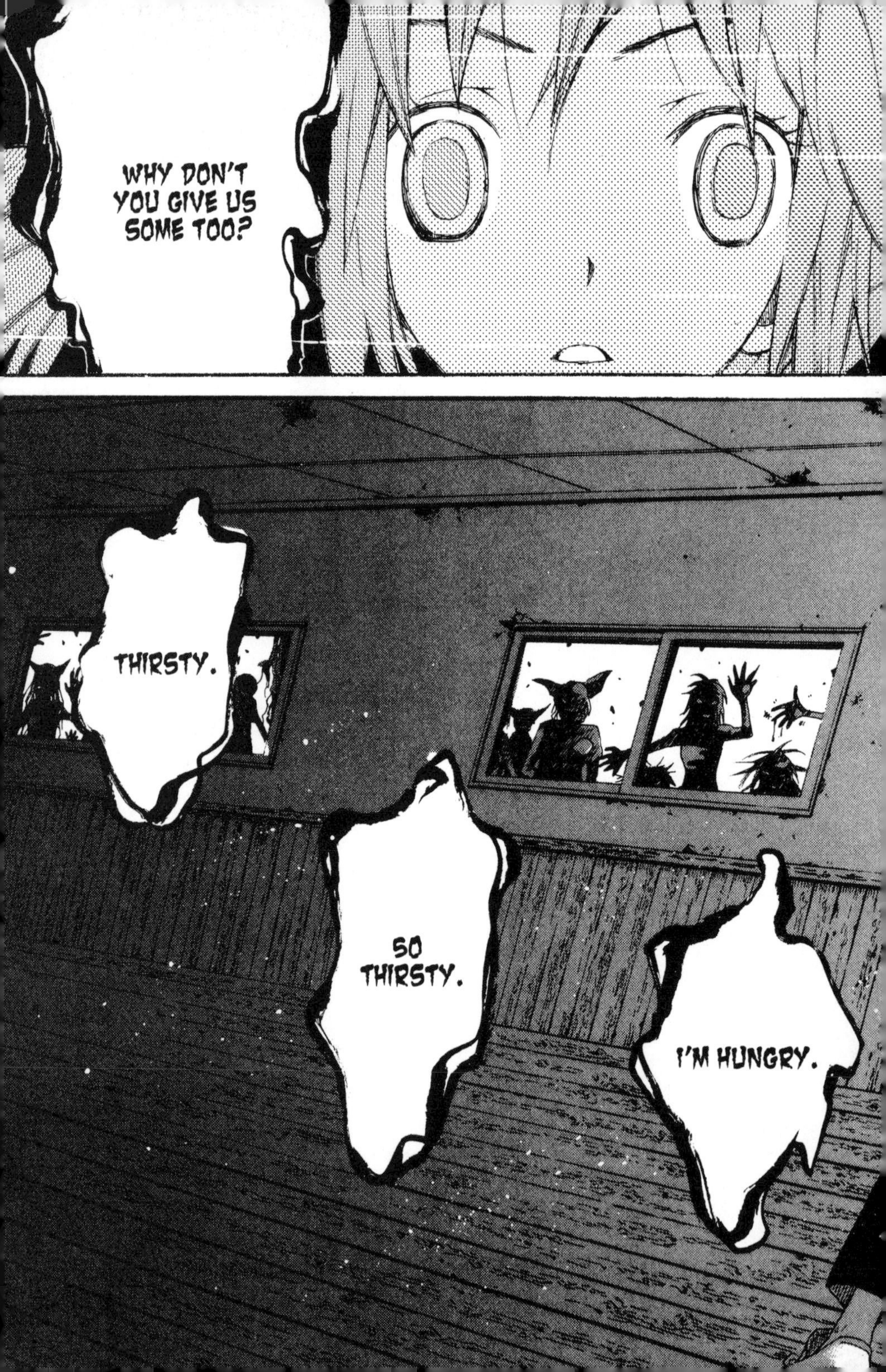
WHY DON'T YOU GIVE US SOME TOO?
THIRSTY.
SO THIRSTY.
I'M HUNGRY.

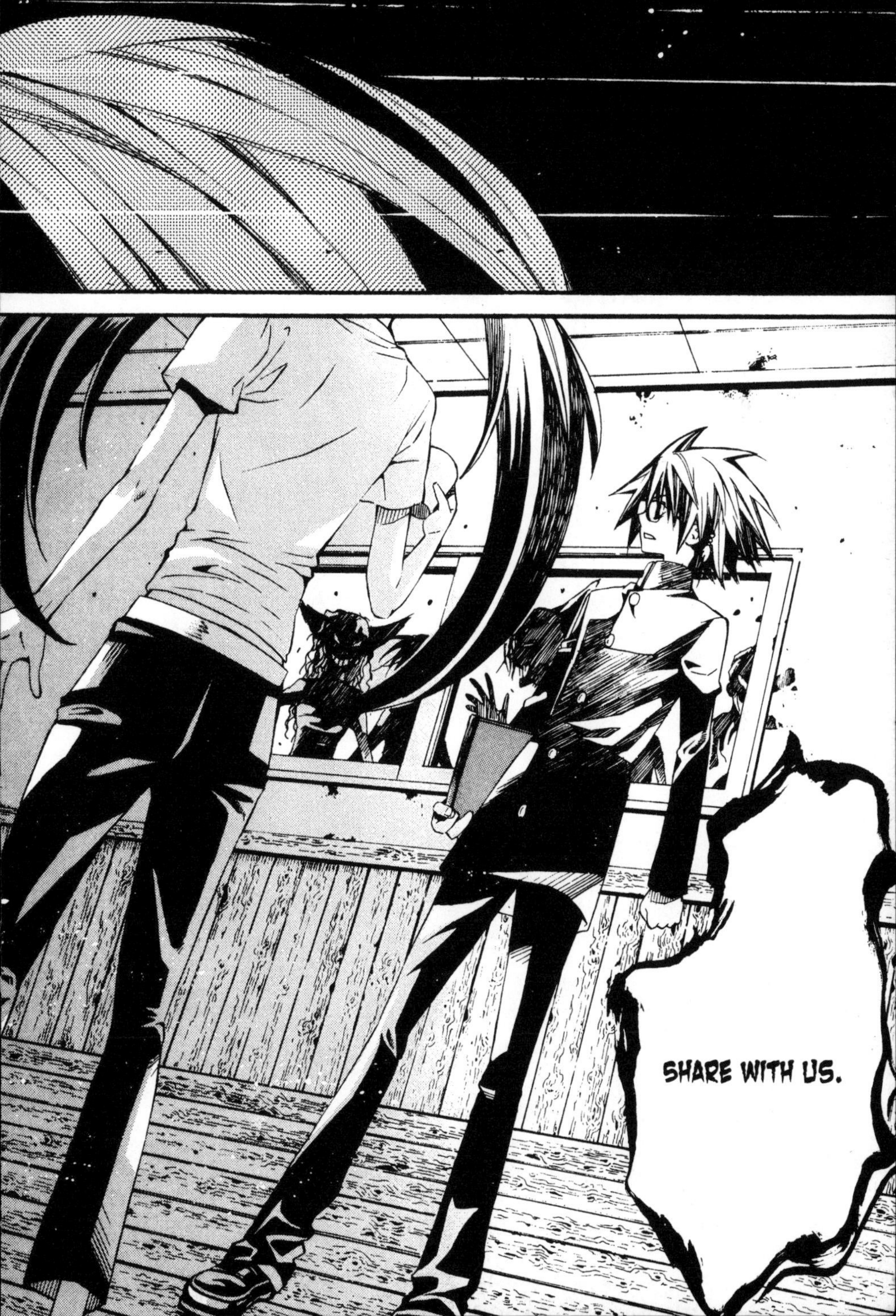
SHARE WITH US.

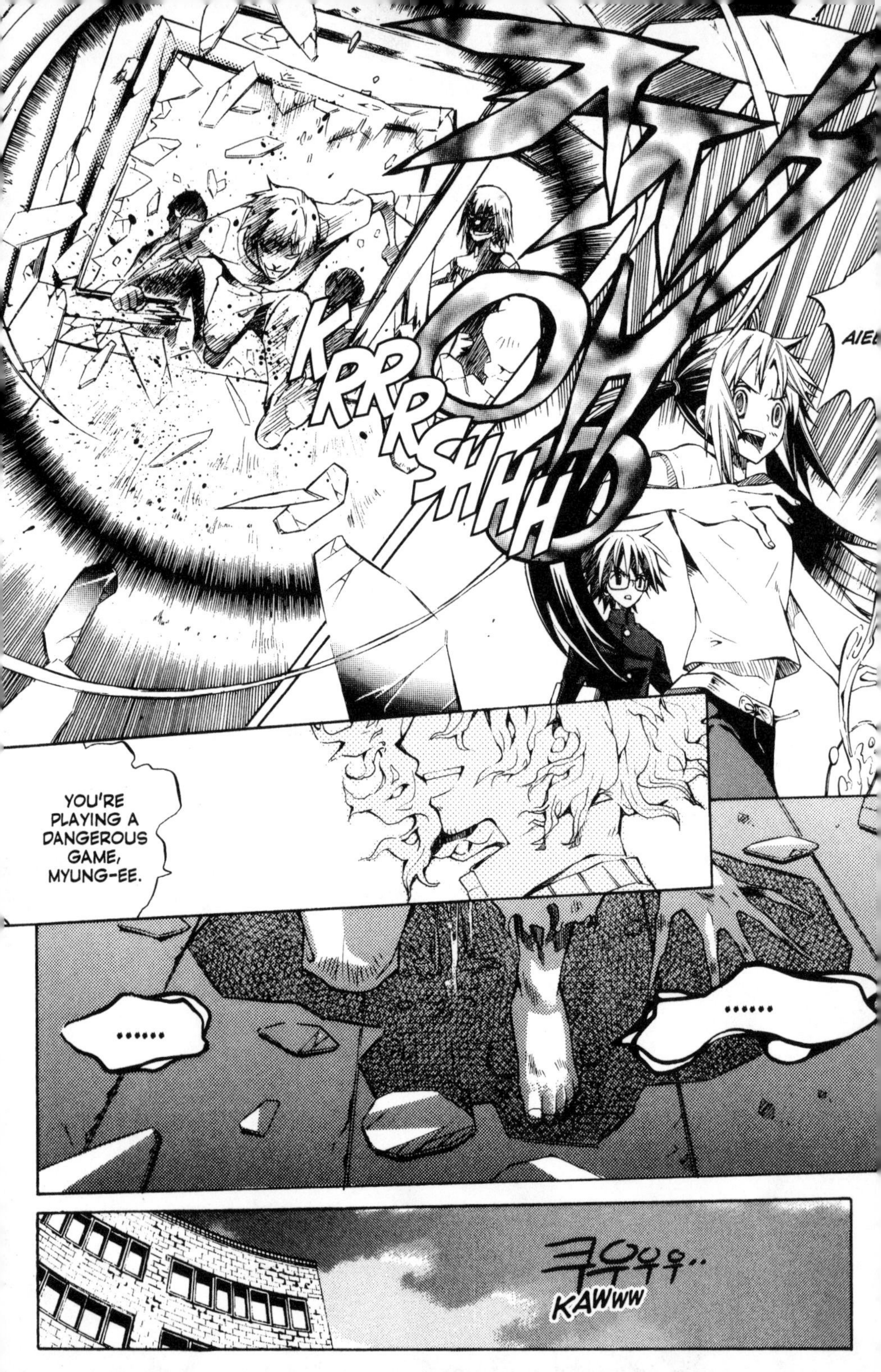
KRRRSHHH
AIE
YOU'RE PLAYING A DANGEROUS GAME, MYUNG-EE.
......
......
쿠우우우..
KAWWW

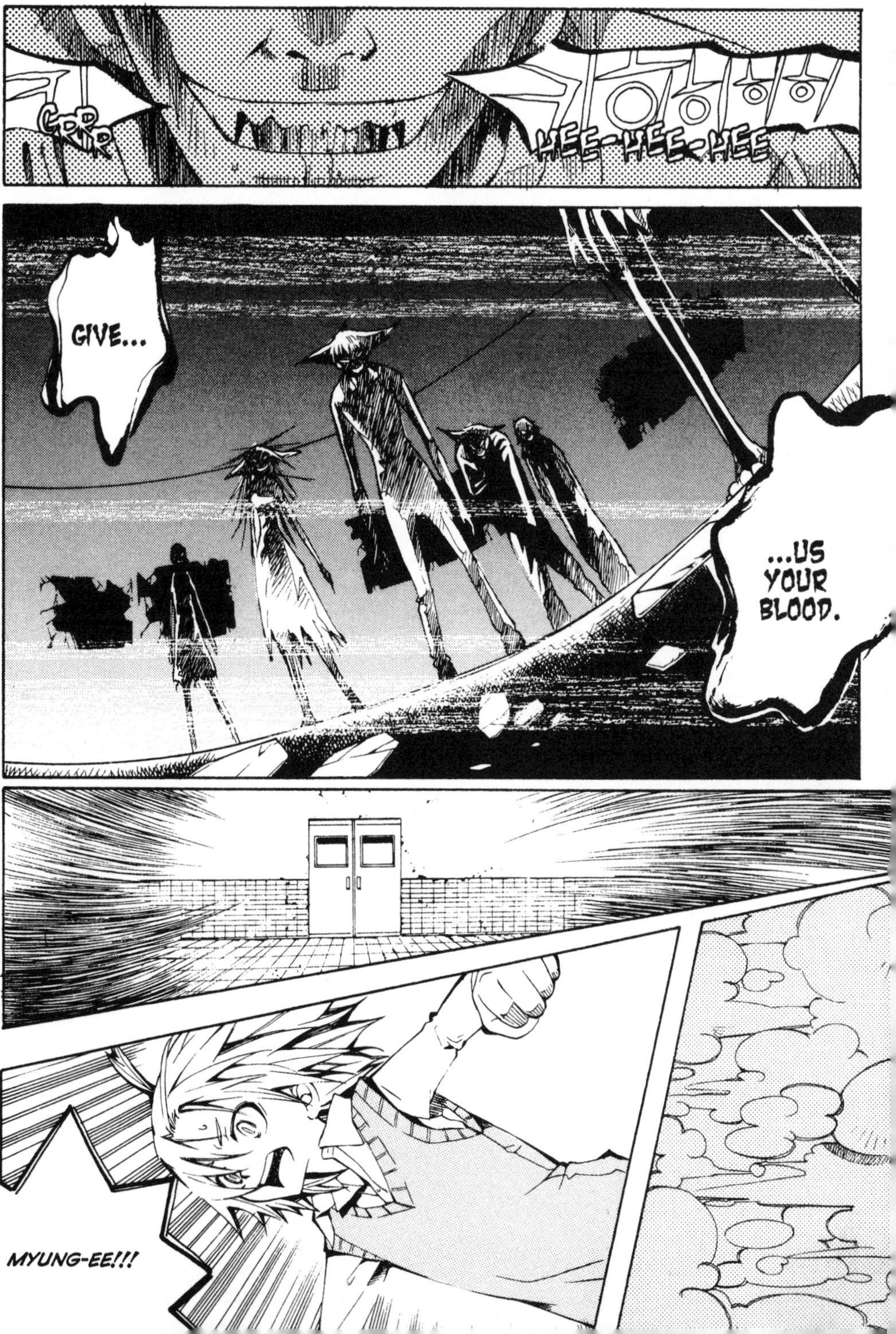
GRRR
HEE-HEE-HEE
GIVE...
...US YOUR BLOOD.
MYUNG-EE!!!

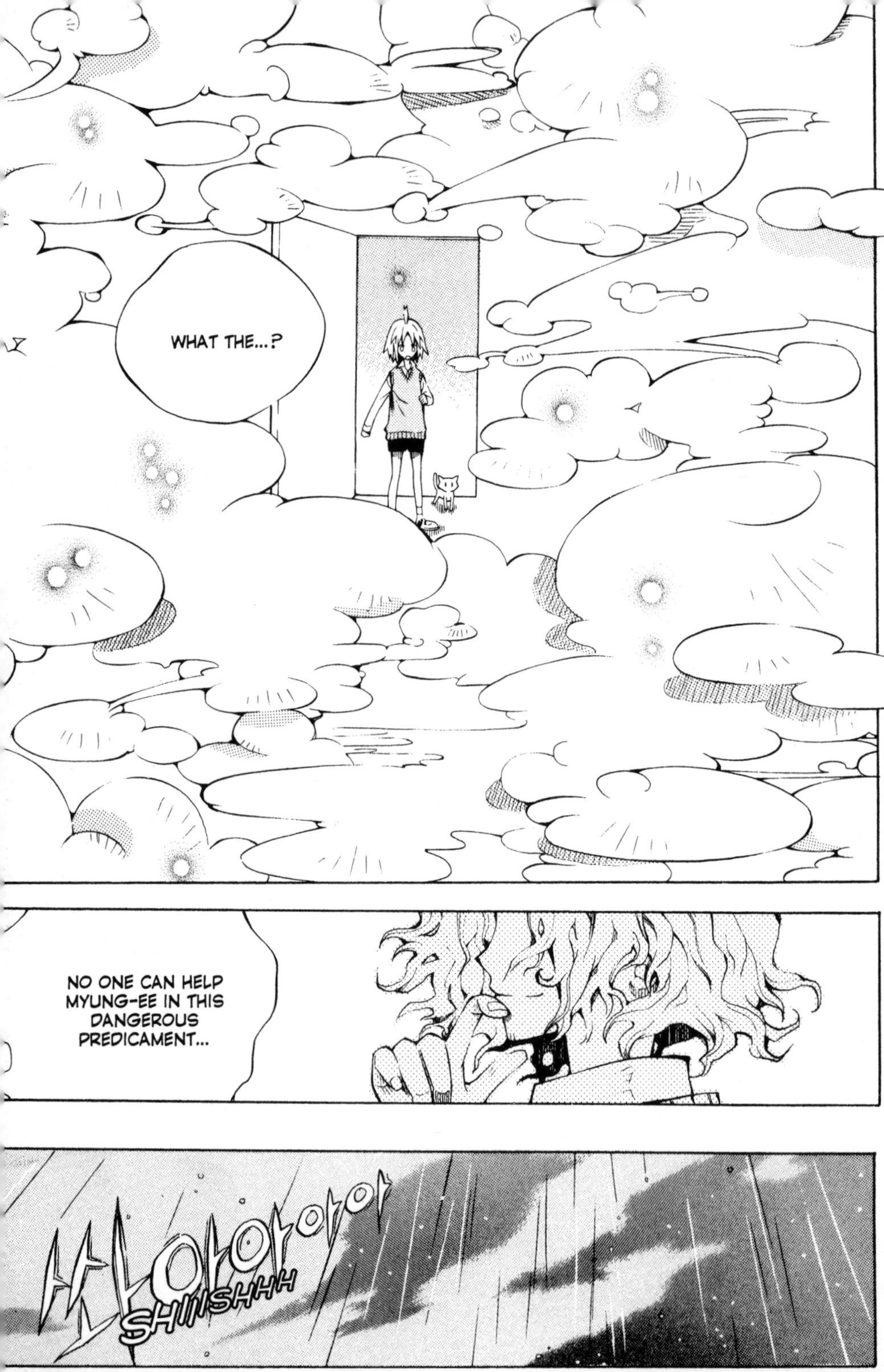
WHAT THE...?
NO ONE CAN HELP MYUNG-EE IN THIS DANGEROUS PREDICAMENT...
쏴아아아아아
SHIIISHHH

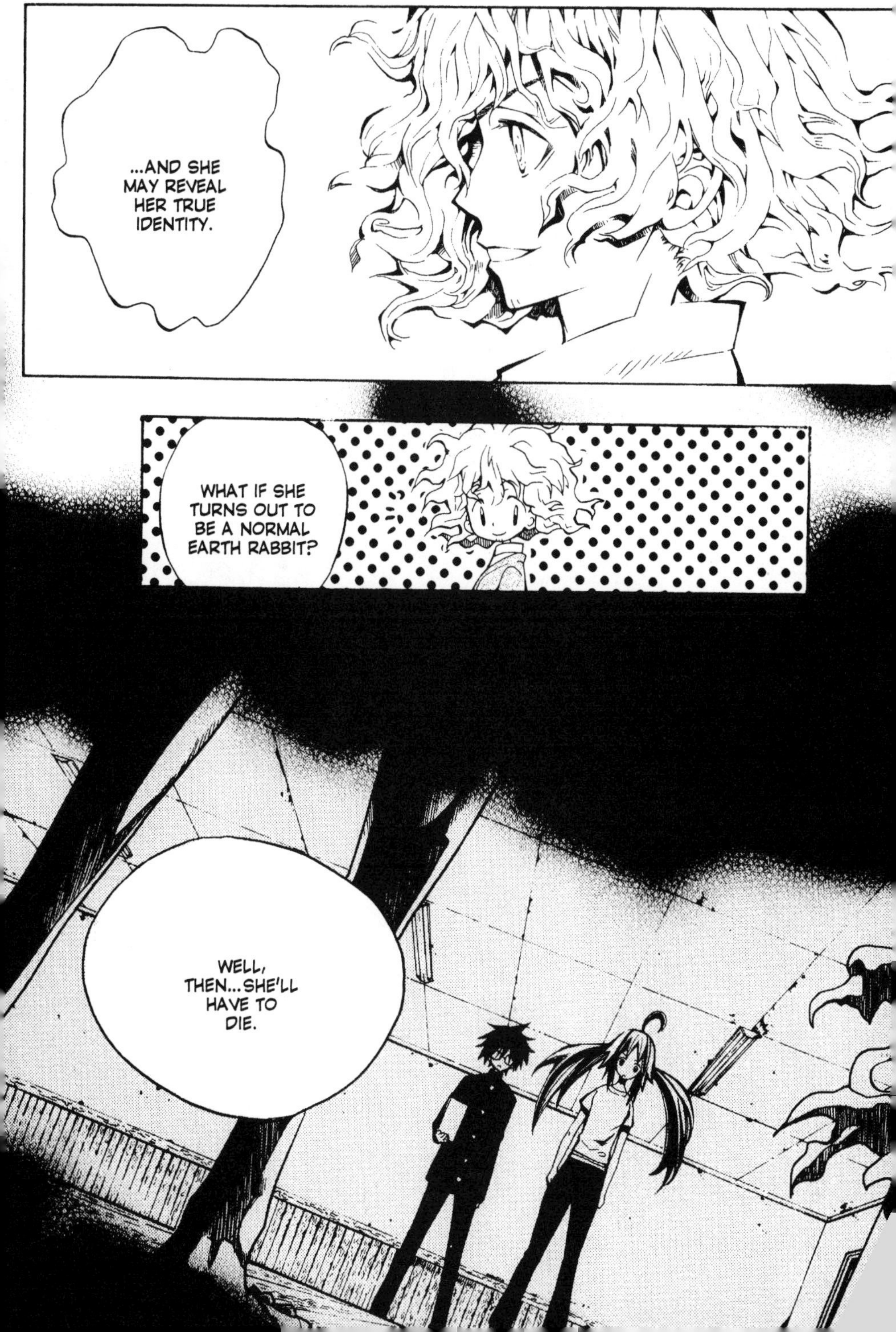
...AND SHE MAY REVEAL HER TRUE IDENTITY.
WHAT IF SHE TURNS OUT TO BE A NORMAL EARTH RABBIT?
WELL, THEN...SHE'LL HAVE TO DIE.

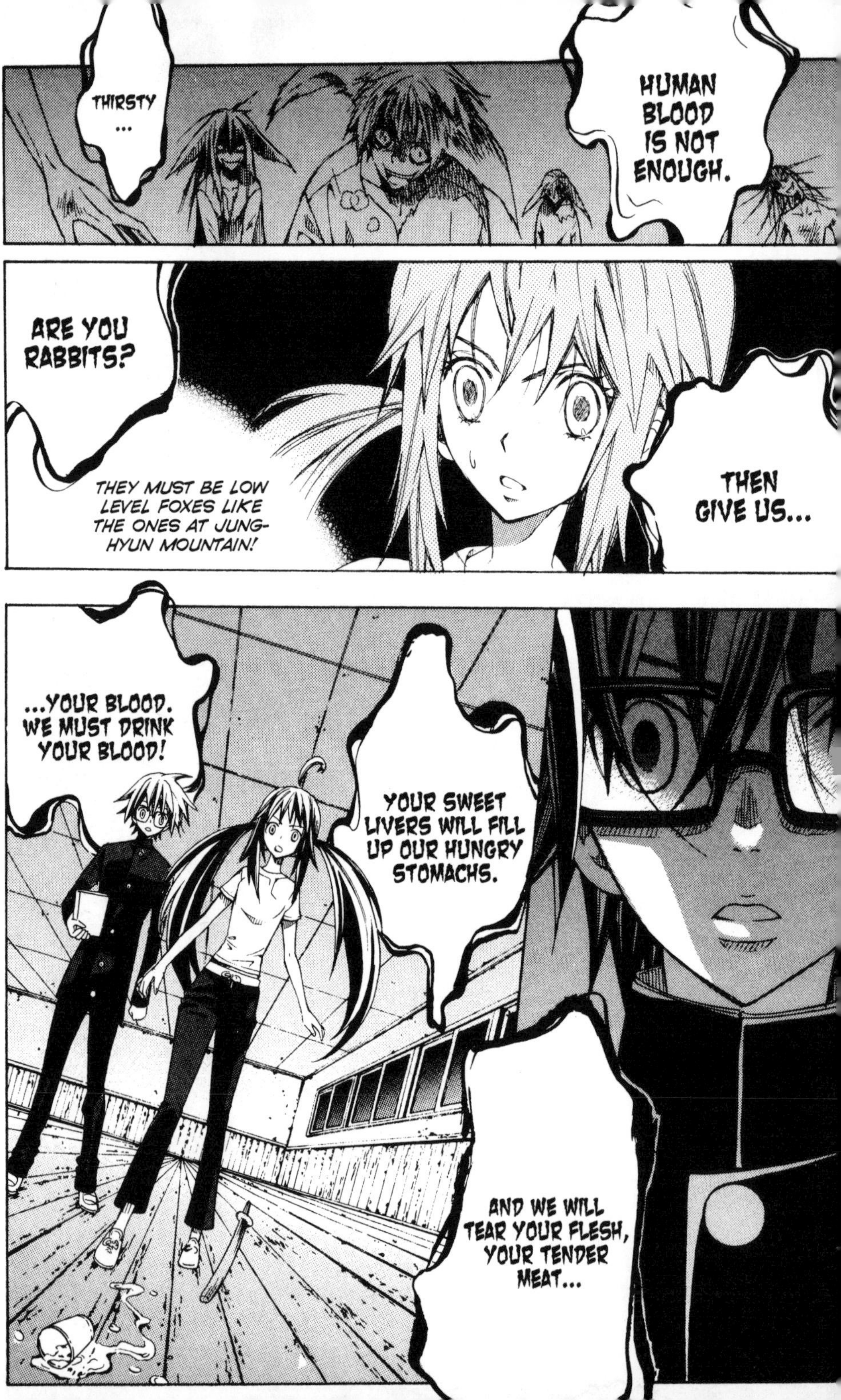
THIRSTY ...
HUMAN BLOOD IS NOT ENOUGH.
ARE YOU RABBITS?
THEY MUST BE LOW LEVEL FOXES LIKE THE ONES AT JUNG-HYUN MOUNTAIN!
THEN GIVE US...
...YOUR BLOOD. WE MUST DRINK YOUR BLOOD!
YOUR SWEET LIVERS WILL FILL UP OUR HUNGRY STOMACHS.
AND WE WILL TEAR YOUR FLESH, YOUR TENDER MEAT...

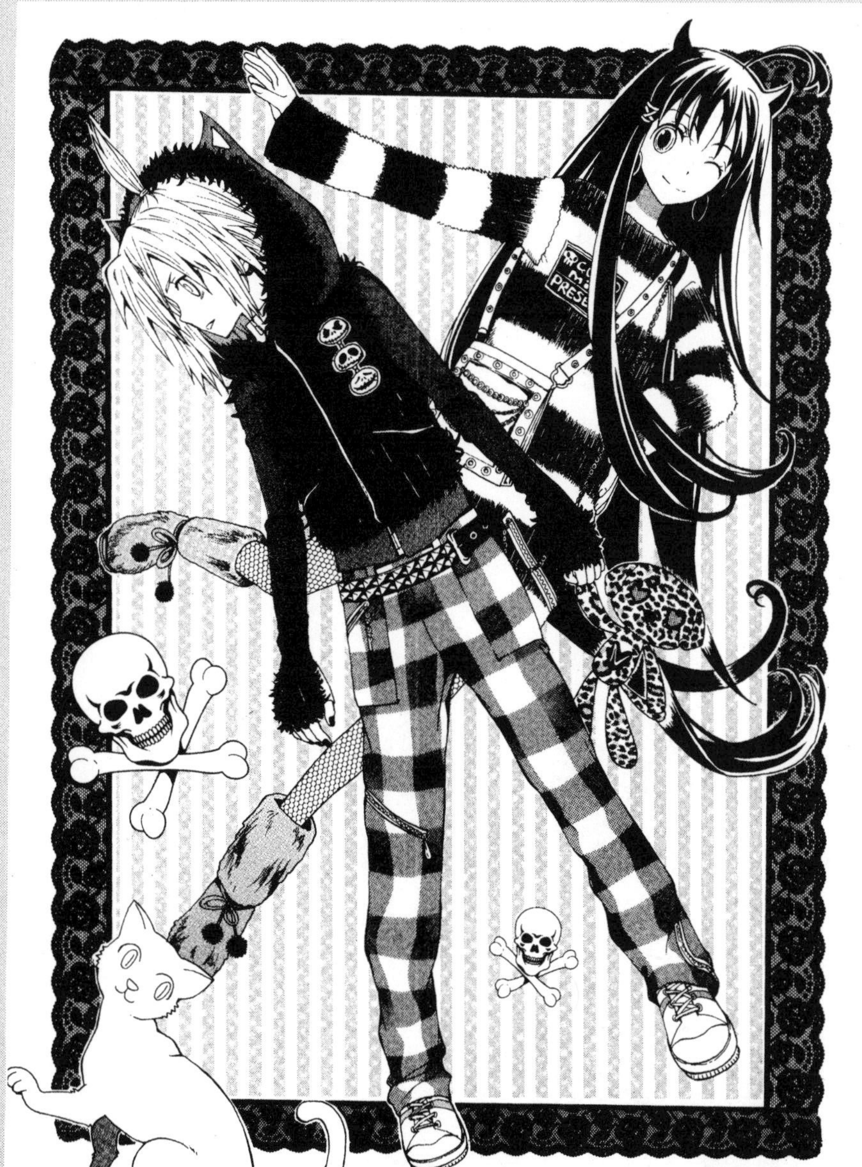

Moon Boy
월요일소년

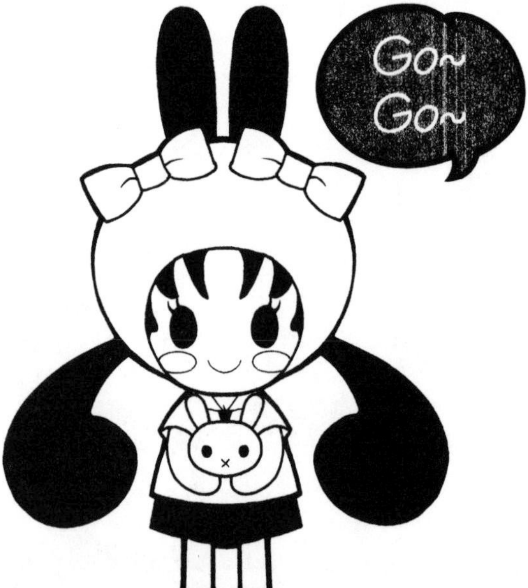
Go~
Go~

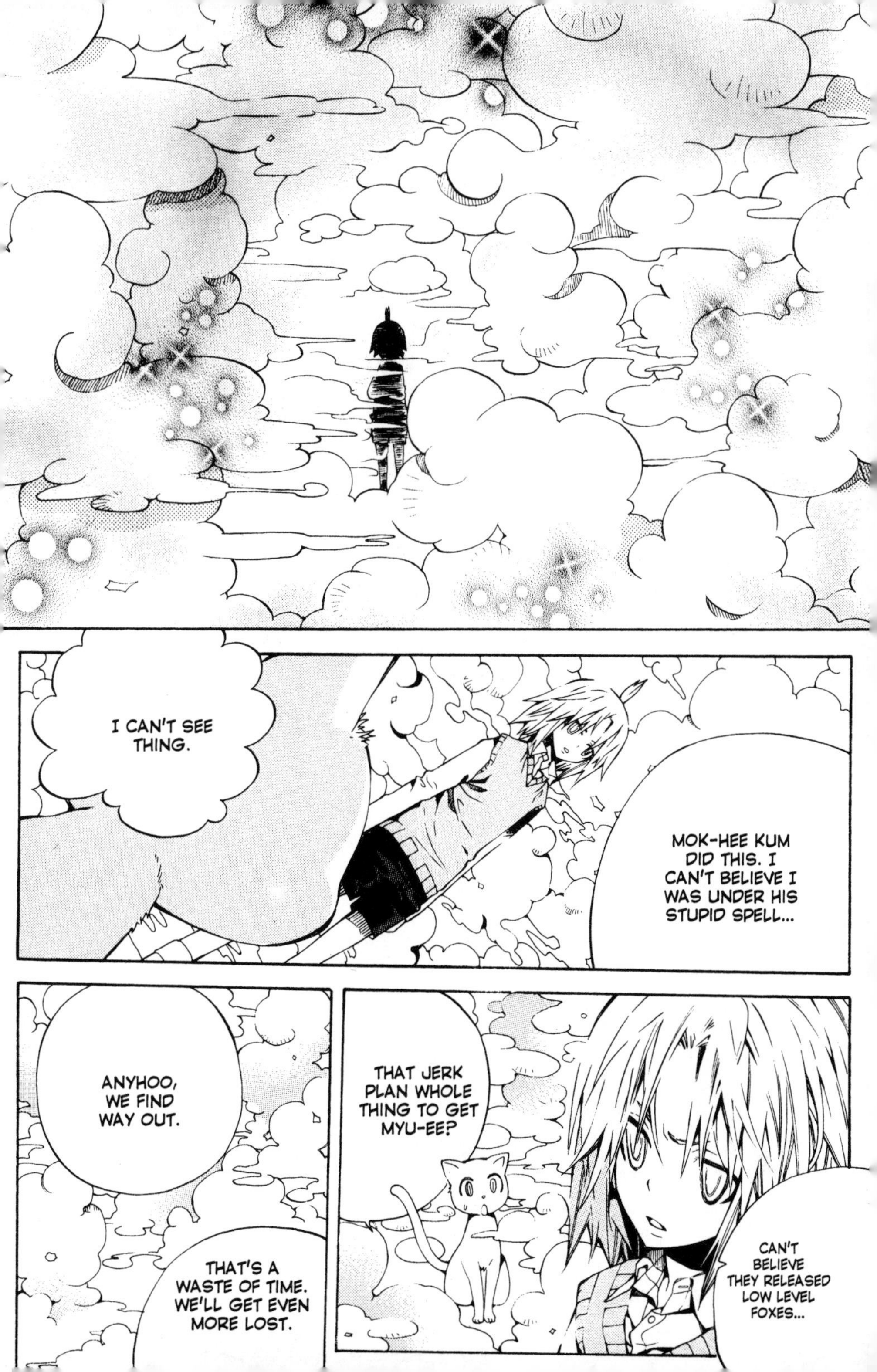
I CAN'T SEE THING.
MOK-HEE KUM DID THIS. I CAN'T BELIEVE I WAS UNDER HIS STUPID SPELL...
ANYHOO, WE FIND WAY OUT.
THAT'S A WASTE OF TIME. WE'LL GET EVEN MORE LOST.
THAT JERK PLAN WHOLE THING TO GET MYU-EE?
CAN'T BELIEVE THEY RELEASED LOW LEVEL FOXES...

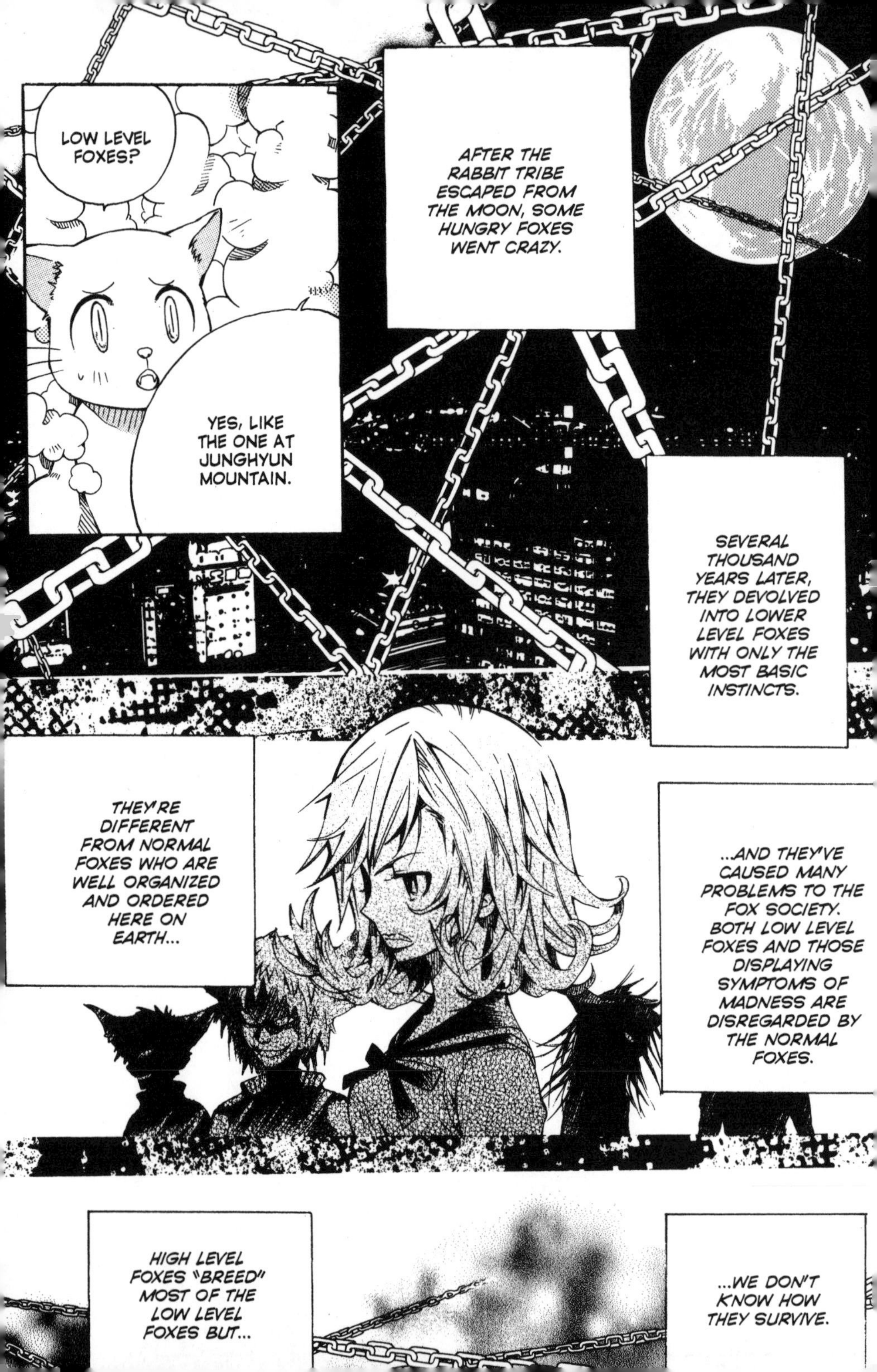
LOW LEVEL FOXES?
YES, LIKE THE ONE AT JUNGHYUN MOUNTAIN.
AFTER THE RABBIT TRIBE ESCAPED FROM THE MOON, SOME HUNGRY FOXES WENT CRAZY.
SEVERAL THOUSAND YEARS LATER, THEY DEVOLVED INTO LOWER LEVEL FOXES WITH ONLY THE MOST BASIC INSTINCTS.
THEY'RE DIFFERENT FROM NORMAL FOXES WHO ARE WELL ORGANIZED AND ORDERED HERE ON EARTH...
...AND THEY'VE CAUSED MANY PROBLEMS TO THE FOX SOCIETY. BOTH LOW LEVEL FOXES AND THOSE DISPLAYING SYMPTOMS OF MADNESS ARE DISREGARDED BY THE NORMAL FOXES.
HIGH LEVEL FOXES "BREED" MOST OF THE LOW LEVEL FOXES BUT...
...WE DON'T KNOW HOW THEY SURVIVE.

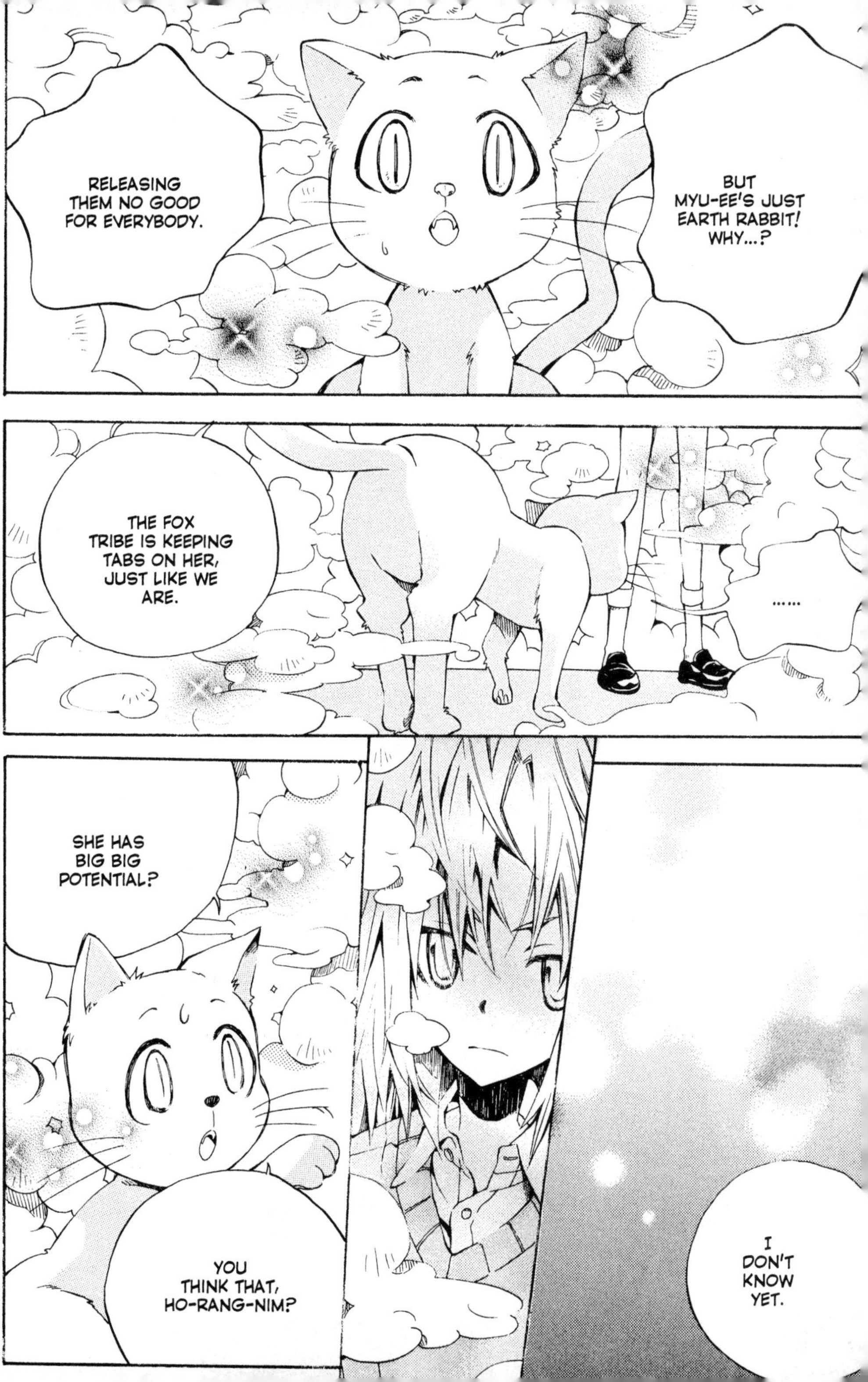
RELEASING THEM NO GOOD FOR EVERYBODY.
BUT MYU-EE'S JUST EARTH RABBIT! WHY...?
THE FOX TRIBE IS KEEPING TABS ON HER, JUST LIKE WE ARE.
......
SHE HAS BIG BIG POTENTIAL?
YOU THINK THAT, HO-RANG-NIM?
I DON'T KNOW YET.

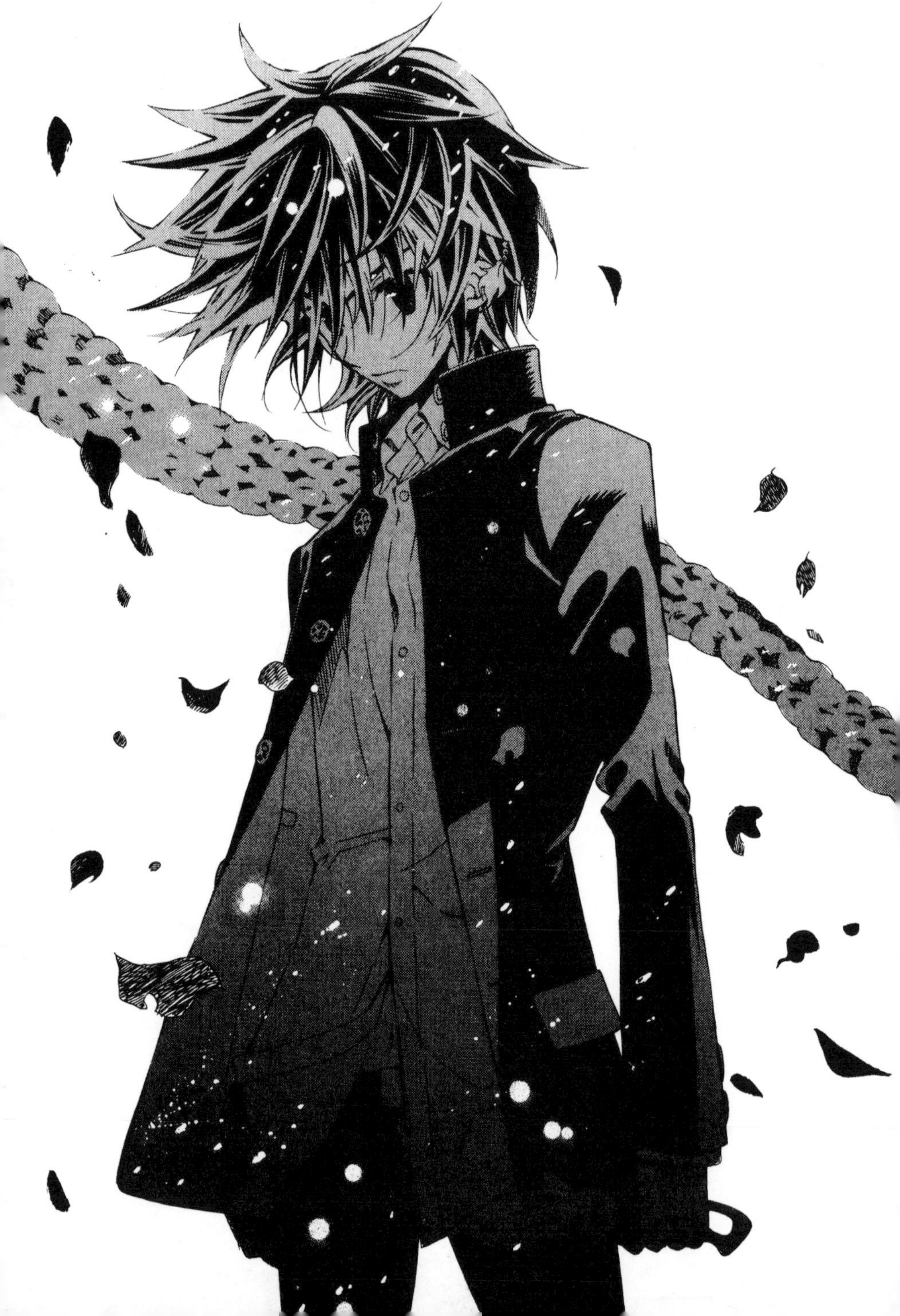

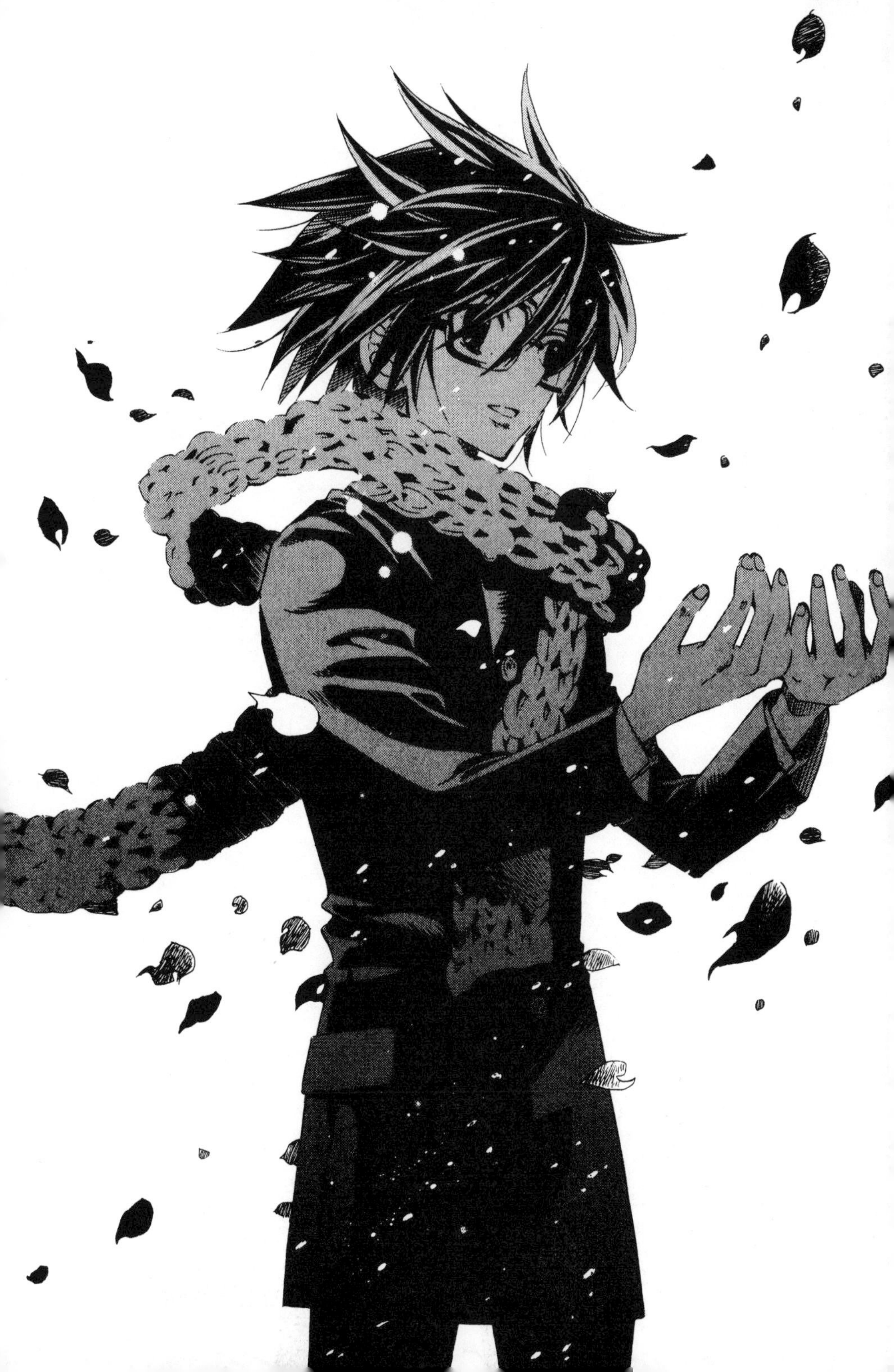

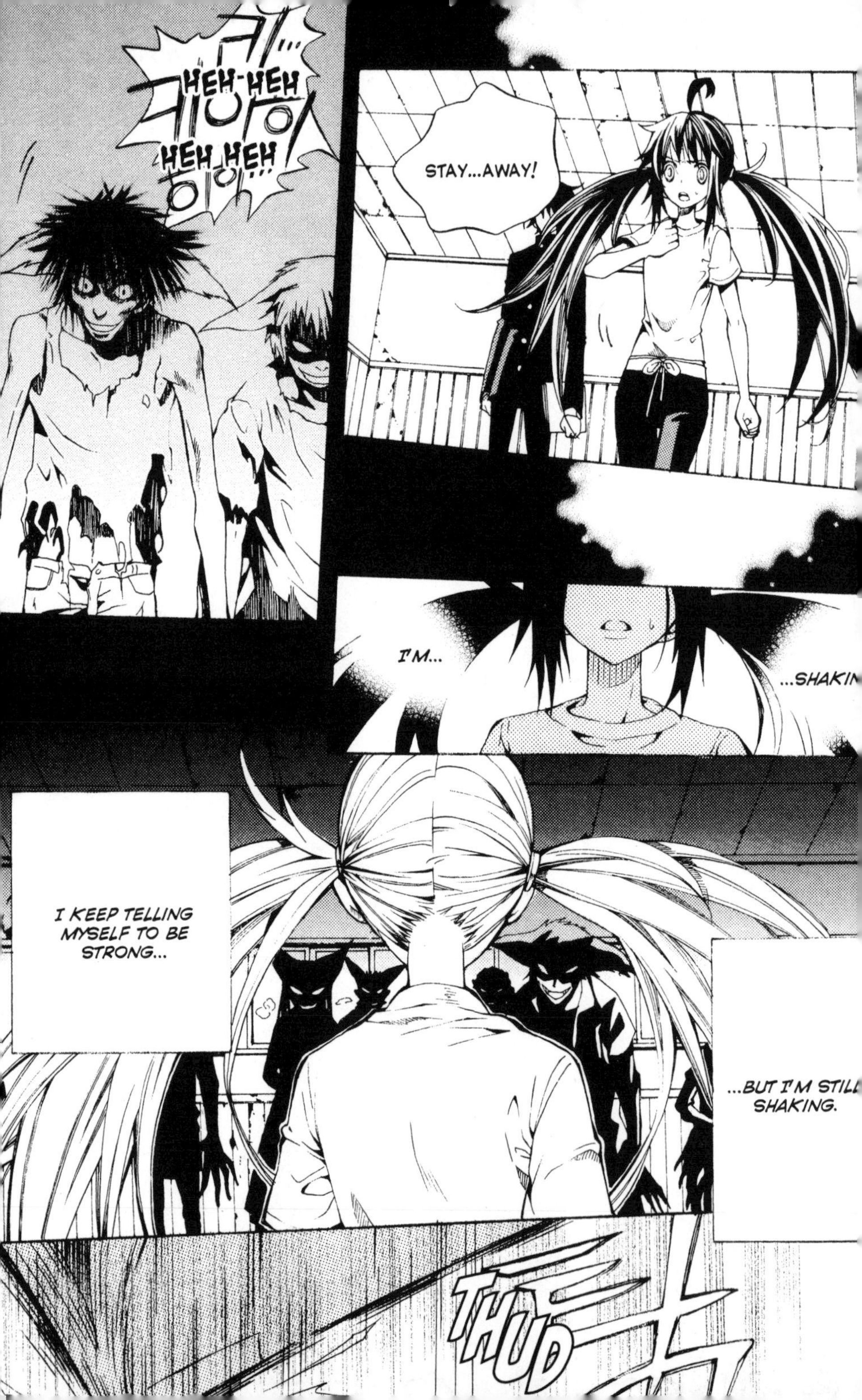
HEH-HEH
HEH HEH
STAY...AWAY!
I'M...
...SHAKIN
I KEEP TELLING MYSELF TO BE STRONG...
...BUT I'M STILL SHAKING.
THUD

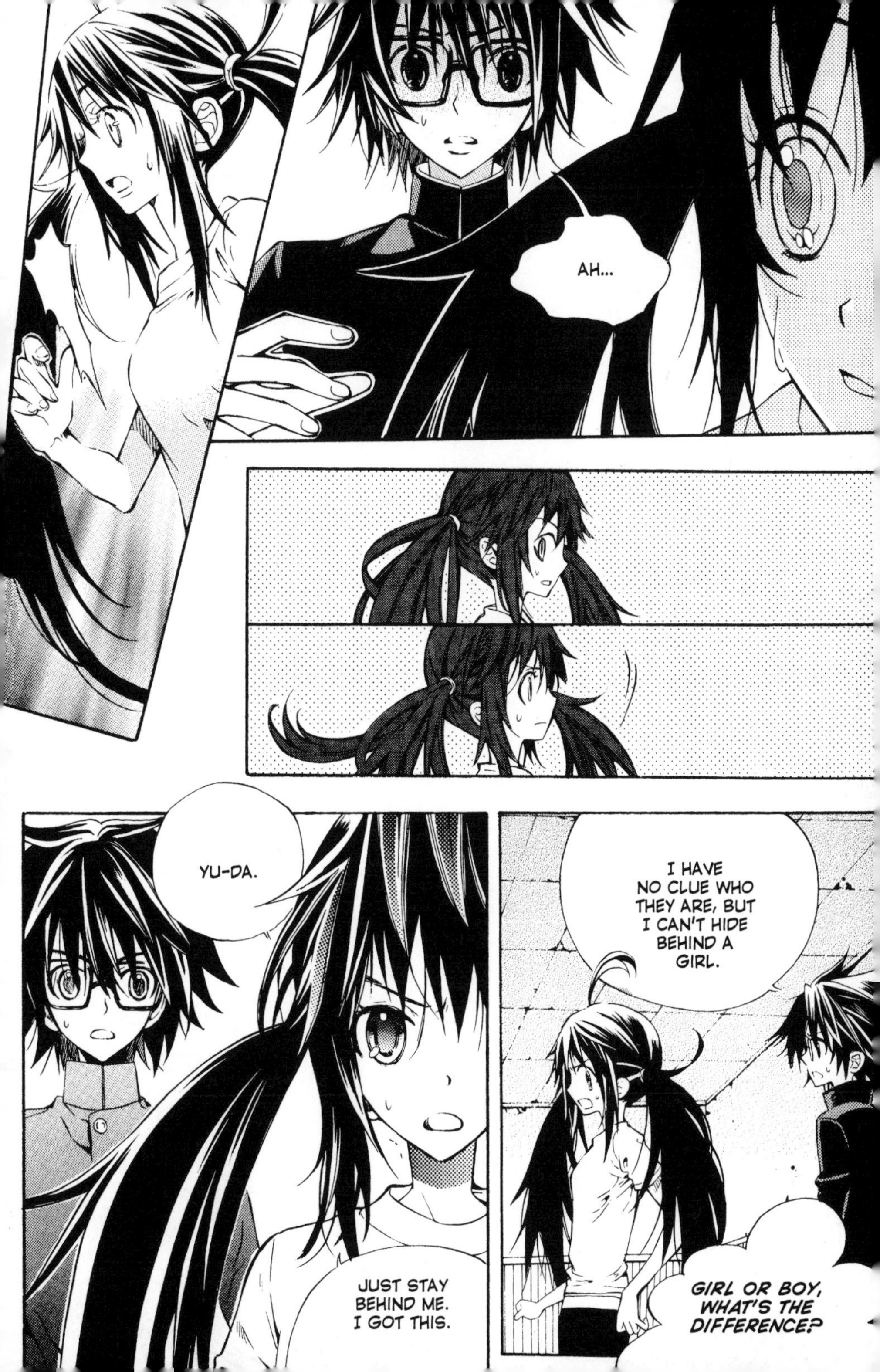
AH...
YU-DA.
JUST STAY BEHIND ME. I GOT THIS.
I HAVE NO CLUE WHO THEY ARE, BUT I CAN'T HIDE BEHIND A GIRL.
GIRL OR BOY, WHAT'S THE DIFFERENCE?

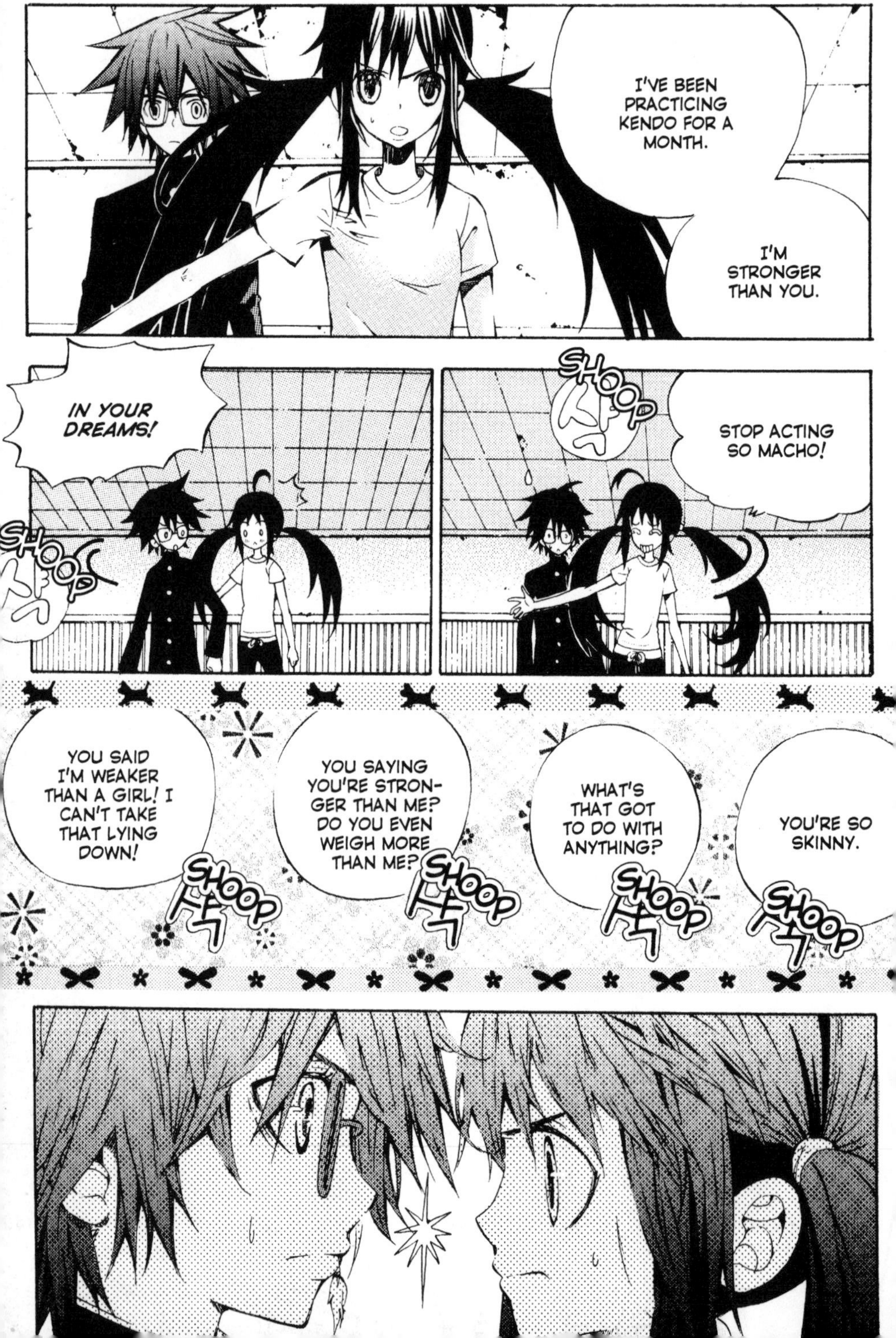
I'VE BEEN PRACTICING KENDO FOR A MONTH.
I'M STRONGER THAN YOU.
IN YOUR DREAMS!
SHOOP
SHOOP
STOP ACTING SO MACHO!
YOU SAID I'M WEAKER THAN A GIRL! I CAN'T TAKE THAT LYING DOWN!
SHOOP
YOU SAYING YOU'RE STRONGER THAN ME? DO YOU EVEN WEIGH MORE THAN ME?
SHOOP
WHAT'S THAT GOT TO DO WITH ANYTHING?
SHOOP
YOU'RE SO SKINNY.
SHOOP

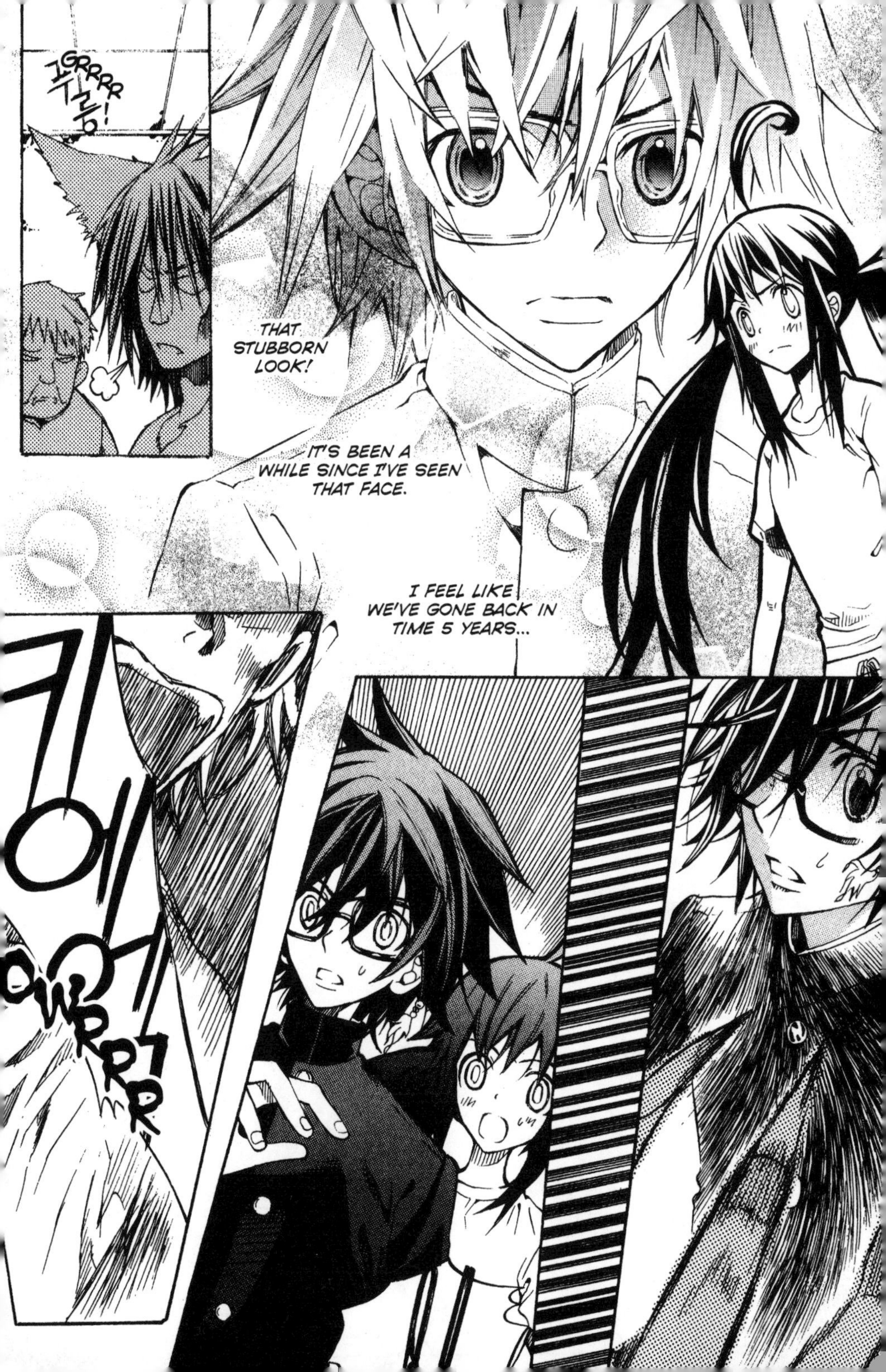
GRRRR
그르릉!
THAT STUBBORN LOOK!
IT'S BEEN A WHILE SINCE I'VE SEEN THAT FACE.
I FEEL LIKE WE'VE GONE BACK IN TIME 5 YEARS...
OWRRRR

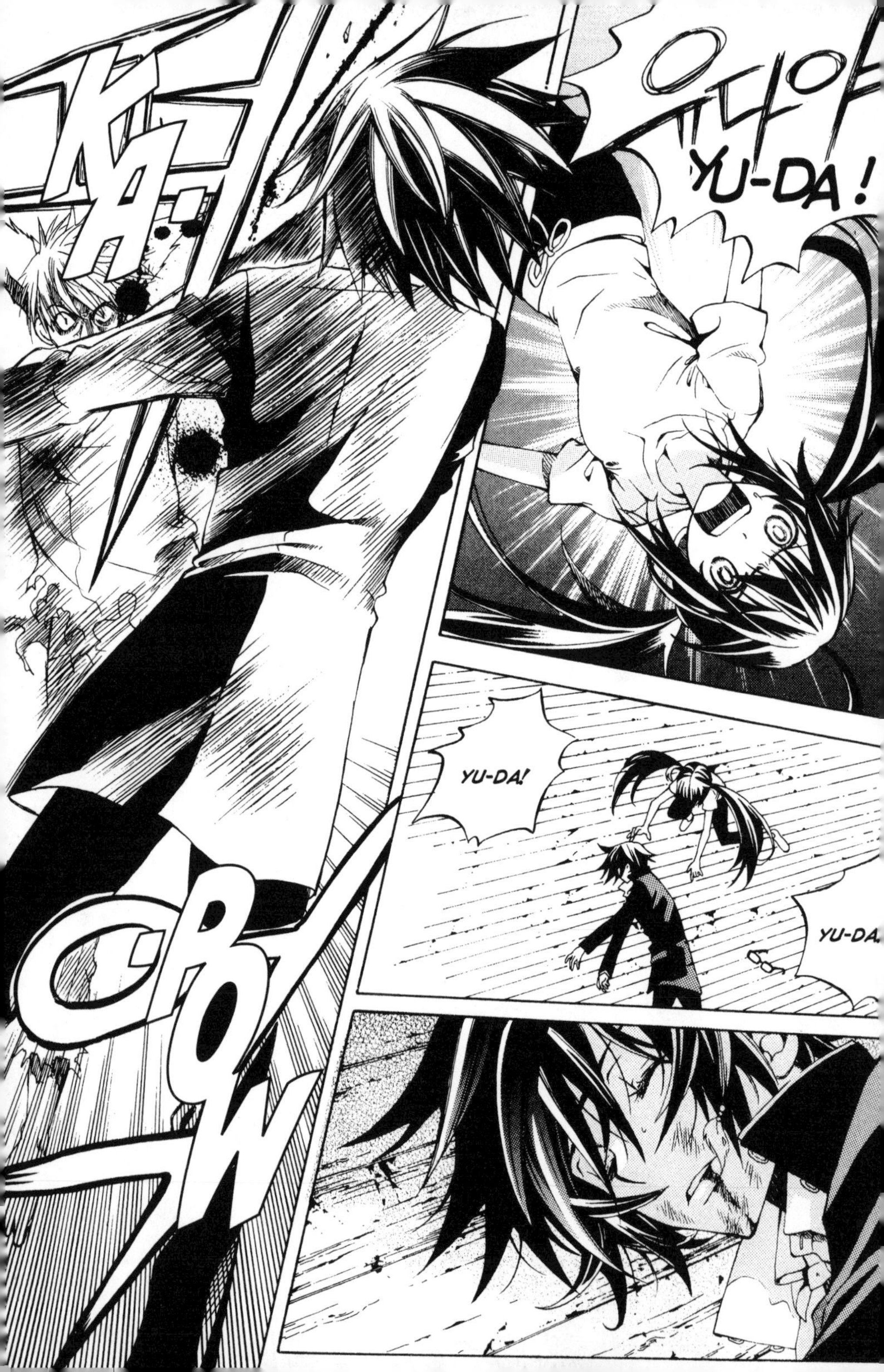
YU-DA !
YU-DA!
YU-DA...

YU-DA...

WHAT AM I GONNA DO?

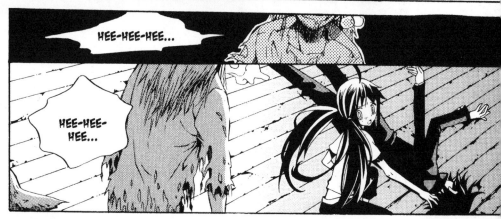

HEE-HEE-HEE...

HEE-HEE-HEE...

PLEASE GOD...

...LET ME...

...PROTECT HIM.

GIVE ME THE COURAGE...

...NO FEAR...

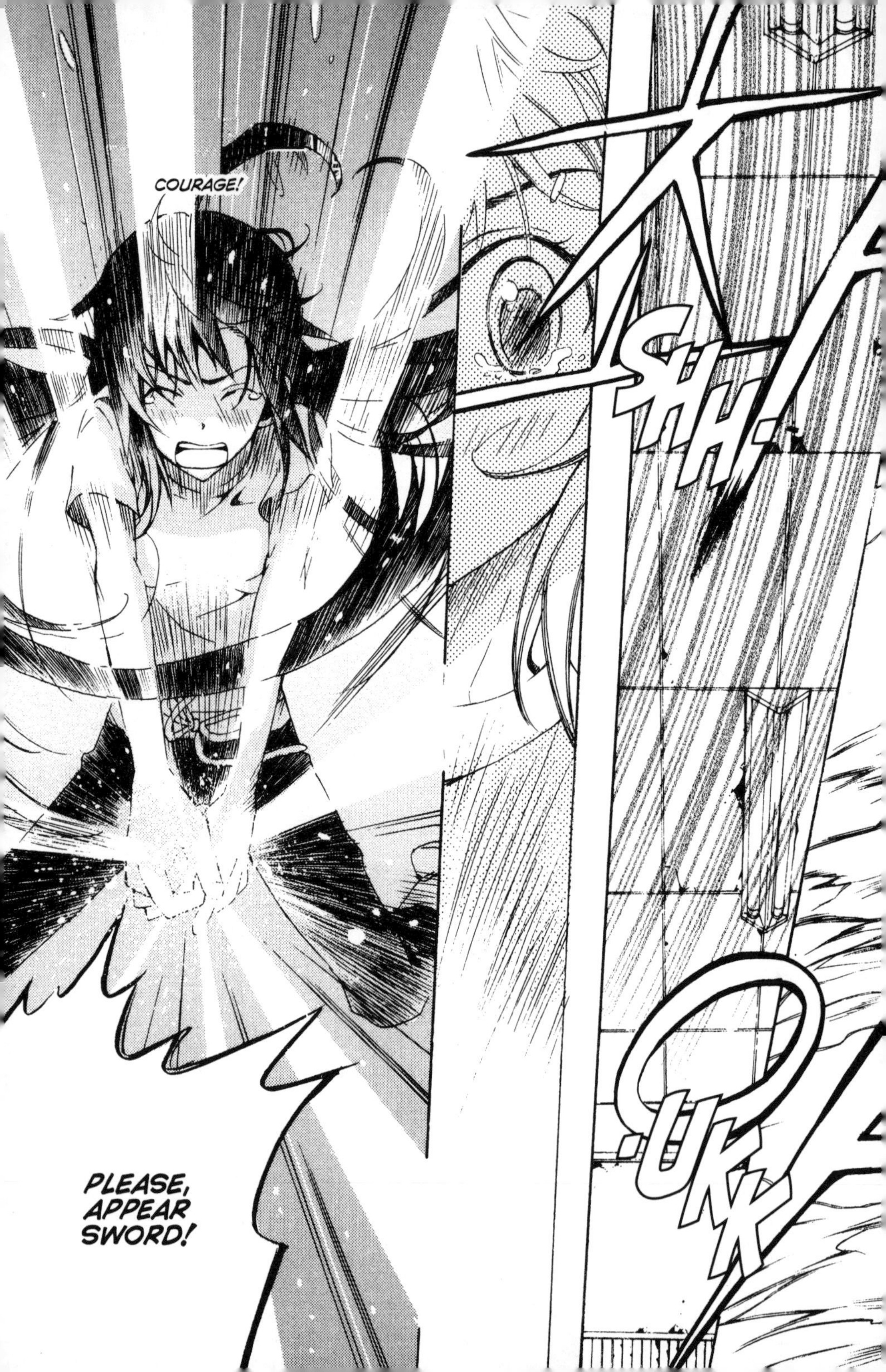
COURAGE!
SHH...
PLEASE, APPEAR SWORD!
...UKK

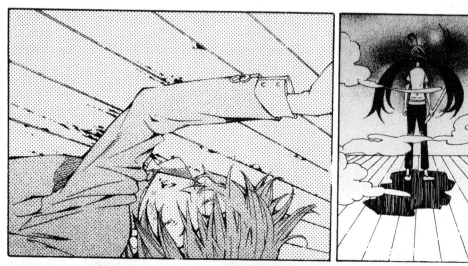

...IS MY HO-SE SWORD.
THE COURAGE THAT OVERCOMES FEAR...
I WON'T ALLOW YOU TO HURT HIM...
...EVER AGAIN.

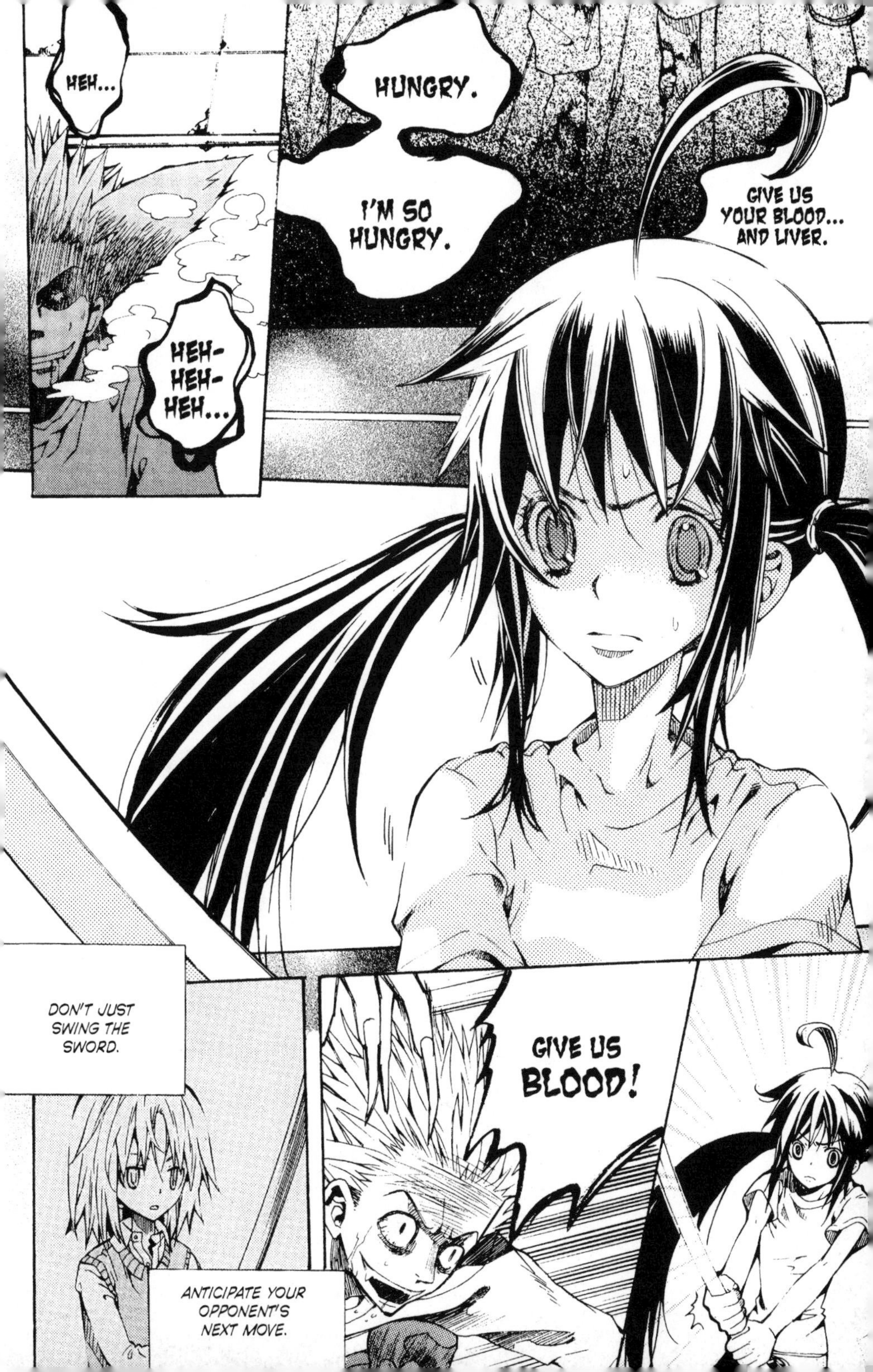
HEH...
HEH-HEH-HEH...
HUNGRY.
I'M SO HUNGRY.
GIVE US YOUR BLOOD... AND LIVER.
DON'T JUST SWING THE SWORD.
ANTICIPATE YOUR OPPONENT'S NEXT MOVE.
GIVE US BLOOD!

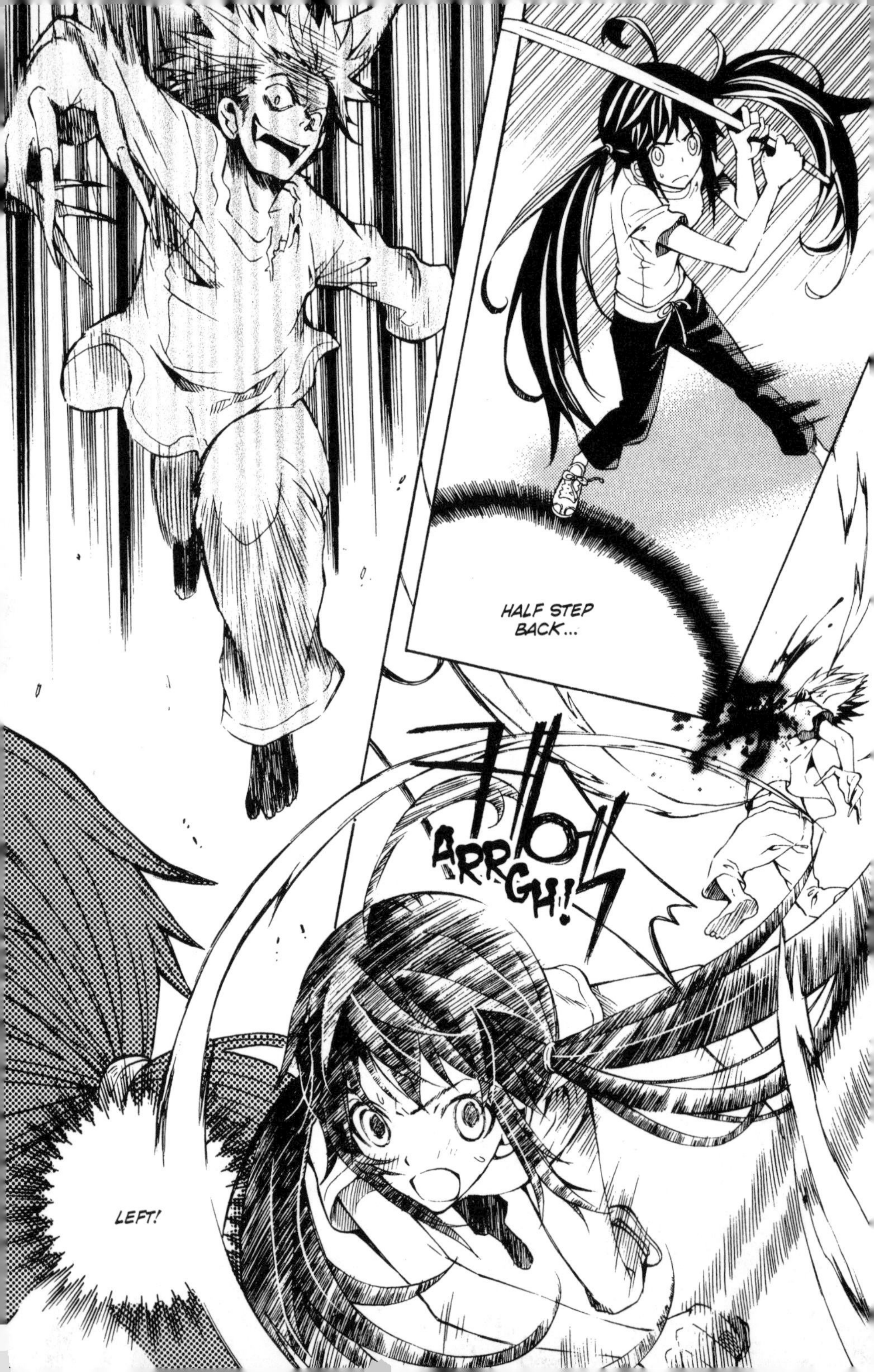
HALF STEP BACK...
ARRGH!
LEFT!

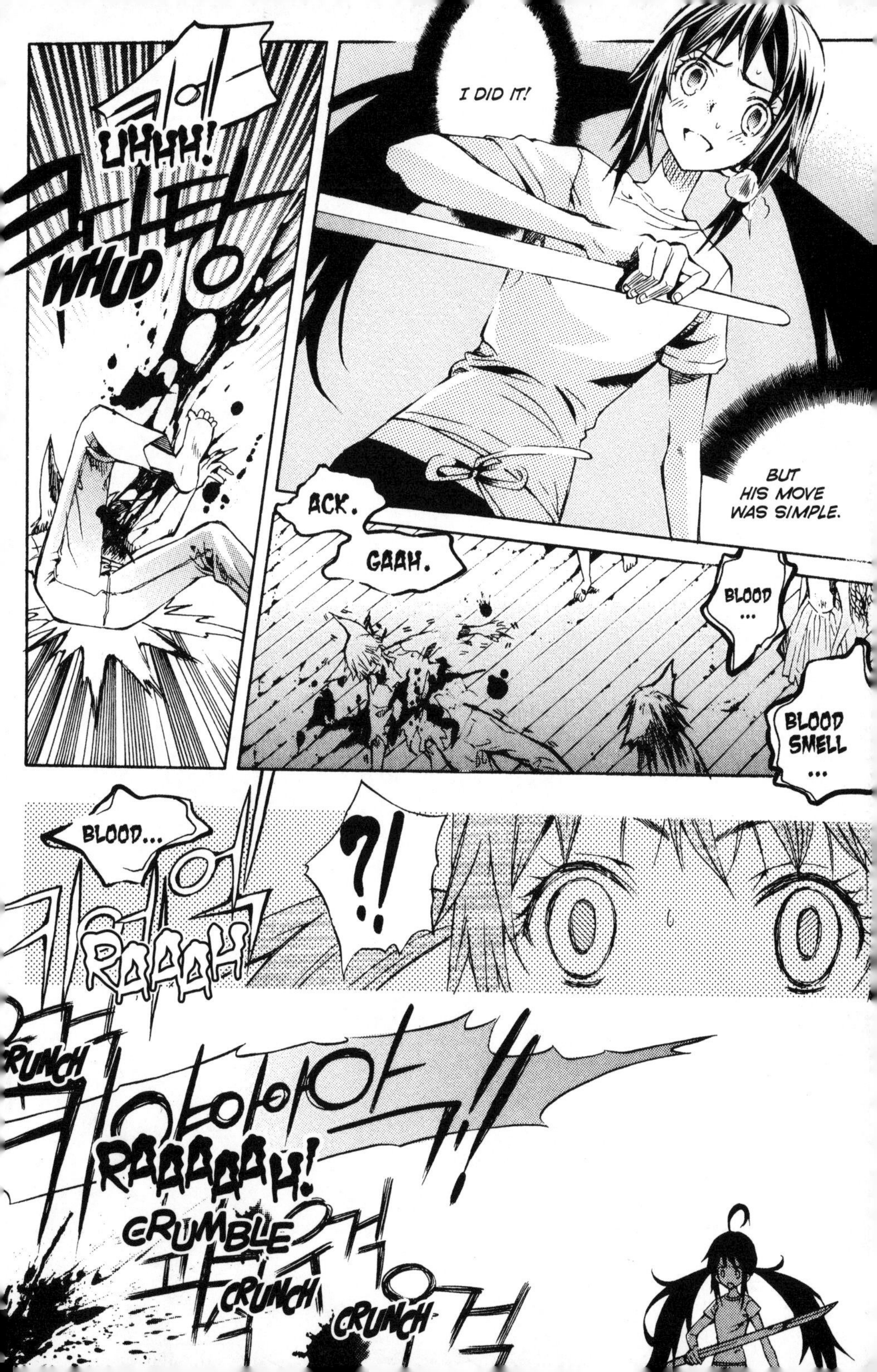
UHHH!
WHUD
I DID IT!
ACK.
GAAH.
BUT HIS MOVE WAS SIMPLE.
BLOOD ...
BLOOD SMELL ...
BLOOD...
RAAAH
?!
CRUNCH
RAAAAAH!
CRUMBLE
CRUNCH
CRUNCH

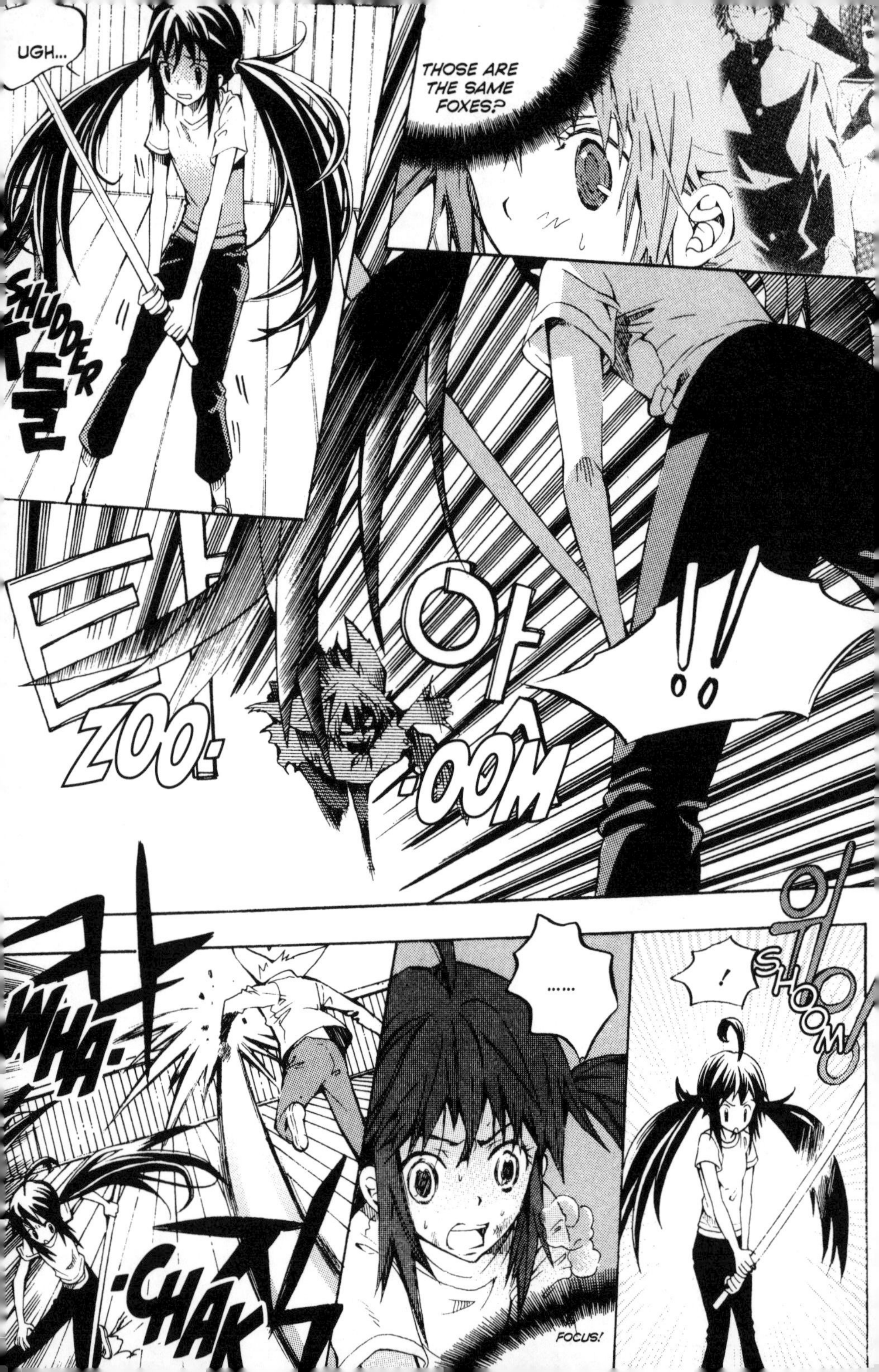

UGH...
SHUDDER
THOSE ARE THE SAME FOXES?
ZOO-
-OOM
!!
WHA-
-CHAK
......
!
SHOOM
FOCUS!

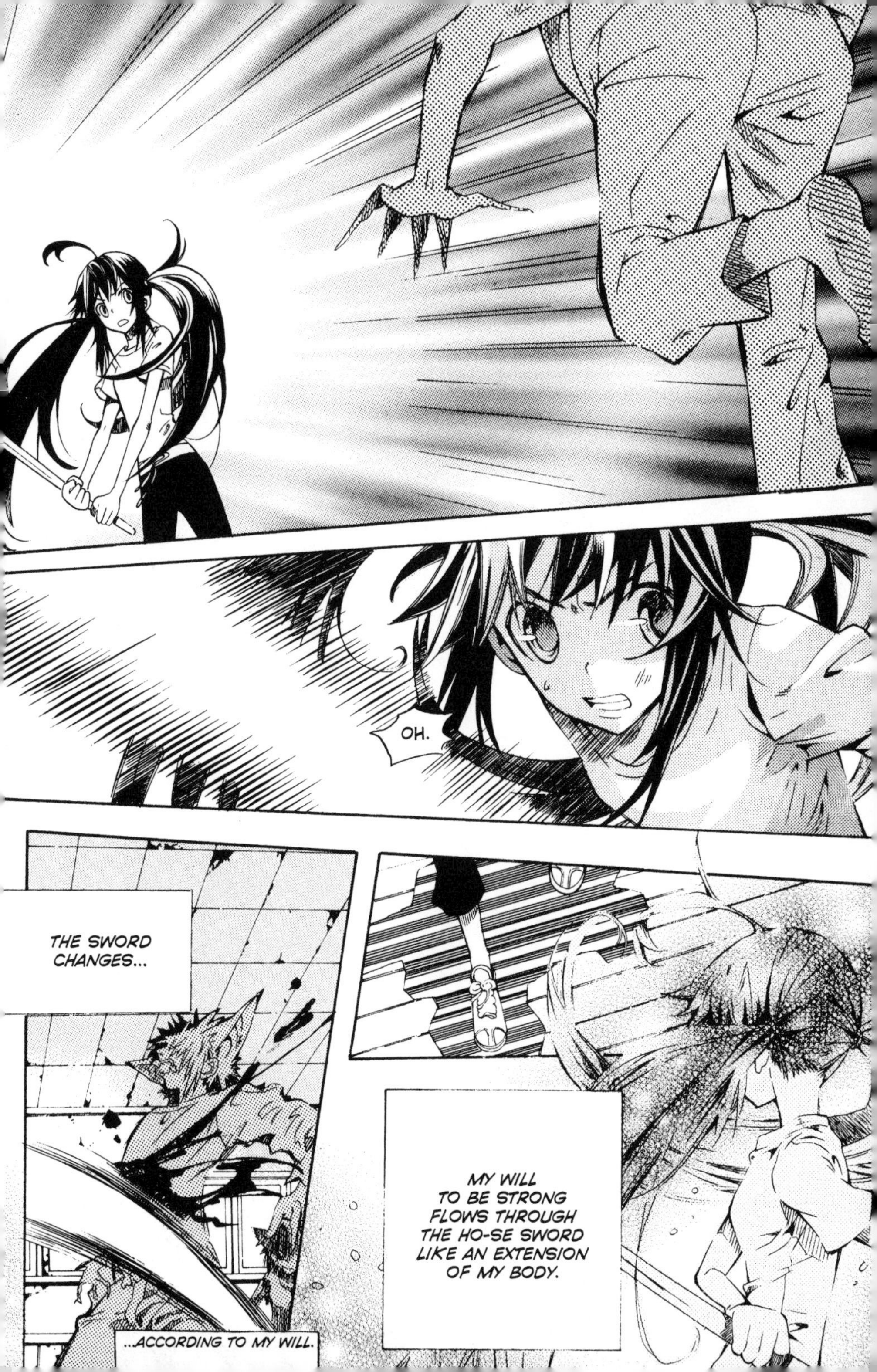
OH.
THE SWORD CHANGES...
...ACCORDING TO MY WILL.
MY WILL TO BE STRONG FLOWS THROUGH THE HO-SE SWORD LIKE AN EXTENSION OF MY BODY.

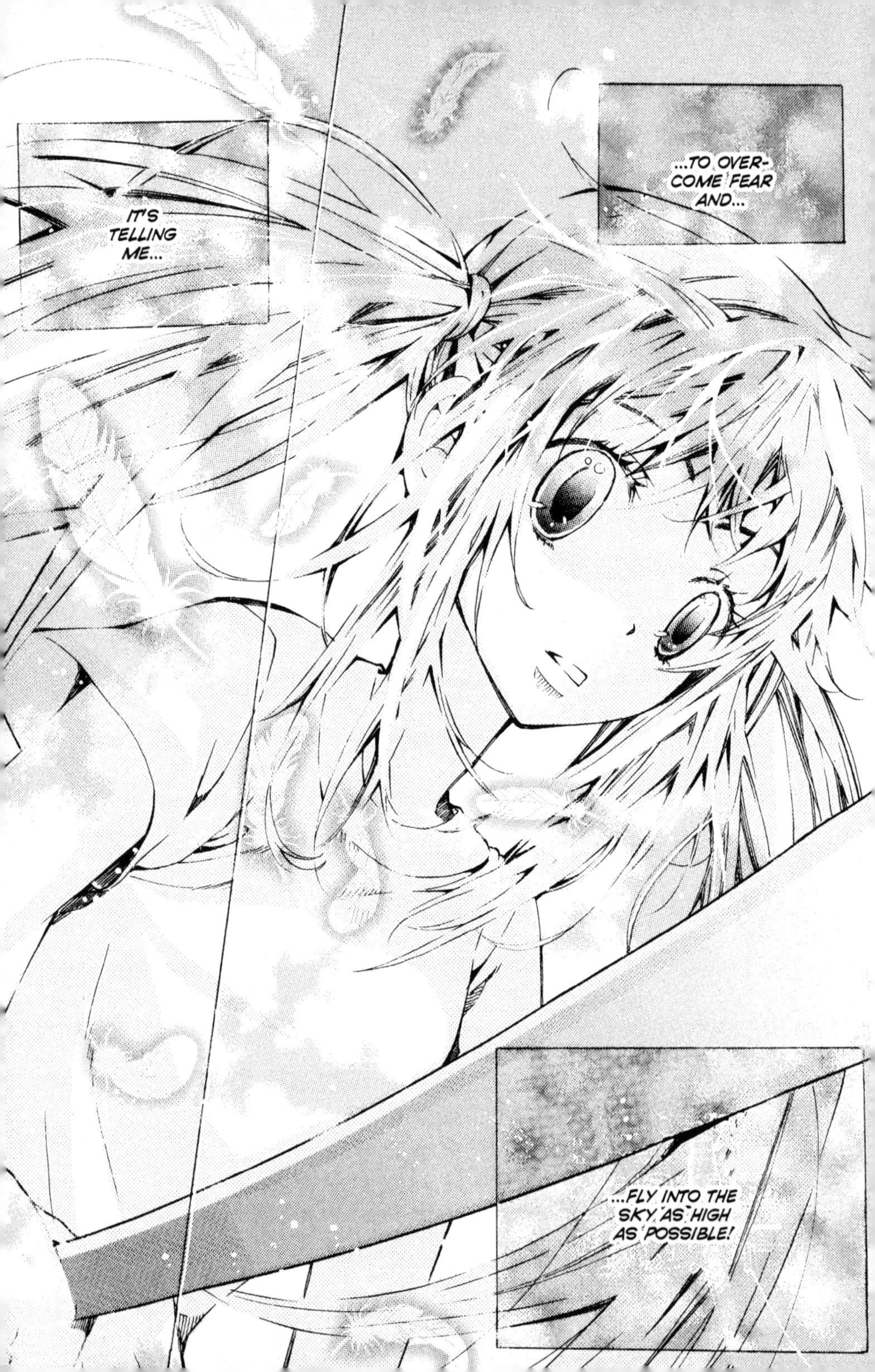
...TO OVER-COME FEAR AND...
IT'S TELLING ME...
...FLY INTO THE SKY AS HIGH AS POSSIBLE!

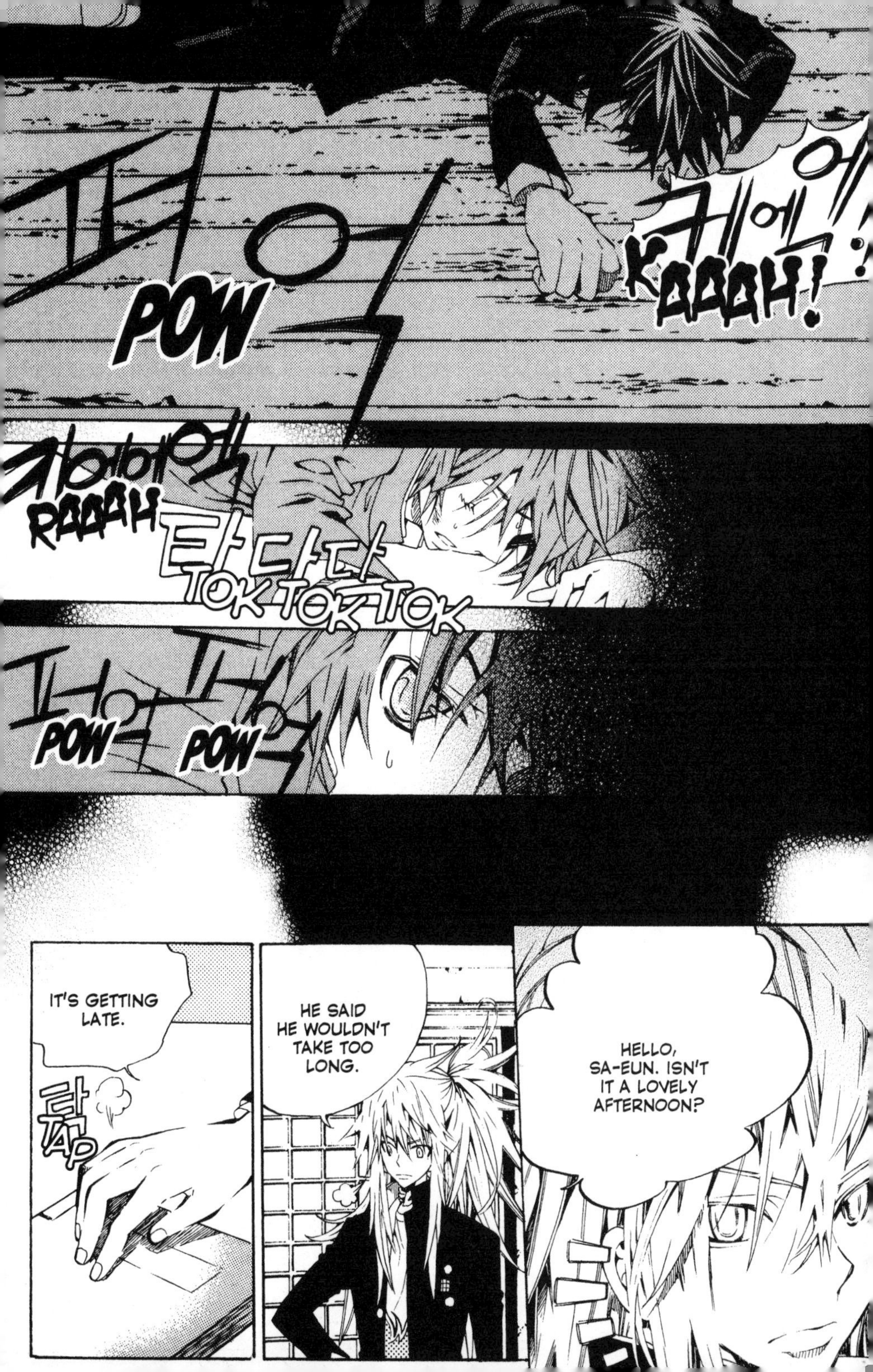
POW
KAAAH!
RAAAH
TOK TOK TOK
POW
POW
IT'S GETTING LATE.
탁
TAP
HE SAID HE WOULDN'T TAKE TOO LONG.
HELLO, SA-EUN. ISN'T IT A LOVELY AFTERNOON?

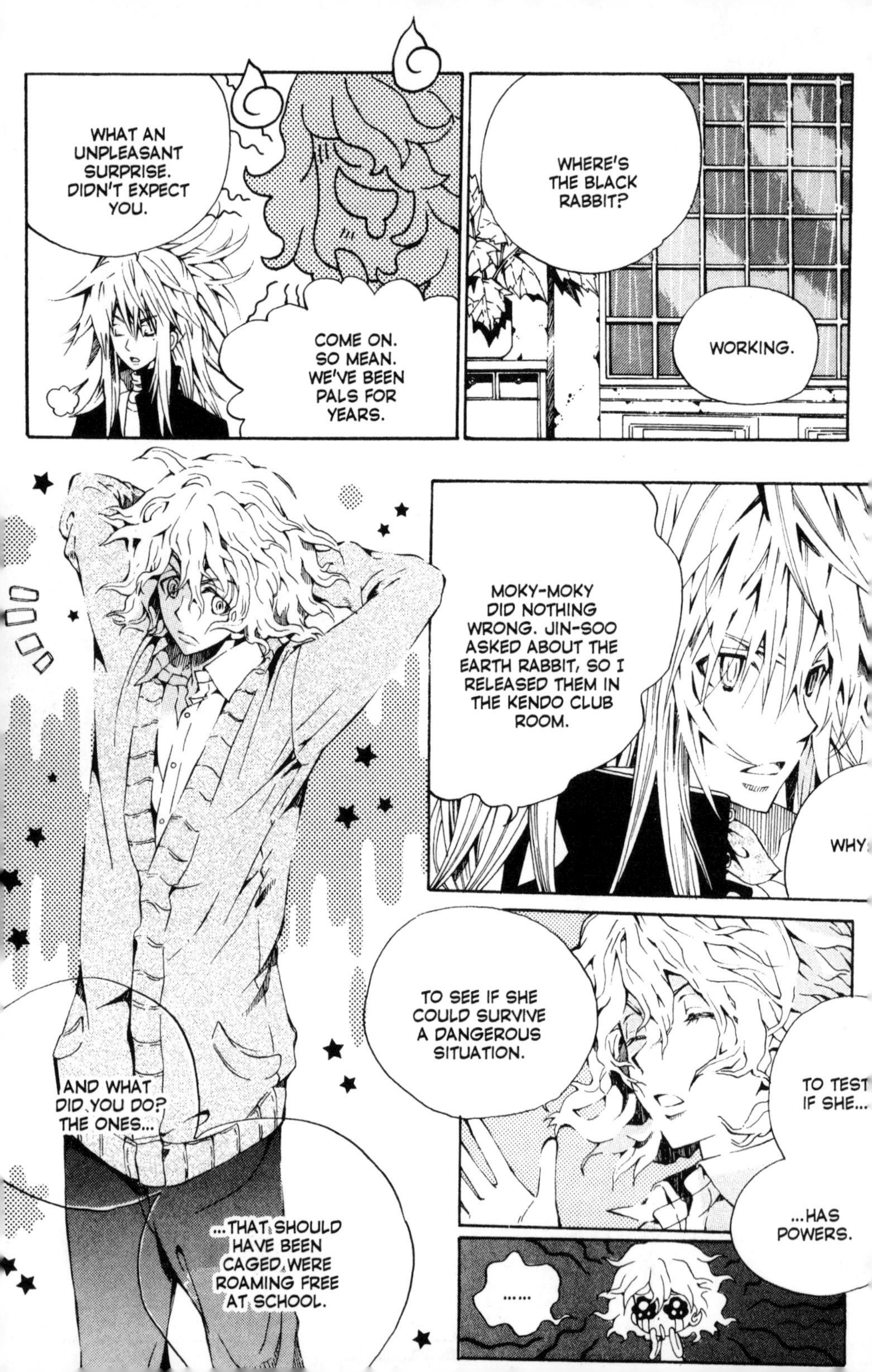
WHAT AN UNPLEASANT SURPRISE. DIDN'T EXPECT YOU.
COME ON. SO MEAN. WE'VE BEEN PALS FOR YEARS.
WHERE'S THE BLACK RABBIT?
WORKING.
AND WHAT DID YOU DO? THE ONES...
...THAT SHOULD HAVE BEEN CAGED WERE ROAMING FREE AT SCHOOL.
MOKY-MOKY DID NOTHING WRONG. JIN-SOO ASKED ABOUT THE EARTH RABBIT, SO I RELEASED THEM IN THE KENDO CLUB ROOM.
WHY
TO SEE IF SHE COULD SURVIVE A DANGEROUS SITUATION.
TO TEST IF SHE...
...HAS POWERS.
......

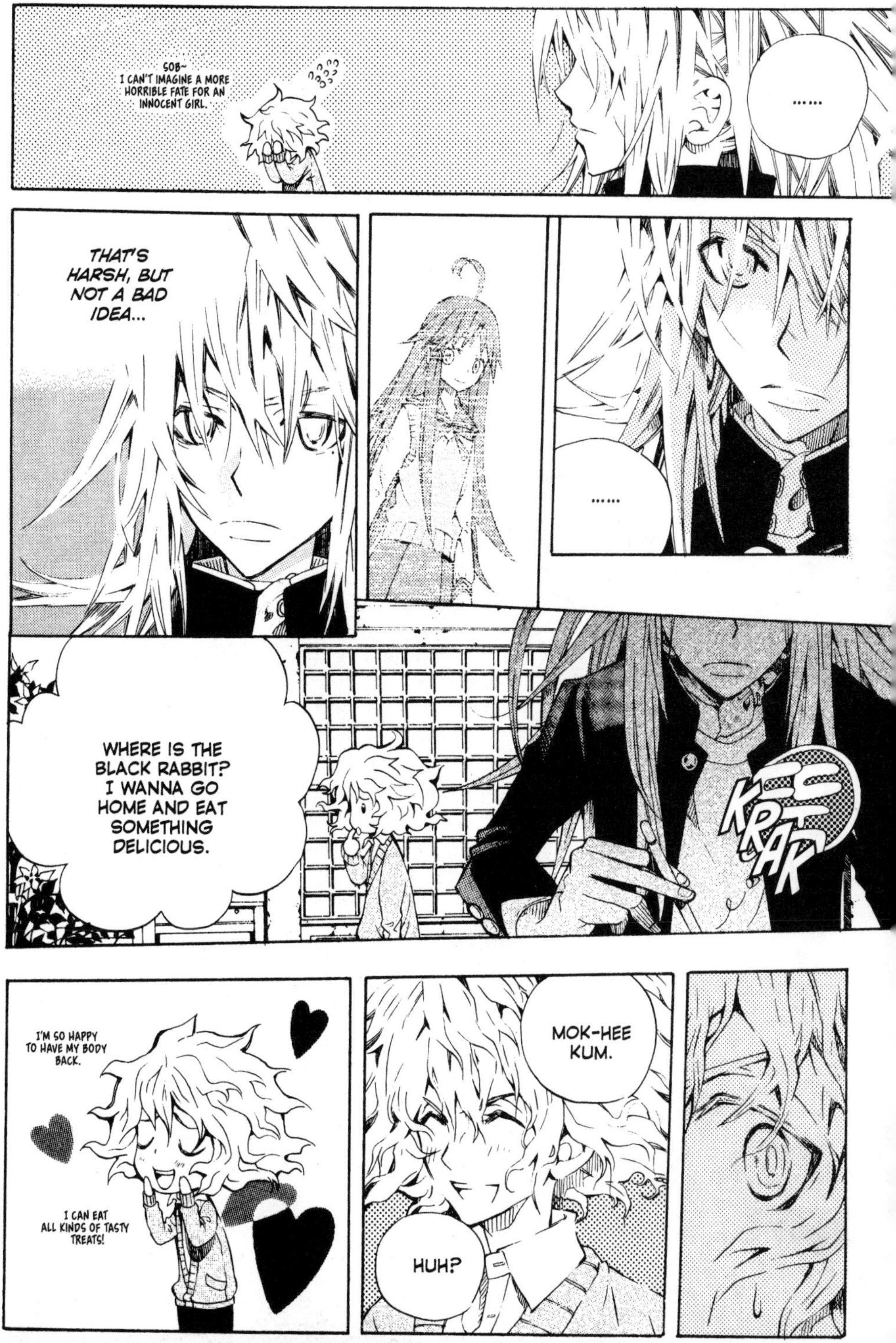
SOB~
I CAN'T IMAGINE A MORE HORRIBLE FATE FOR AN INNOCENT GIRL.
......
THAT'S HARSH, BUT NOT A BAD IDEA...
......
WHERE IS THE BLACK RABBIT? I WANNA GO HOME AND EAT SOMETHING DELICIOUS.
KRAK
I'M SO HAPPY TO HAVE MY BODY BACK.
I CAN EAT ALL KINDS OF TASTY TREATS!
MOK-HEE KUM.
HUH?

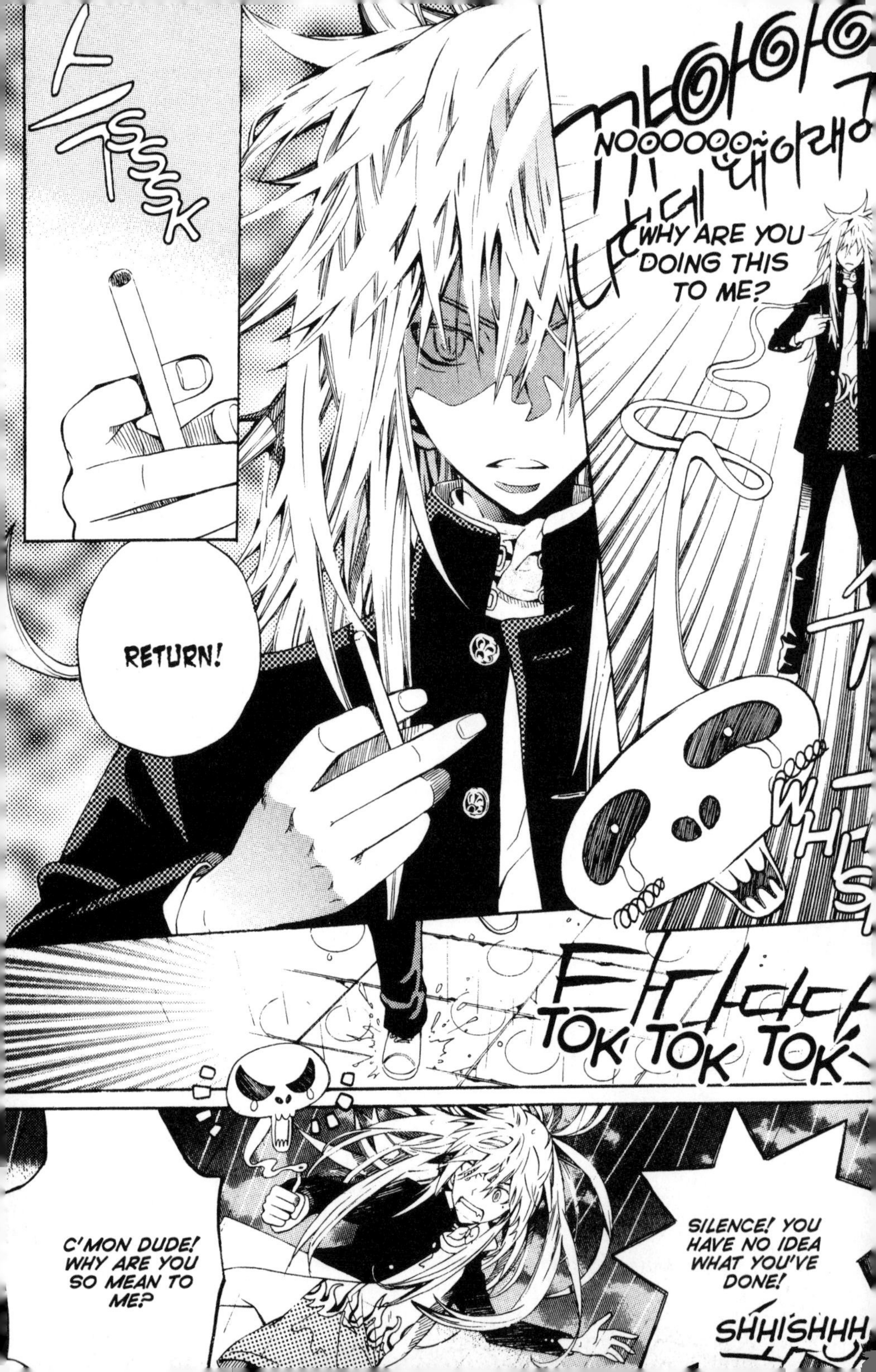
TSSSK
RETURN!
NOOOOOO
WHY ARE YOU DOING THIS TO ME?
WHSH
TOK TOK TOK
C'MON DUDE! WHY ARE YOU SO MEAN TO ME?
SILENCE! YOU HAVE NO IDEA WHAT YOU'VE DONE!
SHHISHHH

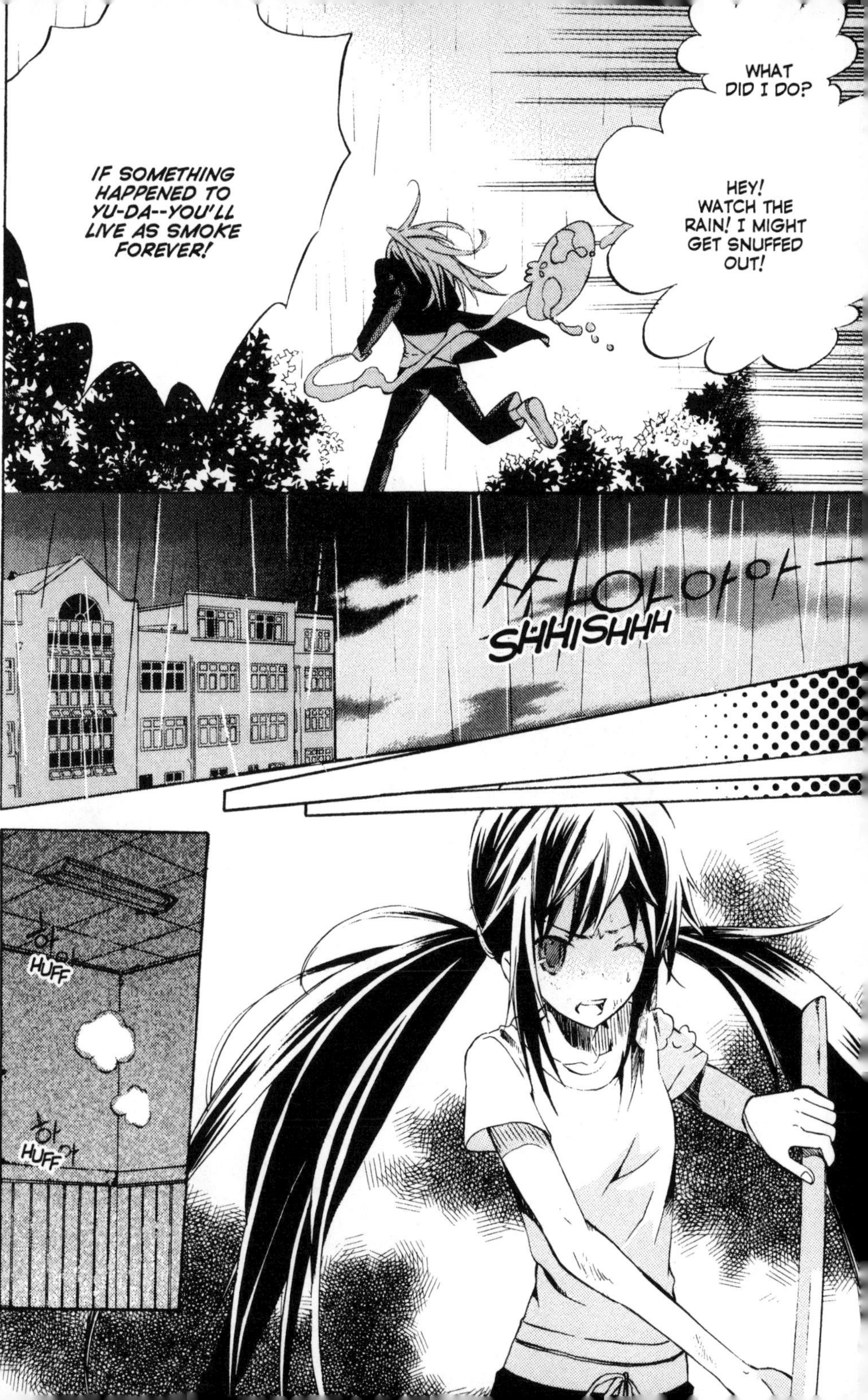
IF SOMETHING HAPPENED TO YU-DA--YOU'LL LIVE AS SMOKE FOREVER!
WHAT DID I DO?
HEY! WATCH THE RAIN! I MIGHT GET SNUFFED OUT!
SHHISHHH
HUFF
HUFF

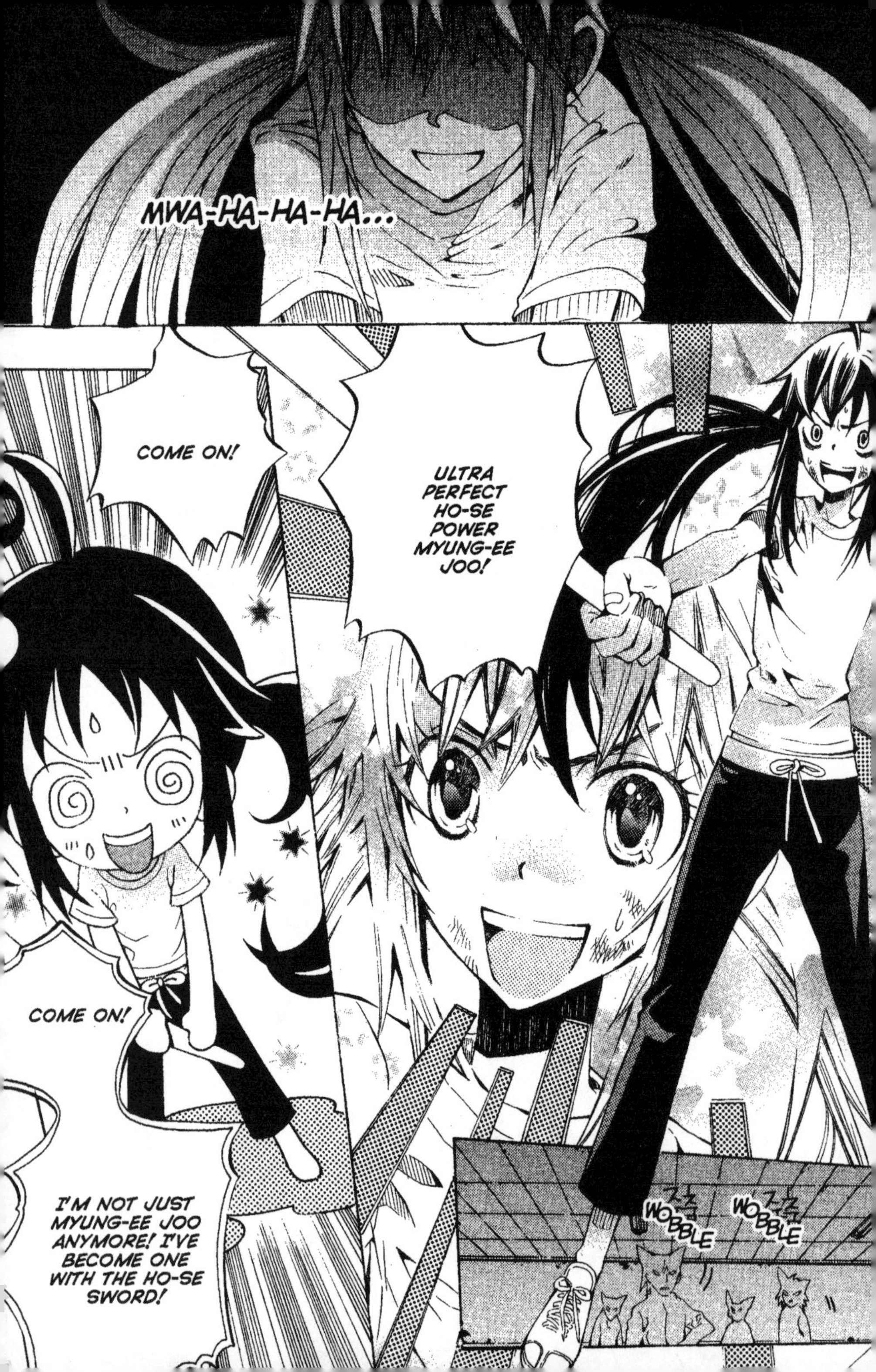
MWA-HA-HA-HA...
COME ON!
COME ON!
I'M NOT JUST MYUNG-EE JOO ANYMORE! I'VE BECOME ONE WITH THE HO-SE SWORD!
ULTRA PERFECT HO-SE POWER MYUNG-EE JOO!
WOBBLE
WOBBLE

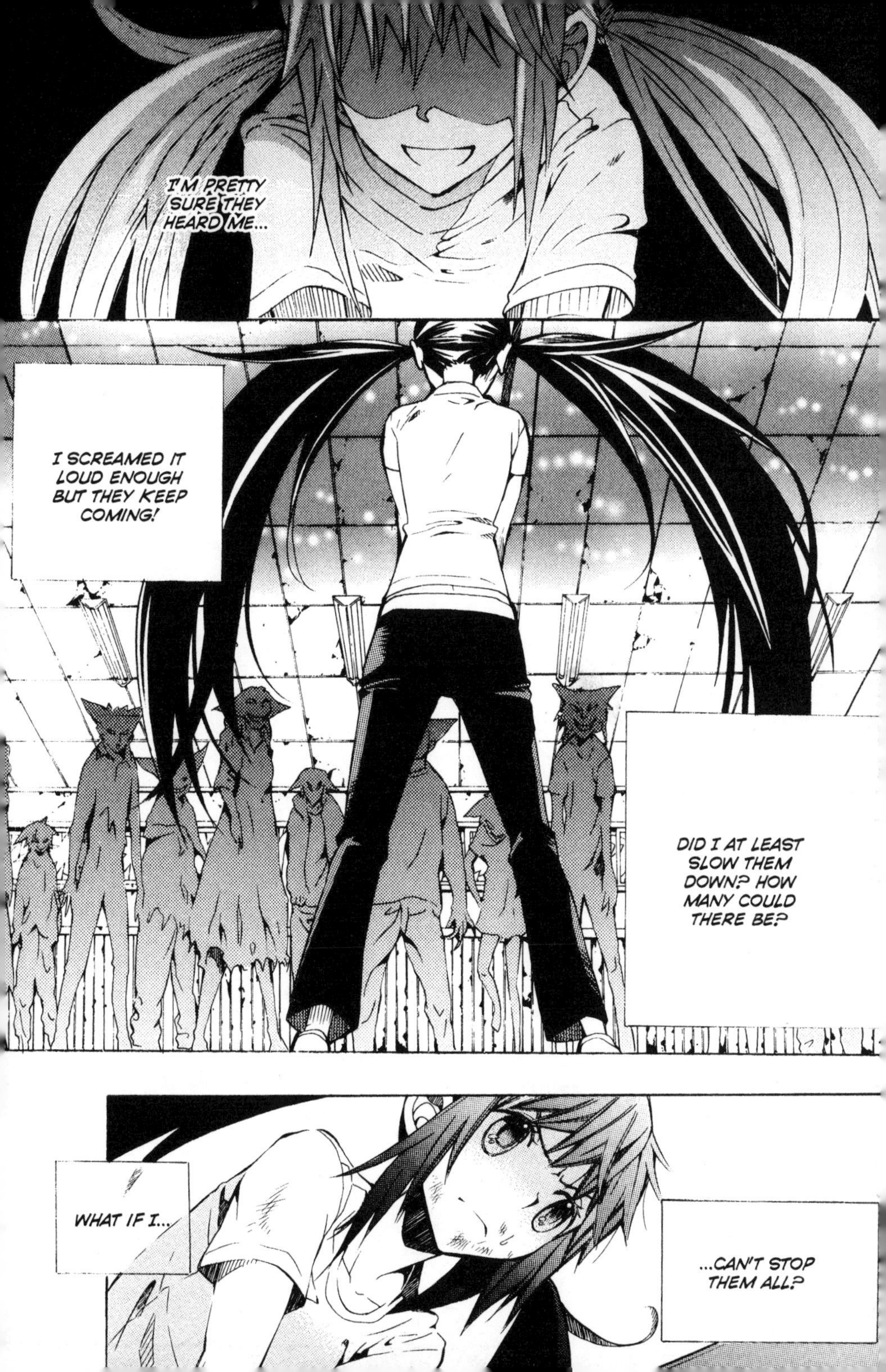
I'M PRETTY SURE THEY HEARD ME...
I SCREAMED IT LOUD ENOUGH BUT THEY KEEP COMING!
DID I AT LEAST SLOW THEM DOWN? HOW MANY COULD THERE BE?
WHAT IF I...
...CAN'T STOP THEM ALL?

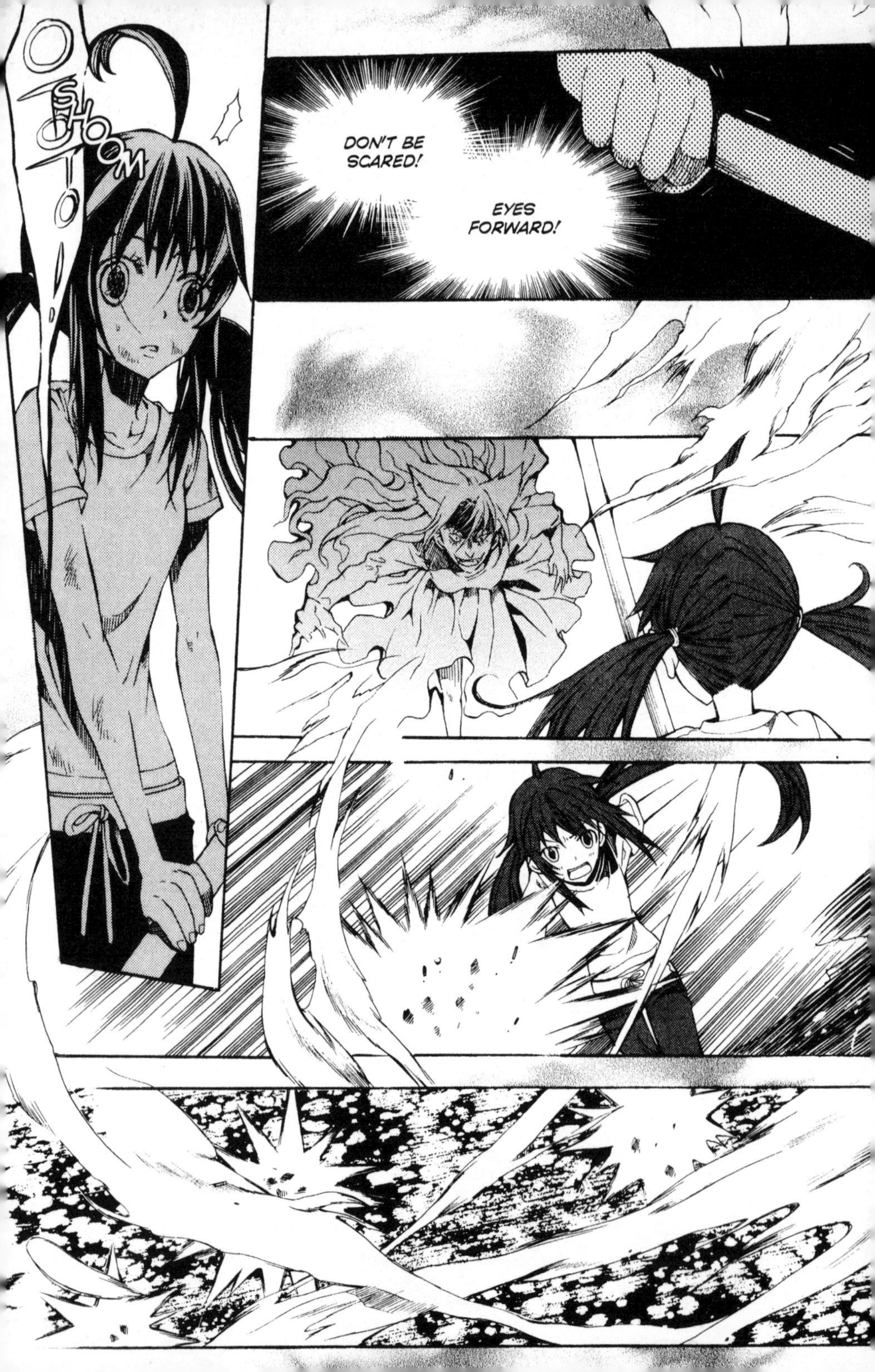

SHOOM
OTTO!
DON'T BE SCARED!
EYES FORWARD!

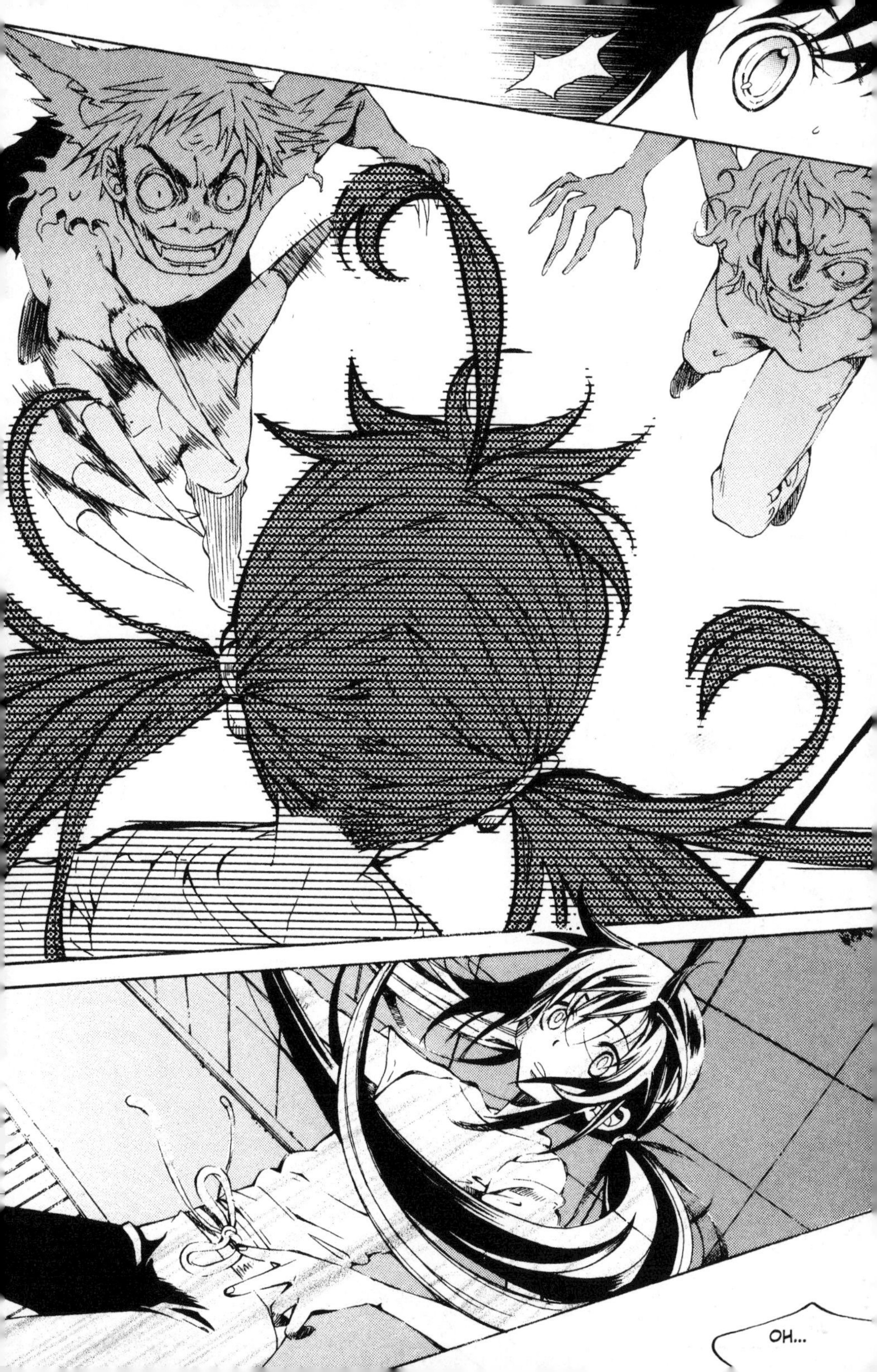
OH...

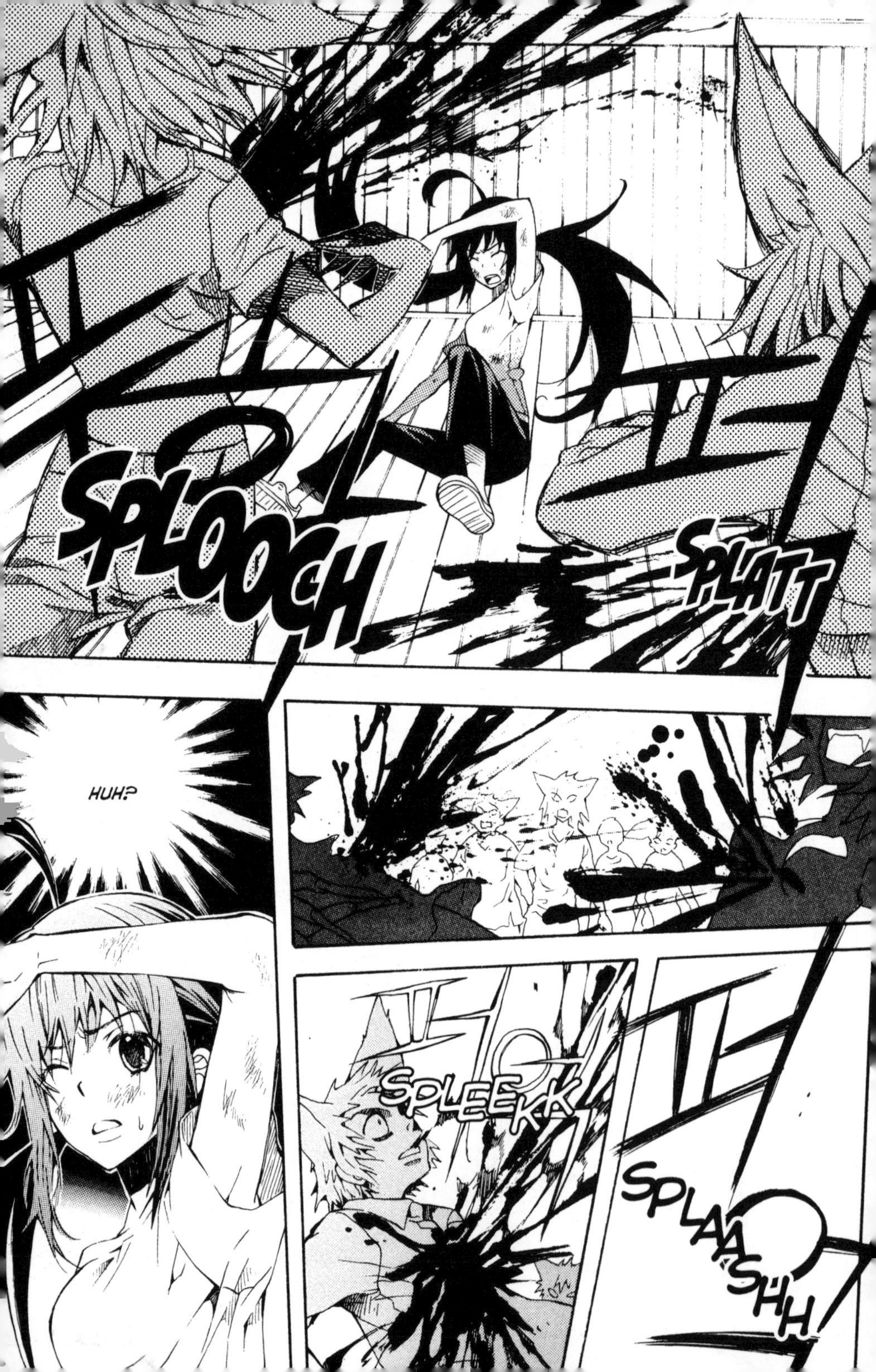
SPLOOCH
SPLATT
HUH?
SPLEEKK
SPLAASHH!

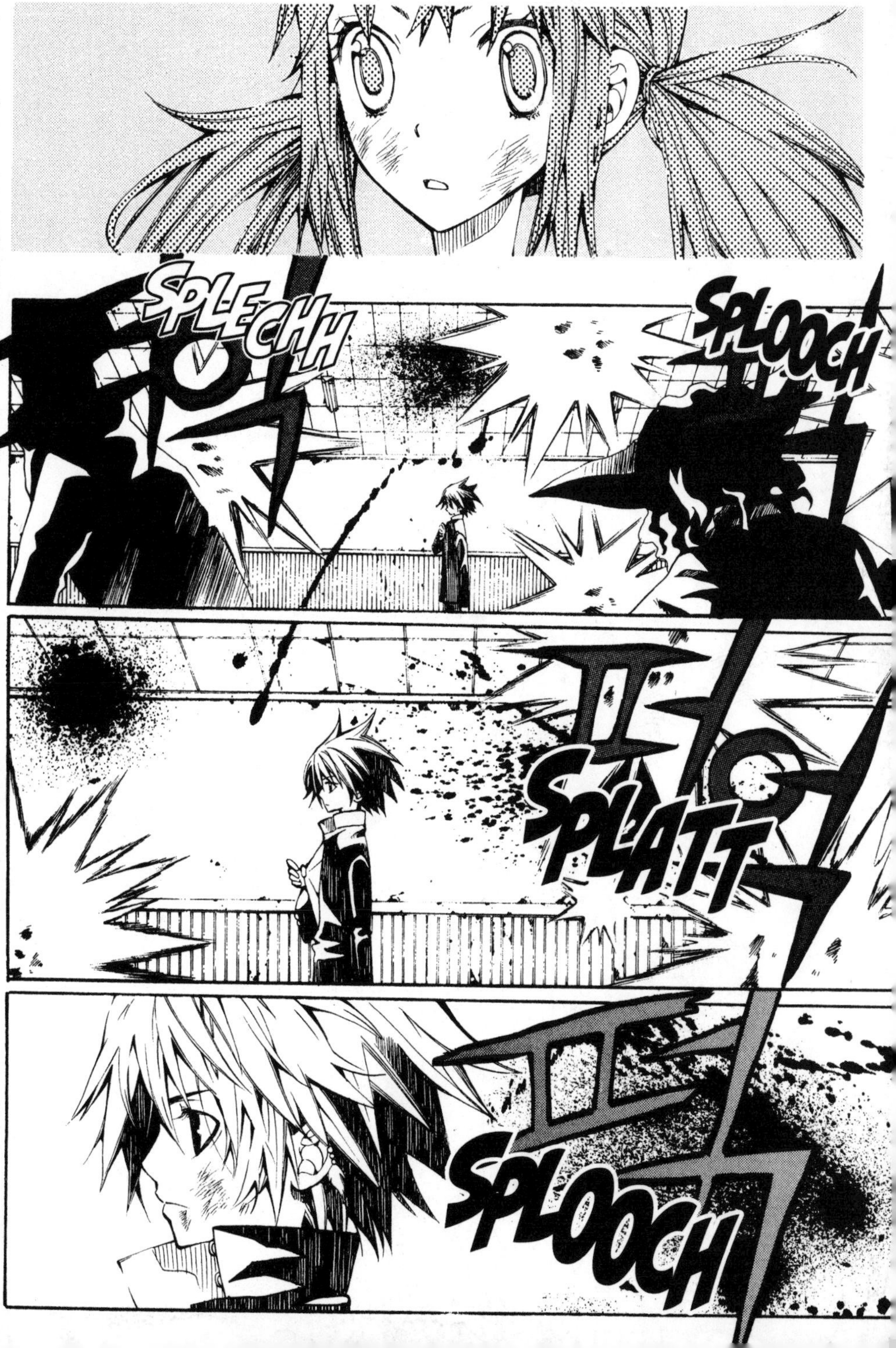
SPLECHH
SPLOOCH
SPLATT
SPLOOCH

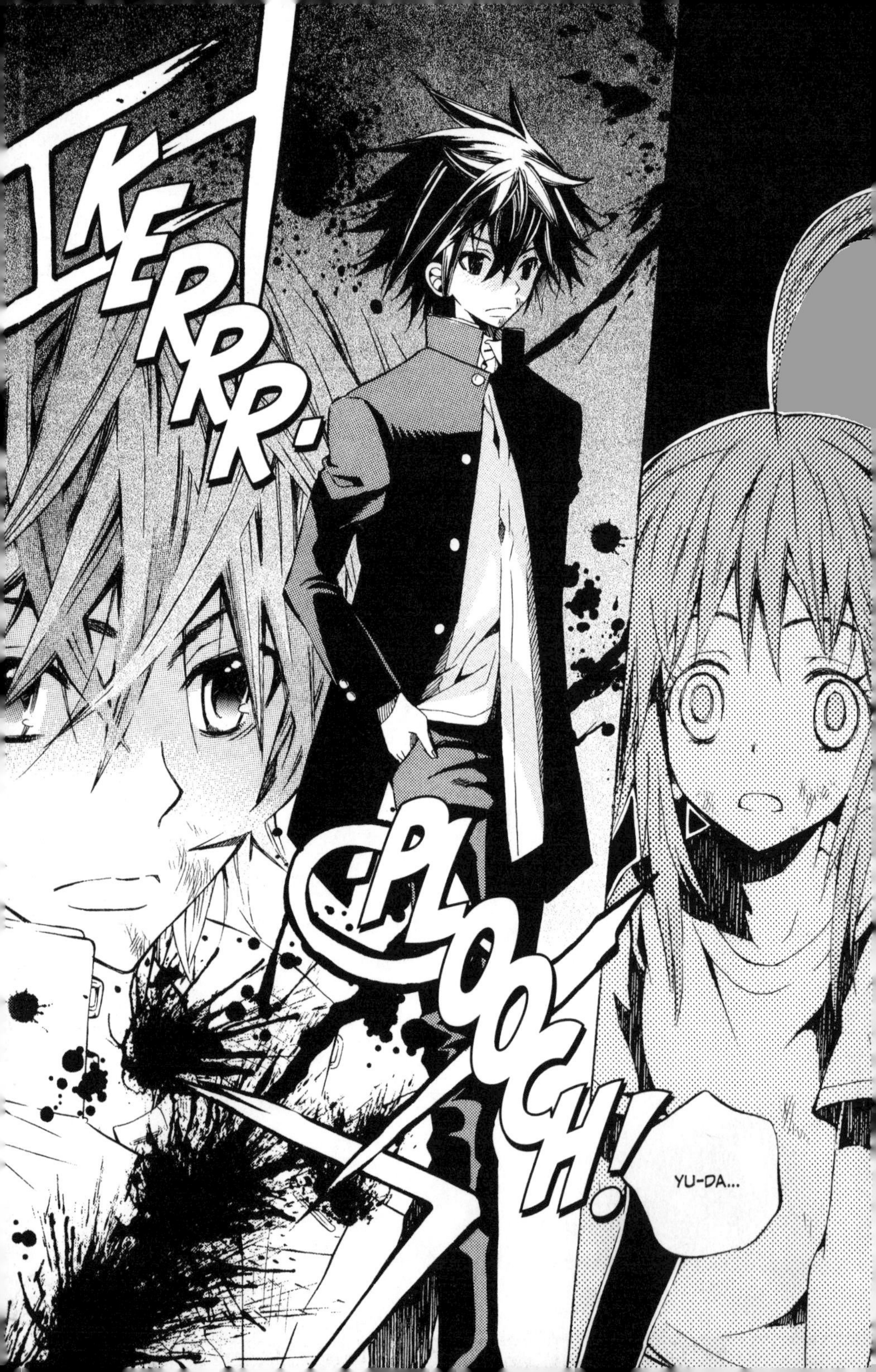
KERRR.
PLOOCH!
YU-DA...

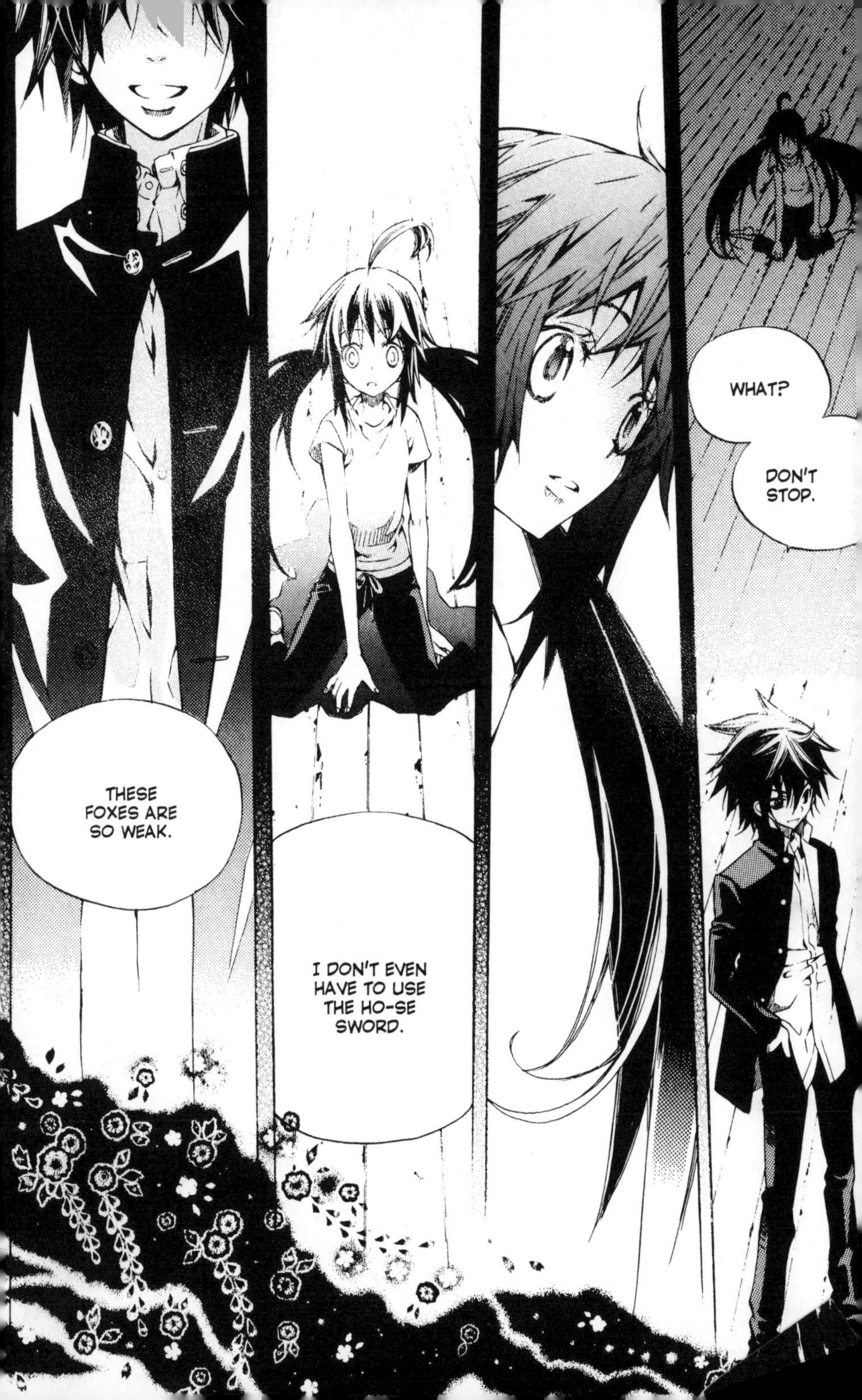
THESE FOXES ARE SO WEAK.
I DON'T EVEN HAVE TO USE THE HO-SE SWORD.
WHAT?
DON'T STOP.

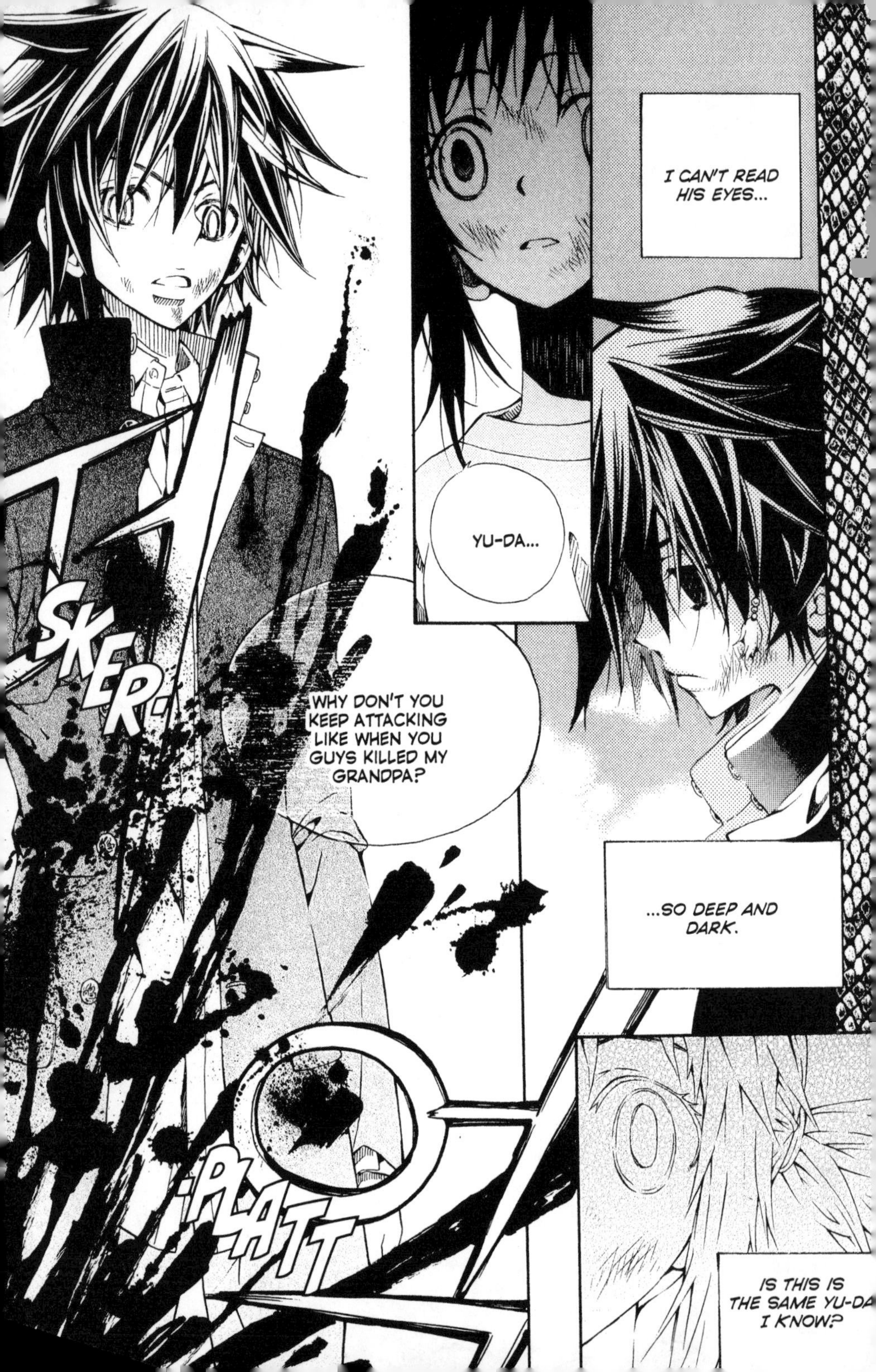
SKER-
WHY DON'T YOU KEEP ATTACKING LIKE WHEN YOU GUYS KILLED MY GRANDPA?
-PLATT
YU-DA...
I CAN'T READ HIS EYES...
...SO DEEP AND DARK.
IS THIS IS THE SAME YU-DA I KNOW?

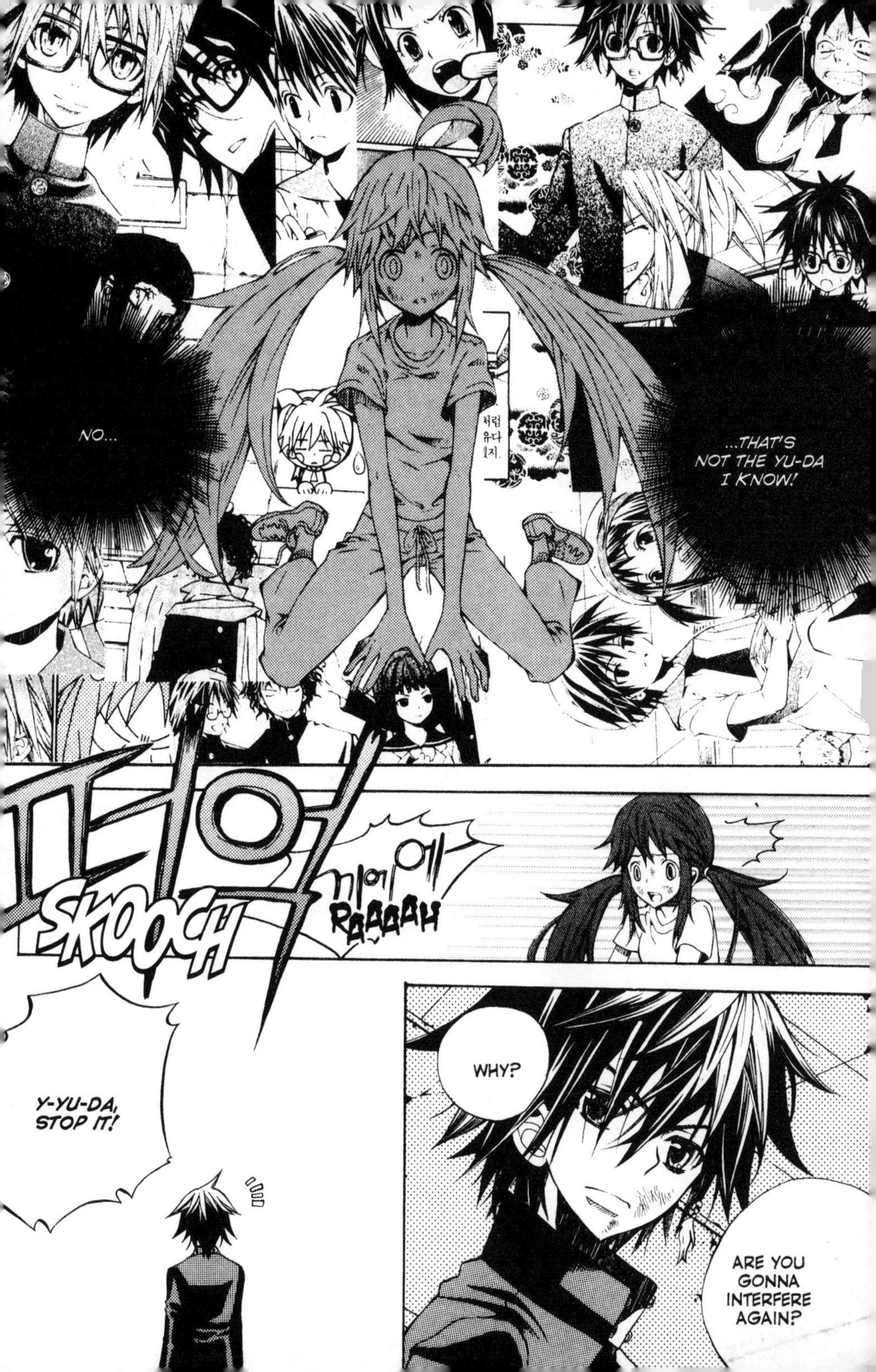

NO...
...THAT'S NOT THE YU-DA I KNOW!
SKOOCH
RAAAH
Y-YU-DA, STOP IT!
WHY?
ARE YOU GONNA INTERFERE AGAIN?

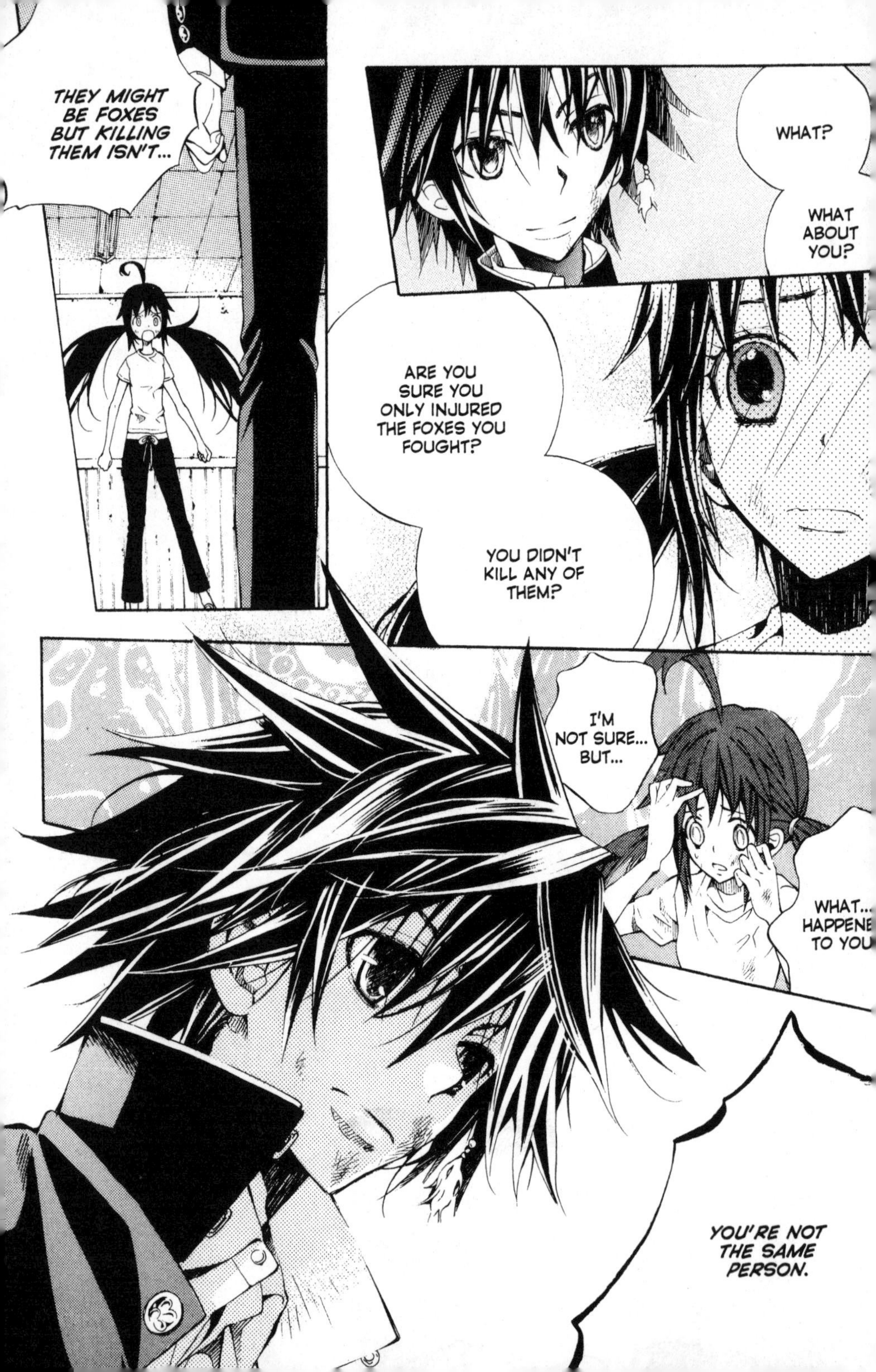
THEY MIGHT BE FOXES BUT KILLING THEM ISN'T...
WHAT?
WHAT ABOUT YOU?
ARE YOU SURE YOU ONLY INJURED THE FOXES YOU FOUGHT?
YOU DIDN'T KILL ANY OF THEM?
I'M NOT SURE... BUT...
WHAT... HAPPENE TO YOU
YOU'RE NOT THE SAME PERSON.

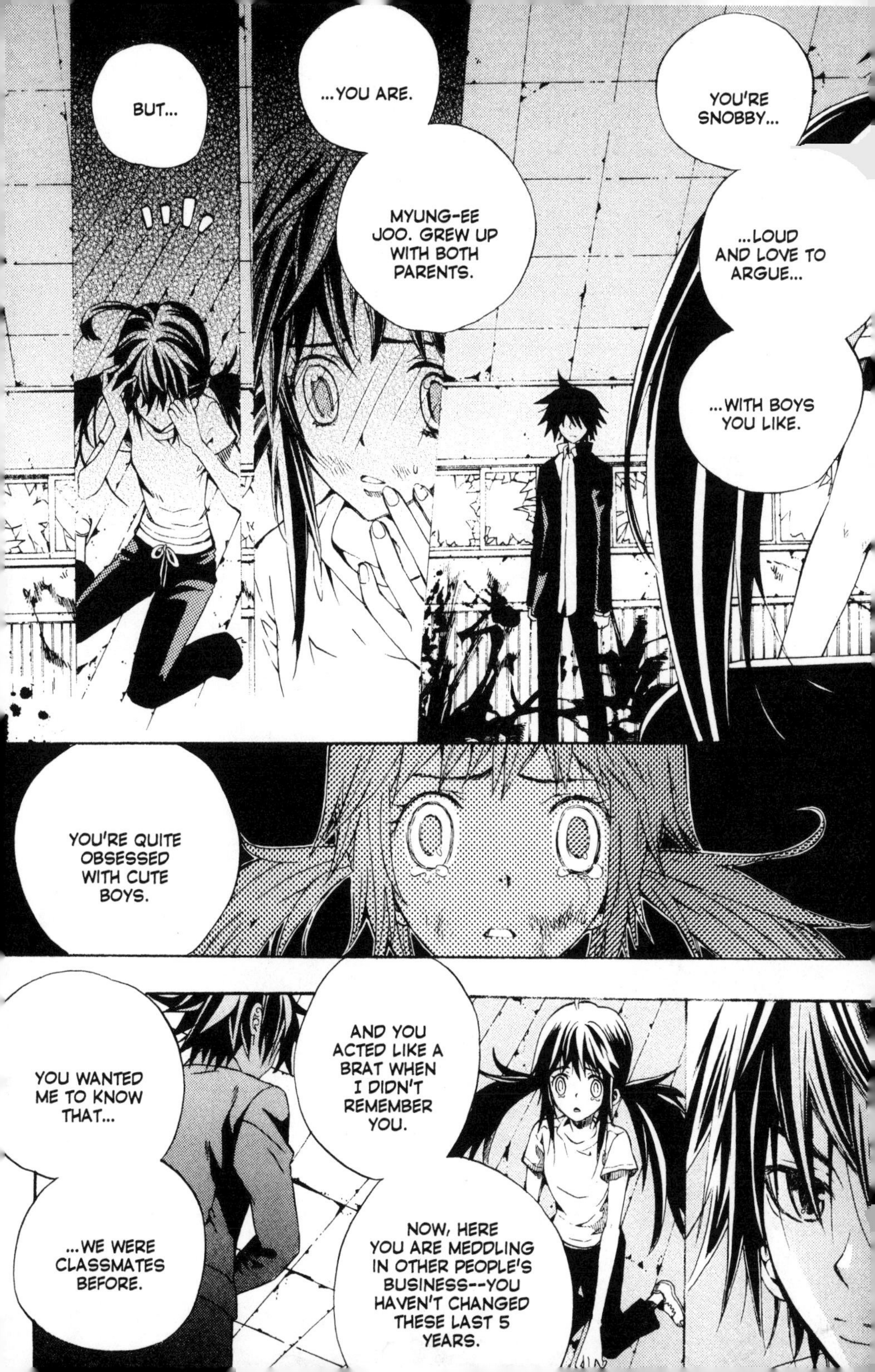
BUT...
...YOU ARE.
MYUNG-EE JOO. GREW UP WITH BOTH PARENTS.
YOU'RE SNOBBY...
...LOUD AND LOVE TO ARGUE...
...WITH BOYS YOU LIKE.
YOU'RE QUITE OBSESSED WITH CUTE BOYS.
YOU WANTED ME TO KNOW THAT...
...WE WERE CLASSMATES BEFORE.
AND YOU ACTED LIKE A BRAT WHEN I DIDN'T REMEMBER YOU.
NOW, HERE YOU ARE MEDDLING IN OTHER PEOPLE'S BUSINESS--YOU HAVEN'T CHANGED THESE LAST 5 YEARS.

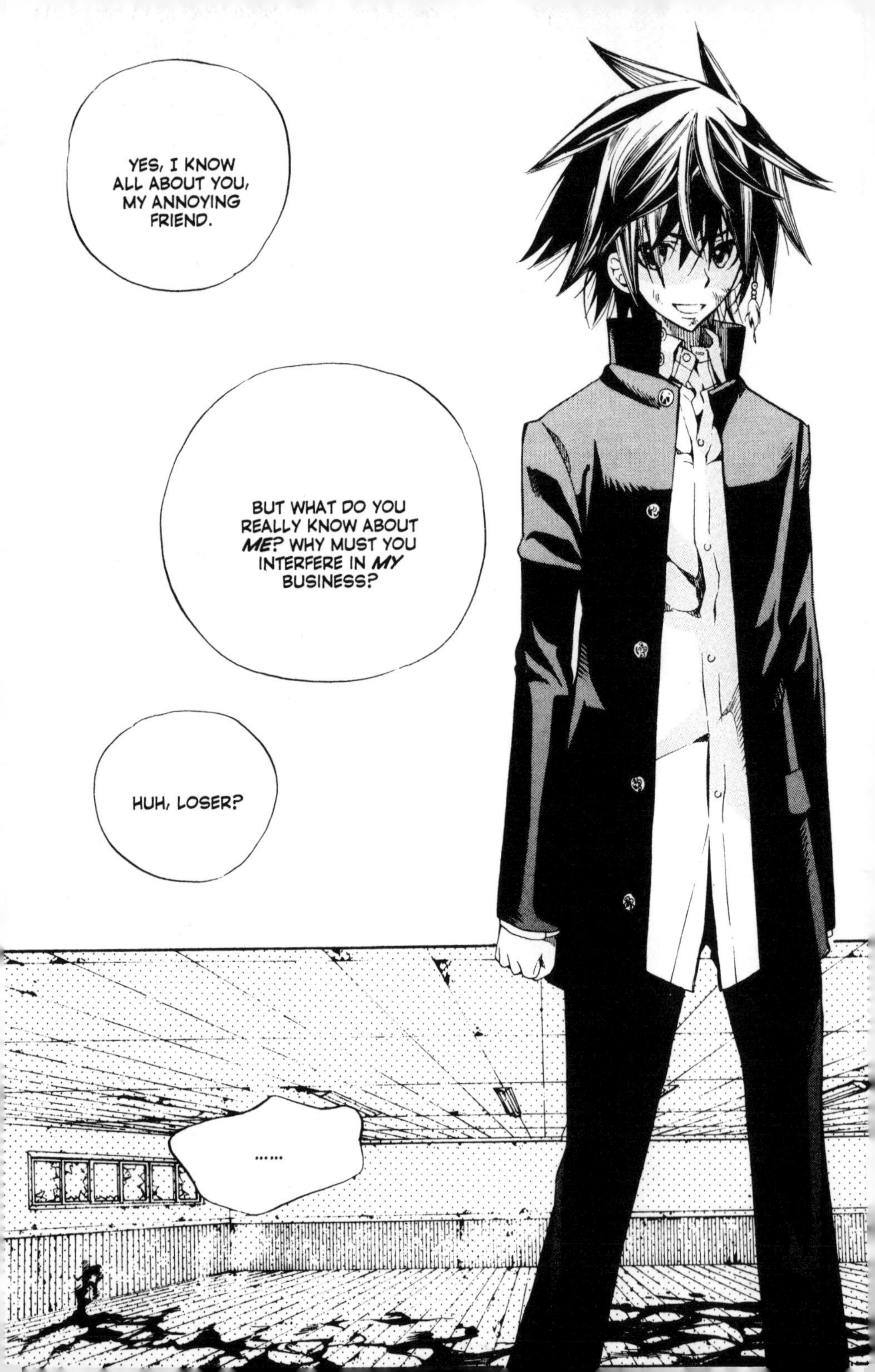

YES, I KNOW ALL ABOUT YOU, MY ANNOYING FRIEND.
BUT WHAT DO YOU REALLY KNOW ABOUT *ME*? WHY MUST YOU INTERFERE IN *MY* BUSINESS?
HUH, LOSER?
......

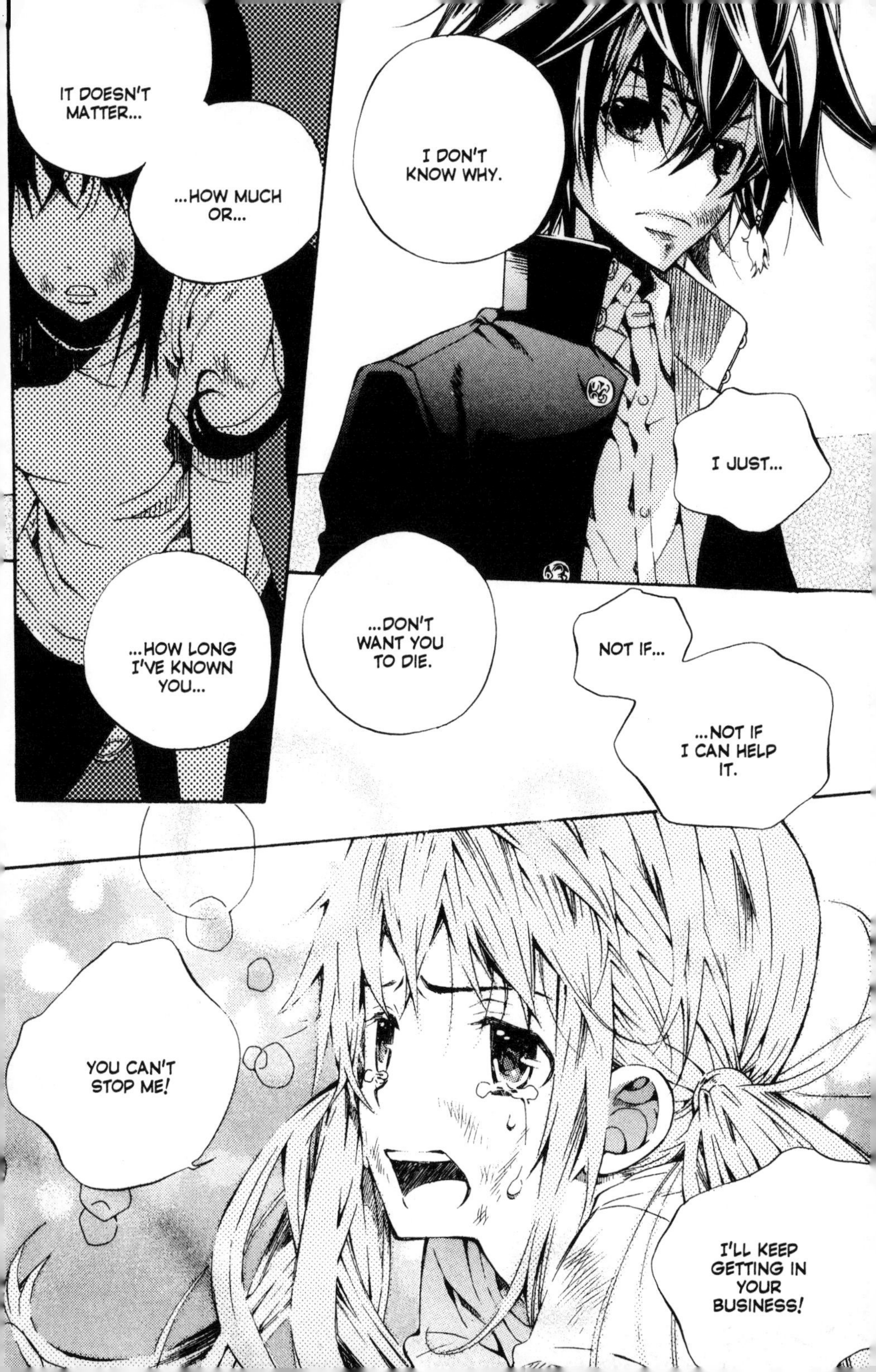
IT DOESN'T MATTER...
...HOW MUCH OR...
...HOW LONG I'VE KNOWN YOU...
I DON'T KNOW WHY.
I JUST...
...DON'T WANT YOU TO DIE.
NOT IF...
...NOT IF I CAN HELP IT.
YOU CAN'T STOP ME!
I'LL KEEP GETTING IN YOUR BUSINESS!

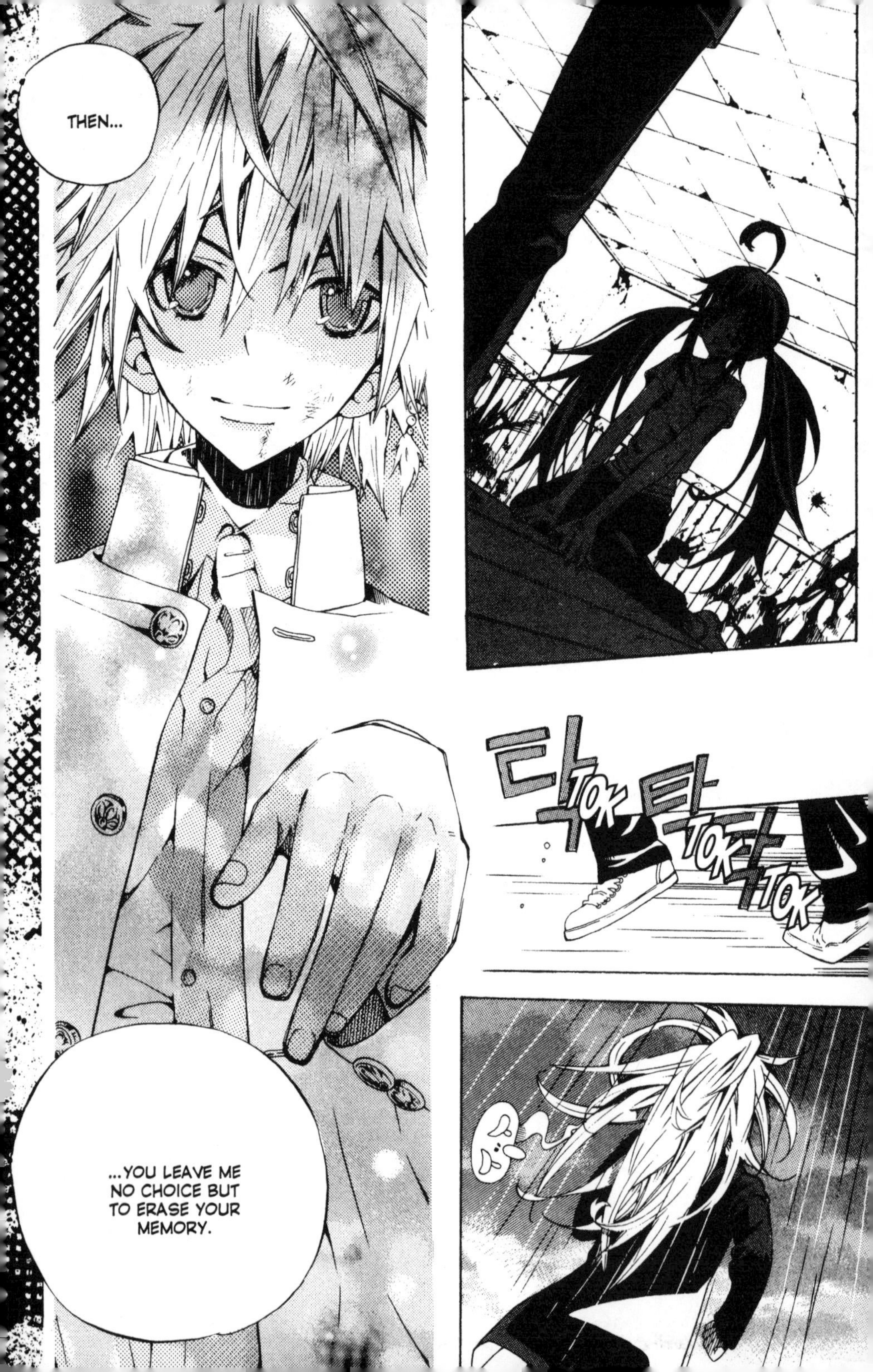
THEN...
...YOU LEAVE ME NO CHOICE BUT TO ERASE YOUR MEMORY.
TOK
TOK
TOK
TOK

KRA-
-KOOM

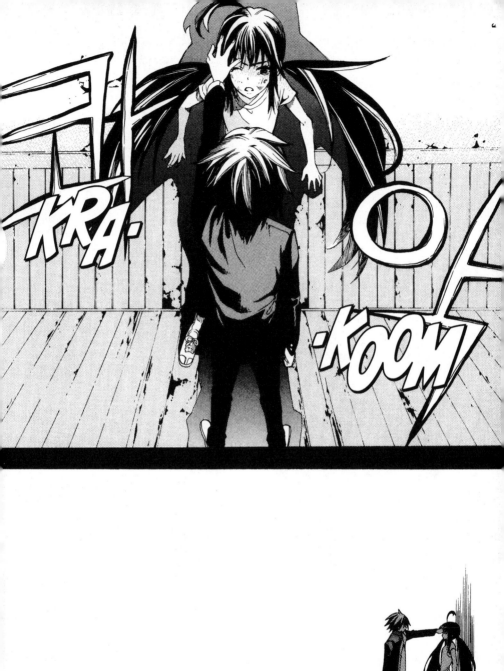

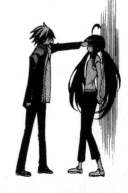

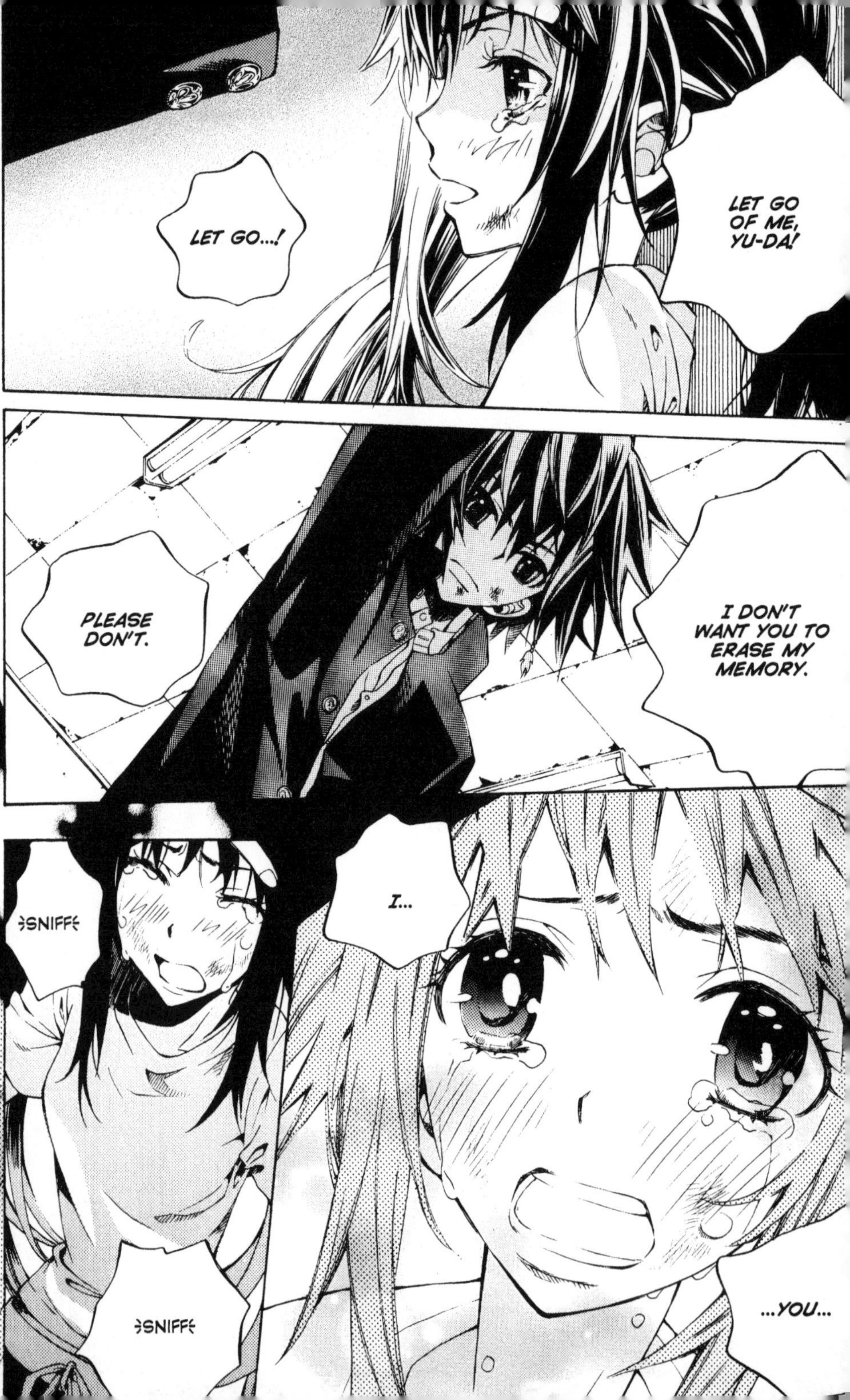
LET GO...!
LET GO OF ME, YU-DA!
PLEASE DON'T.
I DON'T WANT YOU TO ERASE MY MEMORY.
SNIFF
SNIFF
I...
...YOU...

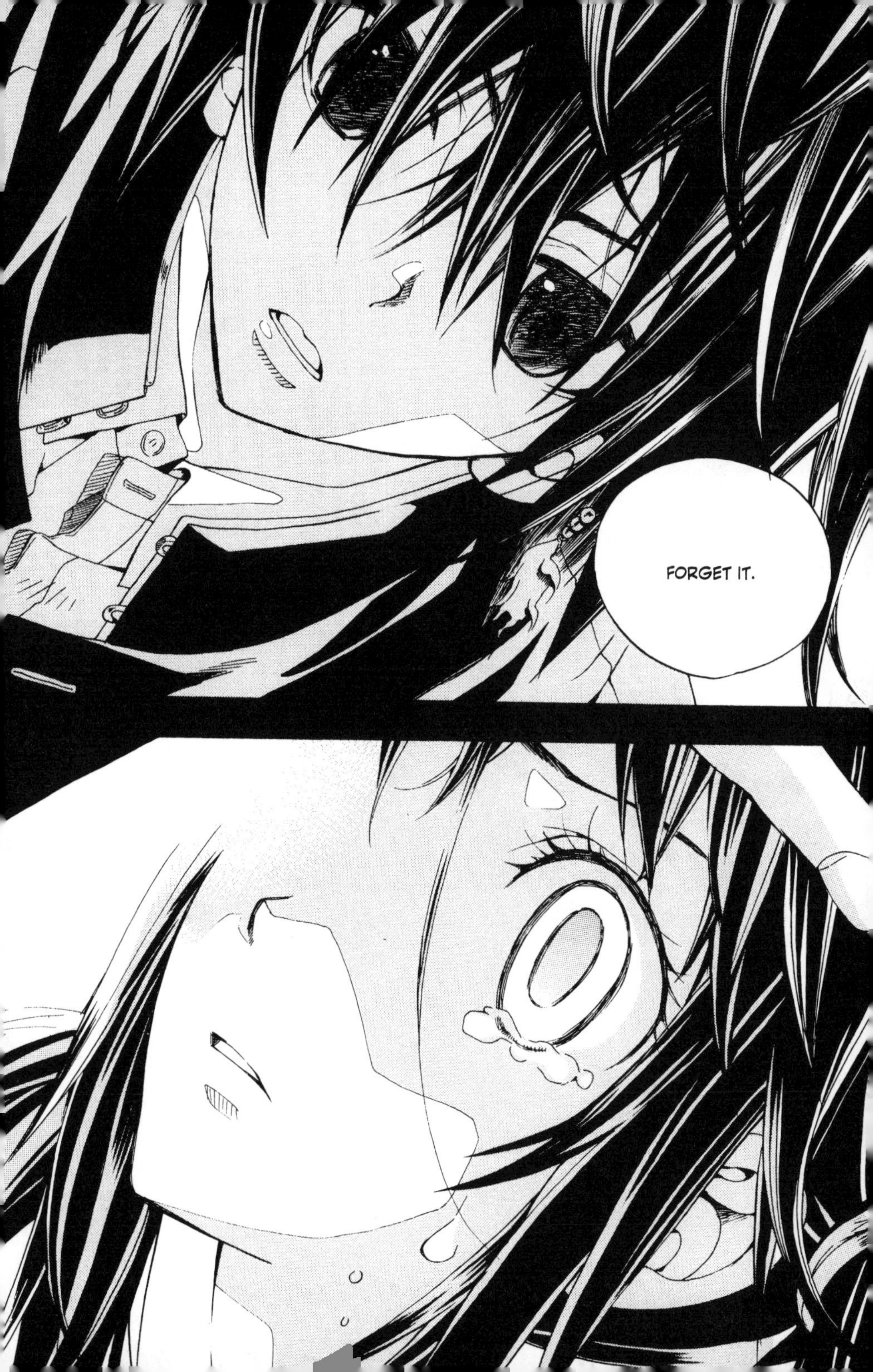
FORGET IT.

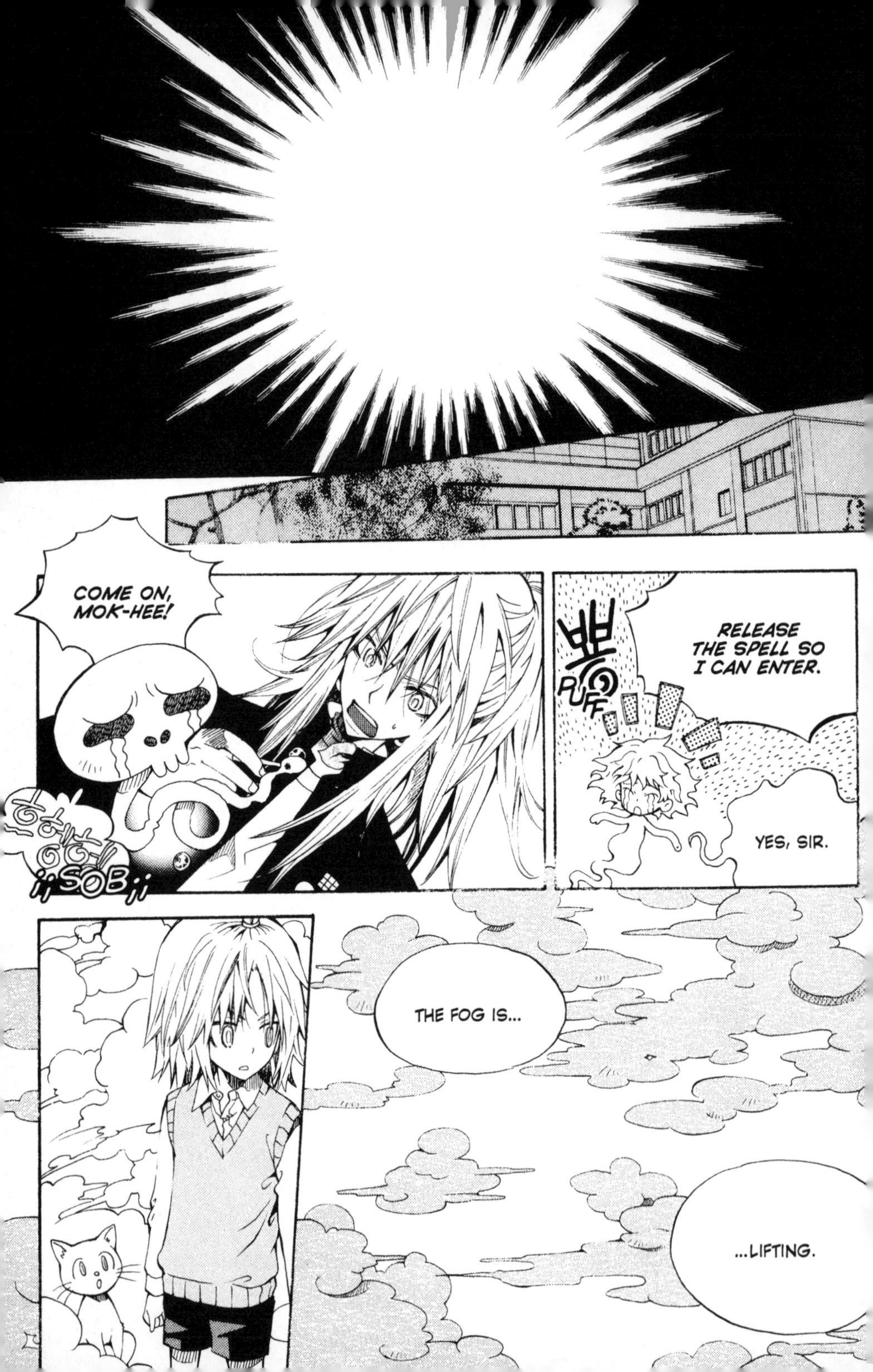
COME ON, MOK-HEE!
¡¡SOB¡¡
PUFF
RELEASE THE SPELL SO I CAN ENTER.
YES, SIR.
THE FOG IS...
...LIFTING.

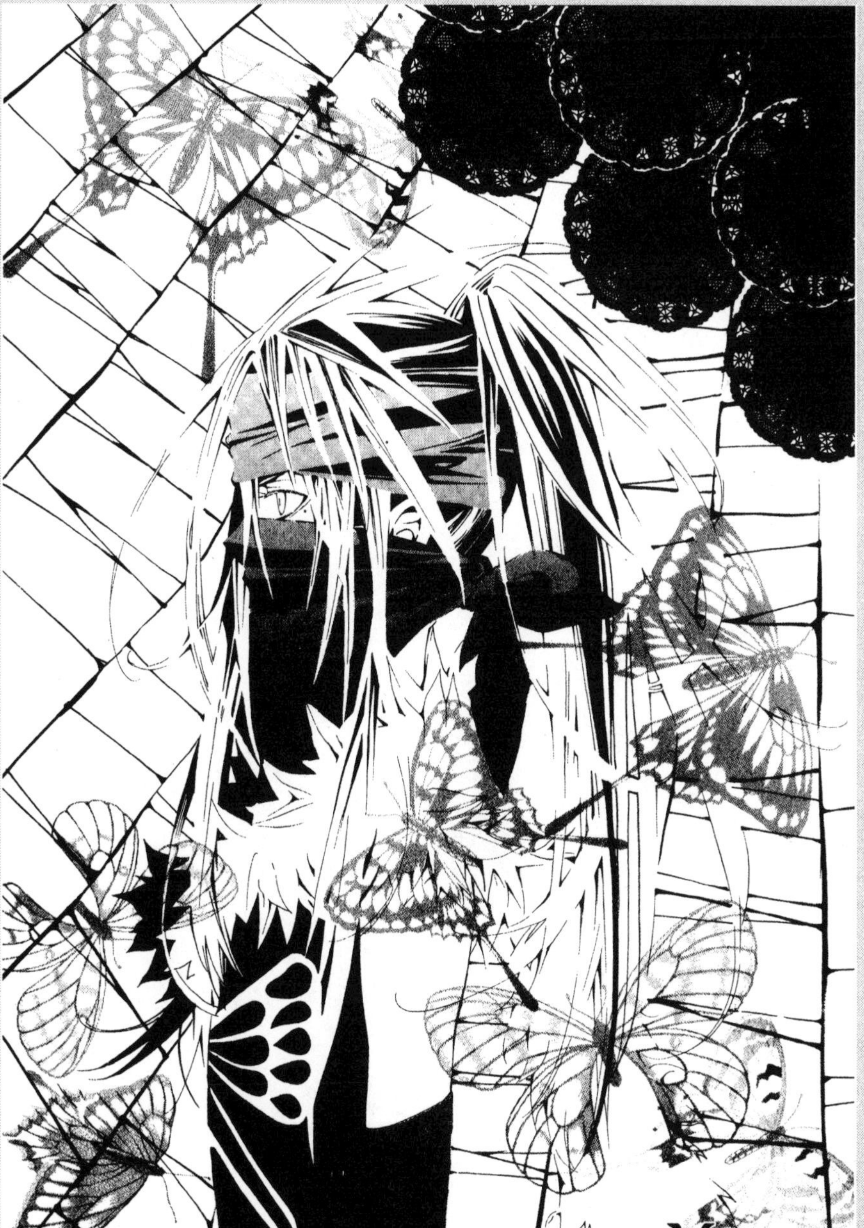
Moon
Boy
월요일 소년

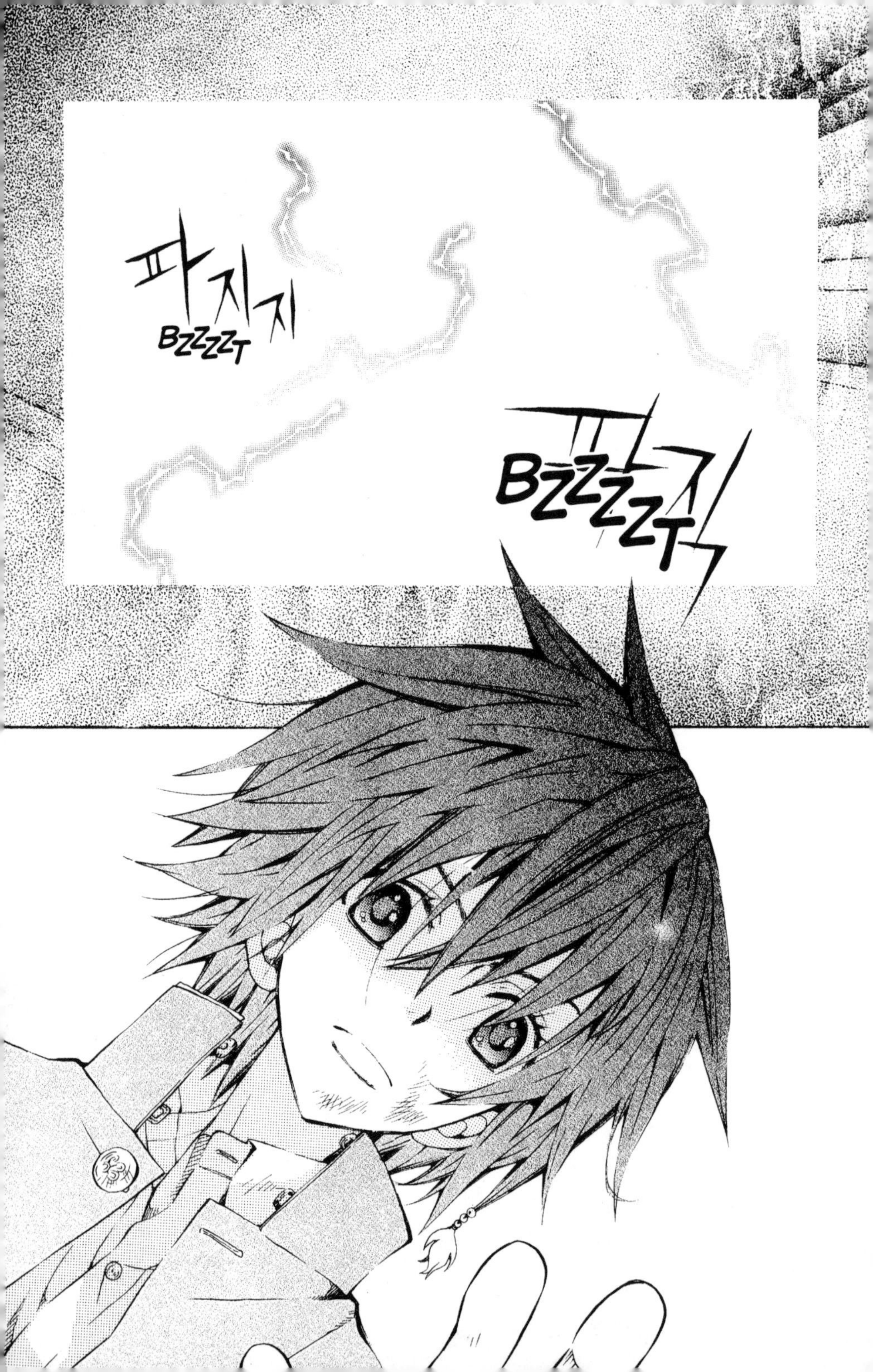
파지지
BZZZZT
파지
BZZZZT

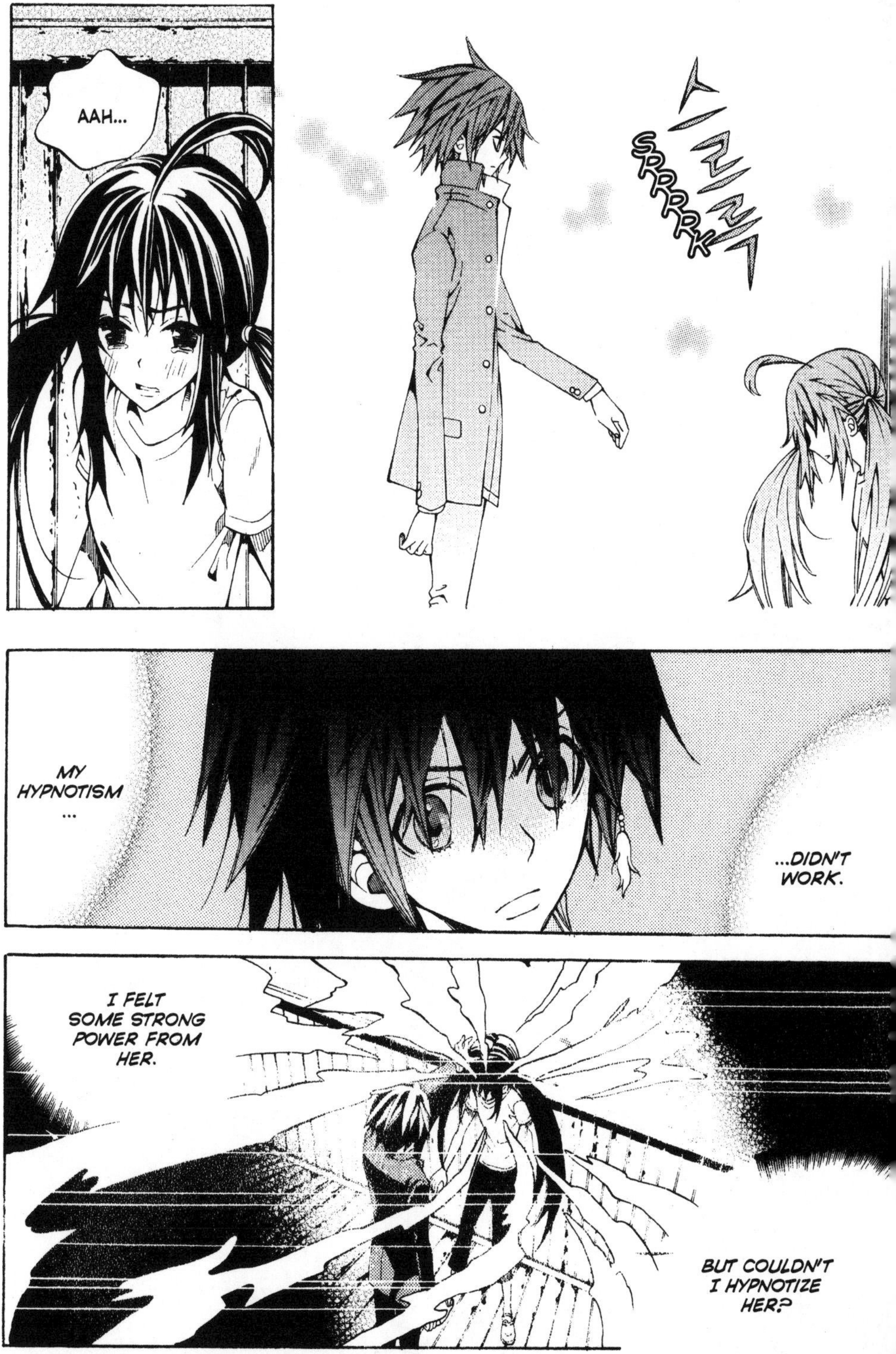
AAH...
SRRRK
MY HYPNOTISM ...
...DIDN'T WORK.
I FELT SOME STRONG POWER FROM HER.
BUT COULDN'T I HYPNOTIZE HER?

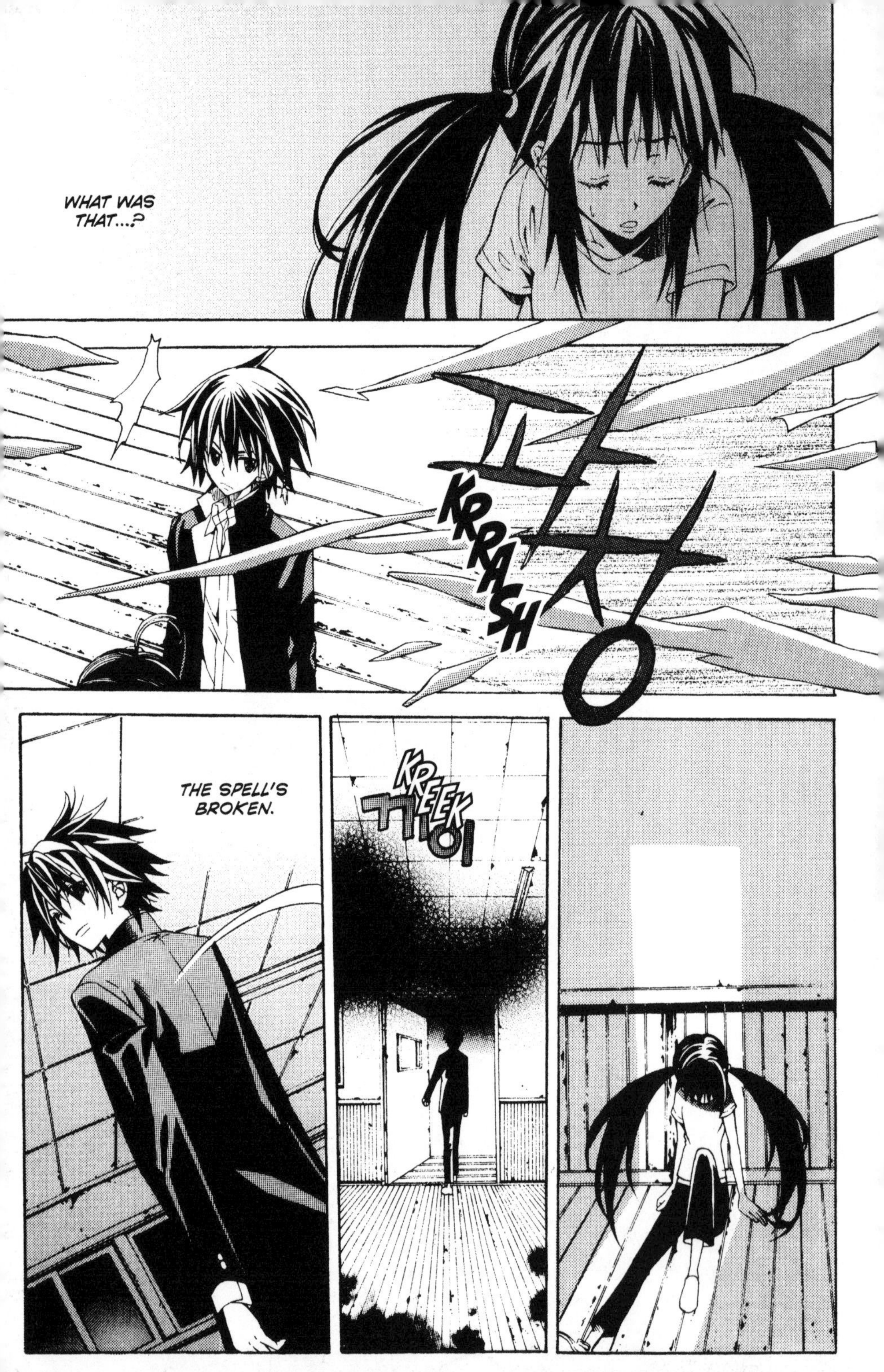

WHAT WAS THAT...?
KRRASH
THE SPELL'S BROKEN.
KREEK

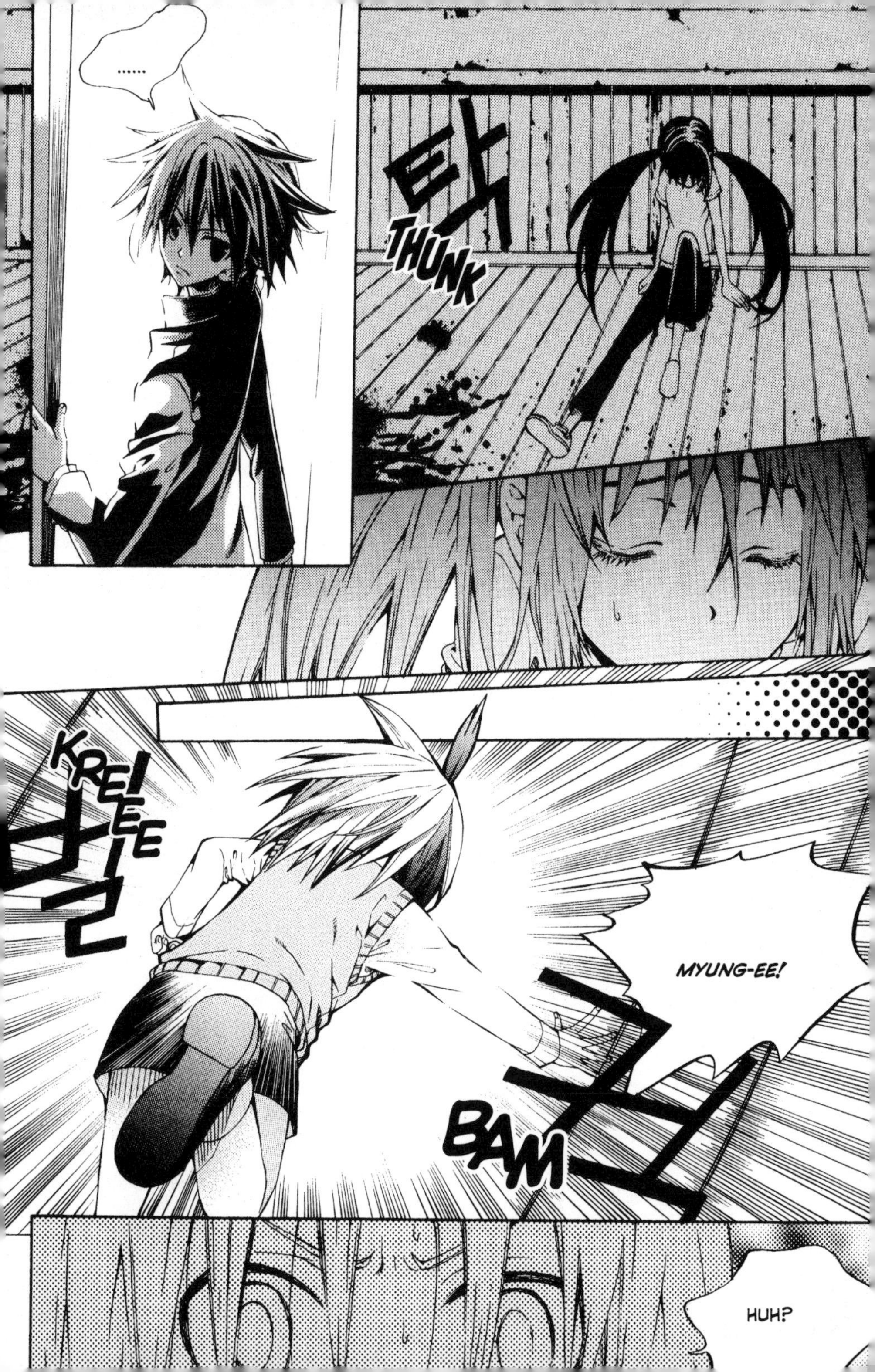
......
탁
THUNK
KREEEE
MYUNG-EE!
BAM
HUH?

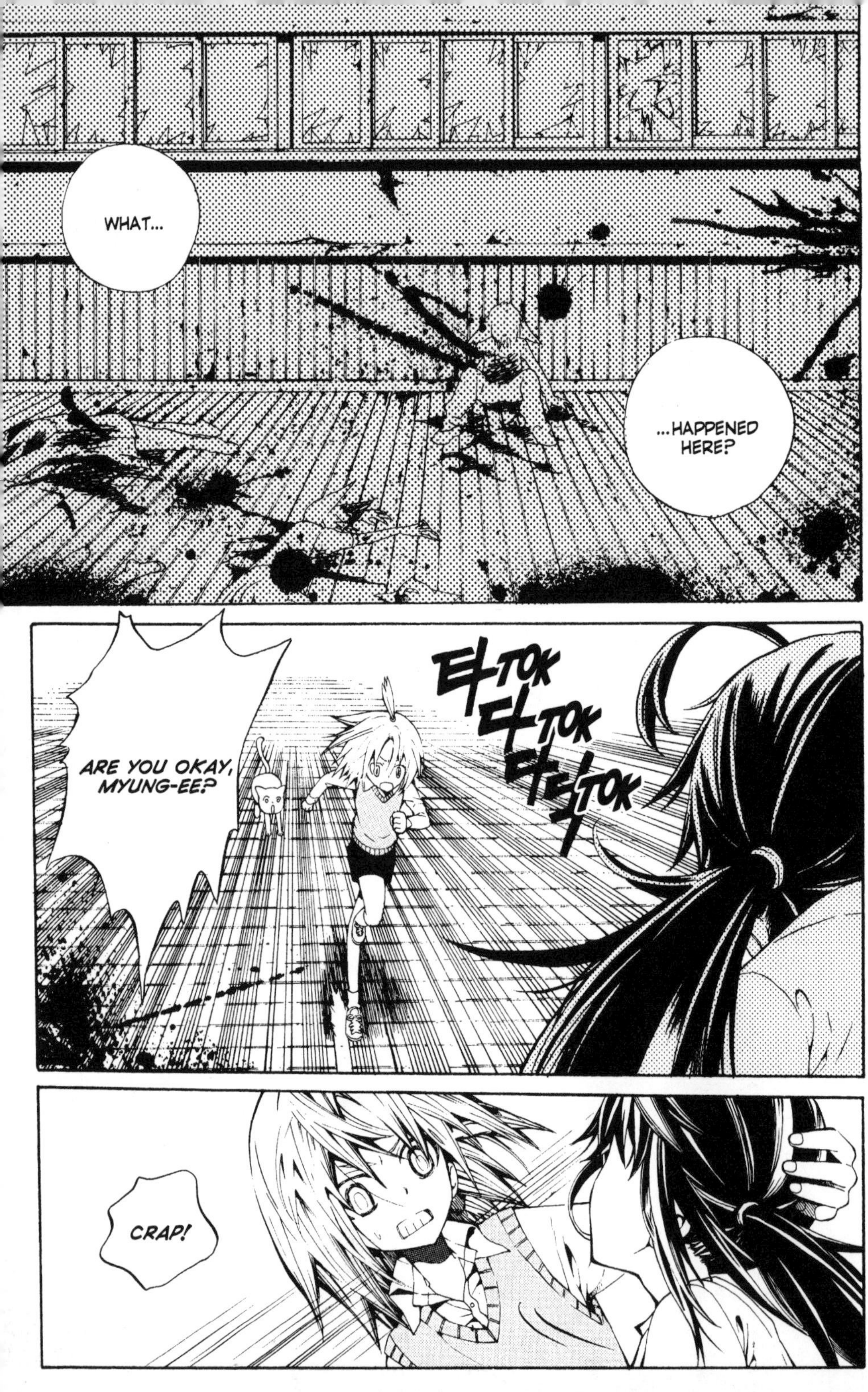
WHAT...
...HAPPENED HERE?
ARE YOU OKAY, MYUNG-EE?
타TOK
다TOK
TOK
CRAP!

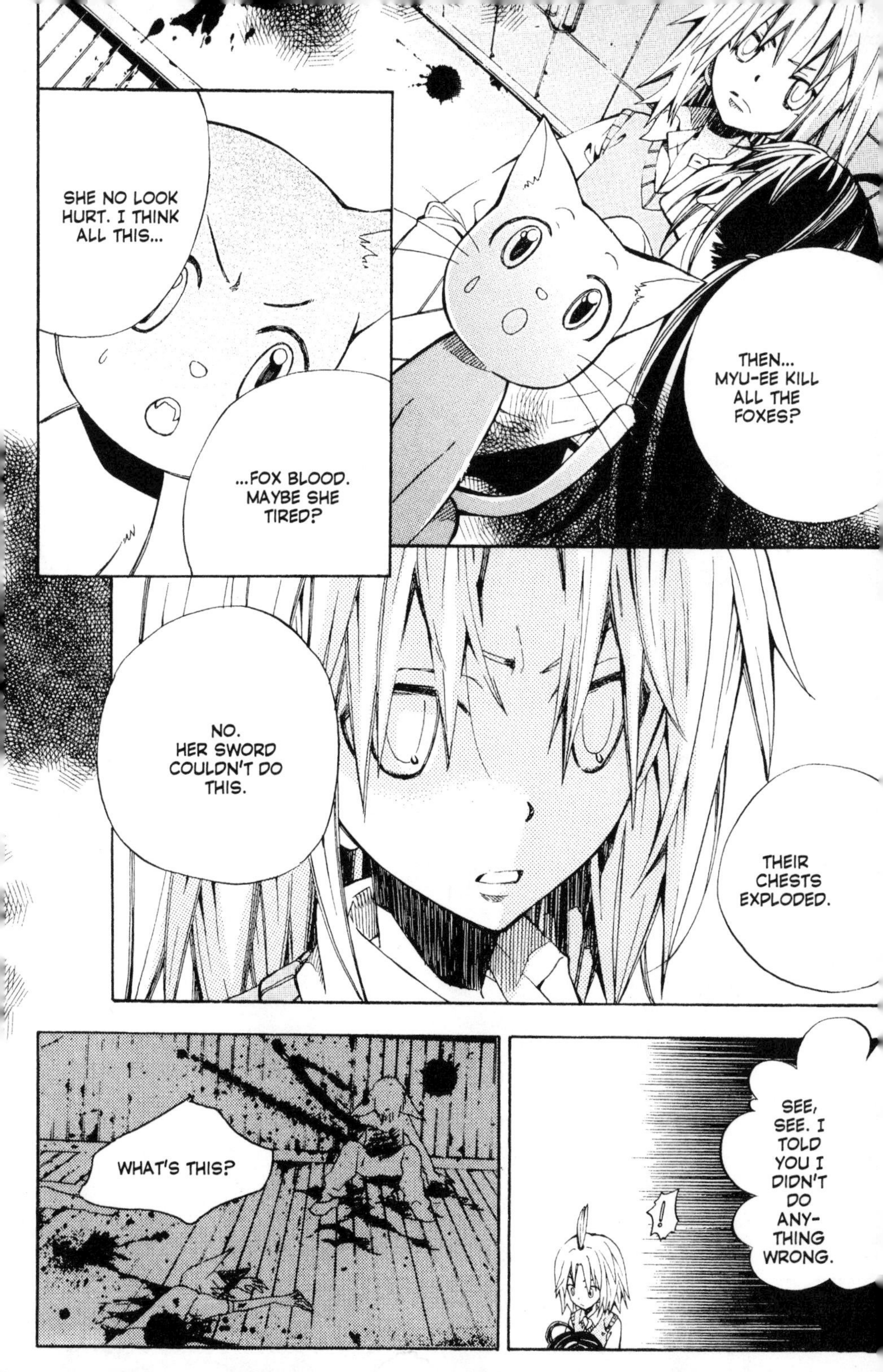
SHE NO LOOK HURT. I THINK ALL THIS...
...FOX BLOOD. MAYBE SHE TIRED?
THEN... MYU-EE KILL ALL THE FOXES?
NO. HER SWORD COULDN'T DO THIS.
THEIR CHESTS EXPLODED.
WHAT'S THIS?
SEE, SEE. I TOLD YOU I DIDN'T DO ANY-THING WRONG.
!

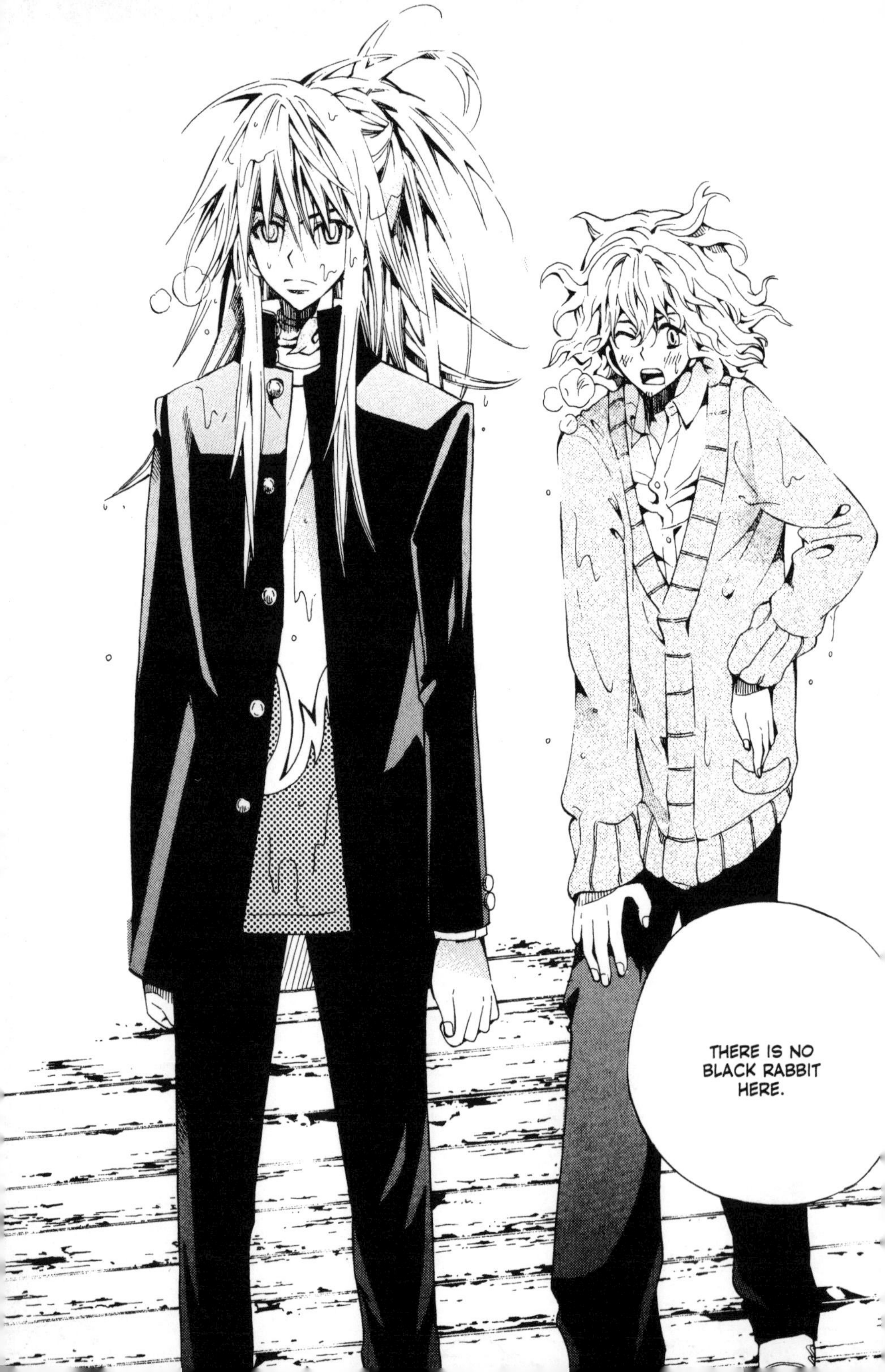
THERE IS NO BLACK RABBIT HERE.

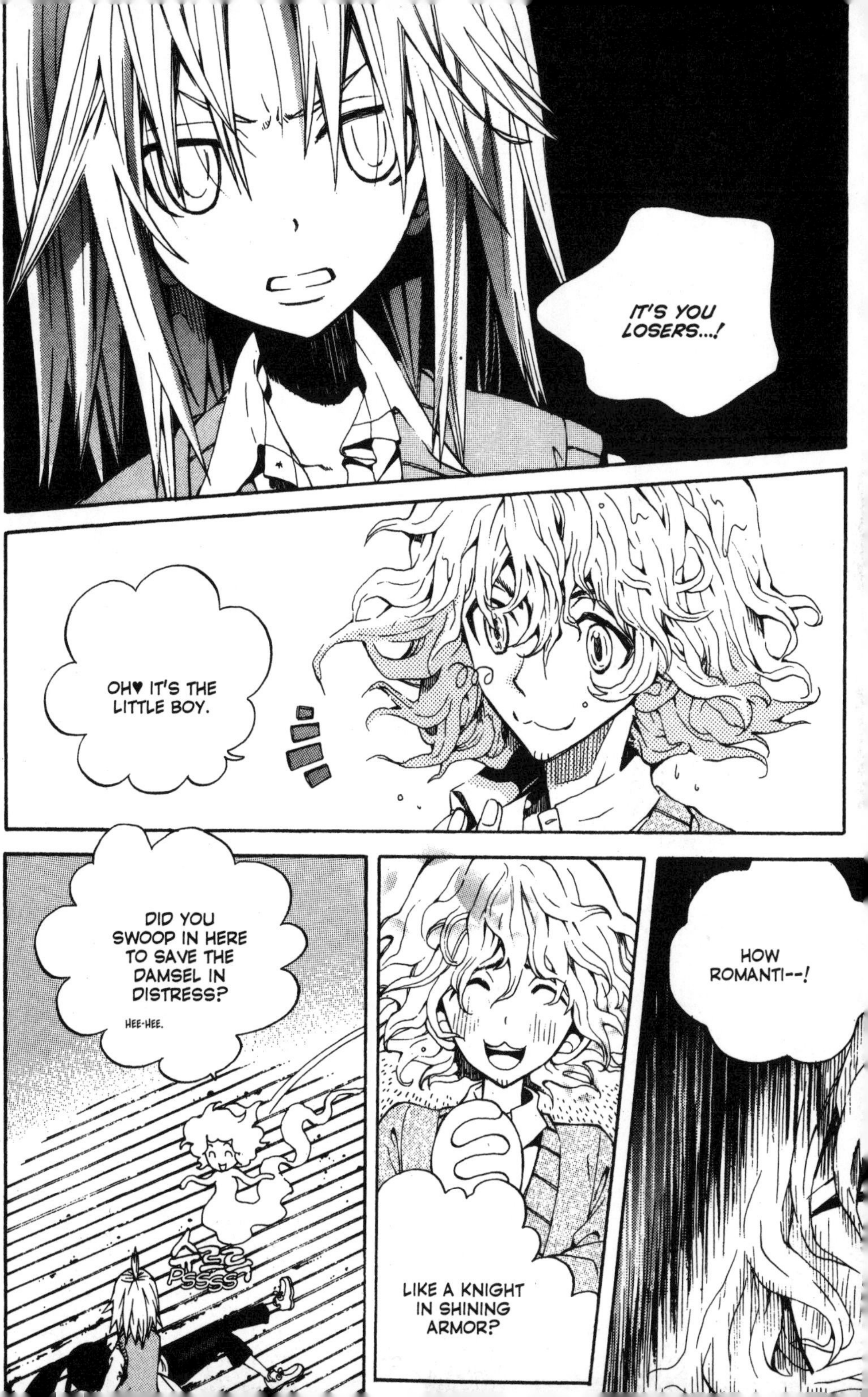
IT'S YOU LOSERS...!
OH♥ IT'S THE LITTLE BOY.
DID YOU SWOOP IN HERE TO SAVE THE DAMSEL IN DISTRESS?
HEE-HEE.
PSSSS
LIKE A KNIGHT IN SHINING ARMOR?
HOW ROMANTI--!

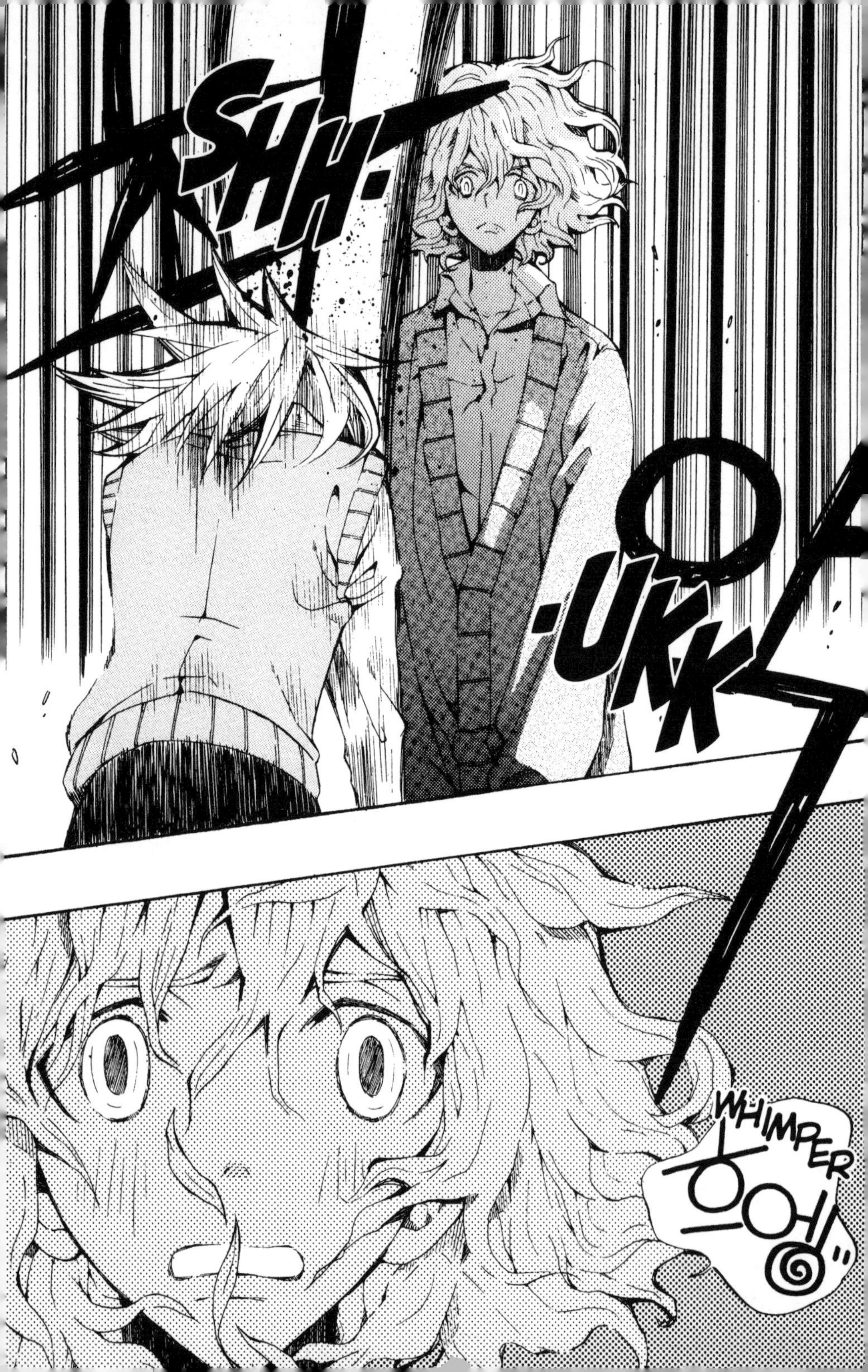
SHH-
OOF
-UKK
WHIMPER
OOH!!

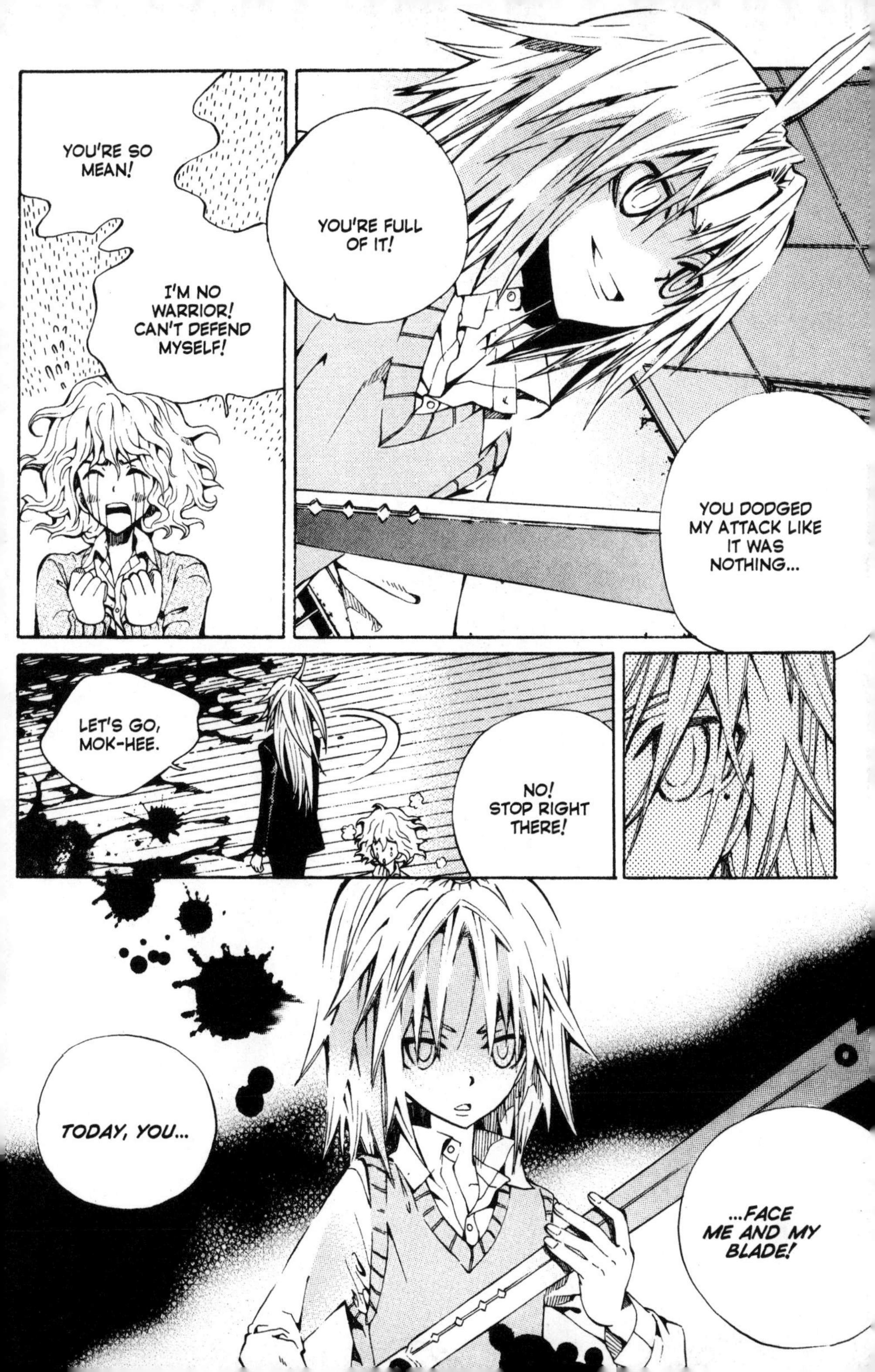
YOU'RE SO MEAN!
I'M NO WARRIOR! CAN'T DEFEND MYSELF!
YOU'RE FULL OF IT!
YOU DODGED MY ATTACK LIKE IT WAS NOTHING...
LET'S GO, MOK-HEE.
NO! STOP RIGHT THERE!
TODAY, YOU...
...FACE ME AND MY BLADE!

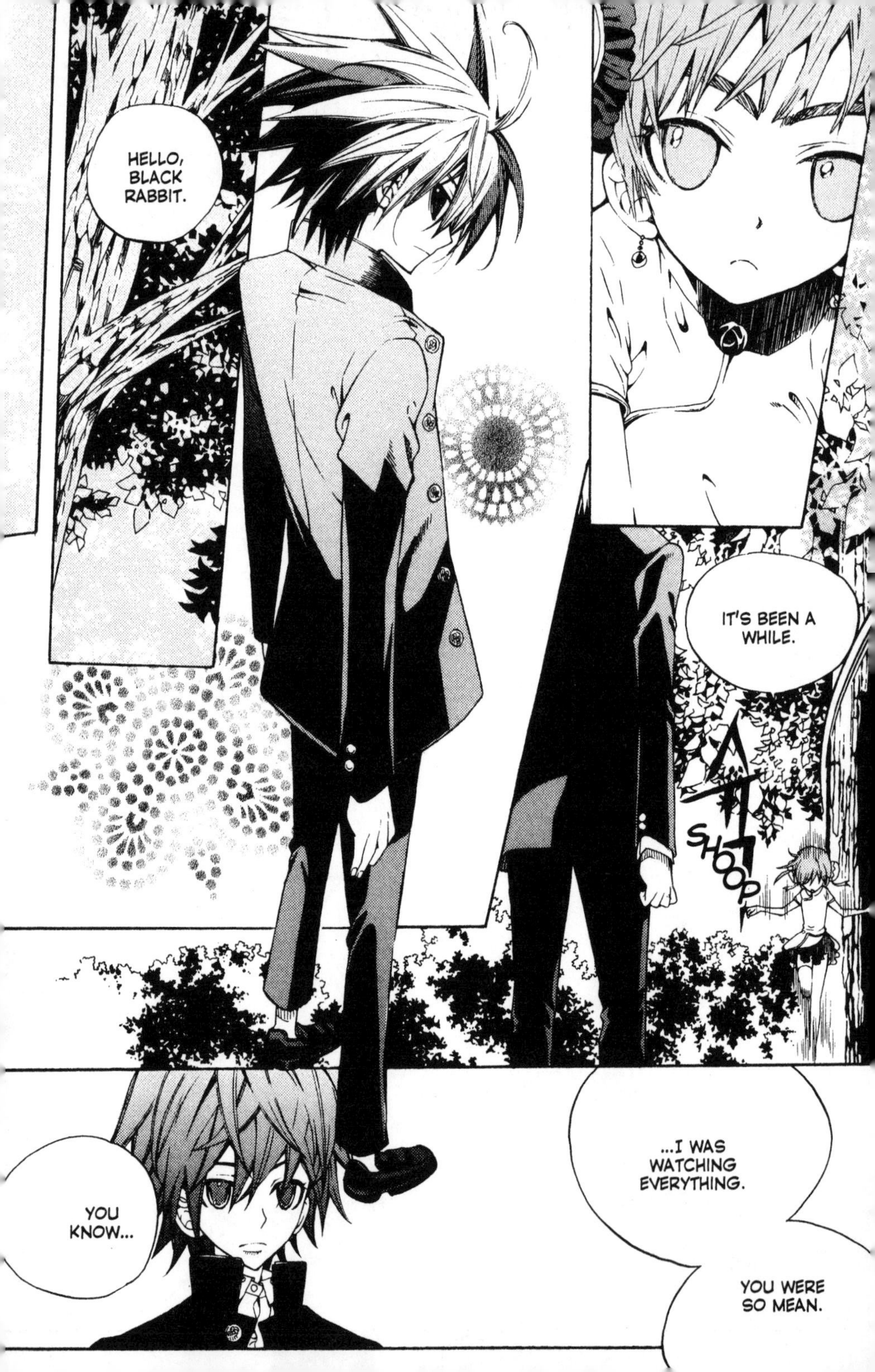
HELLO, BLACK RABBIT.
IT'S BEEN A WHILE.
SHOOP
YOU KNOW...
...I WAS WATCHING EVERYTHING.
YOU WERE SO MEAN.

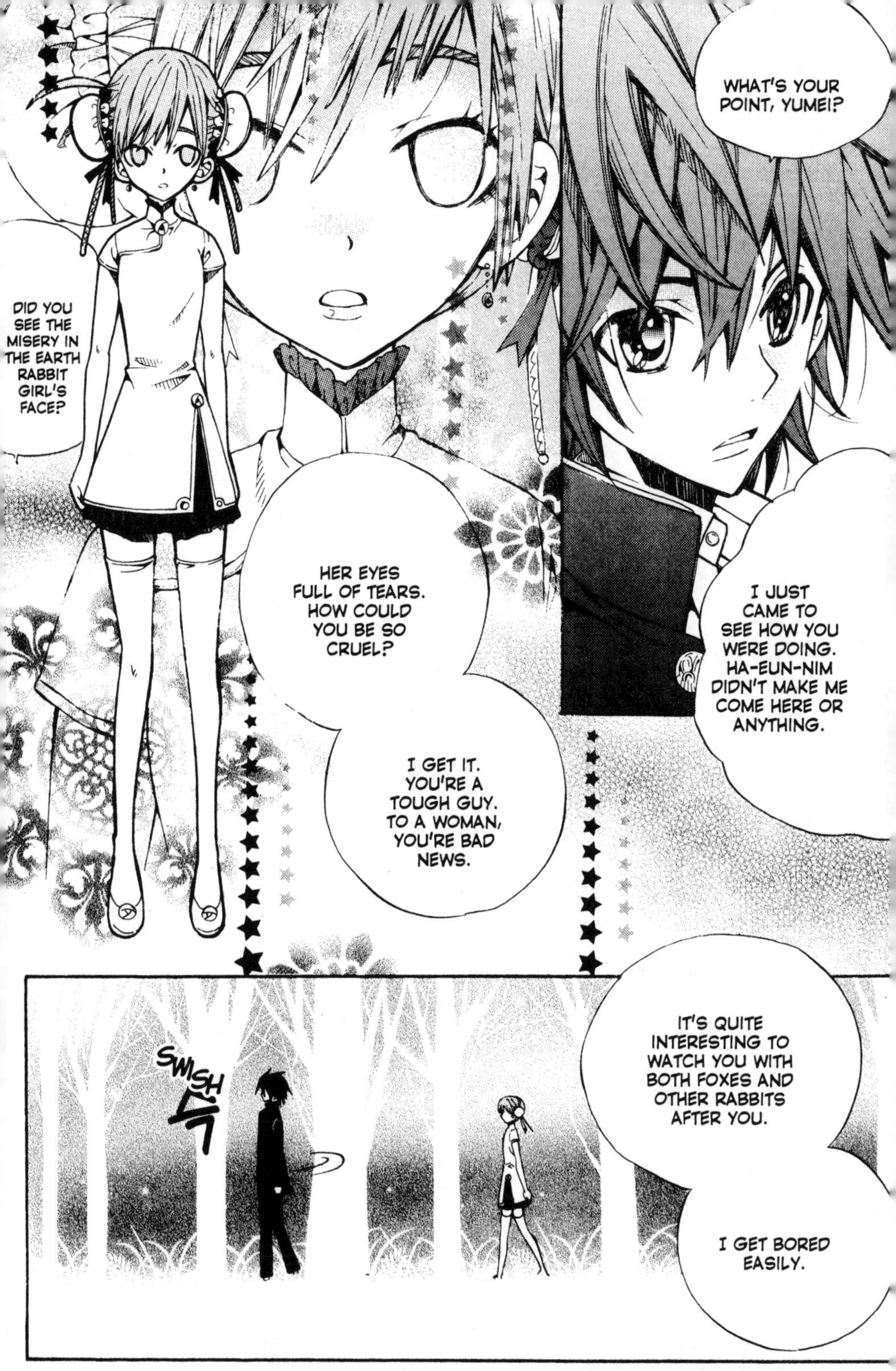
DID YOU SEE THE MISERY IN THE EARTH RABBIT GIRL'S FACE?
WHAT'S YOUR POINT, YUMEI?
HER EYES FULL OF TEARS. HOW COULD YOU BE SO CRUEL?
I GET IT. YOU'RE A TOUGH GUY. TO A WOMAN, YOU'RE BAD NEWS.
I JUST CAME TO SEE HOW YOU WERE DOING. HA-EUN-NIM DIDN'T MAKE ME COME HERE OR ANYTHING.
SWISH
IT'S QUITE INTERESTING TO WATCH YOU WITH BOTH FOXES AND OTHER RABBITS AFTER YOU.
I GET BORED EASILY.

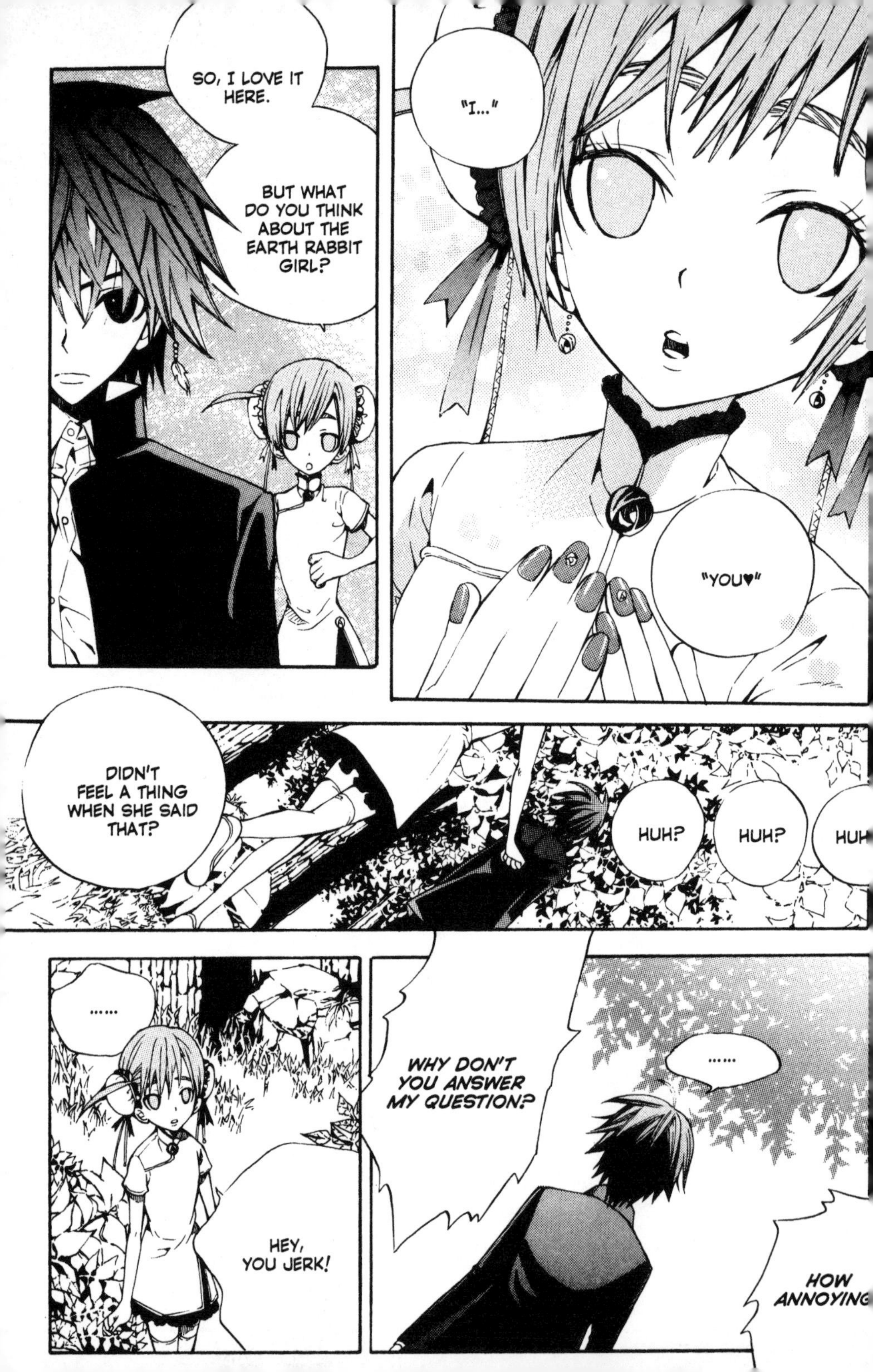
SO, I LOVE IT HERE.
BUT WHAT DO YOU THINK ABOUT THE EARTH RABBIT GIRL?
"I..."
"YOU♥"
DIDN'T FEEL A THING WHEN SHE SAID THAT?
HUH?
HUH?
......
HEY, YOU JERK!
WHY DON'T YOU ANSWER MY QUESTION?
......
HOW ANNOYING

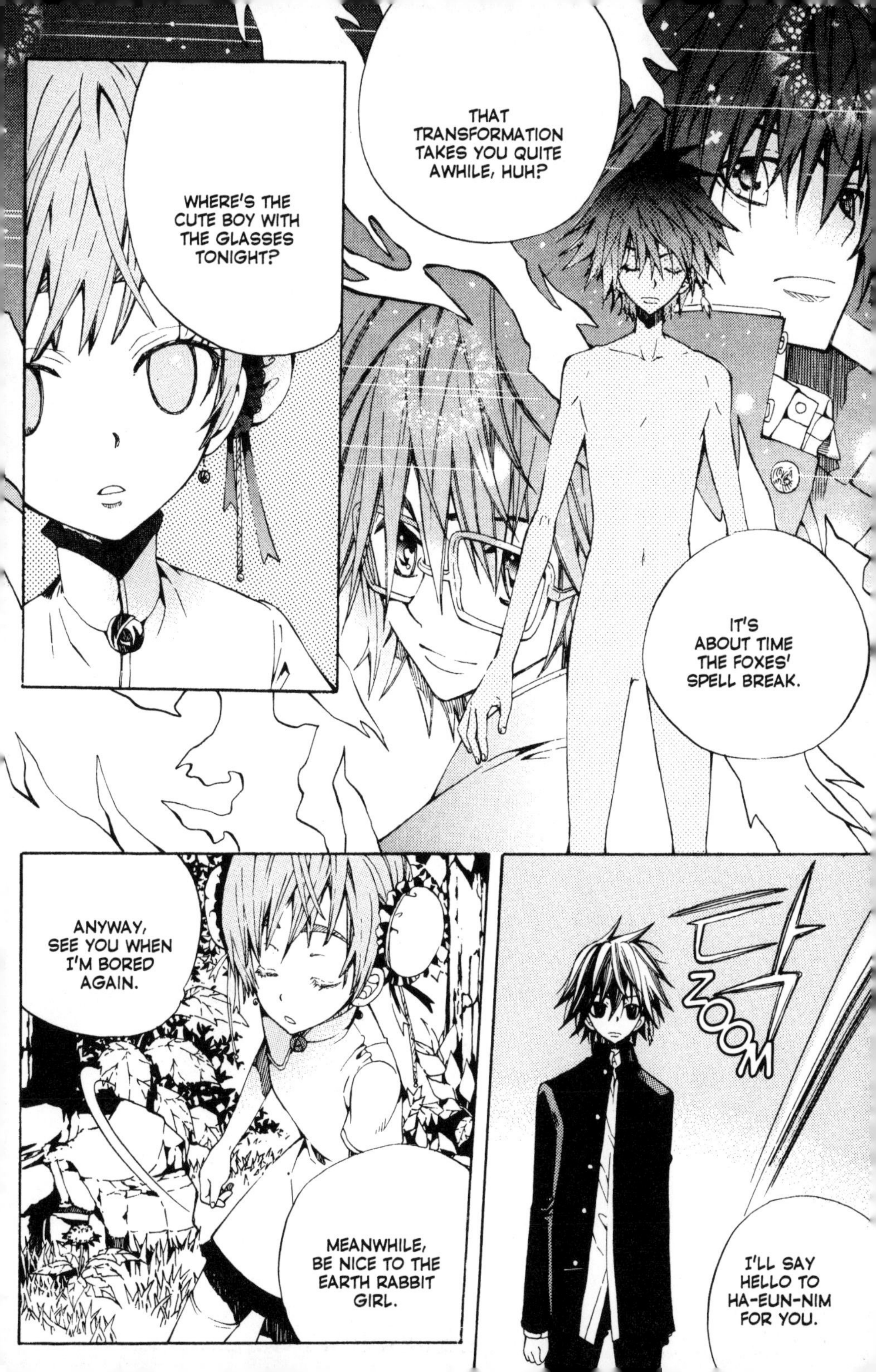
WHERE'S THE CUTE BOY WITH THE GLASSES TONIGHT?
THAT TRANSFORMATION TAKES YOU QUITE AWHILE, HUH?
IT'S ABOUT TIME THE FOXES' SPELL BREAK.
ANYWAY, SEE YOU WHEN I'M BORED AGAIN.
MEANWHILE, BE NICE TO THE EARTH RABBIT GIRL.
ZOOM
I'LL SAY HELLO TO HA-EUN-NIM FOR YOU.

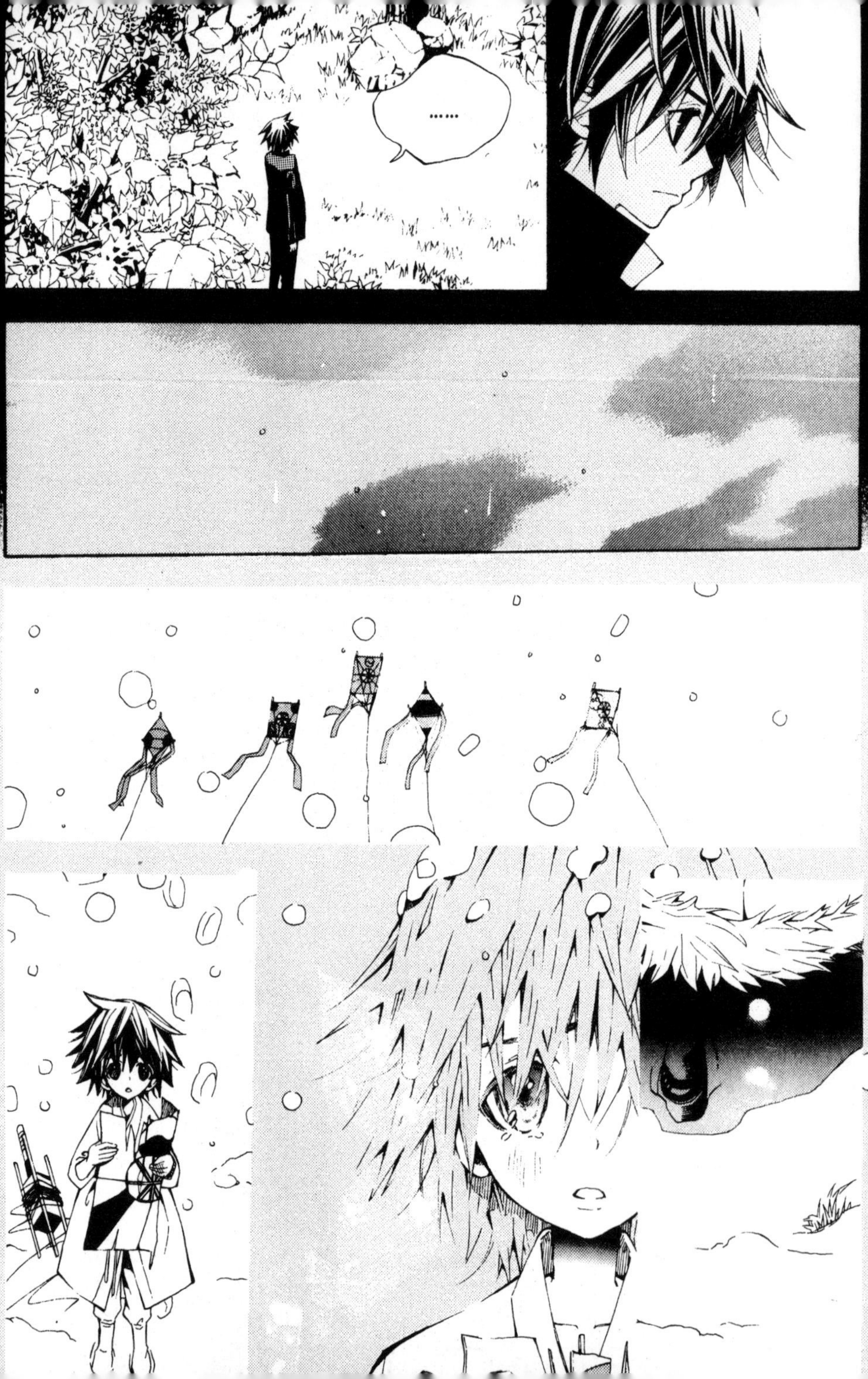
……

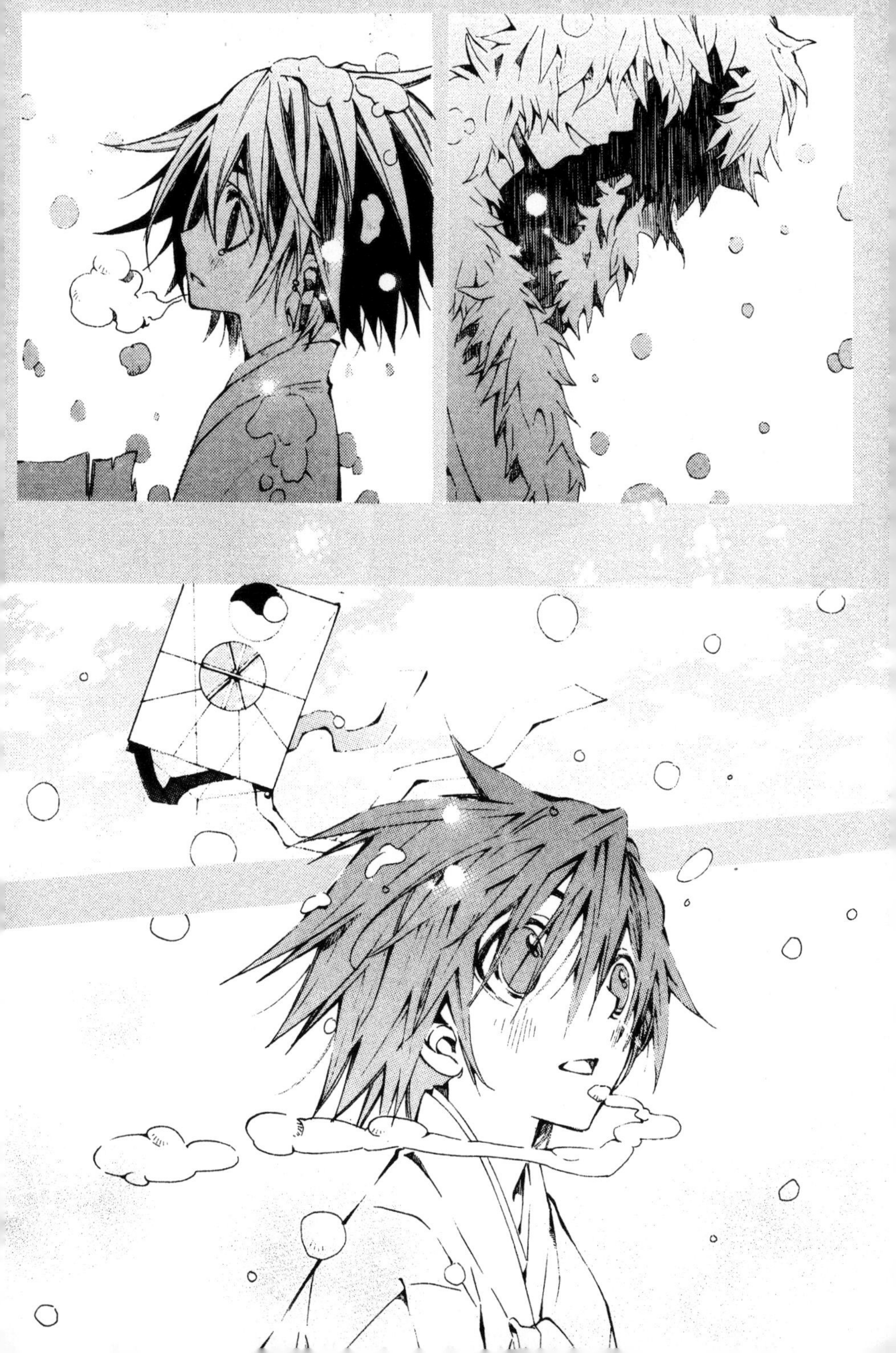

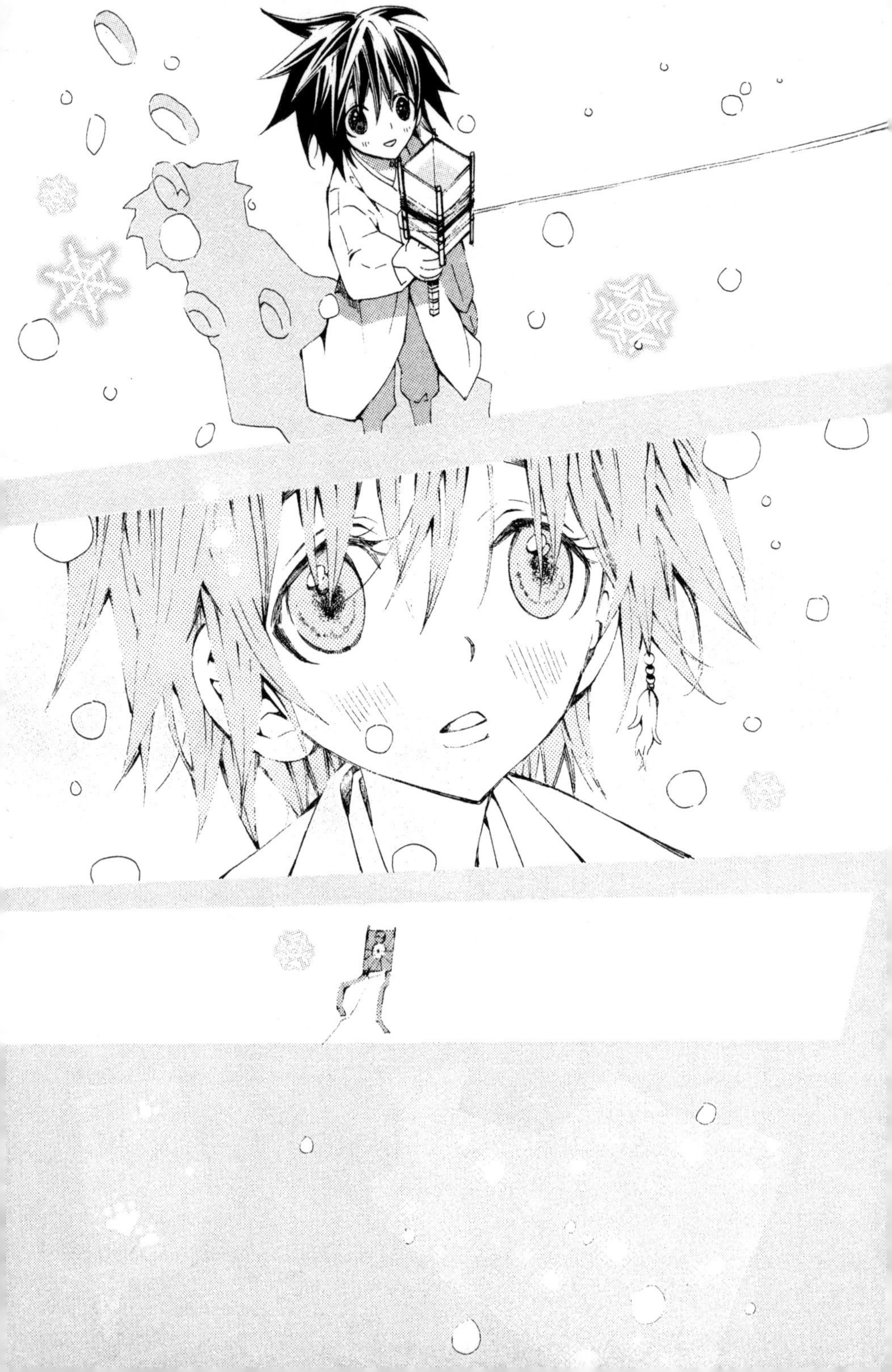

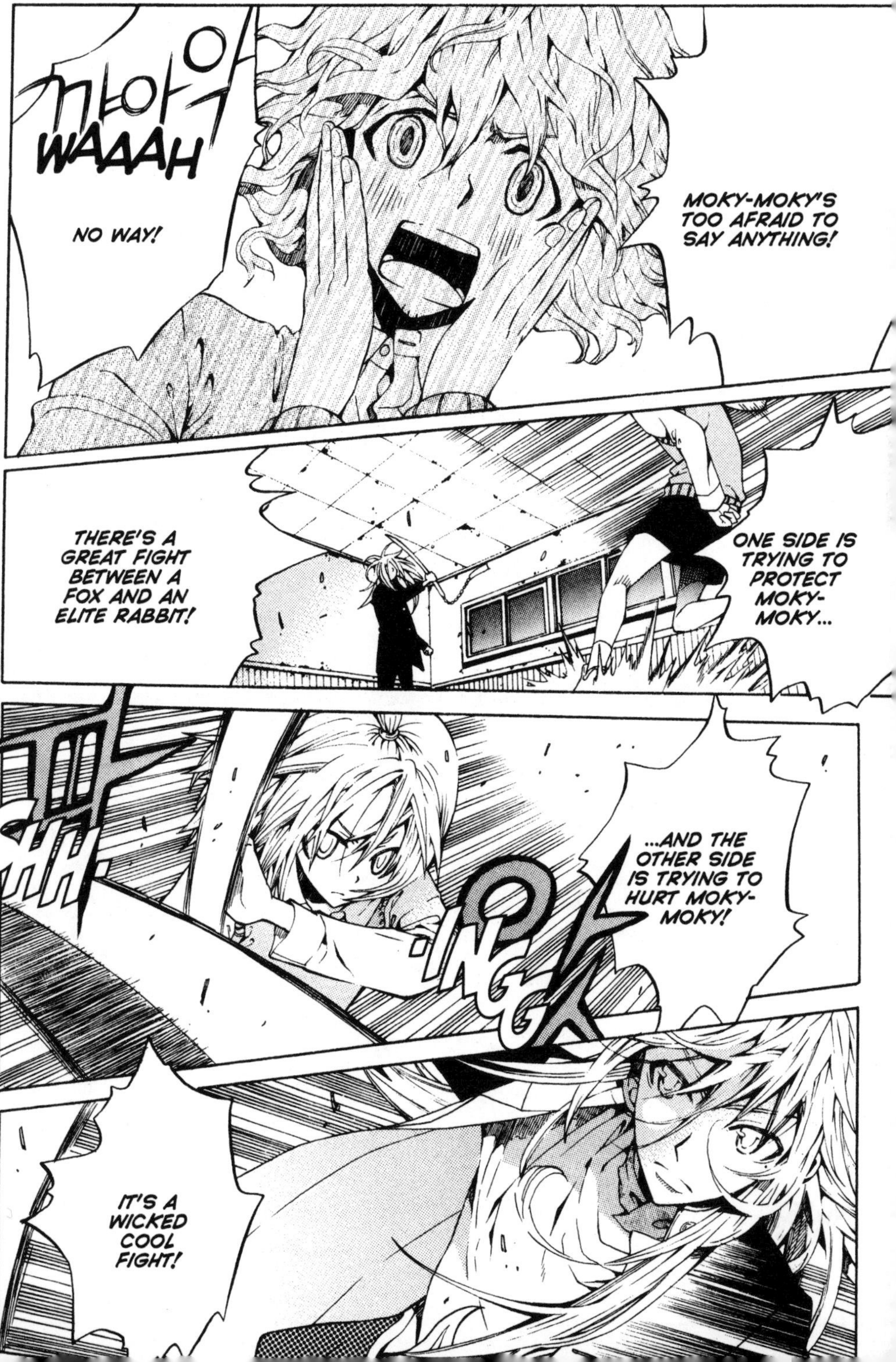
WAAAH
NO WAY!
MOKY-MOKY'S TOO AFRAID TO SAY ANYTHING!
THERE'S A GREAT FIGHT BETWEEN A FOX AND AN ELITE RABBIT!
ONE SIDE IS TRYING TO PROTECT MOKY-MOKY...
...AND THE OTHER SIDE IS TRYING TO HURT MOKY-MOKY!
IT'S A WICKED COOL FIGHT!

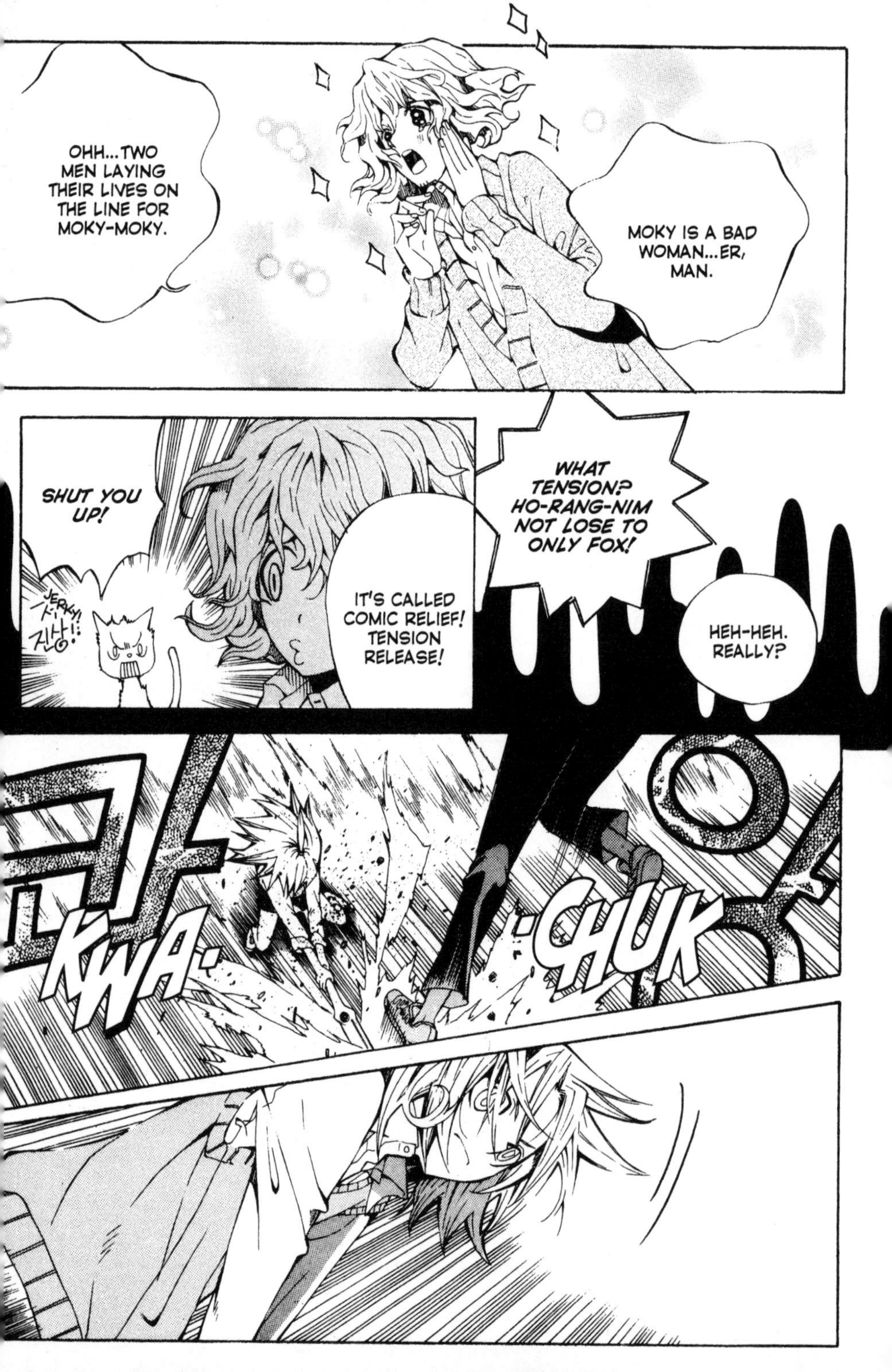
OHH...TWO MEN LAYING THEIR LIVES ON THE LINE FOR MOKY-MOKY.
MOKY IS A BAD WOMAN...ER, MAN.
SHUT YOU UP!
JERKY!
IT'S CALLED COMIC RELIEF! TENSION RELEASE!
WHAT TENSION? HO-RANG-NIM NOT LOSE TO ONLY FOX!
HEH-HEH. REALLY?
KWA-CHUK

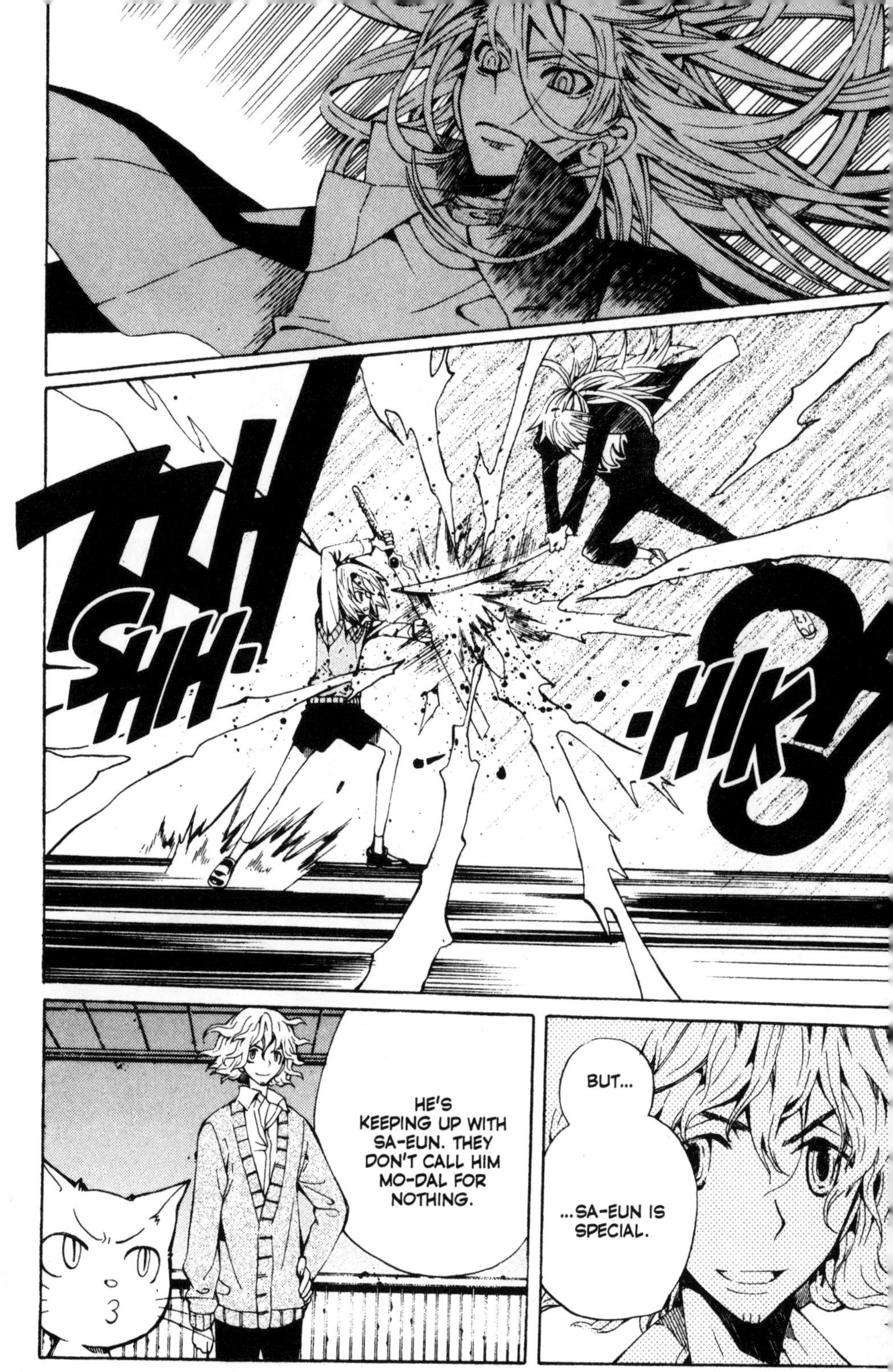
SHH-
-HK
HE'S KEEPING UP WITH SA-EUN. THEY DON'T CALL HIM MO-DAL FOR NOTHING.
BUT...
...SA-EUN IS SPECIAL.

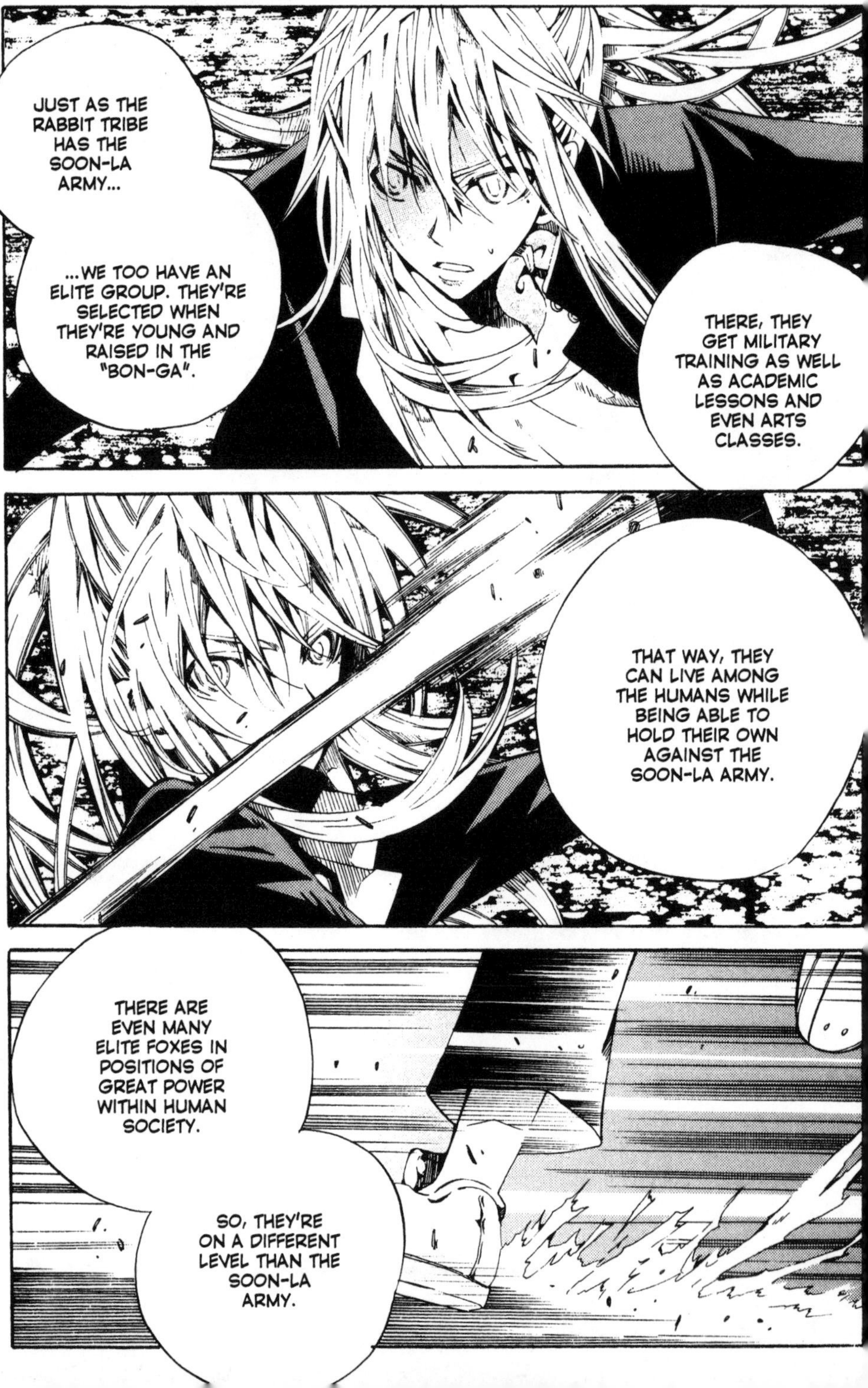
JUST AS THE RABBIT TRIBE HAS THE SOON-LA ARMY...
...WE TOO HAVE AN ELITE GROUP. THEY'RE SELECTED WHEN THEY'RE YOUNG AND RAISED IN THE "BON-GA".
THERE, THEY GET MILITARY TRAINING AS WELL AS ACADEMIC LESSONS AND EVEN ARTS CLASSES.
THAT WAY, THEY CAN LIVE AMONG THE HUMANS WHILE BEING ABLE TO HOLD THEIR OWN AGAINST THE SOON-LA ARMY.
THERE ARE EVEN MANY ELITE FOXES IN POSITIONS OF GREAT POWER WITHIN HUMAN SOCIETY.
SO, THEY'RE ON A DIFFERENT LEVEL THAN THE SOON-LA ARMY.

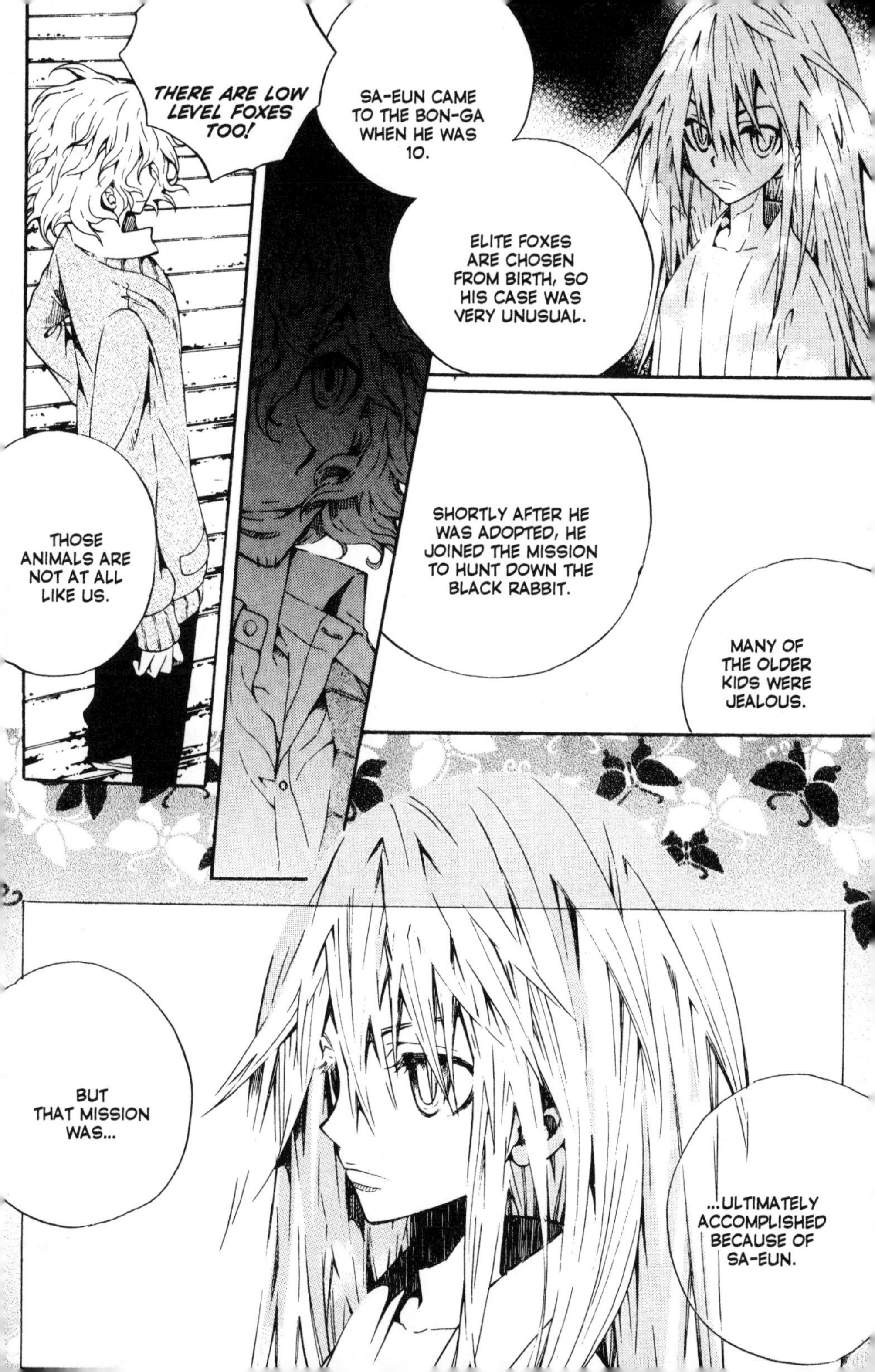
THERE ARE LOW LEVEL FOXES TOO!
THOSE ANIMALS ARE NOT AT ALL LIKE US.
SA-EUN CAME TO THE BON-GA WHEN HE WAS 10.
ELITE FOXES ARE CHOSEN FROM BIRTH, SO HIS CASE WAS VERY UNUSUAL.
SHORTLY AFTER HE WAS ADOPTED, HE JOINED THE MISSION TO HUNT DOWN THE BLACK RABBIT.
MANY OF THE OLDER KIDS WERE JEALOUS.
BUT THAT MISSION WAS...
...ULTIMATELY ACCOMPLISHED BECAUSE OF SA-EUN.

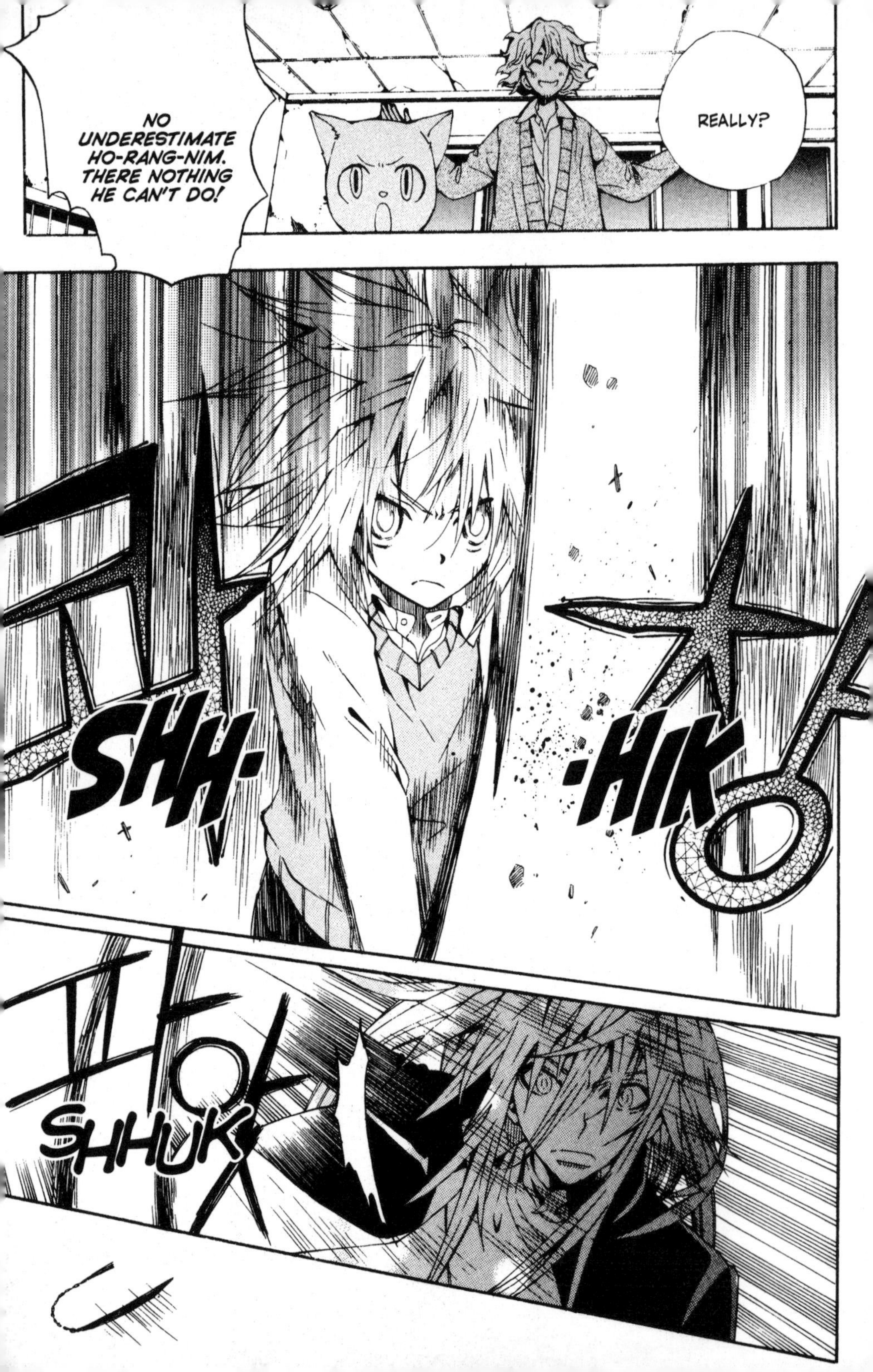
NO UNDERESTIMATE HO-RANG-NIM. THERE NOTHING HE CAN'T DO!
REALLY?
SHH- -HIK
SHHUK

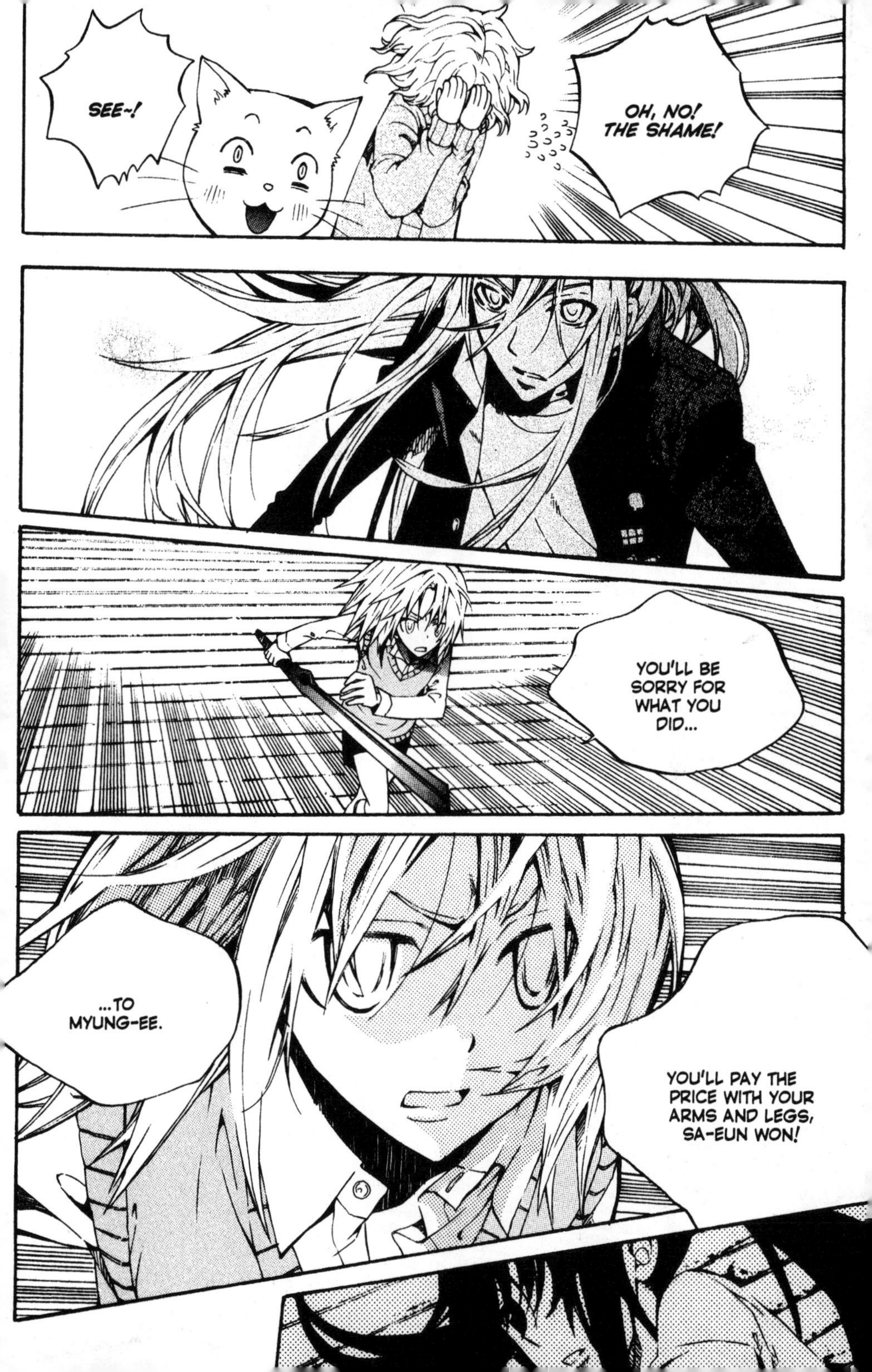
SEE~!
OH, NO! THE SHAME!
YOU'LL BE SORRY FOR WHAT YOU DID...
...TO MYUNG-EE.
YOU'LL PAY THE PRICE WITH YOUR ARMS AND LEGS, SA-EUN WON!

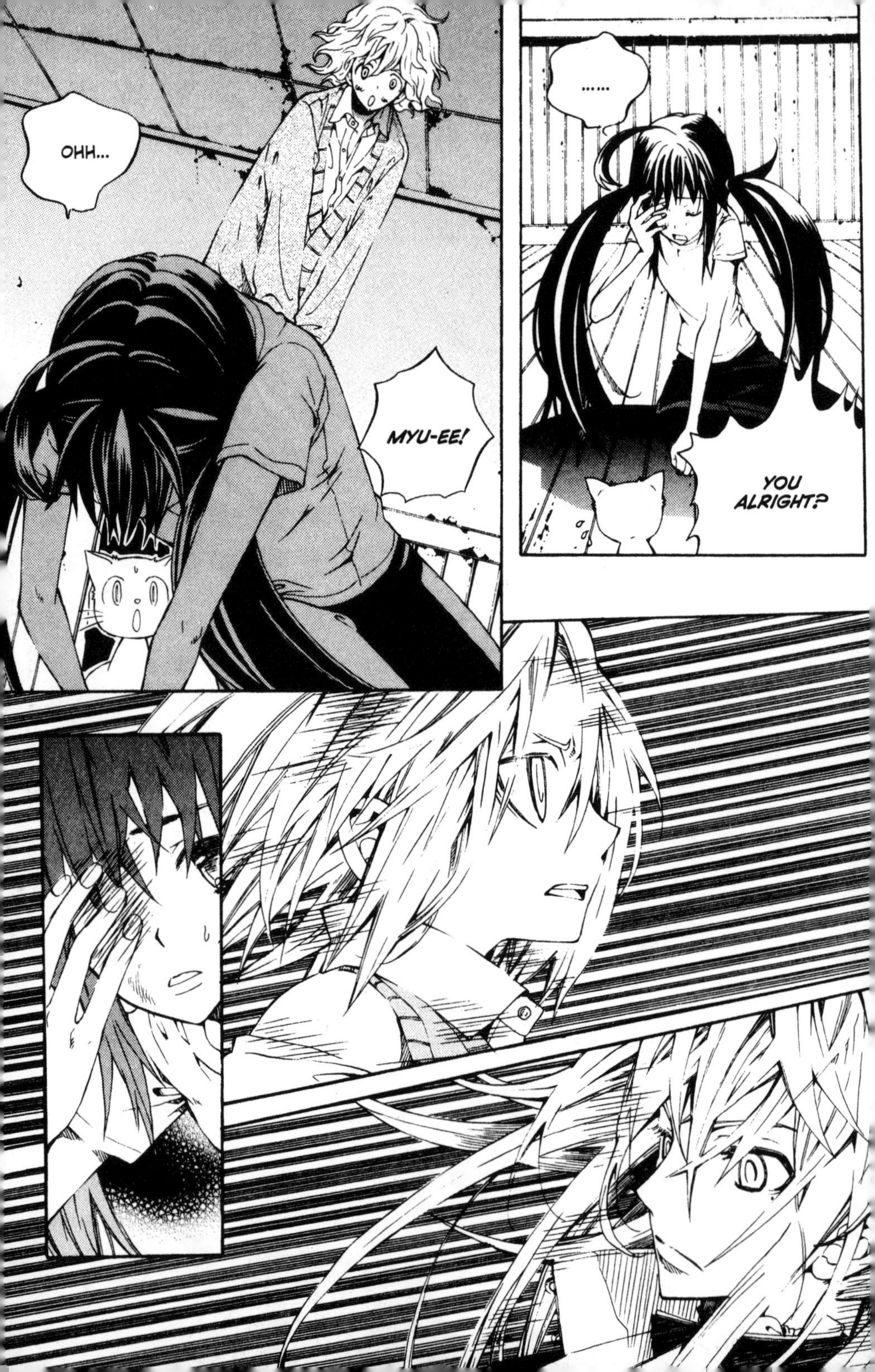
OHH...
MYU-EE!
......
YOU ALRIGHT?

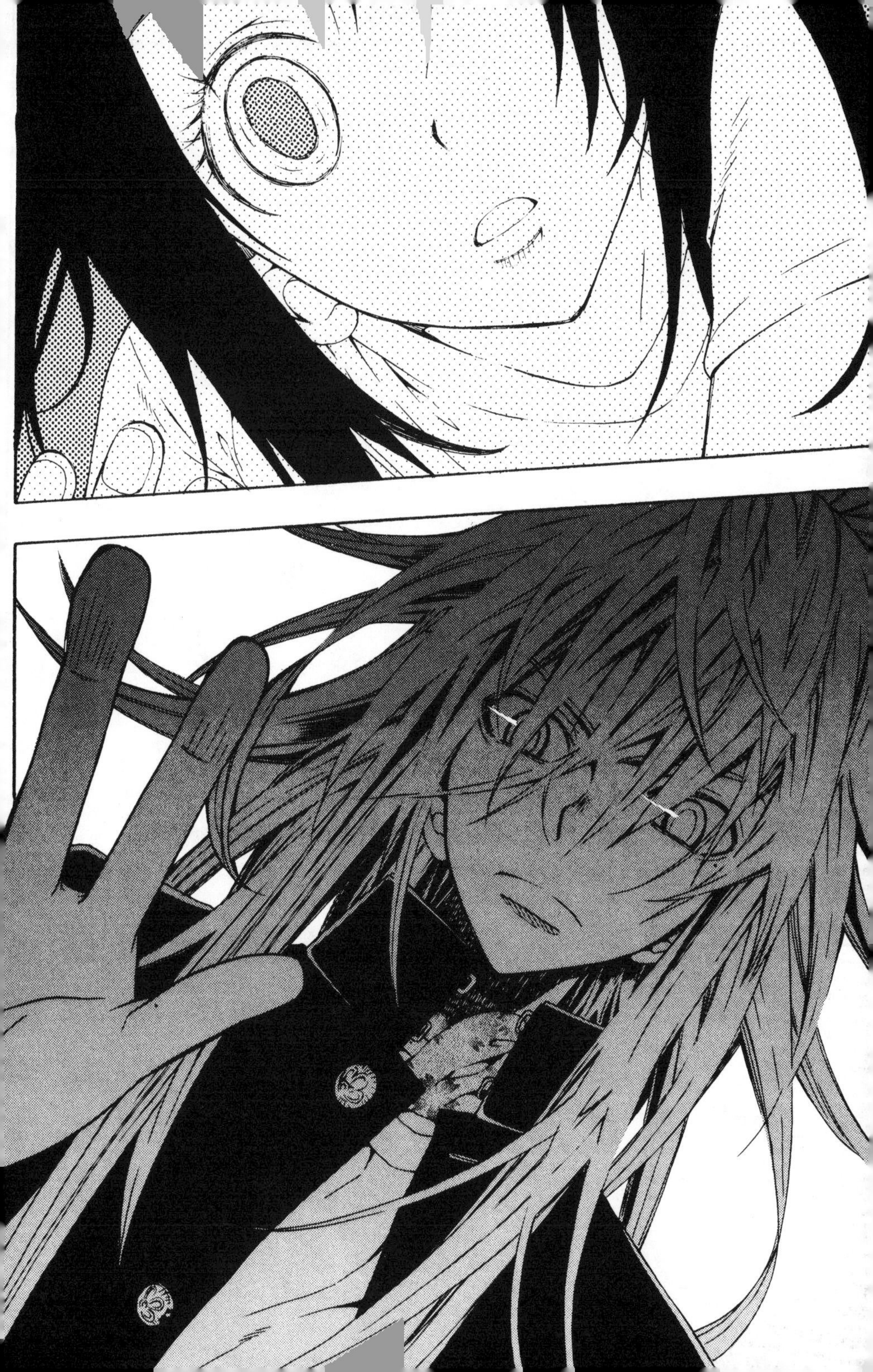

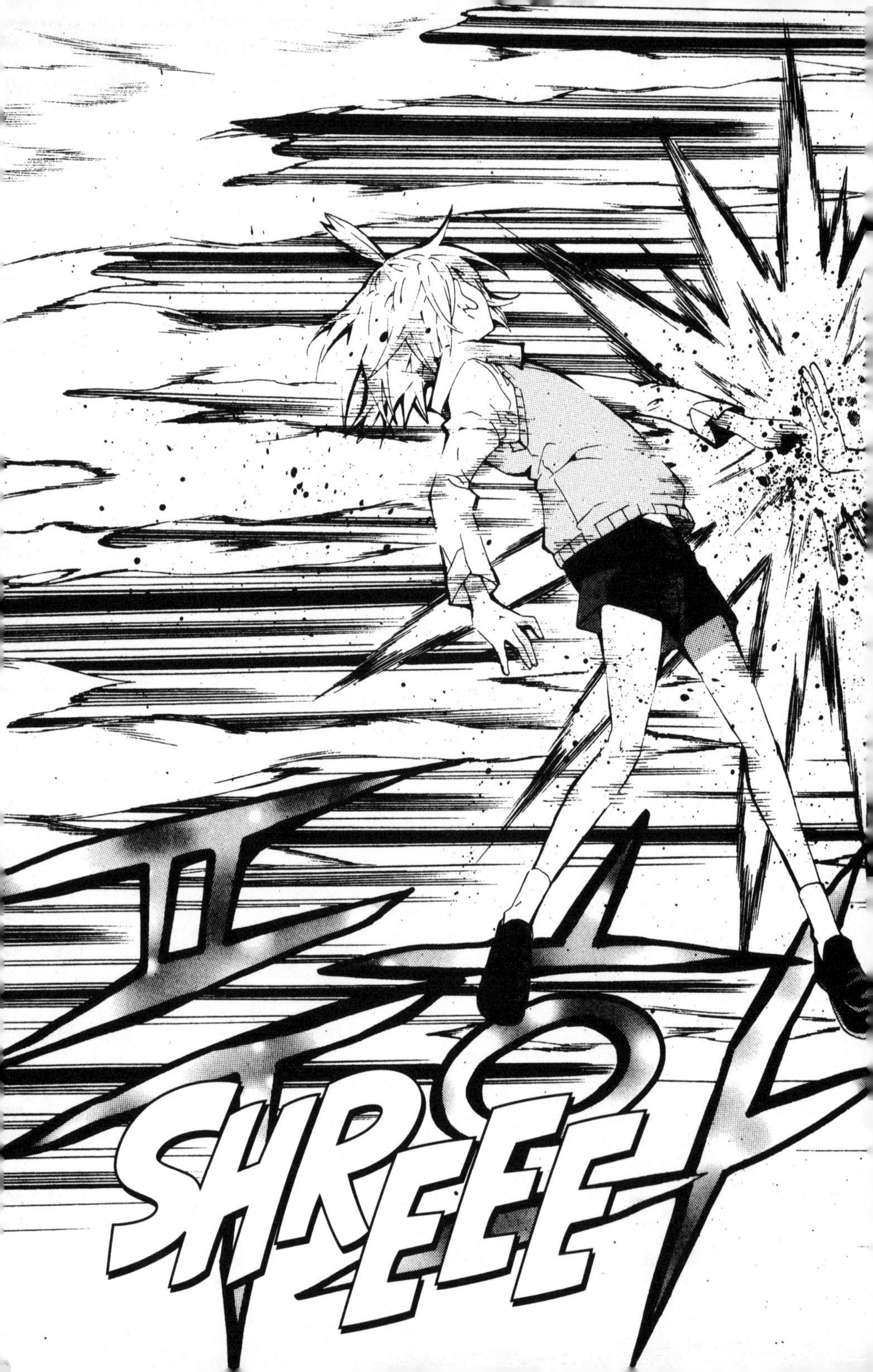
SHREEEK

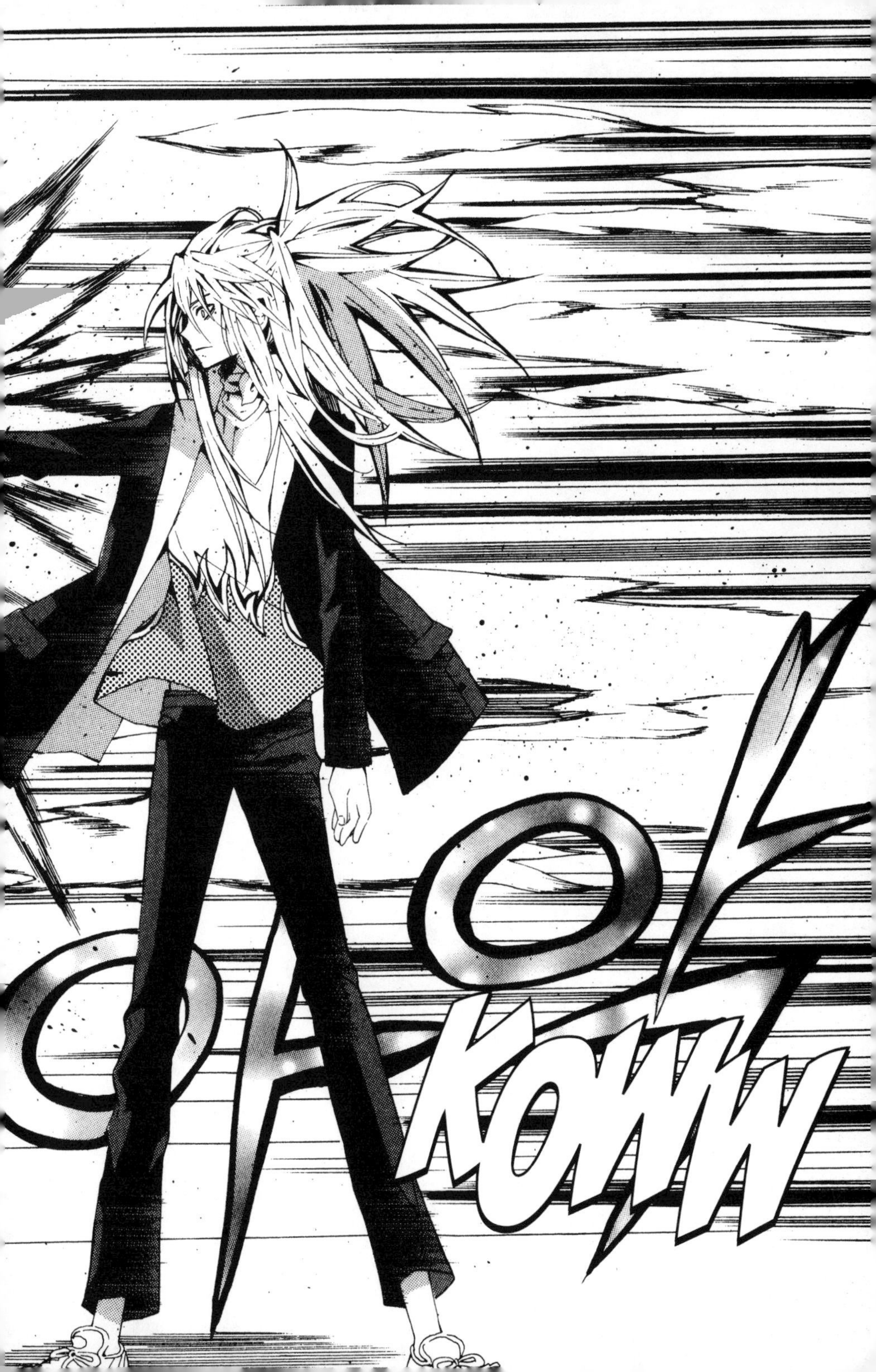
KOWW

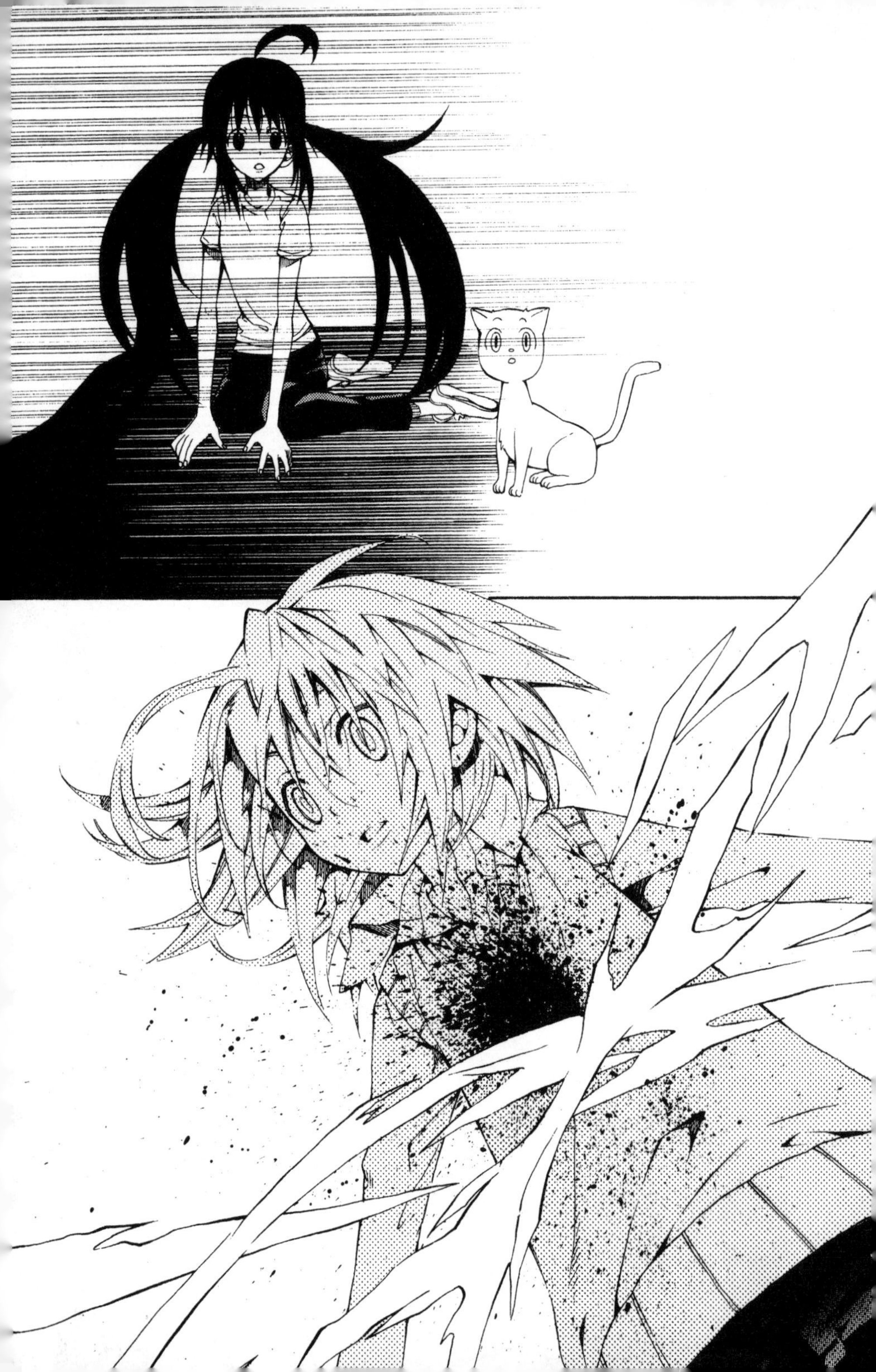

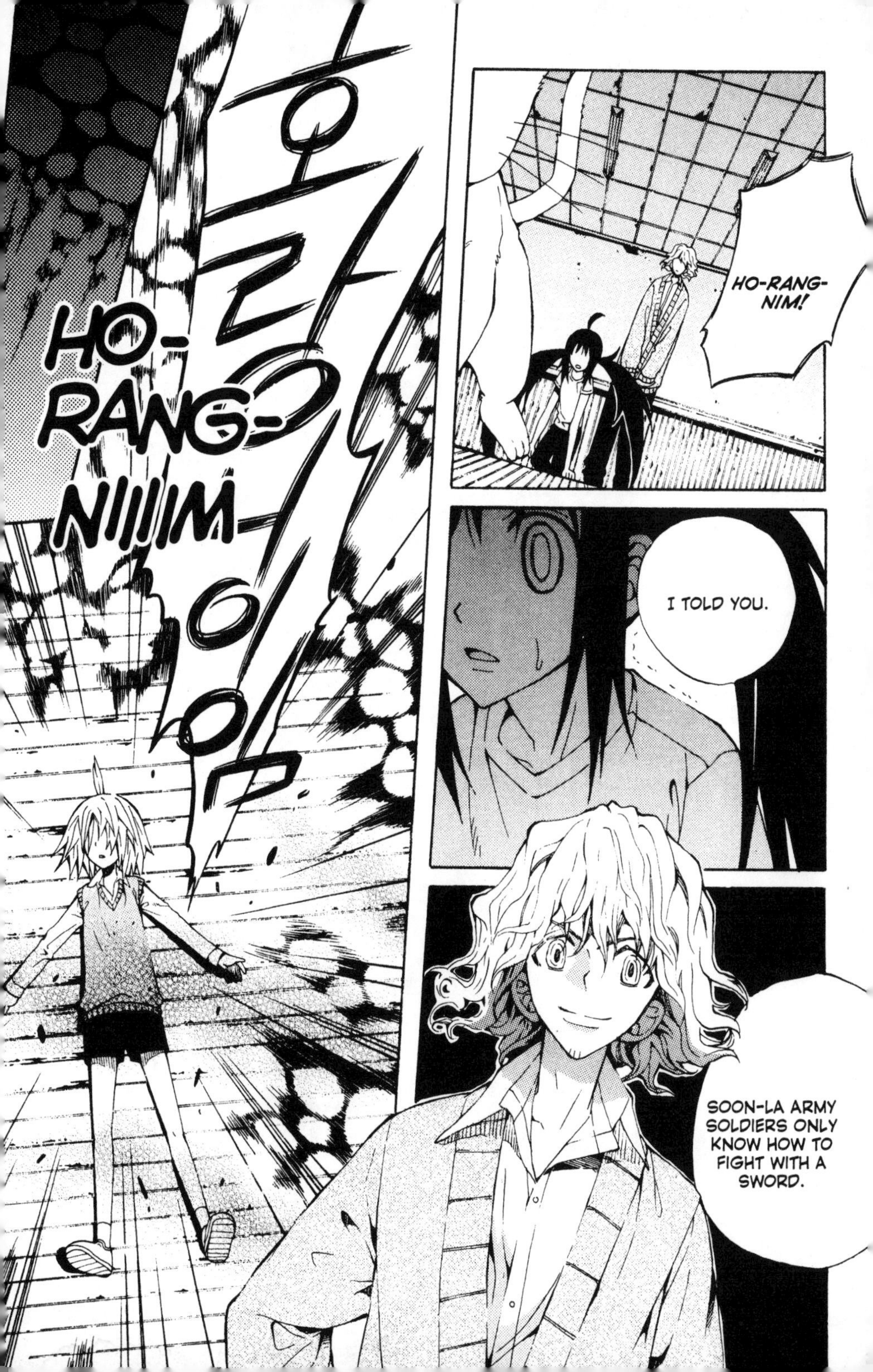
HO-RANG-NIIIIM
HO-RANG-NIM!
I TOLD YOU.
SOON-LA ARMY SOLDIERS ONLY KNOW HOW TO FIGHT WITH A SWORD.

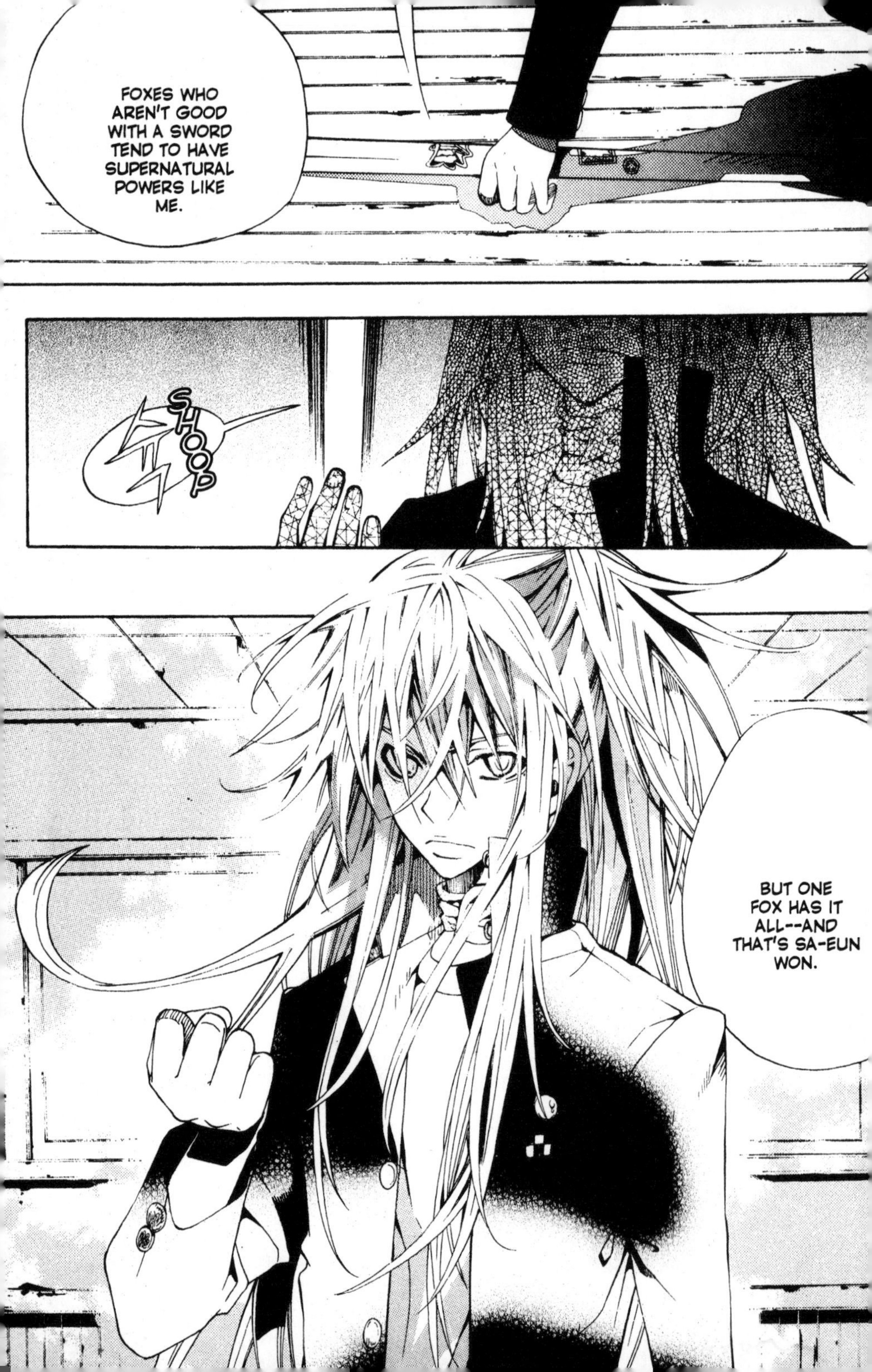
FOXES WHO AREN'T GOOD WITH A SWORD TEND TO HAVE SUPERNATURAL POWERS LIKE ME.
SHOOP
BUT ONE FOX HAS IT ALL--AND THAT'S SA-EUN WON.

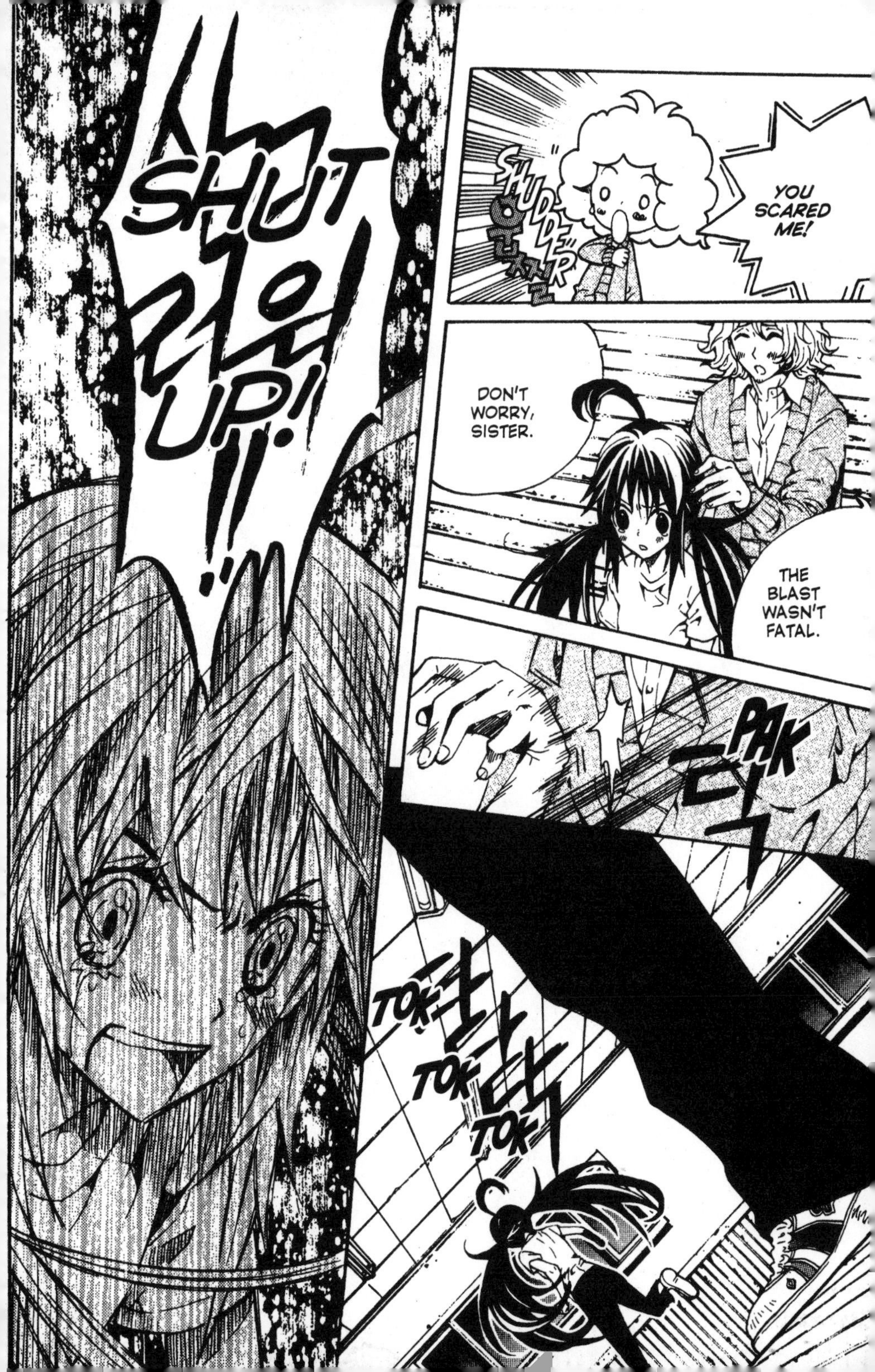
SHUT UP!!
SHUDDER
YOU SCARED ME!
DON'T WORRY, SISTER.
THE BLAST WASN'T FATAL.
PAK
TOK
TOK
TOK

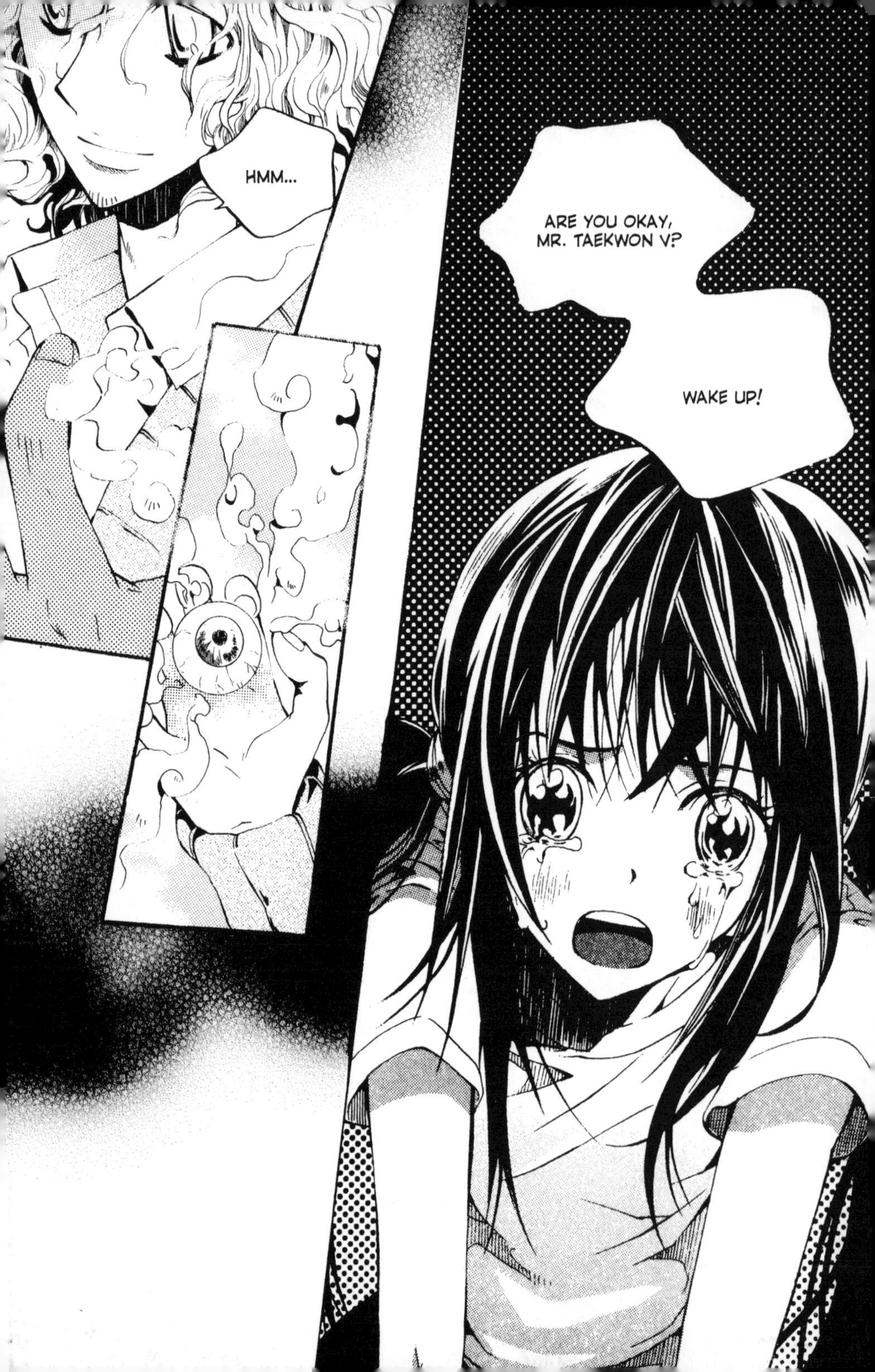
HMM...
ARE YOU OKAY, MR. TAEKWON V?
WAKE UP!

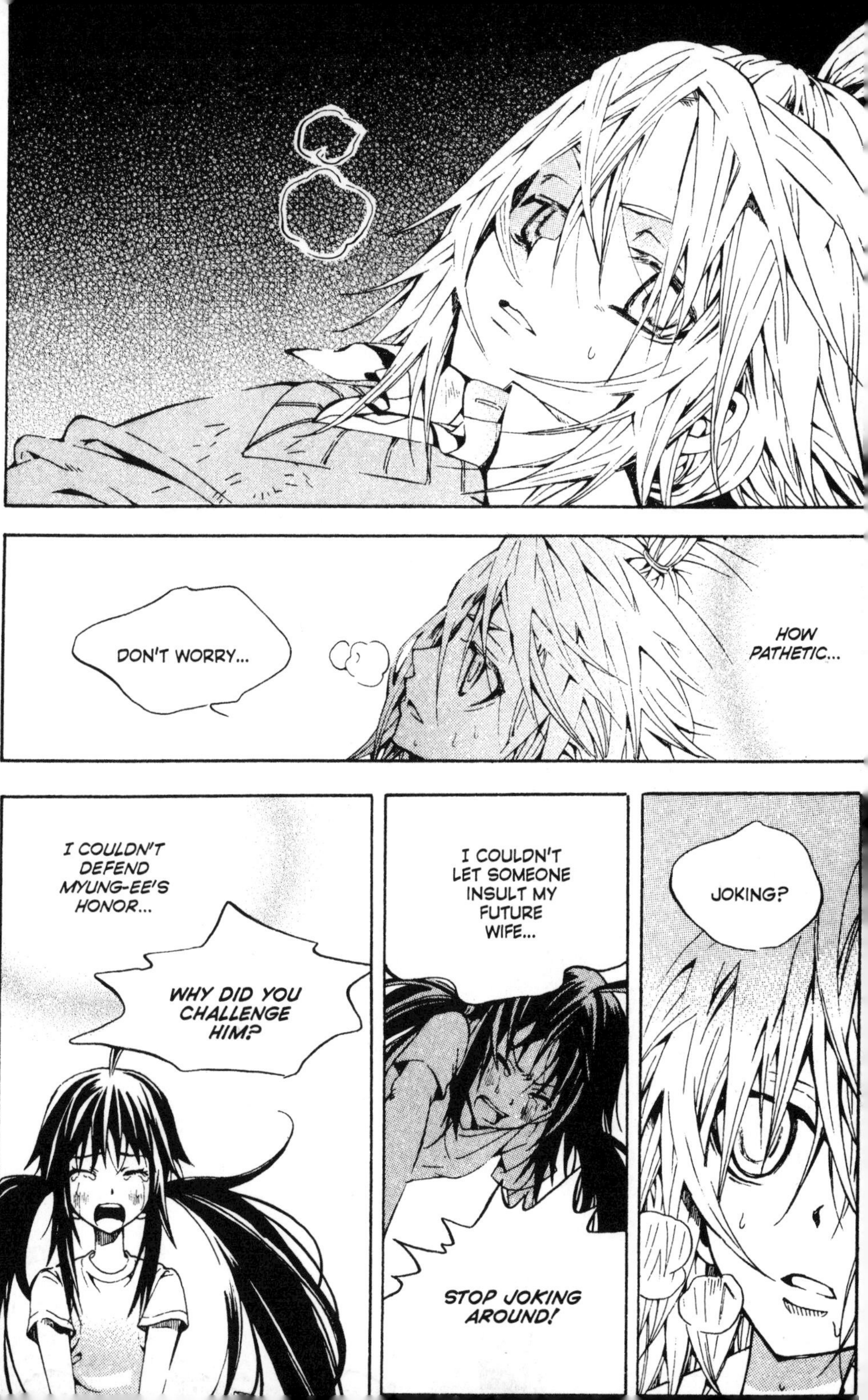
DON'T WORRY...
HOW PATHETIC...
I COULDN'T DEFEND MYUNG-EE'S HONOR...
WHY DID YOU CHALLENGE HIM?
I COULDN'T LET SOMEONE INSULT MY FUTURE WIFE...
STOP JOKING AROUND!
JOKING?

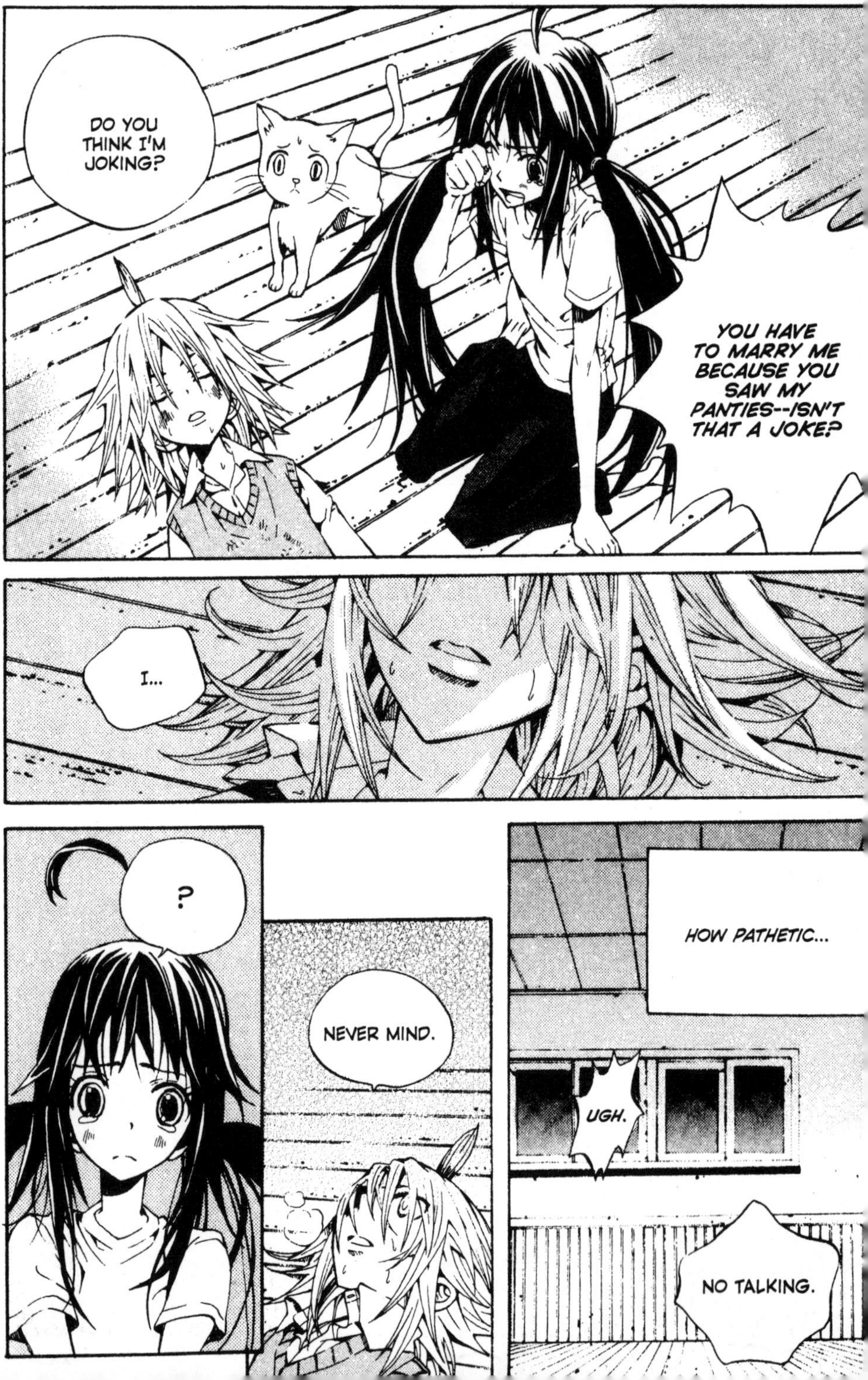
DO YOU THINK I'M JOKING?
YOU HAVE TO MARRY ME BECAUSE YOU SAW MY PANTIES--ISN'T THAT A JOKE?
I...
?
NEVER MIND.
HOW PATHETIC...
UGH.
NO TALKING.

WHAT'S WRONG WITH ME?

I DIDN'T EVEN REALIZE MY OWN FEELINGS...AND NOW...

MR. TAEKWON V IS HURT BECAUSE OF ME...

WHILE I WAS FIGHTING TO KEEP HER HONOR...

I'M WORRIED ABOUT HIM BUT I CAN'T STOP THINKING...

...AFTER I BECAME HURT AND USELESS.

...ABOUT THAT COLD EXPRESSION ON YU-DA'S FACE.

...I REALIZED HOW I FEEL ABOUT HER...

I'M A BAD PERSON.

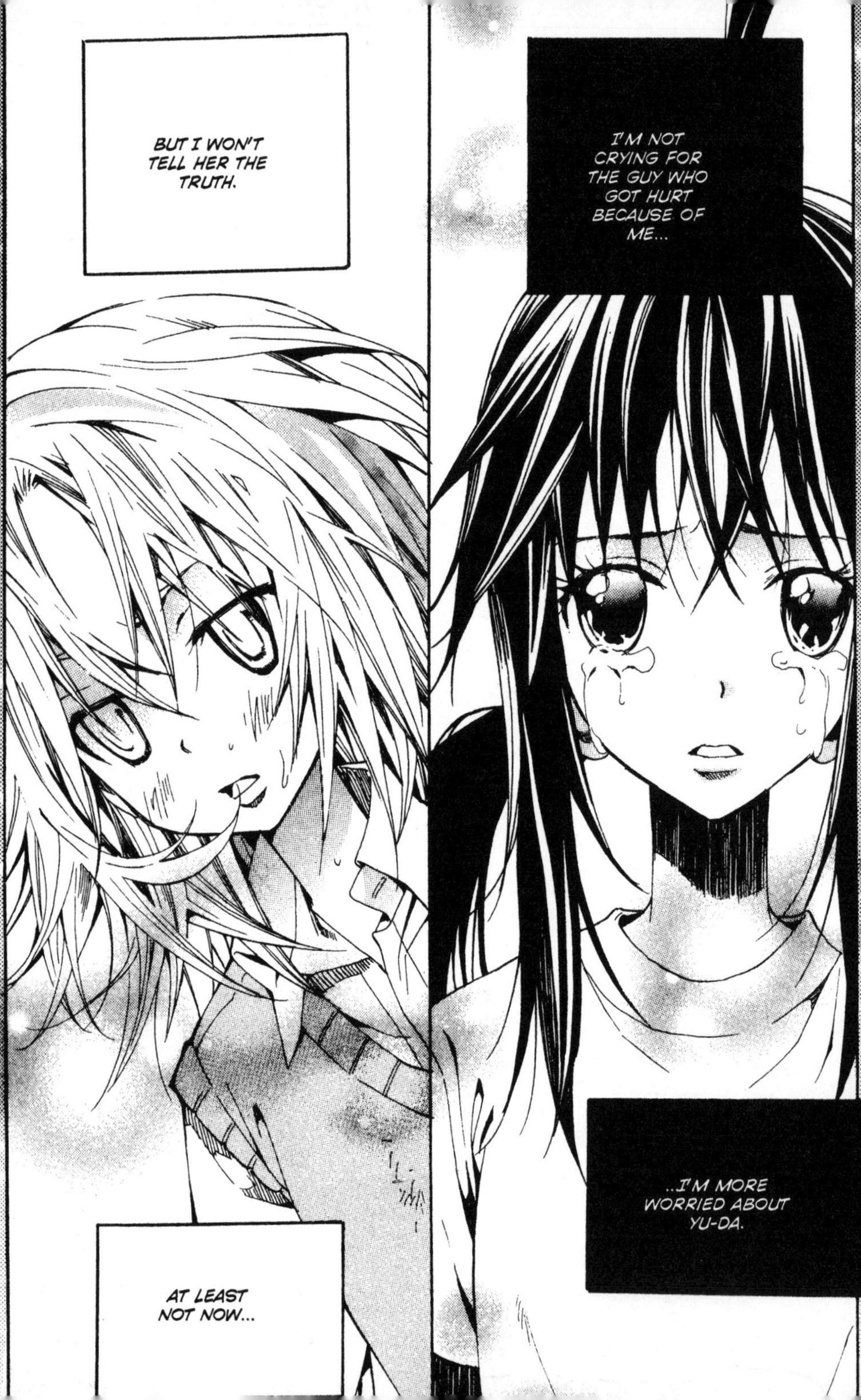
BUT I WON'T TELL HER THE TRUTH.
AT LEAST NOT NOW...
I'M NOT CRYING FOR THE GUY WHO GOT HURT BECAUSE OF ME...
..I'M MORE WORRIED ABOUT YU-DA.

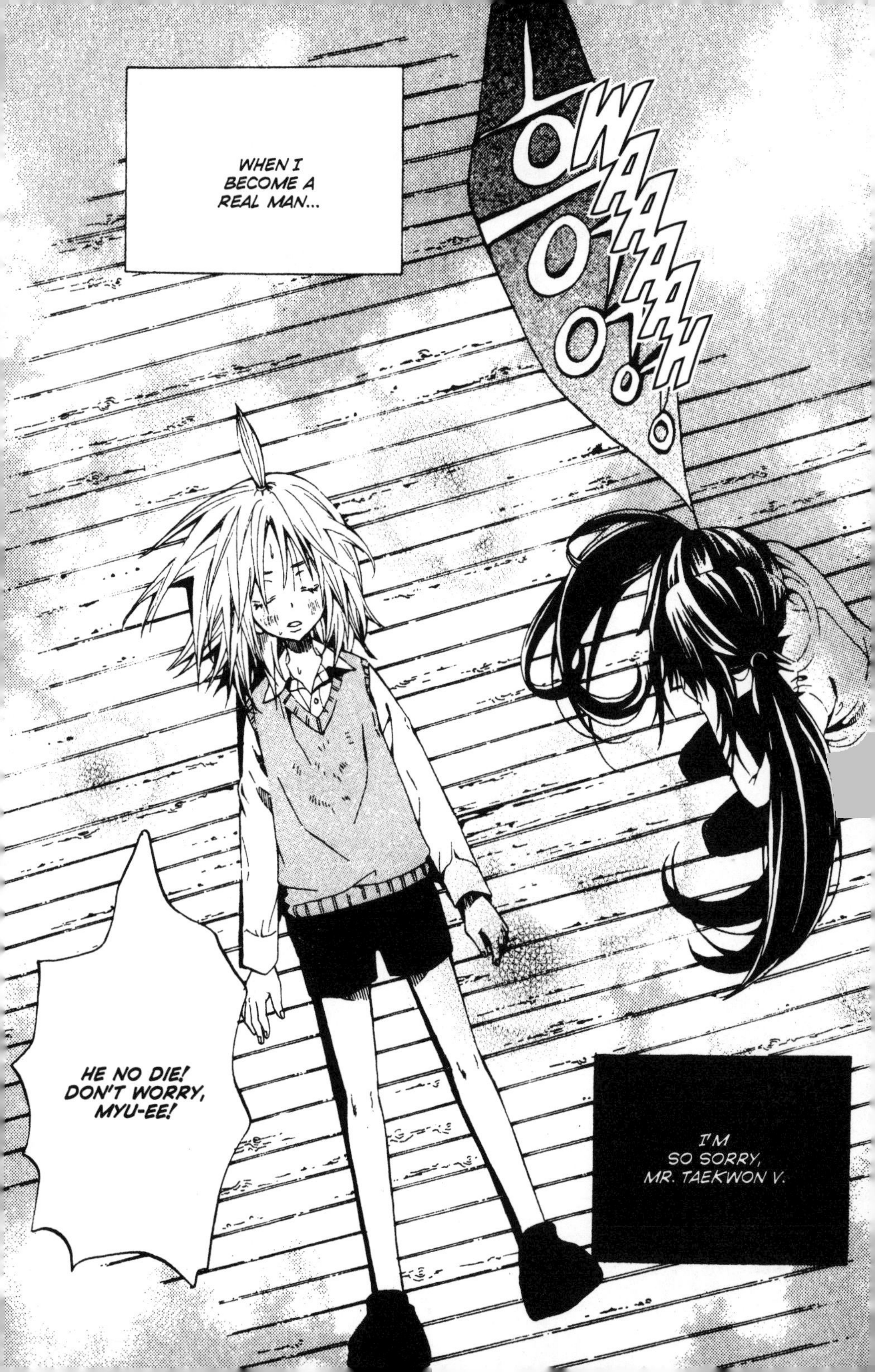
WHEN I BECOME A REAL MAN...
OWAAAAHH OOOO
HE NO DIE! DON'T WORRY, MYU-EE!
I'M SO SORRY, MR. TAEKWON V.

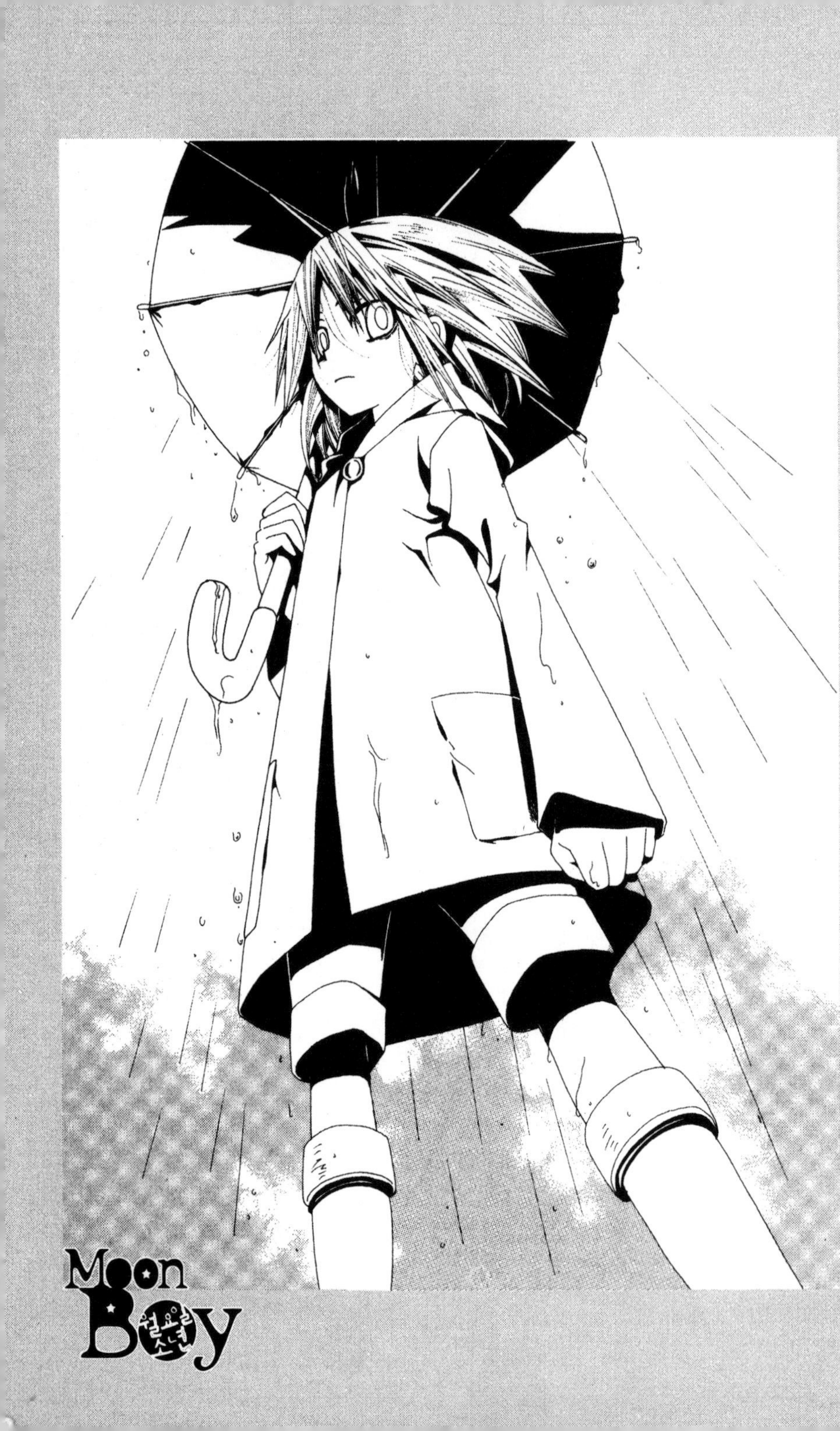

Moon Boy 월요일 소년

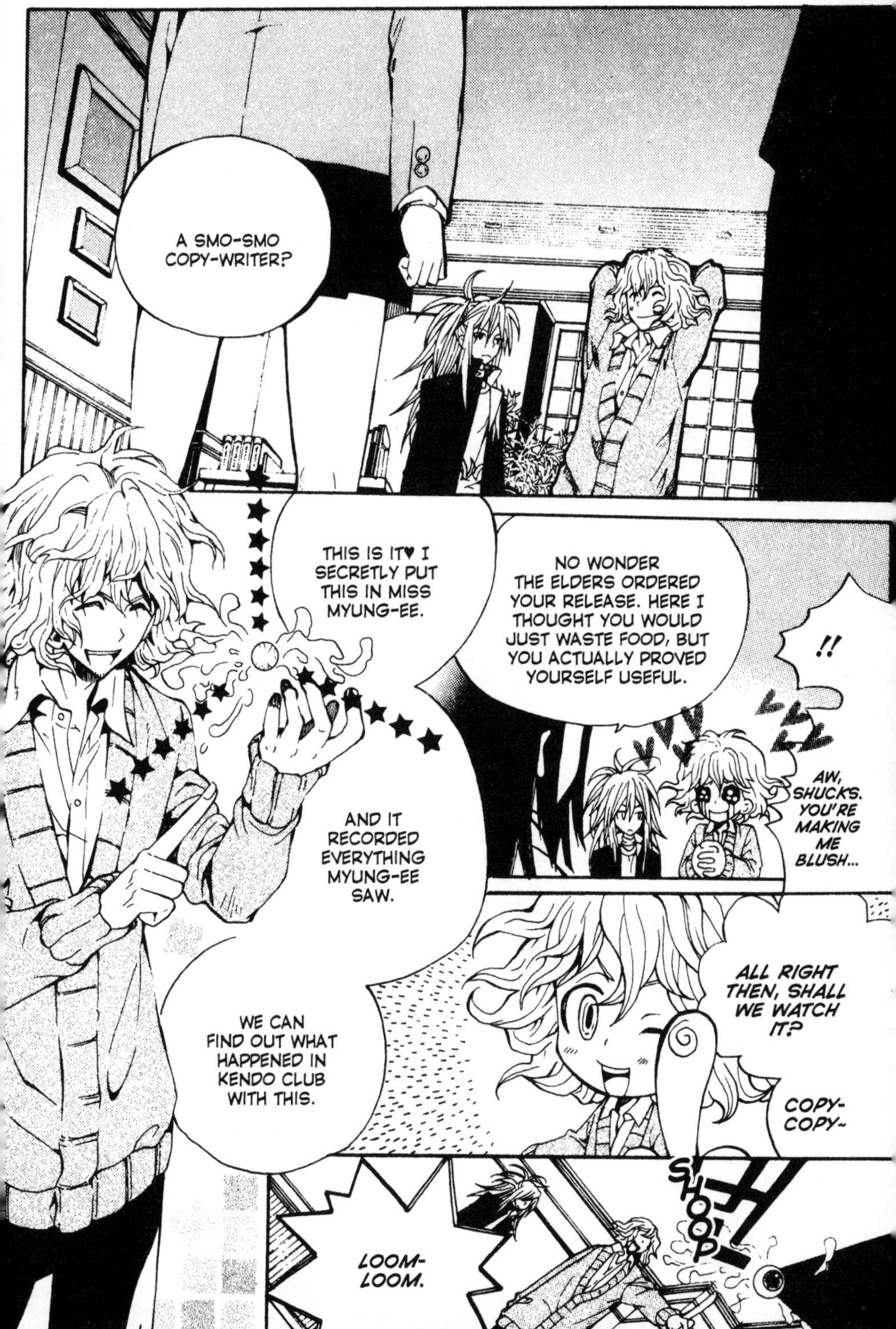
A SMO-SMO COPY-WRITER?
THIS IS IT♥ I SECRETLY PUT THIS IN MISS MYUNG-EE.
AND IT RECORDED EVERYTHING MYUNG-EE SAW.
WE CAN FIND OUT WHAT HAPPENED IN KENDO CLUB WITH THIS.
NO WONDER THE ELDERS ORDERED YOUR RELEASE. HERE I THOUGHT YOU WOULD JUST WASTE FOOD, BUT YOU ACTUALLY PROVED YOURSELF USEFUL.
!!
AW, SHUCKS. YOU'RE MAKING ME BLUSH...
ALL RIGHT THEN, SHALL WE WATCH IT?
COPY-COPY~
LOOM-LOOM.
SHOOP!

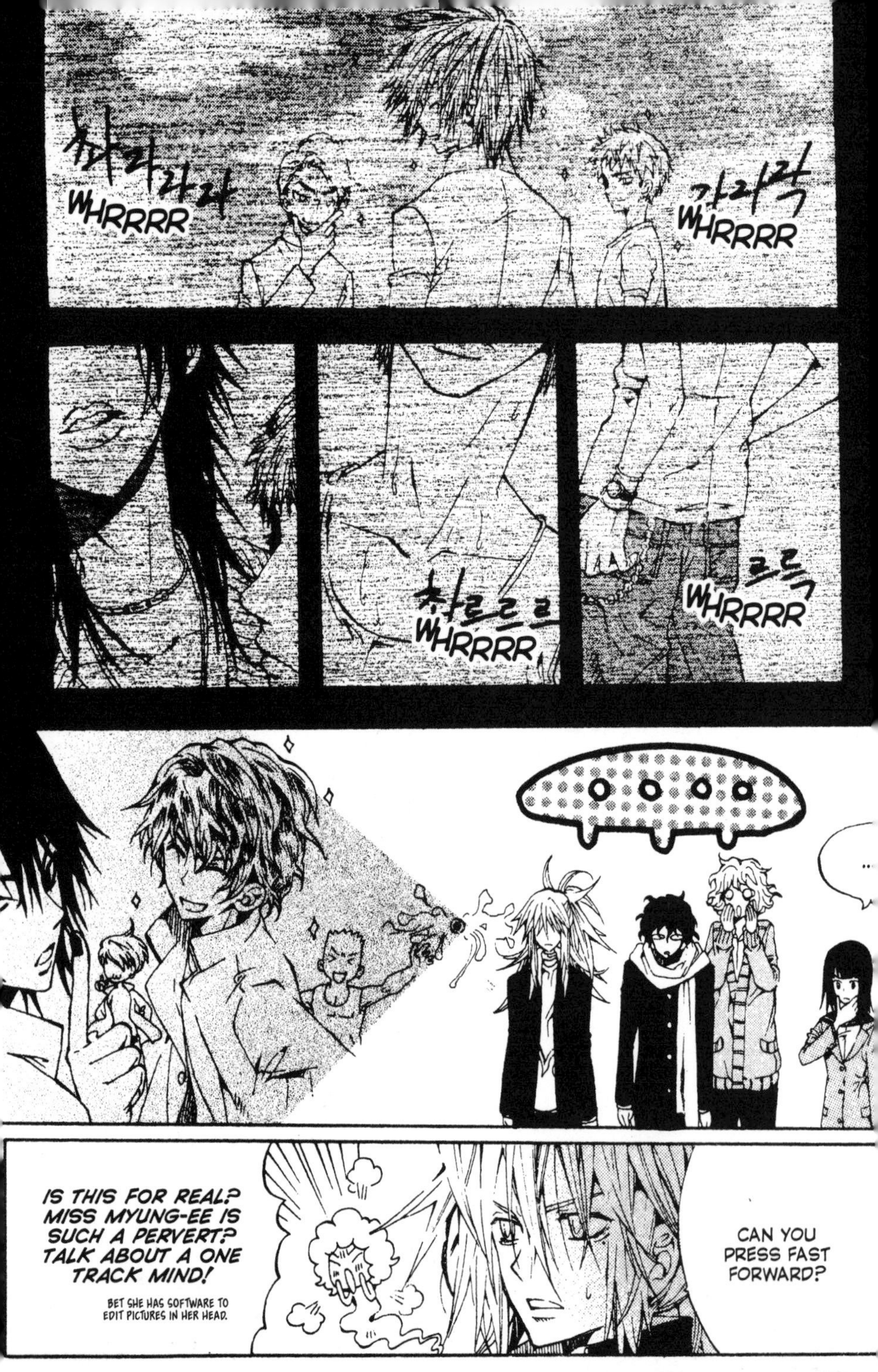
쏴라라라
WHRRRR
가라락
WHRRRR
차르르르
WHRRRR
크득
WHRRRR
...
IS THIS FOR REAL? MISS MYUNG-EE IS SUCH A PERVERT? TALK ABOUT A ONE TRACK MIND!
BET SHE HAS SOFTWARE TO EDIT PICTURES IN HER HEAD.
CAN YOU PRESS FAST FORWARD?

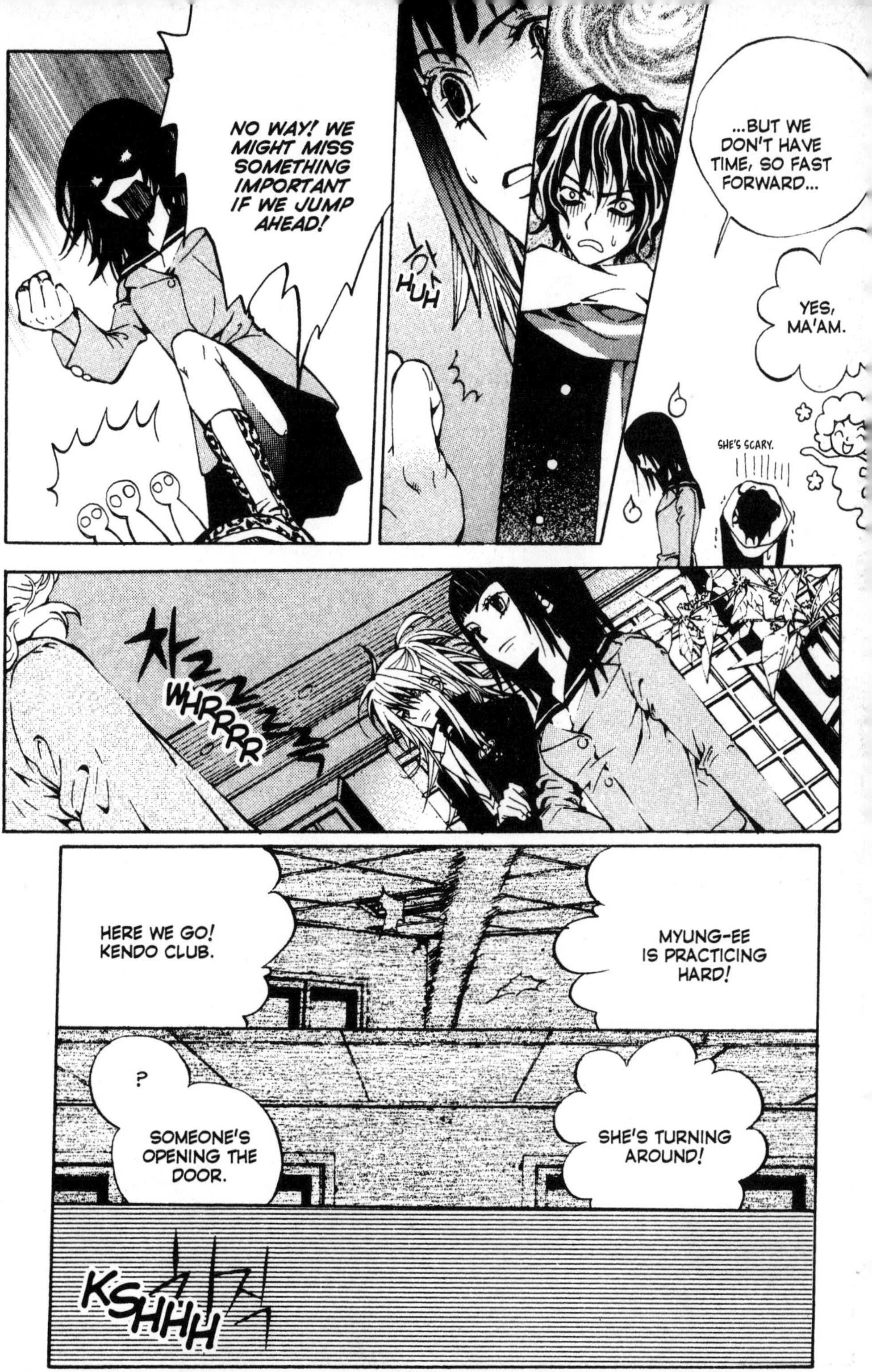
NO WAY! WE MIGHT MISS SOMETHING IMPORTANT IF WE JUMP AHEAD!
HUH
...BUT WE DON'T HAVE TIME, SO FAST FORWARD...
YES, MA'AM.
SHE'S SCARY.
WHRRRR
HERE WE GO! KENDO CLUB.
MYUNG-EE IS PRACTICING HARD!
?
SOMEONE'S OPENING THE DOOR.
SHE'S TURNING AROUND!
KSHHHH

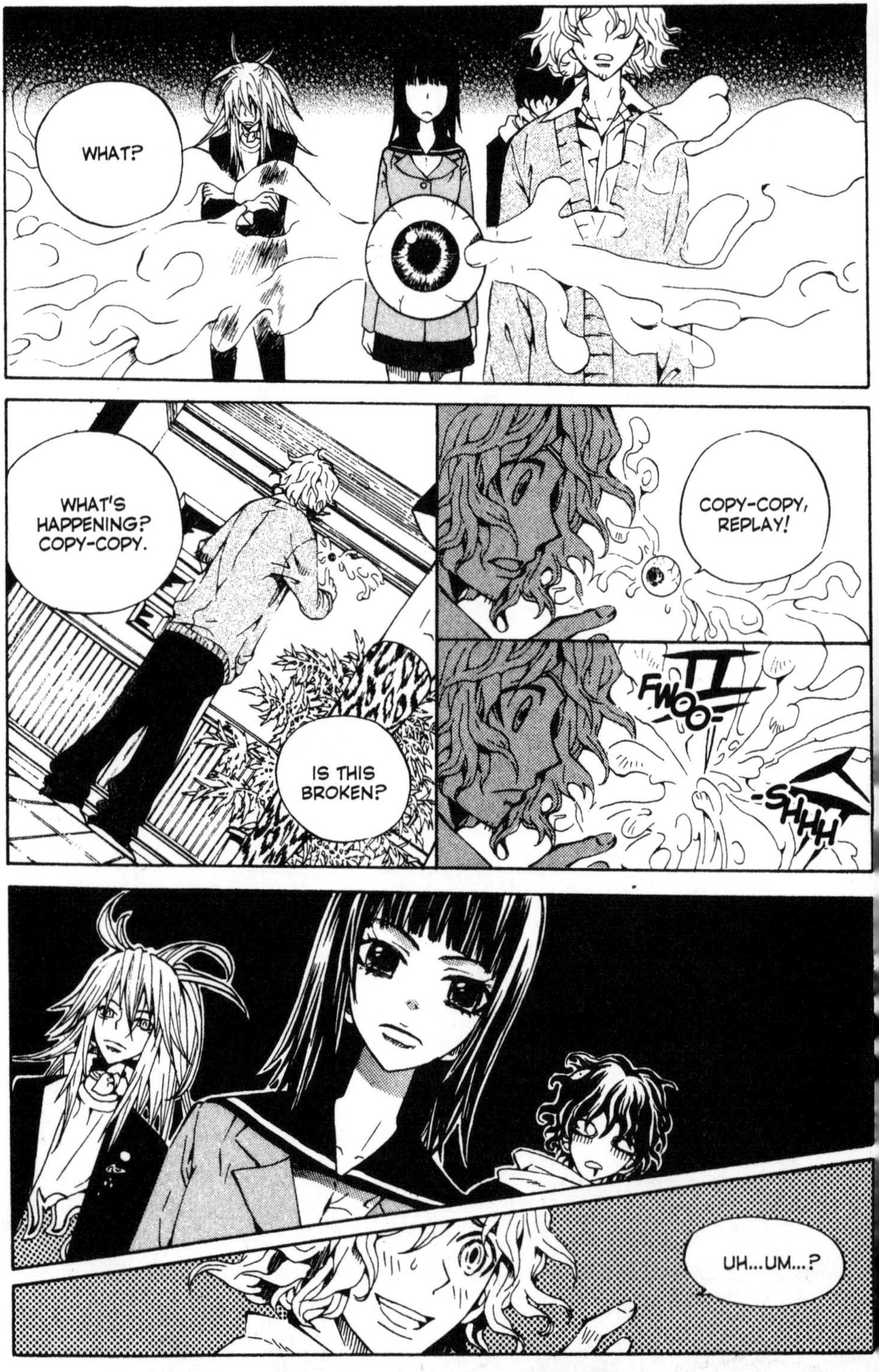
WHAT?
WHAT'S HAPPENING? COPY-COPY.
IS THIS BROKEN?
COPY-COPY, REPLAY!
FWOO-
-SHHH
UH...UM...?

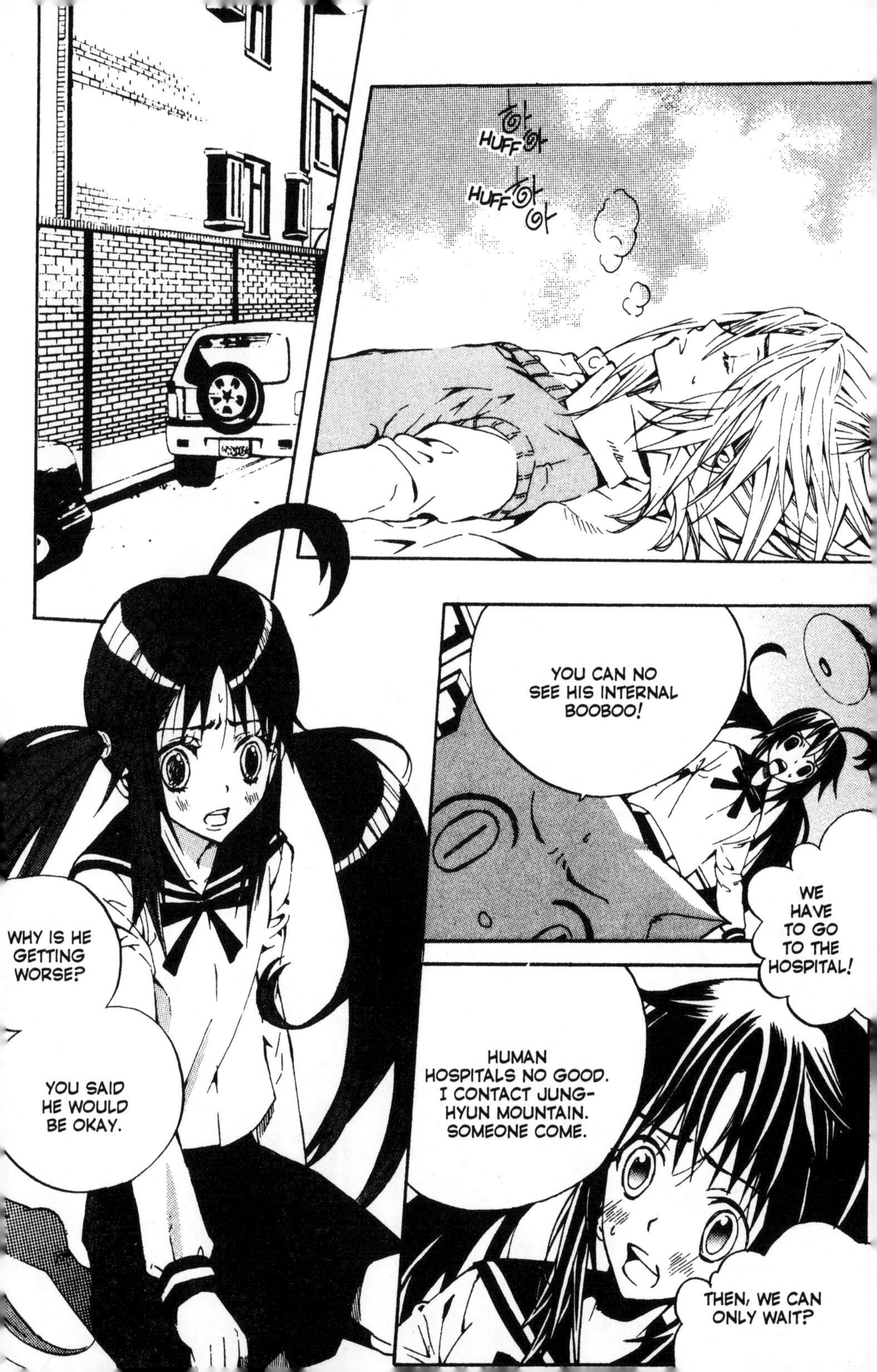
HUFF
HUFF
WHY IS HE GETTING WORSE?
YOU SAID HE WOULD BE OKAY.
YOU CAN NO SEE HIS INTERNAL BOOBOO!
WE HAVE TO GO TO THE HOSPITAL!
HUMAN HOSPITALS NO GOOD. I CONTACT JUNG-HYUN MOUNTAIN. SOMEONE COME.
THEN, WE CAN ONLY WAIT?

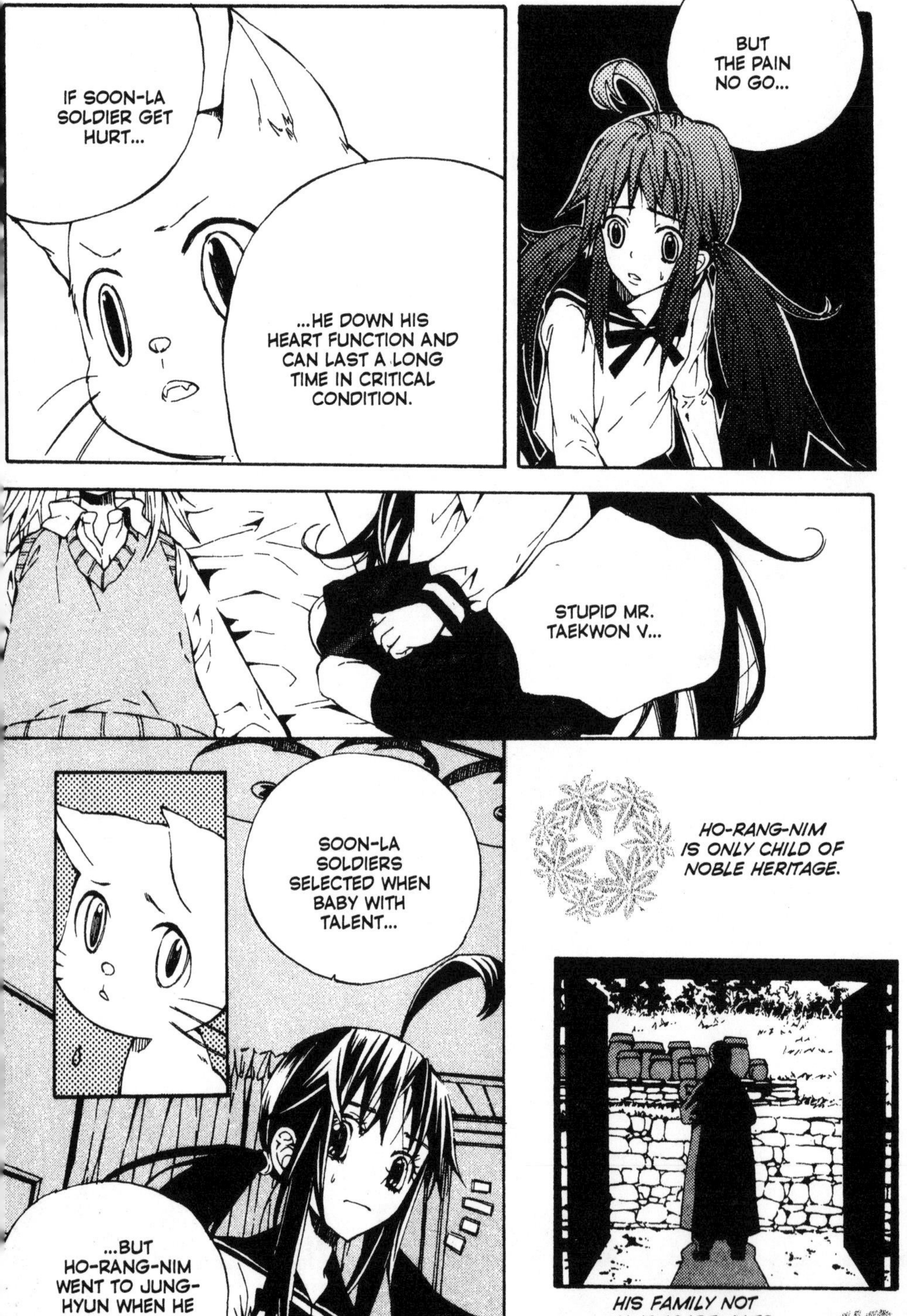
IF SOON-LA SOLDIER GET HURT...
...HE DOWN HIS HEART FUNCTION AND CAN LAST A LONG TIME IN CRITICAL CONDITION.
BUT THE PAIN NO GO...
STUPID MR. TAEKWON V...
SOON-LA SOLDIERS SELECTED WHEN BABY WITH TALENT...
...BUT HO-RANG-NIM WENT TO JUNG-HYUN WHEN HE WAS 7.
HO-RANG-NIM IS ONLY CHILD OF NOBLE HERITAGE.
HIS FAMILY NOT WANT ACADEMY TO TAKE HIM.

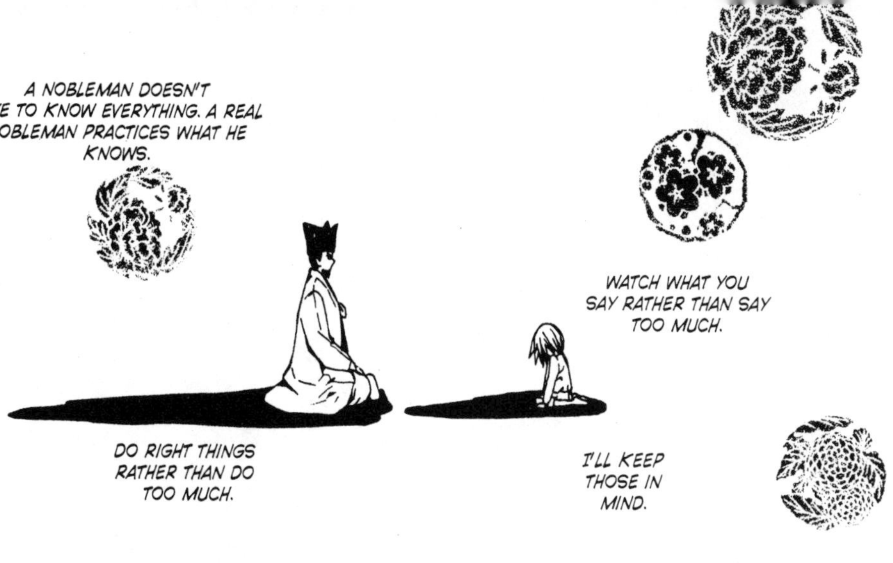
A NOBLEMAN DOESN'T HAVE TO KNOW EVERYTHING. A REAL NOBLEMAN PRACTICES WHAT HE KNOWS.
WATCH WHAT YOU SAY RATHER THAN SAY TOO MUCH.
DO RIGHT THINGS RATHER THAN DO TOO MUCH.
I'LL KEEP THOSE IN MIND.

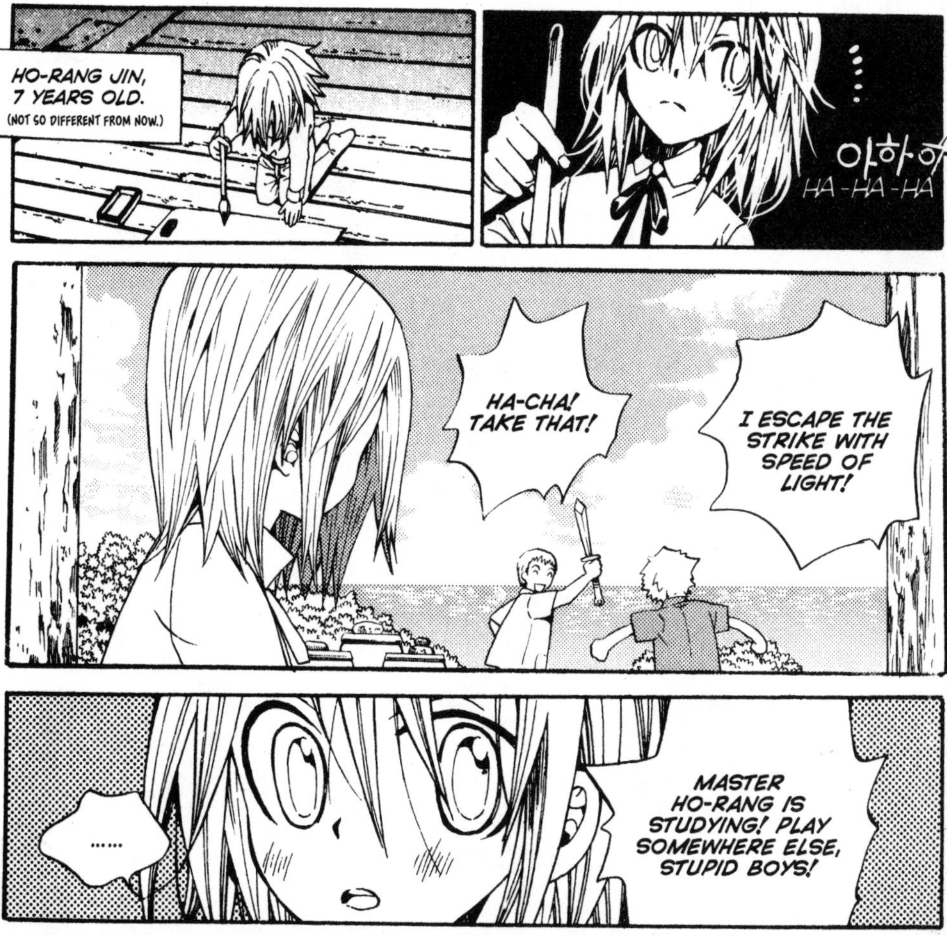
HO-RANG JIN, 7 YEARS OLD.
(NOT SO DIFFERENT FROM NOW.)
아하하
HA-HA-HA
HA-CHA! TAKE THAT!
I ESCAPE THE STRIKE WITH SPEED OF LIGHT!
......
MASTER HO-RANG IS STUDYING! PLAY SOMEWHERE ELSE, STUPID BOYS!

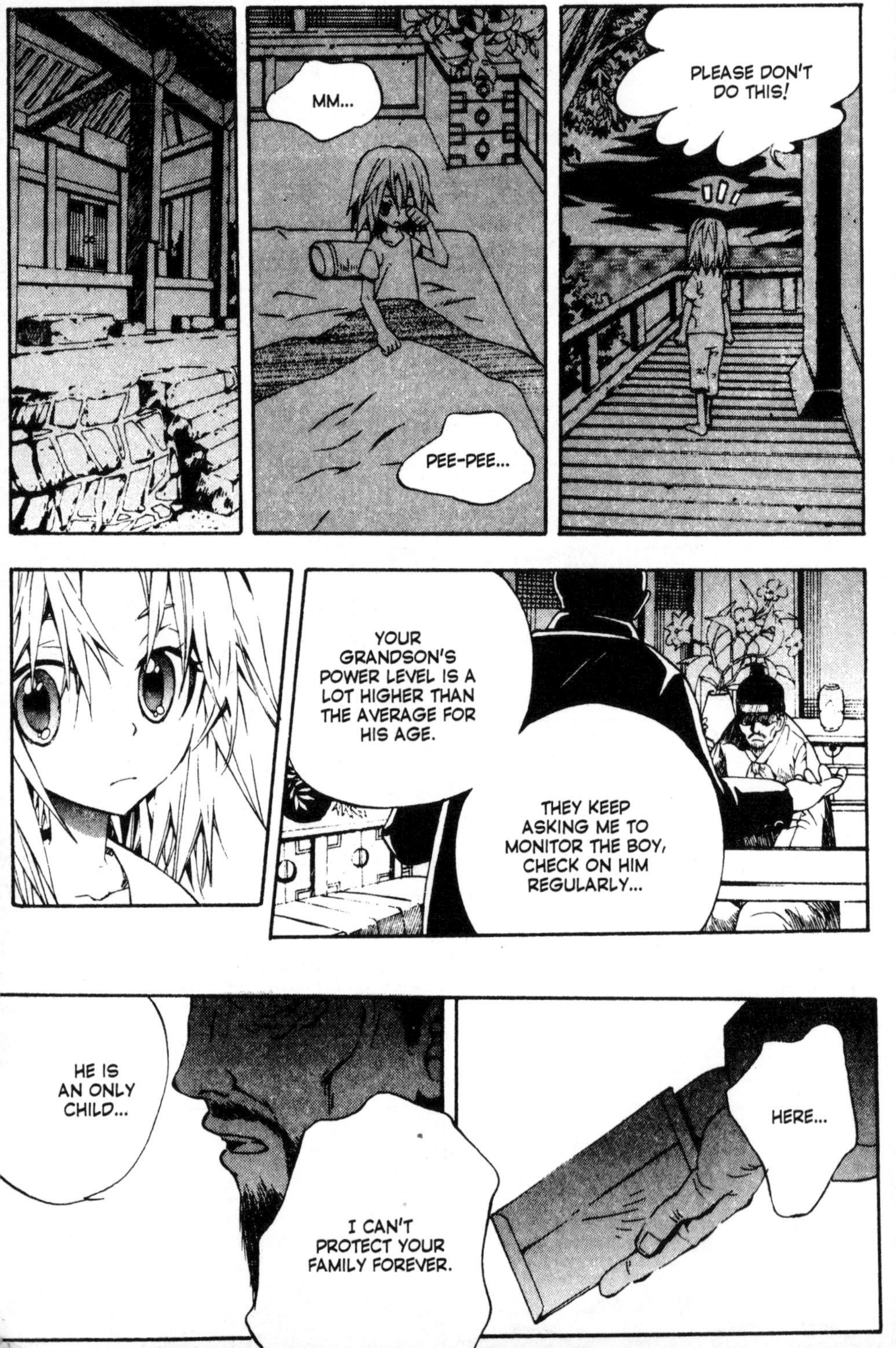
MM...
PEE-PEE...
PLEASE DON'T DO THIS!
YOUR GRANDSON'S POWER LEVEL IS A LOT HIGHER THAN THE AVERAGE FOR HIS AGE.
THEY KEEP ASKING ME TO MONITOR THE BOY, CHECK ON HIM REGULARLY...
HE IS AN ONLY CHILD...
I CAN'T PROTECT YOUR FAMILY FOREVER.
HERE...

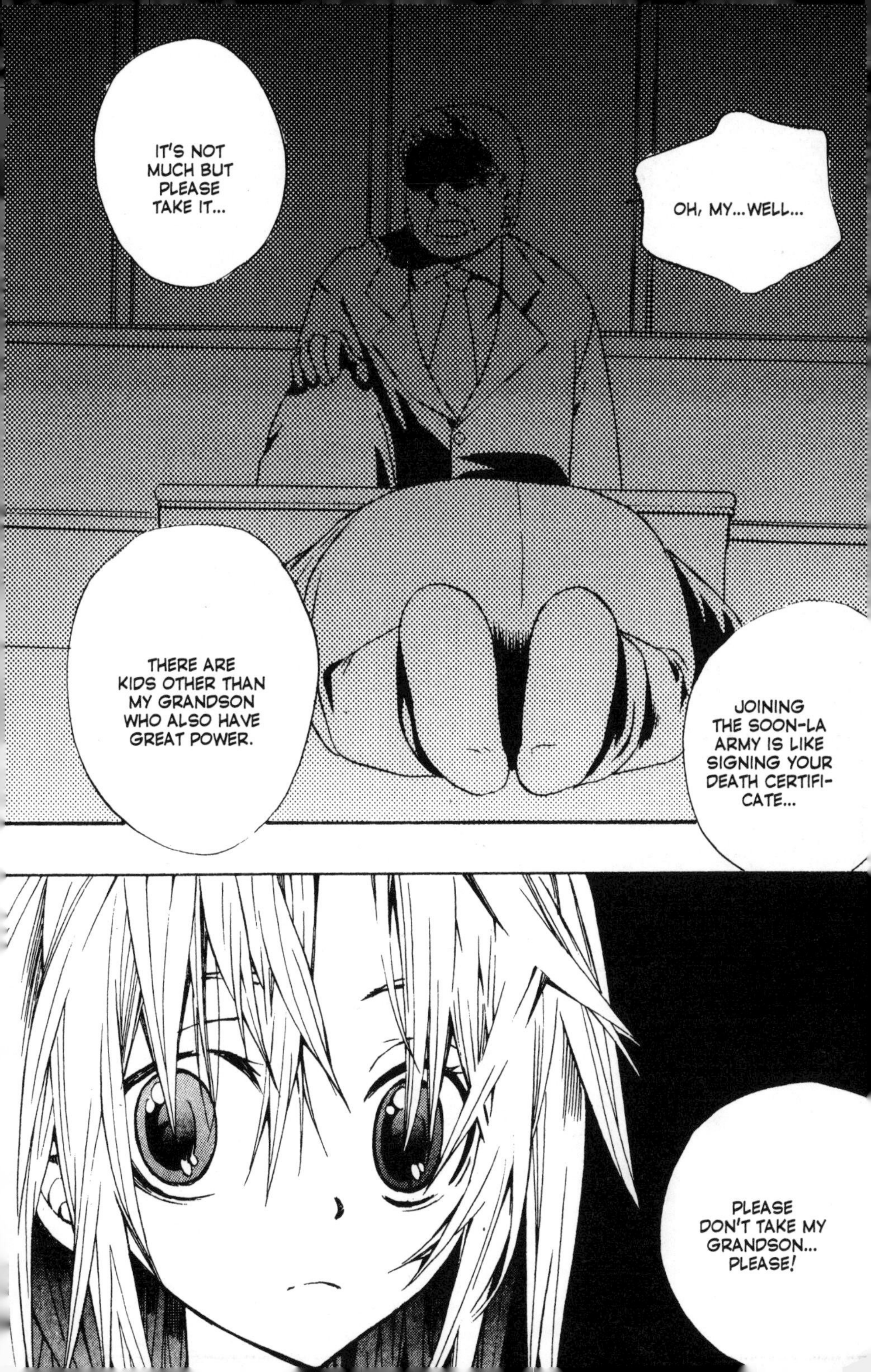
IT'S NOT MUCH BUT PLEASE TAKE IT...
OH, MY...WELL...
THERE ARE KIDS OTHER THAN MY GRANDSON WHO ALSO HAVE GREAT POWER.
JOINING THE SOON-LA ARMY IS LIKE SIGNING YOUR DEATH CERTIFI-CATE...
PLEASE DON'T TAKE MY GRANDSON... PLEASE!

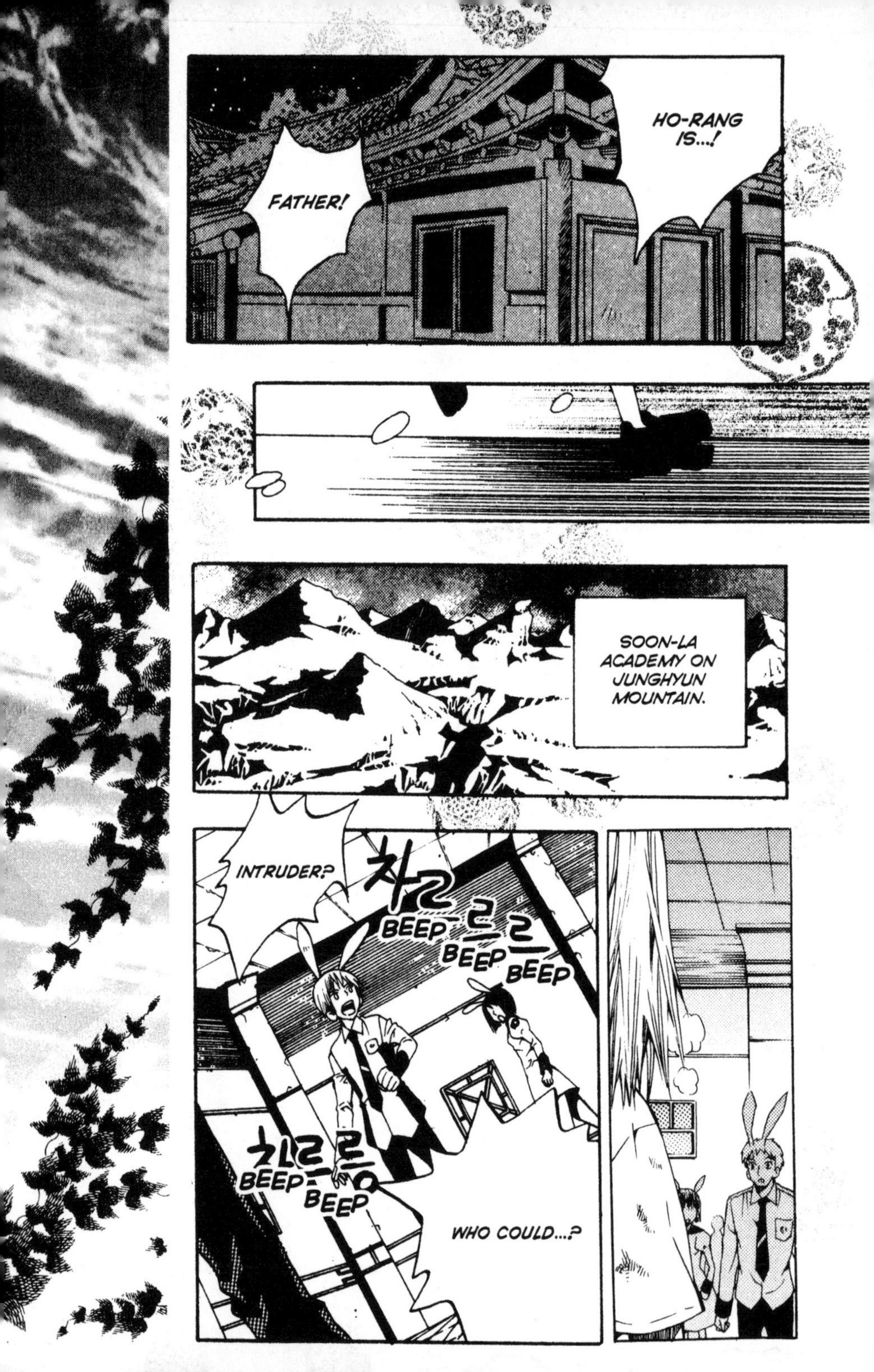
FATHER!
HO-RANG IS...!
SOON-LA ACADEMY ON JUNGHYUN MOUNTAIN.
INTRUDER?
BEEP BEEP BEEP
BEEP BEEP
WHO COULD...?

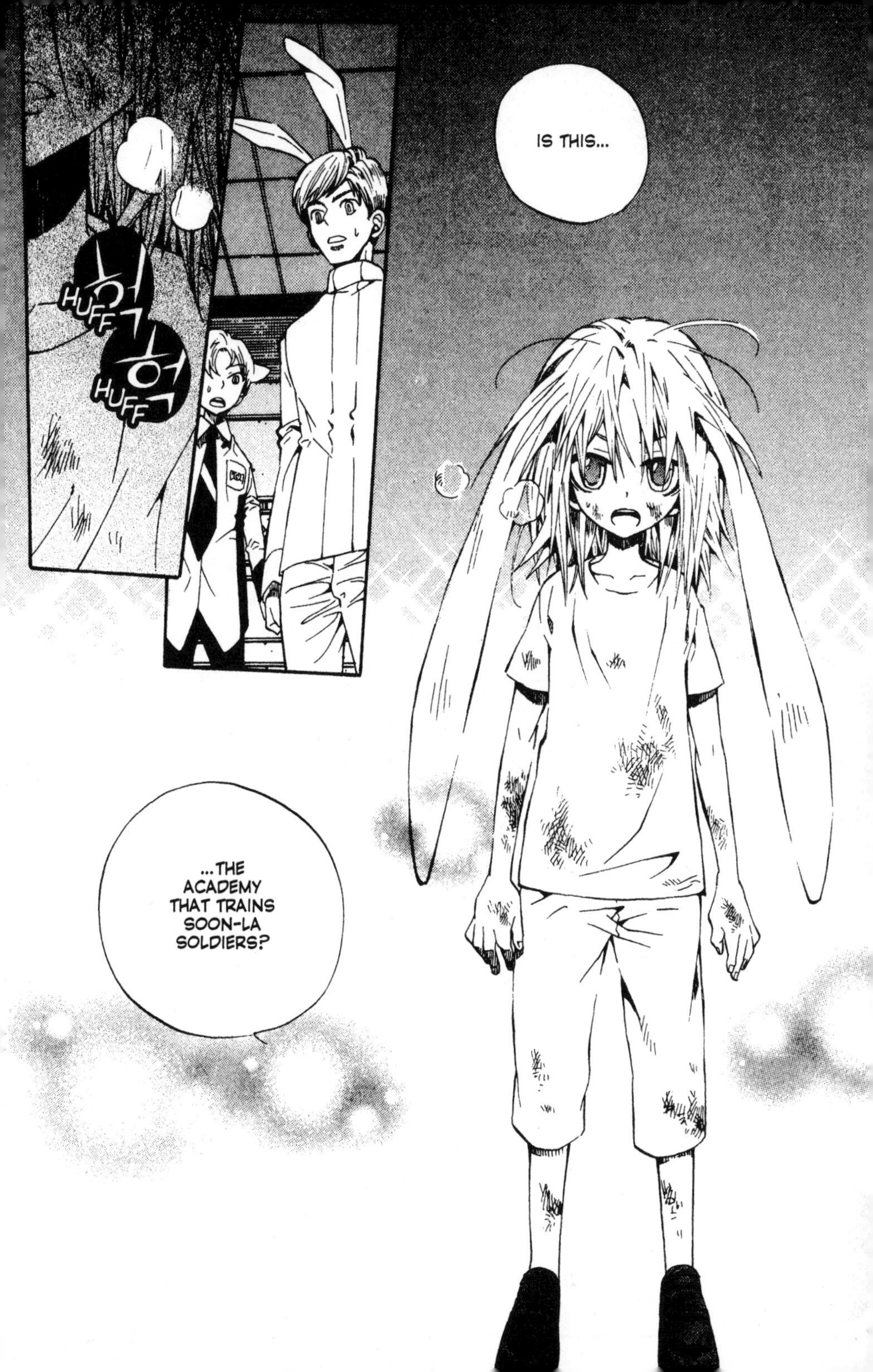
HUFF
HUFF
IS THIS...
...THE ACADEMY THAT TRAINS SOON-LA SOLDIERS?

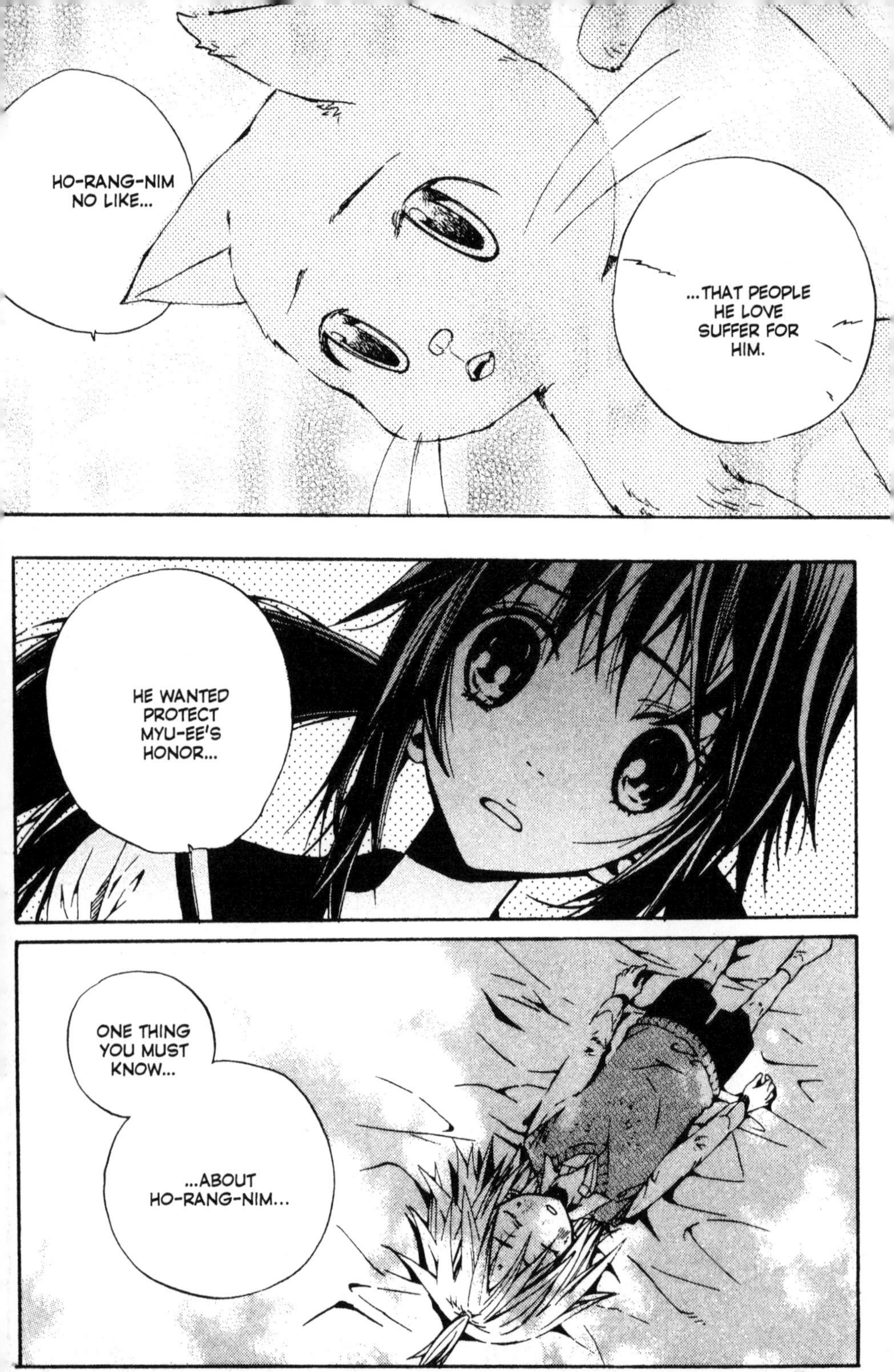
HO-RANG-NIM NO LIKE...
...THAT PEOPLE HE LOVE SUFFER FOR HIM.
HE WANTED PROTECT MYU-EE'S HONOR...
ONE THING YOU MUST KNOW...
...ABOUT HO-RANG-NIM...

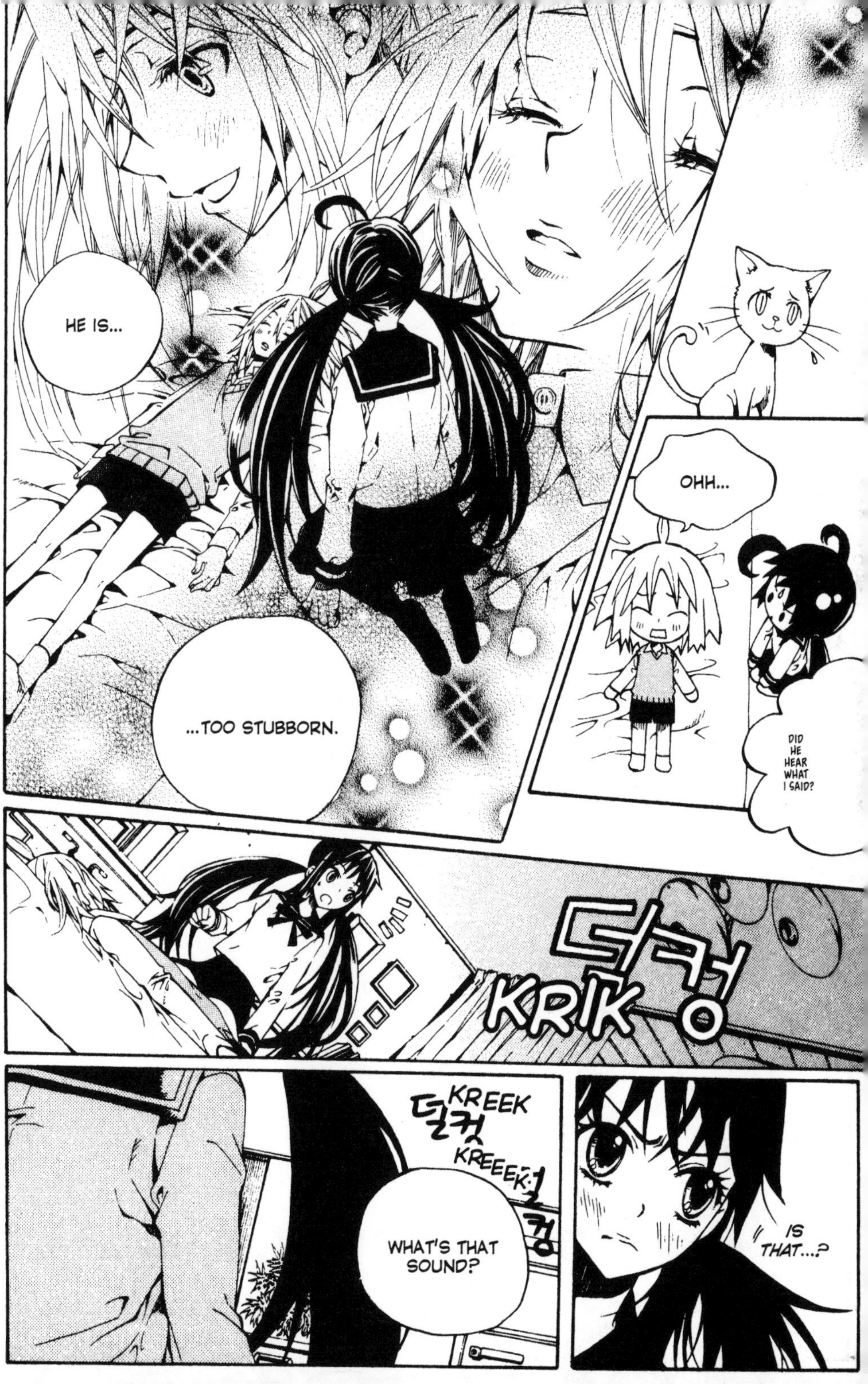
HE IS...
...TOO STUBBORN.
OHH...
DID HE HEAR WHAT I SAID?
덜컹
KRIK
덜컹
KREEK
KREEEK
WHAT'S THAT SOUND?
IS THAT...?

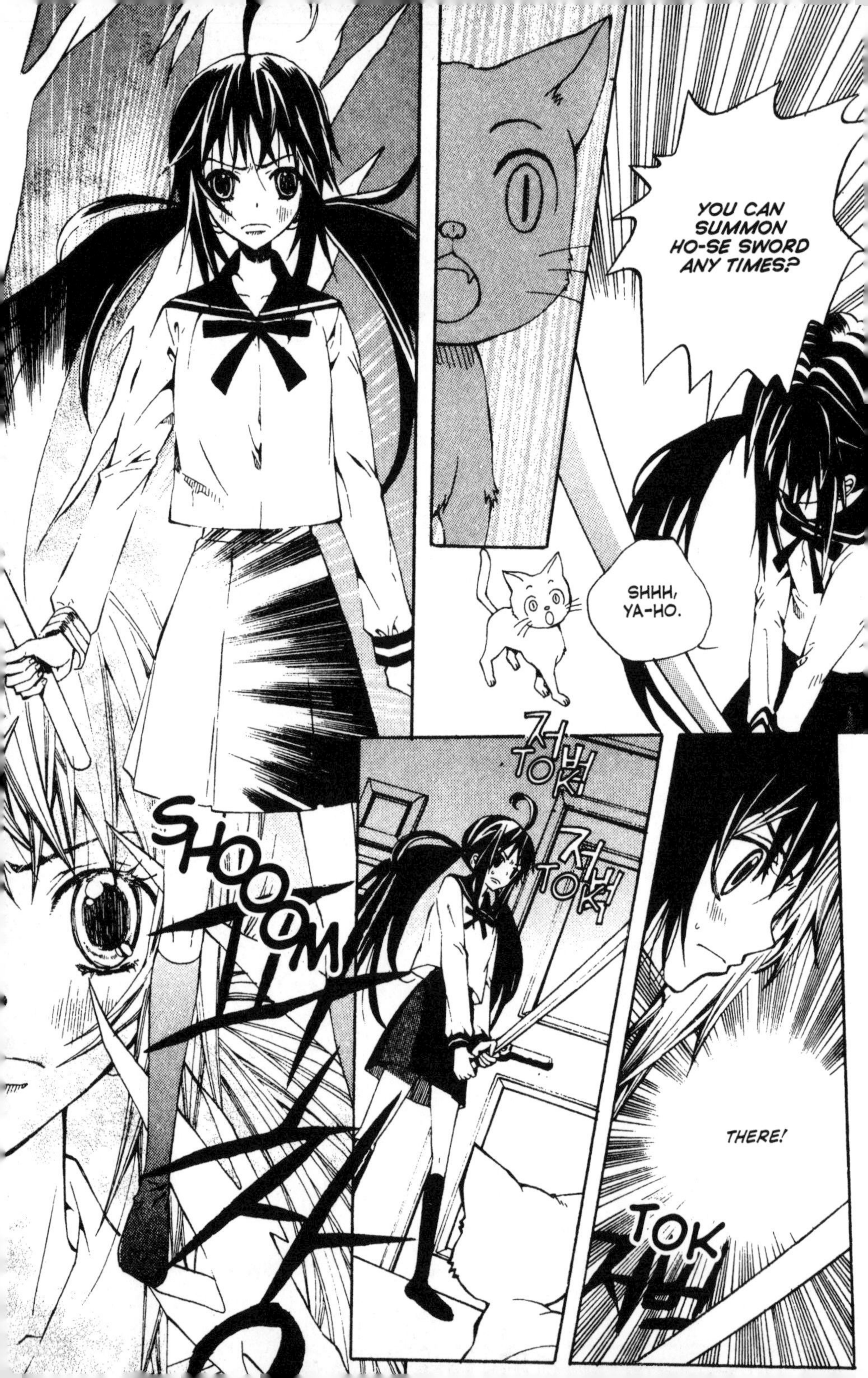
SHOOOOM
YOU CAN SUMMON HO-SE SWORD ANY TIMES?
SHHH, YA-HO.
저벅 TOK
저벅 TOK
THERE!
TOK 저벅

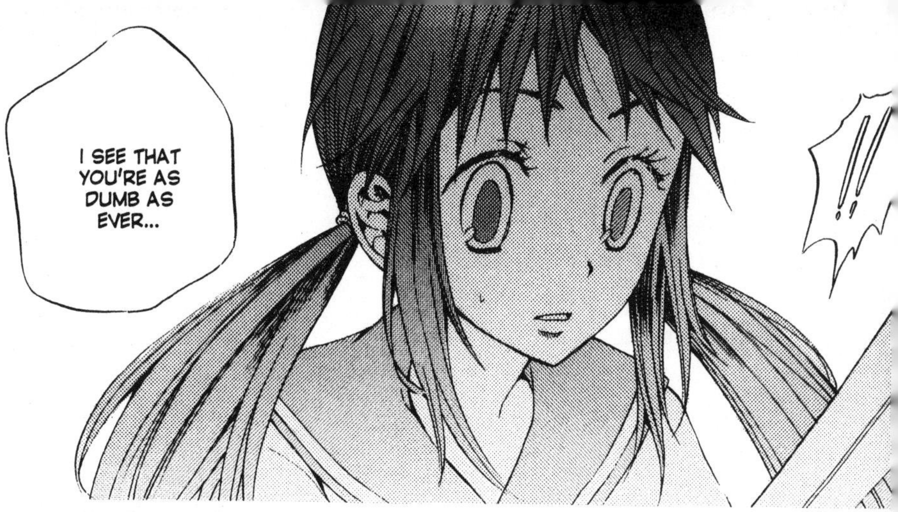
I SEE THAT YOU'RE AS DUMB AS EVER...
!!

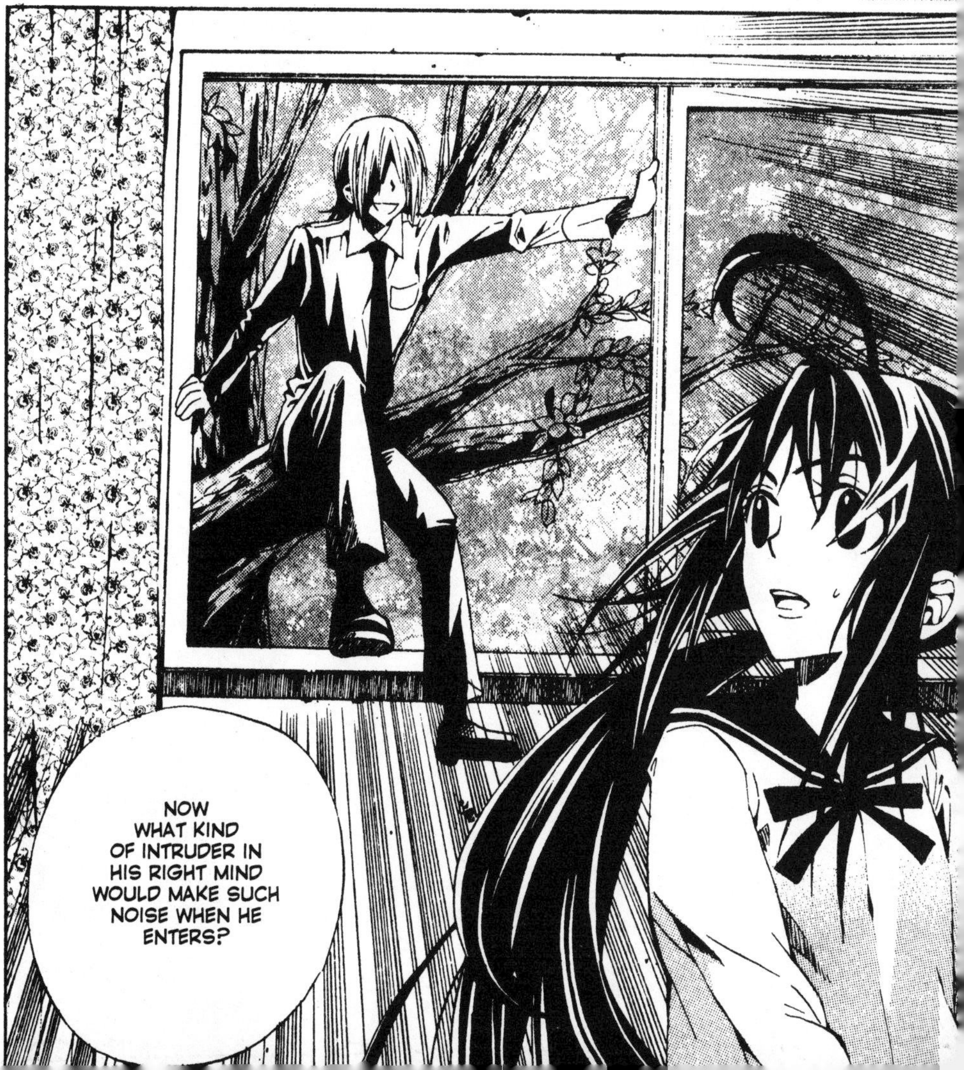
NOW WHAT KIND OF INTRUDER IN HIS RIGHT MIND WOULD MAKE SUCH NOISE WHEN HE ENTERS?

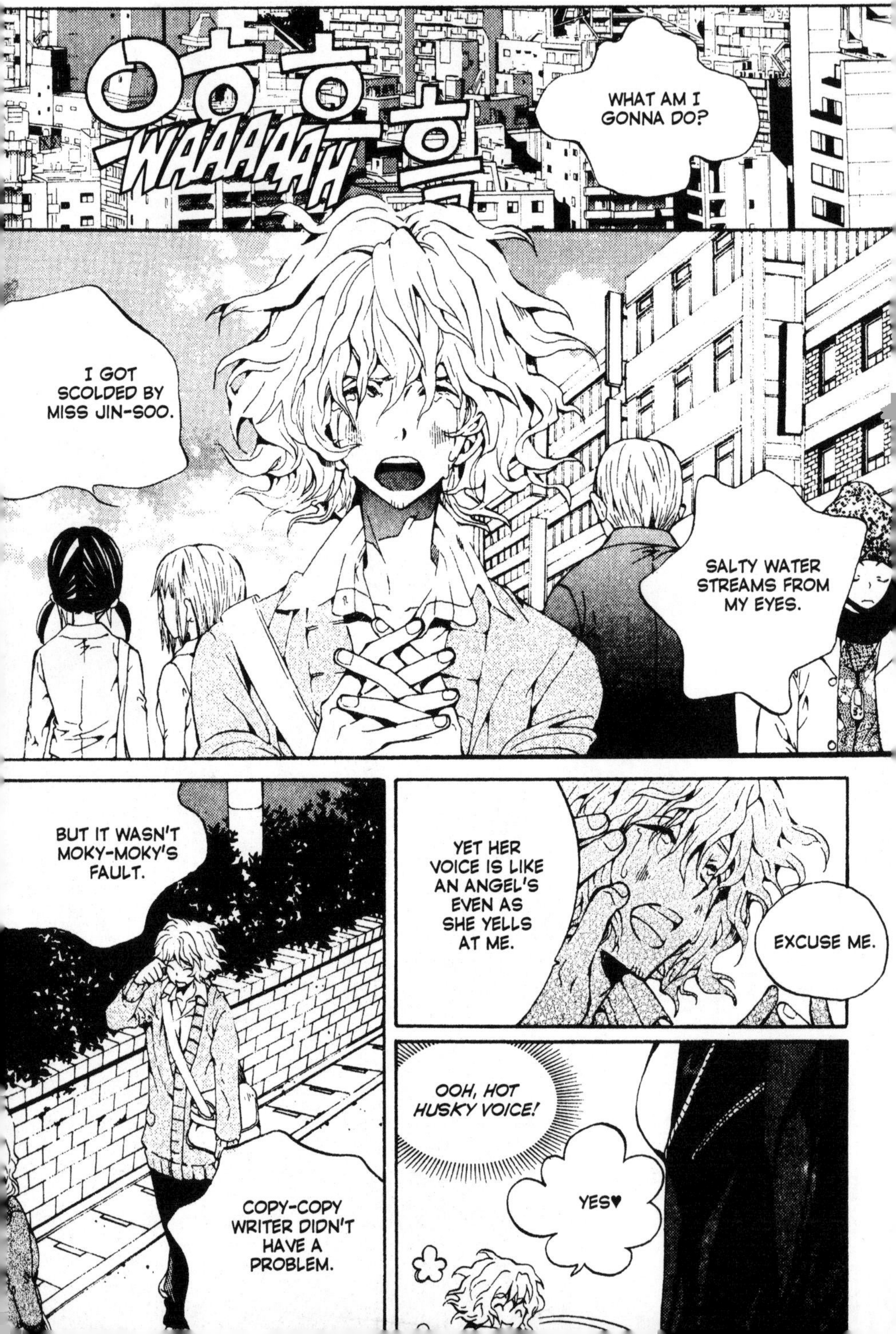
WAAAAAH
WHAT AM I GONNA DO?
I GOT SCOLDED BY MISS JIN-SOO.
SALTY WATER STREAMS FROM MY EYES.
BUT IT WASN'T MOKY-MOKY'S FAULT.
COPY-COPY WRITER DIDN'T HAVE A PROBLEM.
YET HER VOICE IS LIKE AN ANGEL'S EVEN AS SHE YELLS AT ME.
EXCUSE ME.
OOH, HOT HUSKY VOICE!
YES♥

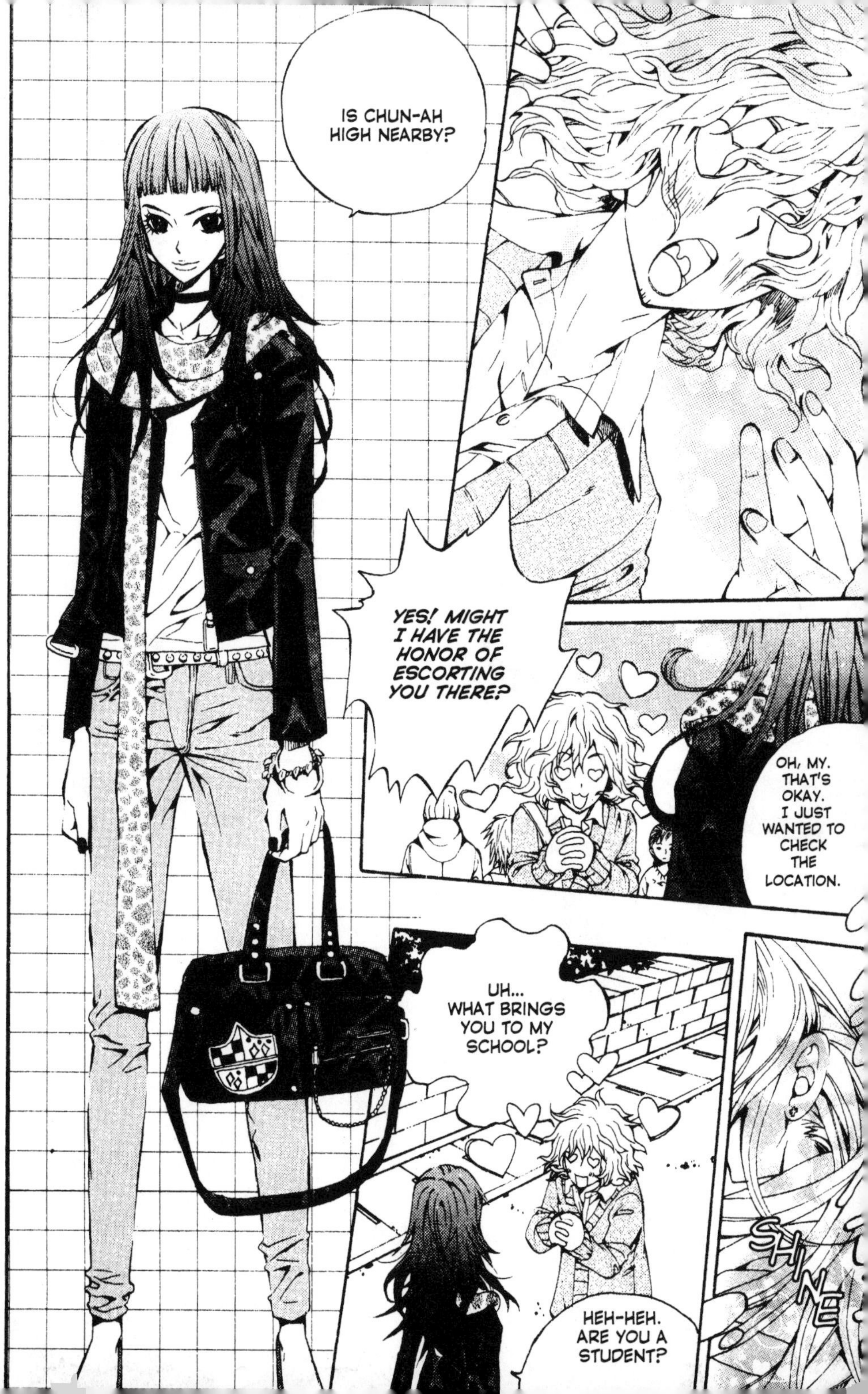
IS CHUN-AH HIGH NEARBY?
YES! MIGHT I HAVE THE HONOR OF ESCORTING YOU THERE?
OH, MY. THAT'S OKAY. I JUST WANTED TO CHECK THE LOCATION.
UH... WHAT BRINGS YOU TO MY SCHOOL?
HEH-HEH. ARE YOU A STUDENT?
SHINE

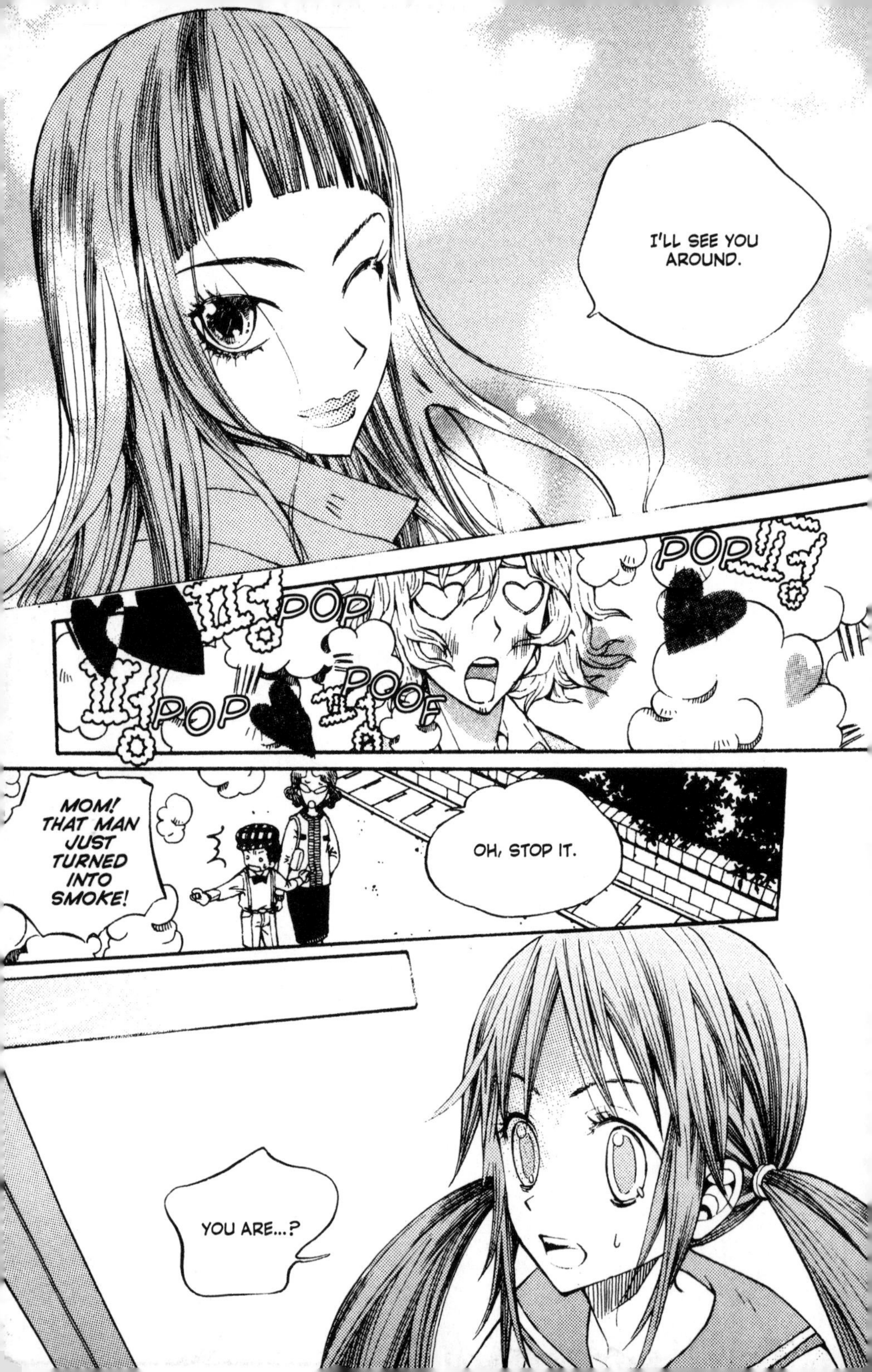
I'LL SEE YOU AROUND.
POP
POP
POOF
POP!?
MOM! THAT MAN JUST TURNED INTO SMOKE!
OH, STOP IT.
YOU ARE...?

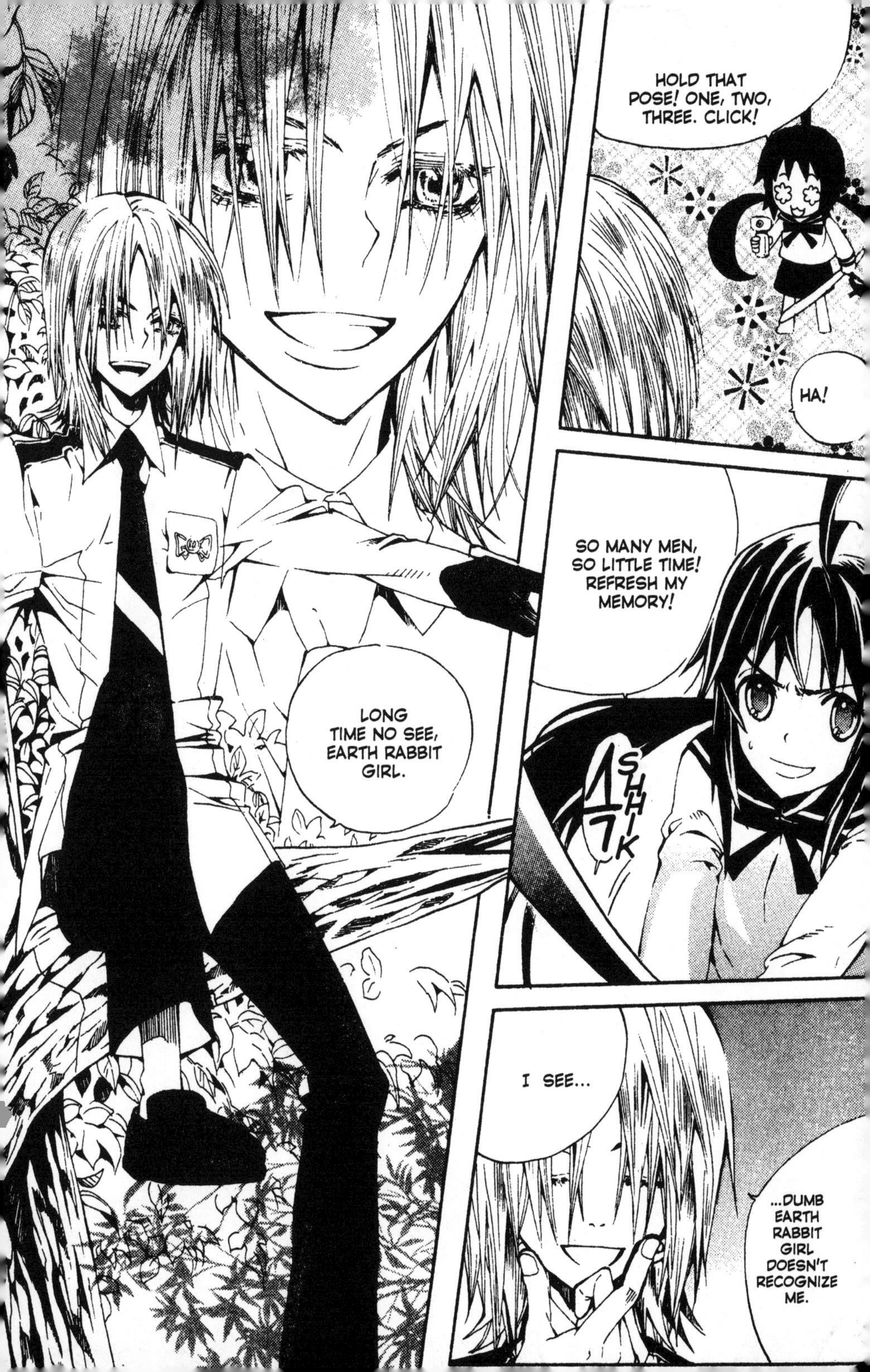
LONG TIME NO SEE, EARTH RABBIT GIRL.
HOLD THAT POSE! ONE, TWO, THREE. CLICK!
HA!
SO MANY MEN, SO LITTLE TIME! REFRESH MY MEMORY!
SHHIK
I SEE...
...DUMB EARTH RABBIT GIRL DOESN'T RECOGNIZE ME.

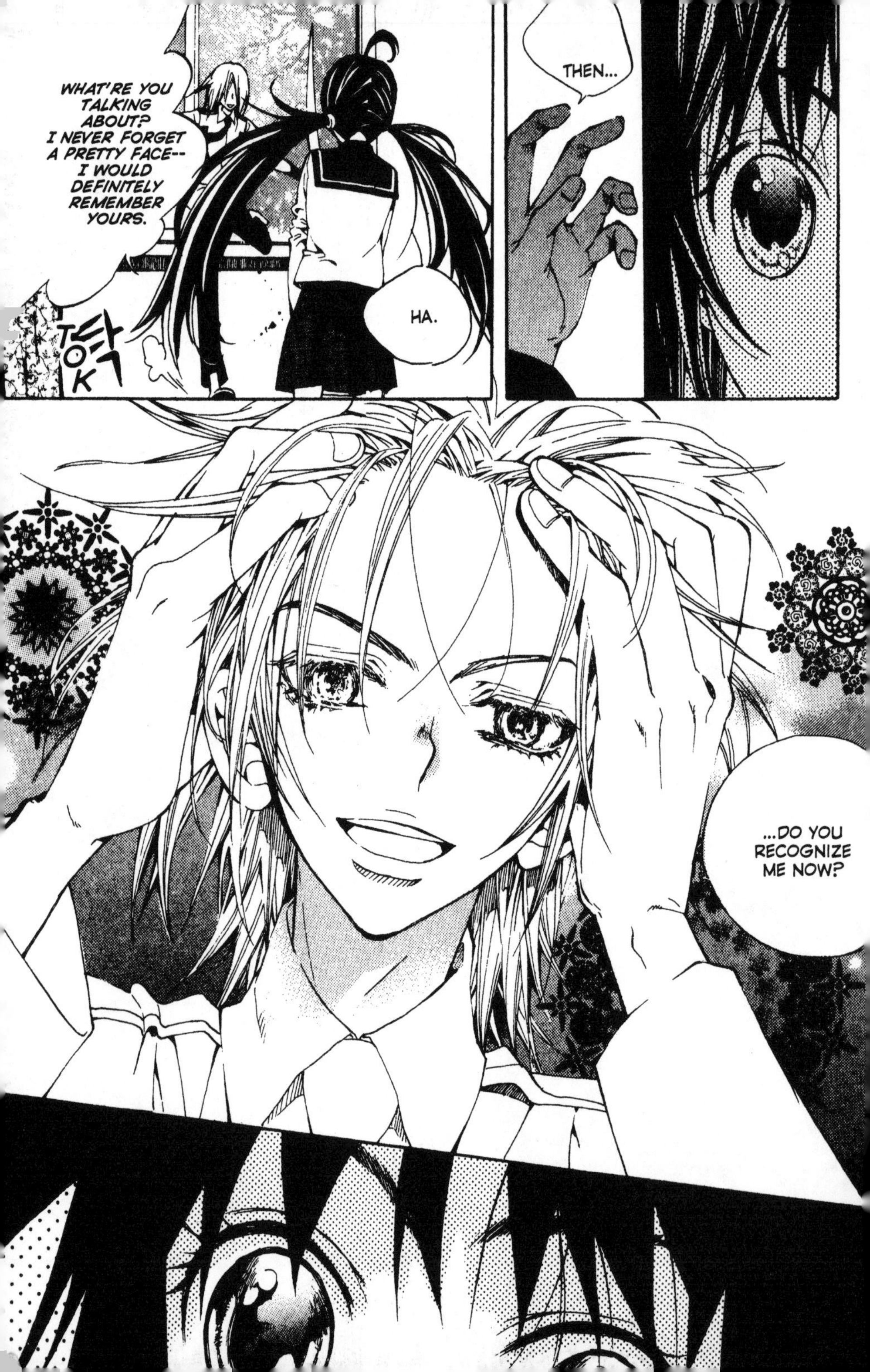
WHAT'RE YOU TALKING ABOUT? I NEVER FORGET A PRETTY FACE-- I WOULD DEFINITELY REMEMBER YOURS.
TEK TOK
HA.
THEN...
...DO YOU RECOGNIZE ME NOW?

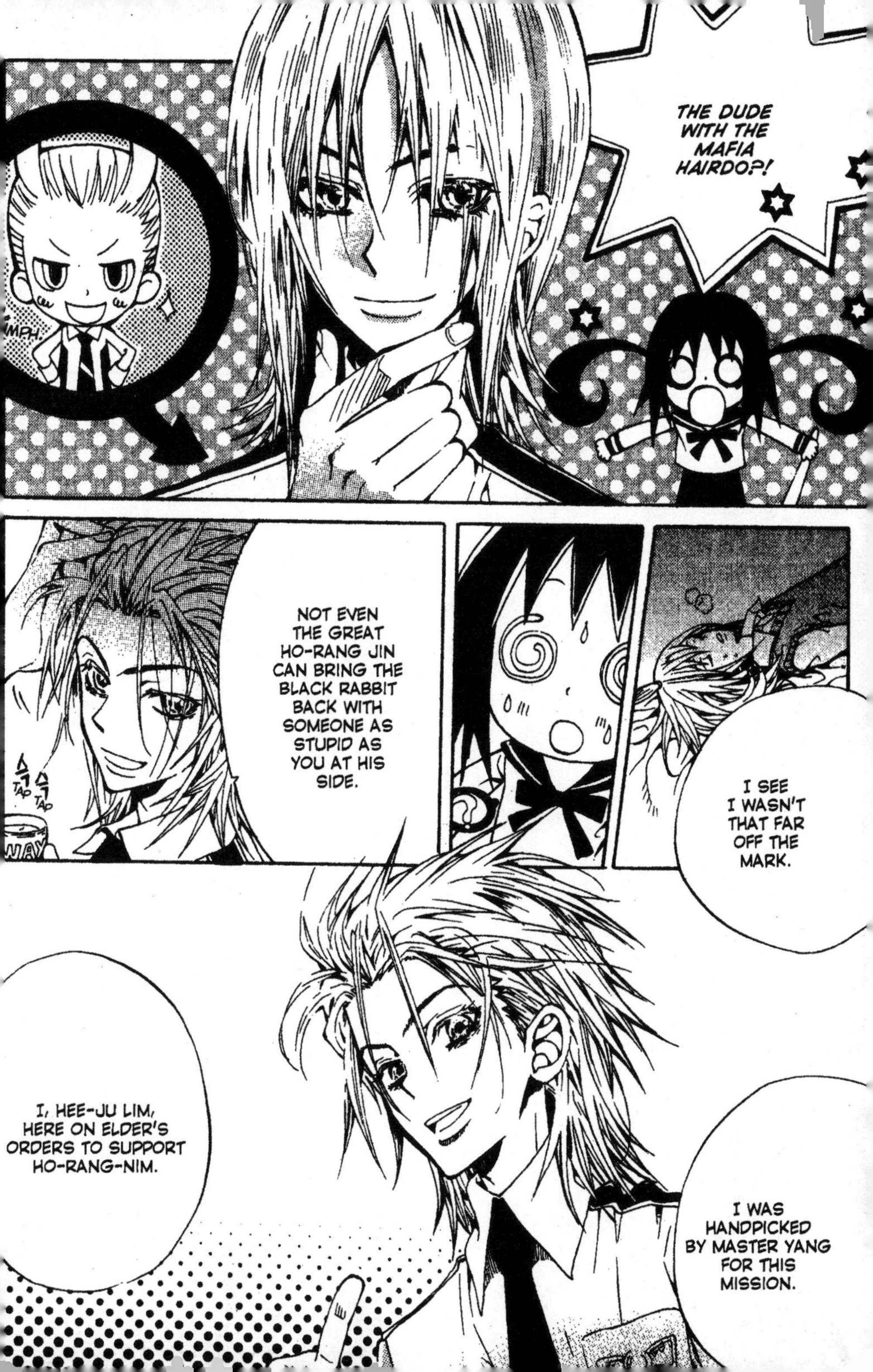
MPH.
THE DUDE WITH THE MAFIA HAIRDO?!
TAP TAP
NOT EVEN THE GREAT HO-RANG JIN CAN BRING THE BLACK RABBIT BACK WITH SOMEONE AS STUPID AS YOU AT HIS SIDE.
I SEE I WASN'T THAT FAR OFF THE MARK.
I, HEE-JU LIM, HERE ON ELDER'S ORDERS TO SUPPORT HO-RANG-NIM.
I WAS HANDPICKED BY MASTER YANG FOR THIS MISSION.

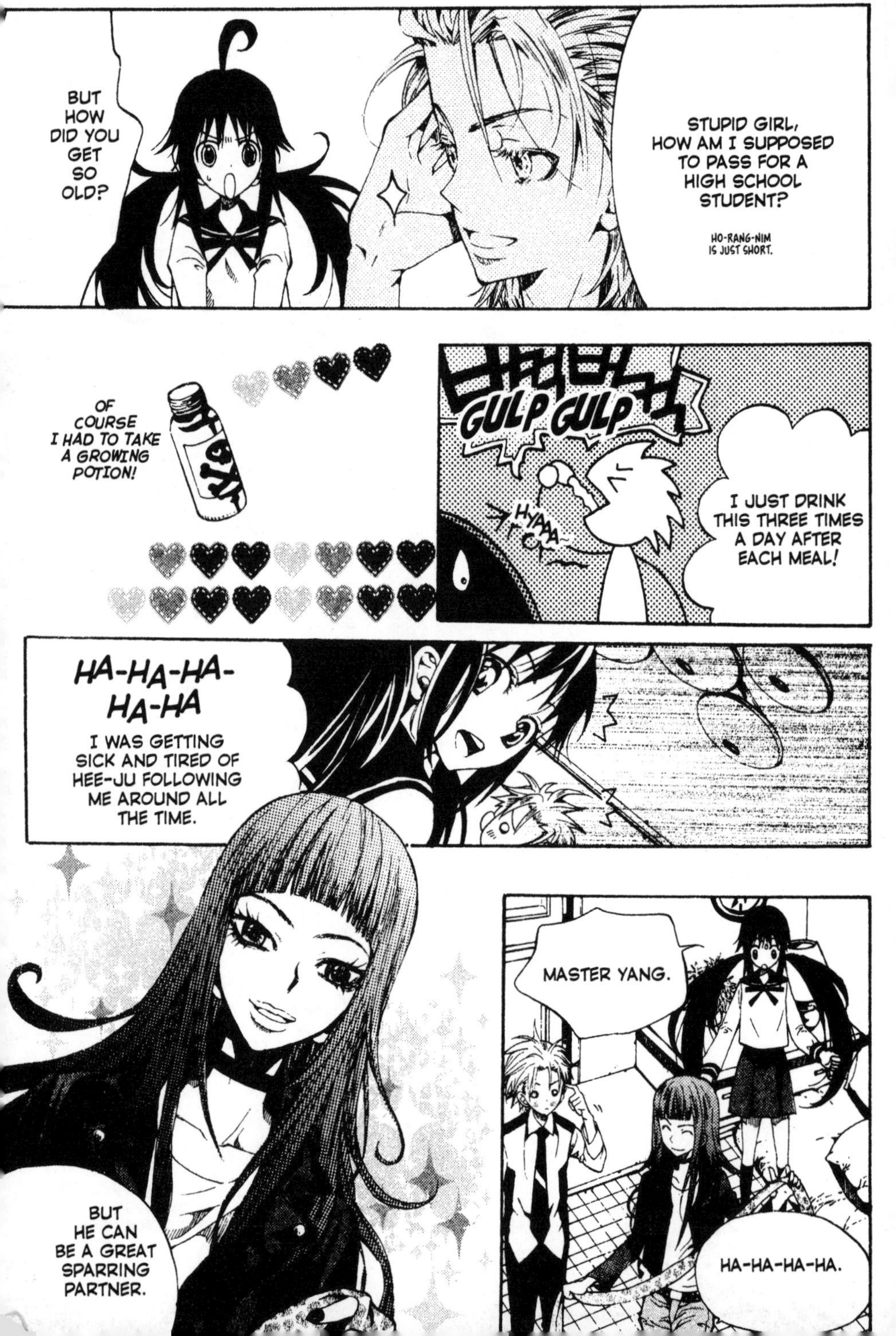
BUT HOW DID YOU GET SO OLD?
STUPID GIRL, HOW AM I SUPPOSED TO PASS FOR A HIGH SCHOOL STUDENT?
HO-RANG-NIM IS JUST SHORT.
OF COURSE I HAD TO TAKE A GROWING POTION!
GULP GULP
HYAAA
I JUST DRINK THIS THREE TIMES A DAY AFTER EACH MEAL!
HA-HA-HA-HA-HA
I WAS GETTING SICK AND TIRED OF HEE-JU FOLLOWING ME AROUND ALL THE TIME.
BUT HE CAN BE A GREAT SPARRING PARTNER.
MASTER YANG.
HA-HA-HA-HA.

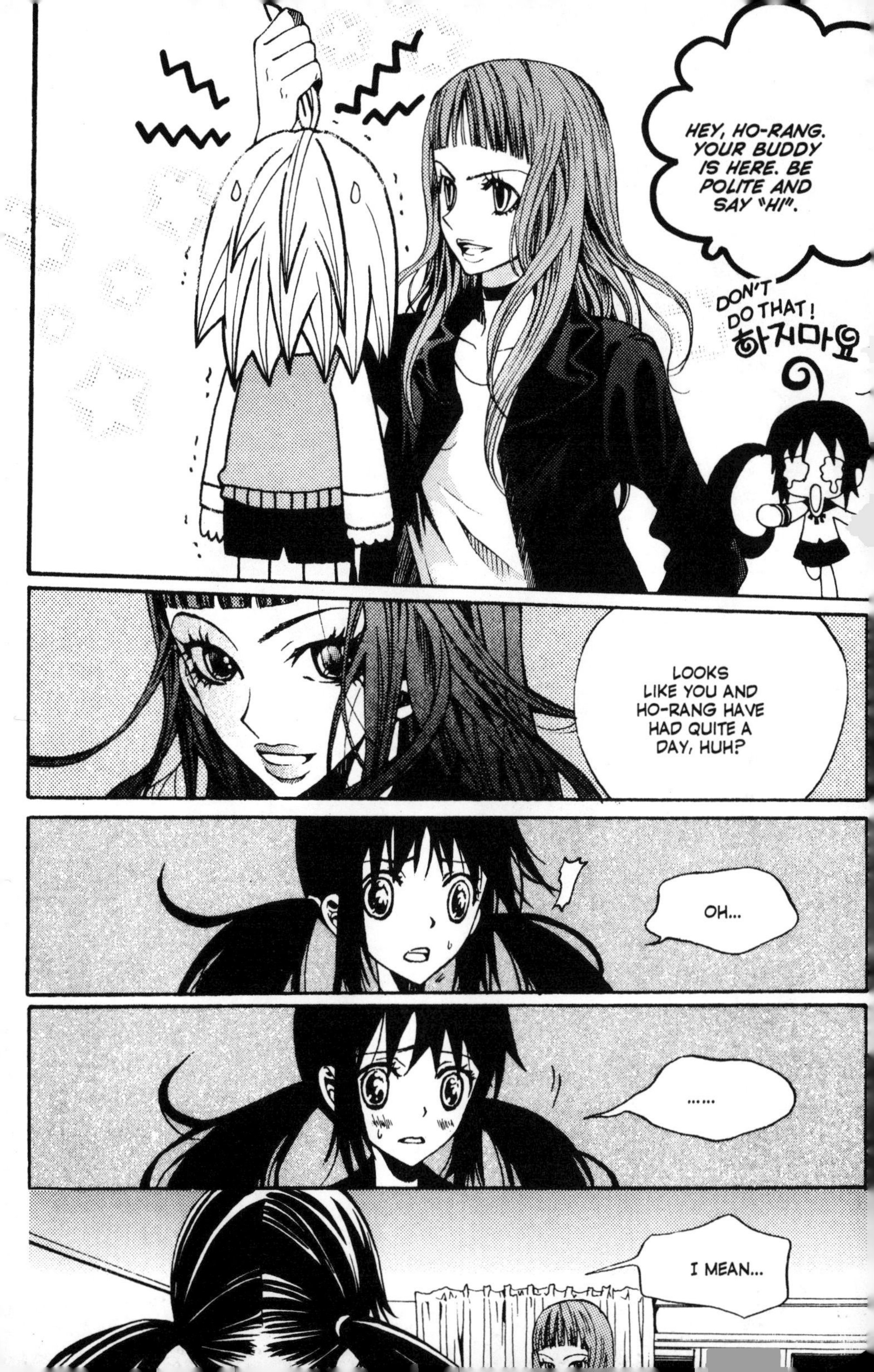
HEY, HO-RANG. YOUR BUDDY IS HERE. BE POLITE AND SAY "HI".
DON'T DO THAT!
하지마요
LOOKS LIKE YOU AND HO-RANG HAVE HAD QUITE A DAY, HUH?
OH...
......
I MEAN...

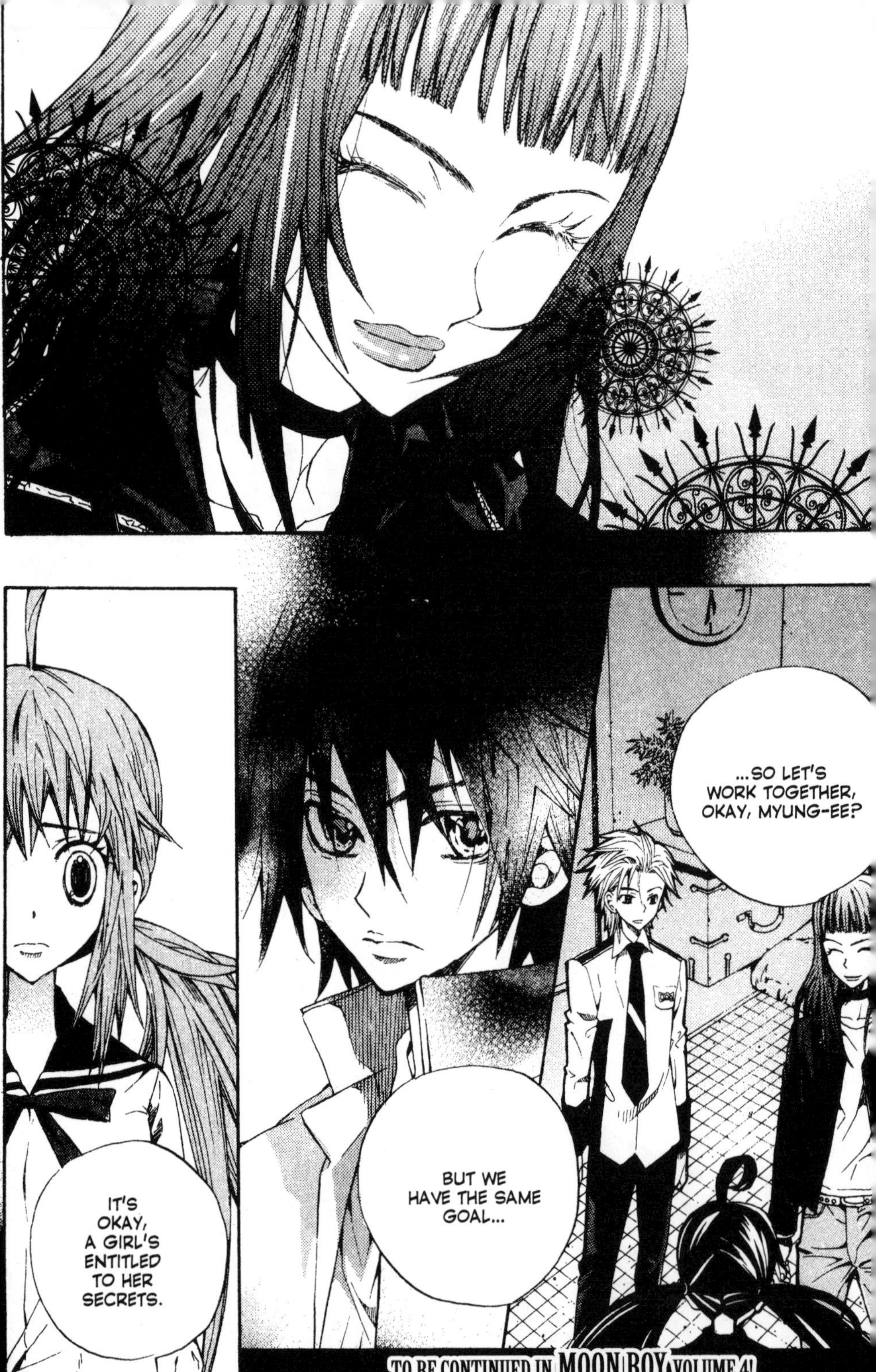
IT'S OKAY, A GIRL'S ENTITLED TO HER SECRETS.
BUT WE HAVE THE SAME GOAL...
...SO LET'S WORK TOGETHER, OKAY, MYUNG-EE?

TO BE CONTINUED IN MOON BOY VOLUME 4!

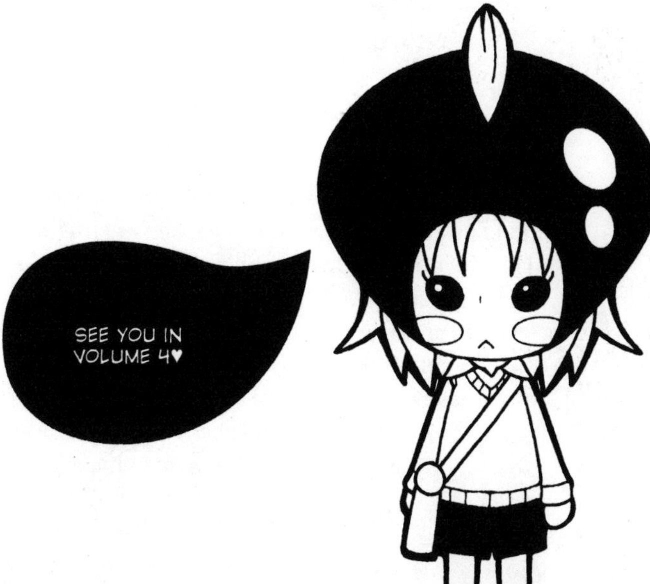
SEE YOU IN VOLUME 4♥

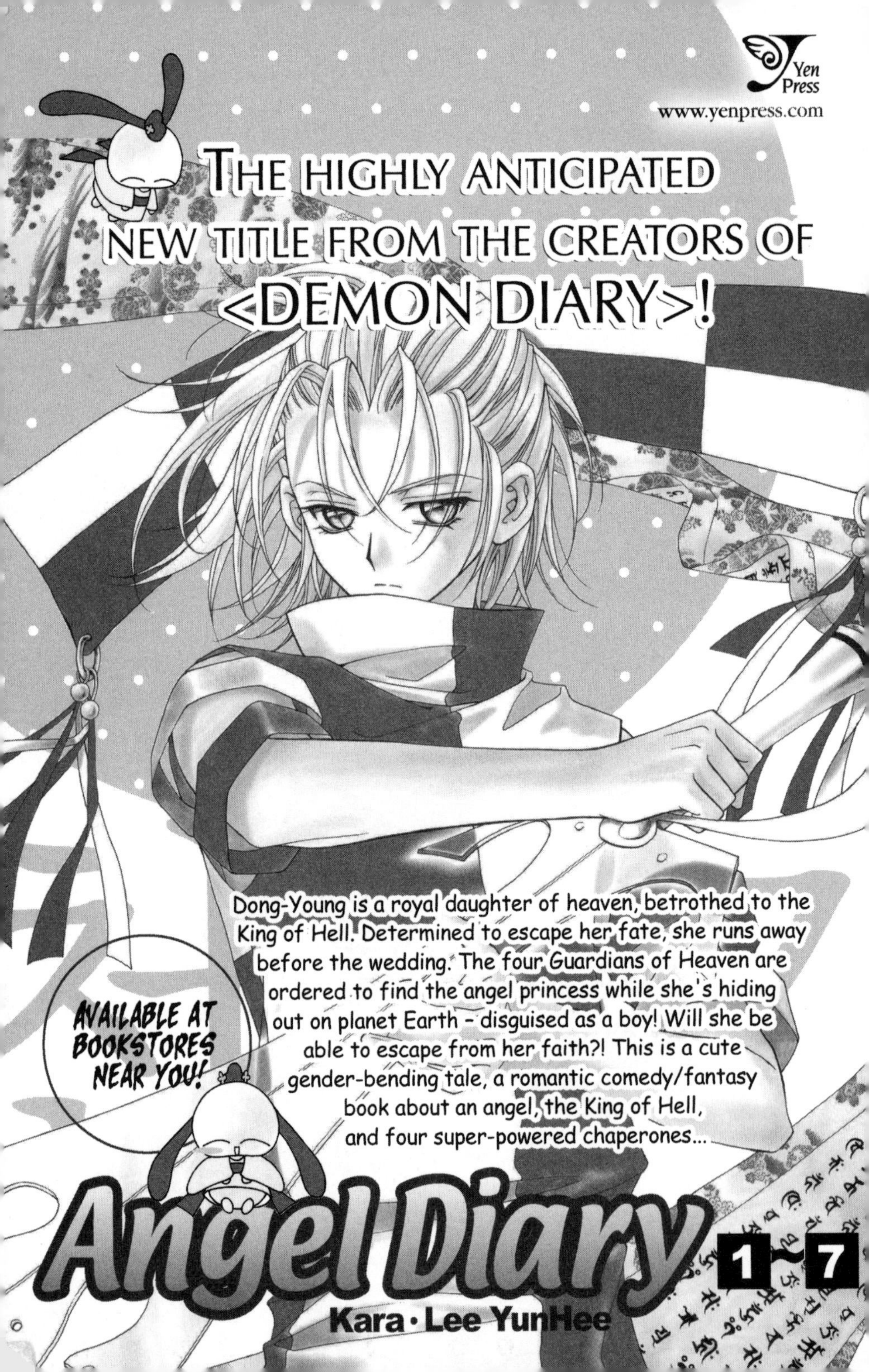
Yen Press
www.yenpress.com
THE HIGHLY ANTICIPATED NEW TITLE FROM THE CREATORS OF <DEMON DIARY>!
Dong-Young is a royal daughter of heaven, betrothed to the King of Hell. Determined to escape her fate, she runs away before the wedding. The four Guardians of Heaven are ordered to find the angel princess while she's hiding out on planet Earth - disguised as a boy! Will she be able to escape from her faith?! This is a cute gender-bending tale, a romantic comedy/fantasy book about an angel, the King of Hell, and four super-powered chaperones...
AVAILABLE AT BOOKSTORES NEAR YOU!
Angel Diary
1~7
Kara · Lee YunHee

The newest title from the creators of <Demon Diary> and <Angel Diary>!

Once upon a time, a selfish king summoned the monstrous Bulkirin into the real world. The monster killed half of all human beings, leaving the rest helpless as to what to do. That is, until one day when a hero appeared and defeated the Bulkirin with the legendary "Seven Blade Sword." But...what does all this have to do with 8th grader Eun-Gyo Sung?! First, she gets suspended from school for fighting. Then, she runs away from home. The last thing she needed was to be kidnapped—and whisked into the past by a mysterious stranger named No-Ah!

Available at bookstores near you!

Legend

1-3

Kara · Woo SooJung

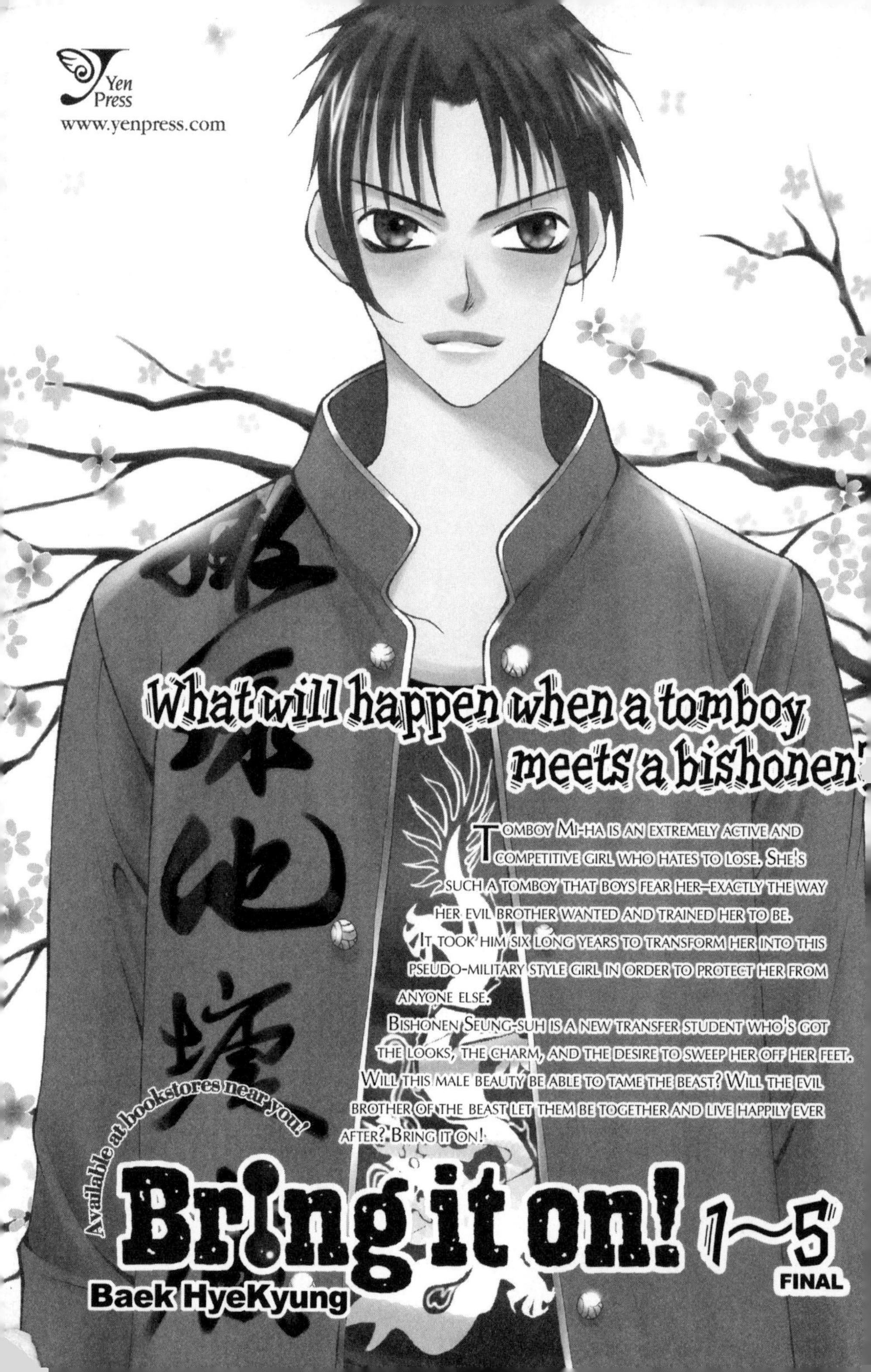
Yen Press
www.yenpress.com
What will happen when a tomboy meets a bishonen?
Tomboy Mi-ha is an extremely active and competitive girl who hates to lose. She's such a tomboy that boys fear her–exactly the way her evil brother wanted and trained her to be.
It took him six long years to transform her into this pseudo-military style girl in order to protect her from anyone else.
Bishonen Seung-suh is a new transfer student who's got the looks, the charm, and the desire to sweep her off her feet. Will this male beauty be able to tame the beast? Will the evil brother of the beast let them be together and live happily ever after? Bring it on!
Available at bookstores near you!
Bring it on! 1~5
FINAL
Baek HyeKyung

Yen Press
www.yenpress.com

Available at bookstores near you!

CHOCOLAT 1~6

Shin JiSang · Geo

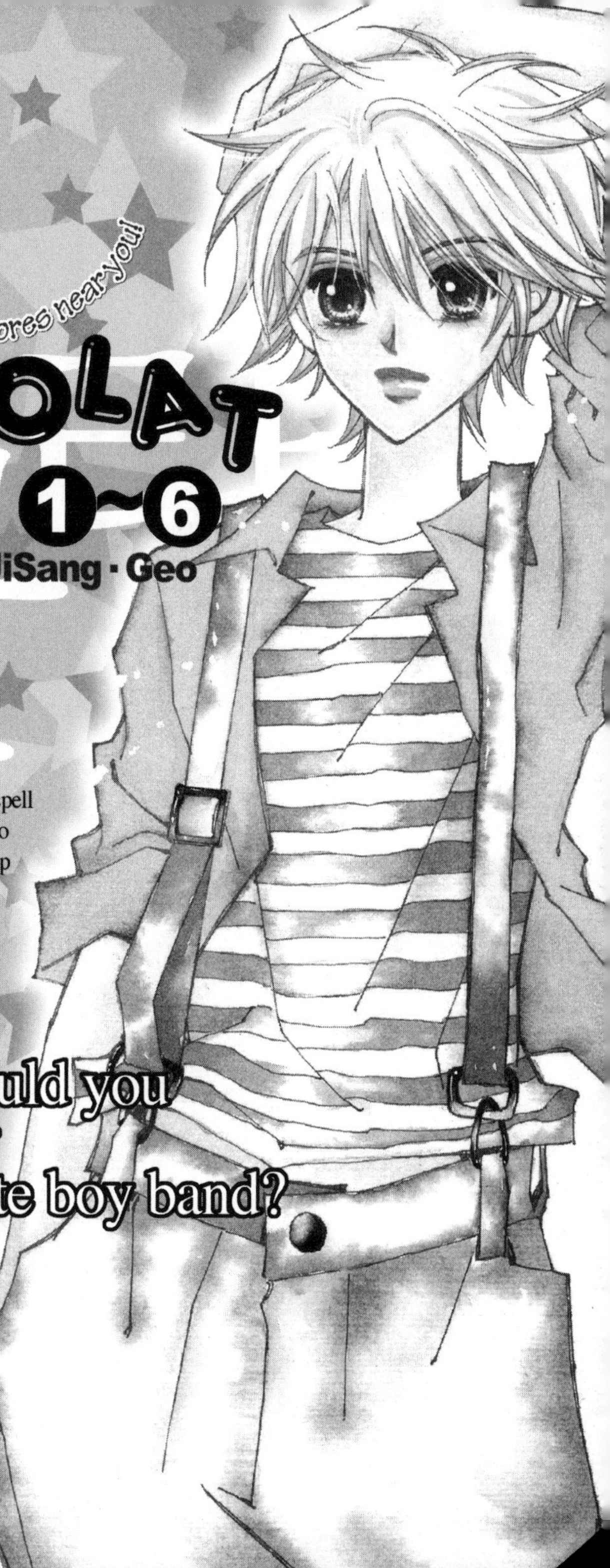

Kum-ji was a little late getting under the spell of the chart-topping band, DDL. Unable to join the DDL fan club, she almost gives up on meeting her idols, until she develops a cunning plan–to become a member of a rival fan club for the brand-new boy band Yo-I. This way she can act as Yo-I's fan club member and also be near Yo-I,

How far would you go to meet your favorite boy band?

who always seem to be in the same shows as DDL. Perfect plan...except being a fanatic is a lot more complicated than she expects. Especially when you're actually a fan of someone else. This full-blown love comedy about a fan club will make you laugh, cry, and laugh some more.

11th CAT

Available at bookstores near you!

Kim MiKyung

1~4 & Special

Cute and charming, yet not so bright little Rika is training to become a real wizard. The first step is to find a magic staff. Ah, that can't be too hard, can it? As Rika and Eujen journey deep into the forest in search of this wonderful magic staff, Rika loses her way. She winds up in an unfortunate chance encounter with the dark sorcerer who kidnapped the princess! Will Rika be able to free the princess and become a real wizard? Follow this cute fantasy story with Rika and find out.

The Cutest Fantasy You've Ever Met!

Sometimes, just being a teenager is hard enough.

Da-Eh, an aspiring manhwa artist who lives with her father and her little brother, comes across Sun-Nam, a softie whose ultimate goal is simply to become a "Tough guy." Whenever these two meet, trouble follows. Meanwhile, Ta-Jun, the hottest guy in town, finds himself drawn to the one girl that his killer smile does not work on–Da-Eh. With their complicated family history hanging on their shoulders, watch how these three teenagers find their way out into the world!

Available at bookstores near you!

HISSING 1~4

Kang EunYoung

The Antique Gift Shop 1~5
Lee Eun

Available at bookstores near you!

Yen Press
www.yenpress.com

CAN YOU FEEL THE SOULS OF THE ANTIQUES? DO YOU BELIEVE?

Did you know that an antique possesses a soul of its own?
The Antique Gift Shop specializes in such items that charm and captivate the buyers they are destined to belong to. Guided by a mysterious and charismatic shopkeeper, the enchanted relics lead their new owners on a journey into an alternate cosmic universe to their true destinies.
Eerily bittersweet and dolefully melancholy, The Antique Gift Shop opens up a portal to a world where torn lovers unite, broken friendships are mended, and regrets are resolved. Can you feel the power of the antiques?

Totally new Arabian nights, where Shahrazad is a guy!

Everyone knows the story of Shahrazad and her wonderful tales from the Arabian Nights. For one thousand and one nights, the stories that she created entertained the mad Sultan and eventually saved her life. In this version, Shahrazad is a guy who wanted to save his sister from the mad Sultan by disguising himself as a woman. When he puts his life on the line, what kind of strange and unique stories would he tell? This new twist on one of the greatest classical tales might just keep you awake for another ONE THOUSAND AND ONE NIGHTS.

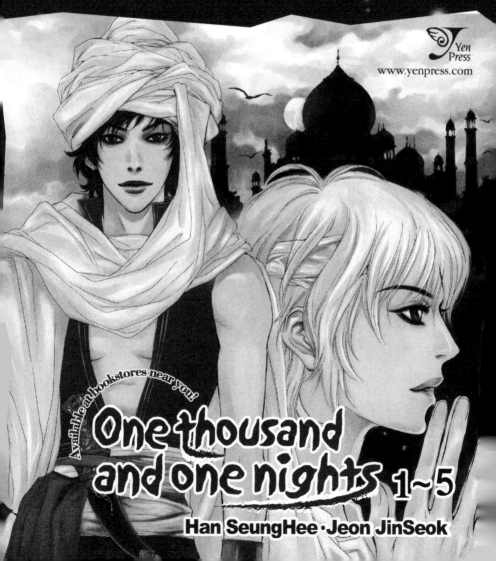

Yen Press
www.yenpress.com

Available at bookstores near you!

One thousand and one nights 1~5

Han SeungHee · Jeon JinSeok

Moon Boy vol. 3

Story and Art by YoungYou Lee

Translation: HyeYoung Im
English Adaptation: J. Torres
Lettering: Terri Delgado · Marshall Dillon

Moonboy, Vol. 3 © 2006 Lee Young You. All rights reserved. First published in Korea in 2006 by Haksan Publishing Co., Ltd. English translation rights in the U.S.A., Canada, UK, and Republic of Ireland arranged by Haksan Publishing Co., Ltd.

Yen Press
Hachette Book Group USA
237 Park Avenue, New York, NY 10017

Visit our Web sites at www.HachetteBookGroupUSA.com and www.YenPress.com.

Yen Press is an imprint of Hachette Book Group USA, Inc. The Yen Press name and logo are trademarks of Hachette Book Group USA, Inc.

First English Printing: December 2006
First Yen Press Edition: September 2008

ISBN-10: 89-527-4609-0
ISBN-13: 978-89-527-4609-2

10 9 8 7 6 5 4 3 2

BVG

Printed in the United States of America